You Want To Be An INTERPRETER?

An Introduction to Sign Language Interpreting for Deaf and hearing students aspiring to become professional practitioners

You Want To Be An
INTERPRETER?

An Introduction to Sign Language Interpreting for Deaf and hearing students aspiring to become professional practitioners

Janice H. Humphrey, Ed.D.
LeWana M. Clark, Ph.D.

William F. Ross III, M.A.
Joseph Featherstone, M.A.

5th Edition

H & H Publishing Co. Inc.
Vancouver, Washington

H & H Publishing Co. Inc.
Vancouver, Washington
844-207-0174

Copyright © 1994, 1995, 2001, 2007, 2020 by Janice H. Humphrey.

You Want To Be An Interpreter?
An Introduction to Sign language Interpreting
Fifth Edition

All rights reserved. Published 2020
Printed in the United States of America
By H & H Publishing Co.

No part of this book may be reproduced, storied or transmitted in any form by print, photoprint, microfilm or any other means, without written permission from the publisher, except as permitted under the Copyright, Design and Patents Act, 1988. Inquiries concerning reproduction outside those terms should be sent to the publishers.

Cover Photo Credit: Rebecca Silva: RsilvaASL@gmail.com

ISBN 13: 978-0-970 4355-5-2

HandHPublishingOnline@gmail.com
HandHPublishingBilling@gmail.com
https://hhpublishingonline.com

H & H Publishing Co. Inc.
PO Box 822792
Vancouver, WA

rev: c

Remembering Bob J. Alcorn

Bob J. Alcorn (1945-1996) was born in a tent beside the Lampasas River in Texas where his family lived off the fish they could catch and vegetables grown on the forest floor. He lost his hearing at the age of 4 from spinal meningitis. He was always grateful, saying that becoming Deaf opened the door to life in the vibrant community and culture of Deaf Americans, as well as providing access to education that would never have been available to him as a child born into poverty. He entered the Texas State School for the Deaf at the age of 5, going on to graduate from Gallaudet with a Bachelor's degree in English and Texas A & M University with a Master's degree in education.

A native Texan, Bob became a tremendous voice for the Deaf community and for interpreters. He made a career of introducing students of all ages to the language and culture of "people of the eye," teaching American Sign Language starting in 1975 and interpreting in 1981. Bob was a beloved professor who encouraged and nurtured his students, a caring mentor, a dedicated Deaf interpreter who closed the communication gap for marginalized members of his community, a Deaf rights advocate, and a friend extraordinaire – always ready to lend his support, make you laugh or encourage you on a dark day.

The 5th edition is dedicated to the memory of Bob Alcorn, the co-author of the first and second editions of this text. He was lauded by many of his students for his contribution to this text, who said it was "the key" to their ability to bridge communication between people who could hear and those who were Deaf.

At the time of his unexpected passing in 1996, Bob was teaching ASL at the University of Texas in Austin. Following his death, the Texas Society of Interpreters for the Deaf (TSID) established the "Bob Alcorn Award." They designed the award to reflect many of Bob's endearing characteristics. They sandblasted the award from Texas granite to represent Bob's strength, courage, his power and lasting impact on all he met. They carved a stone image of two hands coming together, representing dDeaf and hearing individuals working toward a single goal; the base is made of rugged and sturdy wood, representing Bob's rugged, reliable, and solid nature.

Hats off to this humble hero who spent his life fighting for the rights of members of the Deaf community and working to improve the quality of interpreting services nation-wide!

Thank You

It has been a delight working with a tight knit team of four authors, each bringing their own experiences, unique interpreting histories and perspectives which allowed each of us to focus on our particular areas of strength and experience in giving birth to the expanded 5th Edition of this textbook. We believe you will appreciate the content which focuses on:

- Power, privilege, diversity and multiculturalism
- Communication, interpretation, and professional collegiality
- The work of Deaf interpreters and the lives of dDeaf individuals who are differently abled
- A global perspective on sign language interpreting

We are particularly indebted to those who reviewed draft chapters, gave us feedback and suggestions, as well as accolades for the complete updating of the content from the first to the last chapters and for our consistent tone of inclusion.

In short, this edition of the text has benefited from the work of an entire community of scholars involved in the fields of ASL/English interpretation, with input from Canadian Anglophone/ASL and Francophone/LSQ interpreters.

We cannot name everyone who's encouragement and support pushed us forward in writing this 5th edition, but in particular we wish to thank:

- Marilu Santos, Emma Rosa Carbonell and Regina Daniels – interpreters of color who took a preliminary look at the chapter addressing interpreting with colleagues and consumers of color and gave us invaluable feedback

- Regina Daniels, Topher Gonzales, Aleksandr Riabinin and Stephanie Mathis, all Deaf Interpreters who shared personal perspectives on the work of our Deaf interpreting colleagues and the challenges they encounter

- Debra Russell and Christopher Stone, who provided an international look at the work of sign language interpreters

- Barbara Mykle-Hotzon, director of the Douglas College Interpreter Education Program in Vancouver, BC, who was able to refer us to individuals who could assist us with the extensive Canadian content in this edition

- Betty Colonomos for allowing us to share her Integrated Model of Interpreting (IMI), as well as her notes of explanation, and two additional graphics

- Doug Stringham – for his contribution of the "Comparative ASL/English Language Continuum"

- Big hugs and kisses to our spouses – Gary, Christine, Mickell, and BJ, for letting us work long hours and going days without seeing us in the last few weeks leading up to publishing this exciting text

- And a special shout out of thanks to Cierra Ross who stepped in at the last minute to complete some weighty tasks which allowed us to have this amazing edition available to readers for the Fall of 2020!

TABLE OF CONTENTS

**1	Are You Ready to Begin?**	1
Communication and Interpersonal Skills	2
Common Interpreter Characteristics	3
Multilingual and Multicultural Competence	6
Becoming an Interpreter	11
Chapter Review	11
**2	In The Beginning...**	14
The Beginning of Interpreting as a Profession	16
Registry of Interpreters for the Deaf (RID) Established	17
The Canadian Association of Sign Language Interpreters (CASLI)	21
Chapter Review	25
**3	Communication**	28
Culture and Communication	29
Chapter Review	36
**4	Identity, Family, & Culture**	41
The Relationship of Culture and Language	44
Chapter Review	54
**5	Power, Privilege, & Oppression**	59
The Influence of Audism	59
The Impact of Oppression from Interpreters	64
Stereotyping, Oppression, and the Deaf Community	69
Characteristics of Oppressive "Benefactors"	72
Chapter Review	77
**6	People of Color**	81
Interpreting with Indigenous dDeaf People	86
The Transmission of Traditional Knowledge	88
Interpreting with African American dDeaf People and Colleagues	90
Interpreting with dDeaf People and Colleagues Who Are Hispanic/Latinx	94
Complexities of Trilingual Interpreting	98
Other Ethnic/Racial Groups in the United States	99

vii

Chapter Review	101

7 | The Deaf Journey — 104

Chapter Review	117

8 | Mediating Ways of Being — 118

Understanding dDeaf and Non-Deaf Ways of Being	121
Chapter Review	130

9 | Interpreting Process Models — 132

Terminology	134
The Work of Interpreters	136
Mediated Language	138
Message Formulation	139
Pochhacker's Interactant Model	140
Constructing a Message	141
Process Models	143
Dennis Cokely I A Sociolinguistic Model	145
Betty M. Colonomos I IMI Model	146
Integrated Model of Interpreting (IMI)	147
Sandra Gish I The Gish Approach	148
Daniel Gile I The Effort Model	151
The Finer Points of Interpreting	152
Interpreters Working as a Team	154
Chapter Review	155

10 | dDeaf & Differently Abled — 160

Deaf and Physically Challenged	161
Deaf and Intellectually Delayed/Challenged	162
DeafBlind	163
Touch and Communication	164
Chapter Review	169

11 | Where the Jobs Are — 171

Interpreting in Educational Settings	174
VRS/VRI Interpreting	177

Freelance Interpreting | 178

Other Thoughts | 180

Chapter Review | 181

12 | Principles of Practice | 182

What Distinguishes Professionals? | 183

Role Space | 185

What are Ethics? | 187

NAD-RID Code of Professional Conduct | 189

Canadian Association of Sign Language Interpreters (CASLI) | 189

CASLI Code of Ethics | 190

Values of the CASLI Code of Ethics & Guidelines for Professional Conduct | 190

Knowing Yourself: The Foundation of Ethics | 190

Learning to Make Ethical Decisions | 191

Precepts of the Codes | 199

Beyond Graduation | 200

Chapter Review | 201

13 | International Perspectives | 204

International Interpreting Organisations | 205

Interpreter Education Around the Globe | 208

The Reality of Interpreting Outside North America | 210

International Trends Through a Personal Lens | 212

Chapter Review | 215

ToolBox | 217

References | 247

Index | 263

x

Foreword

This text reflects the work and life experience of four authors who, together, have more than 200 years of experience in the dDeaf community, serving as interpreters in almost every setting imaginable. Joseph is Deaf and grew up in a family with 3 brothers who can hear and 2 brothers who are dDeaf; LeWana and Jan have both been deeply involved in the Deaf community since ages 10 and 15; and Bill has Deaf parents and extended family members who are Deaf. As this book goes to press, we all teach interpreting in both formal and informal settings and work as professional interpreters.

We are writing this edition in a year which, speaking honestly, has changed the way of life for everyone globally as a result of COVID-19. This is particularly true for marginalized communities as COVID has affected them more harshly than others around the world who are working virtually in order to obey the "shelter in place" orders in countries near and far. Masks and physical distancing are the new norm. On top of that, the "Black Lives Matter" movement has exploded as a result of the cruel death of George Floyd, resulting in sustained protests and demands for the cessation of racist acts perpetrated against people of color. It is past time for the inclusion of all voices in public and private life, influencing and changing political decisions; time for each of us to develop and demonstrate a respect for the full humanity of every person and for the sanctity of all lives, by examining our assumptions about those like us and about those who are different from us.

In the world where sign language interpreters live and work, we are experiencing greater inclusion of and respect for Deaf interpreters and interpreters of color, embracing dDeaf-parented/heritage interpreters and those who have chosen to immerse themselves in the language and culture of those who are dDeaf — recognizing and honoring Deaf *ways of being*. For readers who can hear, it is our hope that you will recognize that you have privilege – unearned advantages in life simply because you can hear and speak in a world based on sound or that having white skin and speaking English without an accent opens doors to you that are denied to people of color and immigrants. And to those dDeaf individuals who study this book, developing interpreting skills to close the gaps of missing or inaccurate communication between your dDeaf brothers and sisters and those who can hear, we trust you realize that as a *language broker* and *bridge builder* you have the opportunity to fight for inclusion, language rights, and respect for the larger dDeaf community. Each of us has the potential to leave a mark that changes the world in large and small ways, like Bob Alcorn and many others who have gone before us.

So, the authors of this text invite you to open your eyes and minds, jump into the challenge of seeing the world from the view of others, including *"people of the eye."* It is our hope that this text will influence your journey going forward. Some of you may realize from reading this text and doing some honest soul searching, that this is not the field for you. Others may realize that while they are drawn to dDeaf culture and enjoy Deaf community events, along with the company of dDDb friends, your dreams and talents are leading you in a different direction. You may decide to become a counselor, teacher, business owner, or politician who can champion the inclusion of dDeaf and other marginalized people. And to those of you who will choose to take life-changing steps and accept the challenge of becoming an interpreter...***we welcome you!***

Regardless of where you go, we challenge each of you to use the *privilege* you have, whether based on speaking without an accent, your ability to see or walk, having a sound mind, and others because of the color of your skin. To live and move in this world, open to and respectful of the life experiences of those who live in a different reality than yours. Come ready to engage in personal acts of respect and inclusion to those who have been excluded and disrespected for far too long.

TERMS TO KNOW:

- Ethnocentrism
- Communication norms
- High-Context
- Low-Context
- Tacit culture

1 | Are You Ready to Begin?

So, you want to be an interpreter? That's a great decision! You are probably wondering what it takes to go from where you are right now to where you need to be. Being able to facilitate communication between people who are dDeaf who use American, Mexican, or any signed language and people who can hear and speak English, Spanish, or some other spoken language is a skill. Maybe you grew up around interpreters, dDeaf individuals or have seen the interpreting process; perhaps you have no real experience in this area but feel drawn to interpreting as a profession – either way, this is the book for you!

There are many ways Deaf and hard of hearing individuals self-identify in today's society:

- **Deaf** – denoting adherence to the language and culture of the Deaf Community and the native sign language used in the local Deaf Community – American, Puerto Rican, Brazilian
- **deaf** – signifying a person who has a significant hearing loss or may be unable to hear but who chooses to identify with the spoken language and culture of people who hear in their community. As a result a deaf individual may choose to speak for himself rather than sign or in addition to signing. Individuals who fit into this category are not recognized as members of the culturally Deaf community
- **Deafblind or deaf blind** – denoting a person who has a significant loss of hearing in addition to a significant loss of vision. A person who identifies as Deafblind typically uses sign language to communicate; if they have adequate residual vision, they may communicate by standing or sitting close to the person with whom they are signing. However, if they are legally blind, they typically communicate by lightly resting their hands on top of the hands of the person with whom they are interacting with. Rather than identifying with the Deaf community, DeafBlind individuals have their own cultural community, with norms, values and traditions differ from those of both 'deaf' individuals or members of the 'Deaf' community
- **hard of hearing or hearing impaired** – this identification is typically used by an individual who has a hearing loss, often requiring the use of a hearing aid or cochlear implant. Individuals who identify with either of these labels are less likely to learn sign language or to interact socially in the Deaf community

In order to recognize the many ways people with hearing loss identify themselves, the authors of this text are introducing two new label conventions. Throughout the text, you will see the notation of '**dDeaf**' which couples members of deaf community and individuals who are culturally Deaf. In addition to the dDeaf convention, we have adopted the

Chapter 1

NOTES

convention of **'dDDb'** to recognize the DeafBlind community and their unique culture.

The chapters that make up this text will guide you through a range of topics that will move you toward becoming an interpreter. This introduction provides you with a comprehensive list of things you need to know, should understand, think about, and be capable of doing *before* beginning your journey as an interpreter. Welcome to the world of sign language interpreters.

COMMUNICATION AND INTERPERSONAL SKILLS

Interpreting is a task performed when individuals coming from different cultures and different languages strive to communicate with one another. In this text, we are discussing individuals unable to access spoken language because they cannot hear it and people who use spoken language to communicate but do not understand signed languages. Interactions between people who can hear and people who are dDeaf can happen almost anywhere. Any place there are people interacting may have the need for an interpreter – medical appointments, funerals, weddings, concerts, job interviews, or events within the legal system, to name just a few. If you want to be an interpreter, you should ask yourself the following questions:

- Am I a "people person," comfortable meeting and learning about new people?
- Can I navigate new and unfamiliar settings without becoming visibly anxious?
- Do I multitask well while remaining flexible and open to new ideas?
- Do I require knowing what is happening in an interaction or can I successfully manage the stress of being unsure, not knowing what may happen during an event or interaction?
- Can I typically "read" a room or a person accurately?
- Am I open to perspectives, judgments, and values that are different from my own?
- Can I resist passing judgement on others, temporarily suspending my beliefs of right and wrong, good and bad?
- Do I possess fluency in more than one language – at least one signed and one spoken?
- When it comes to a moral right or wrong, am I able to take a stand and not yield when pressed?
- Am I a lifelong learner – curious and learning for the sake of learning?

As you begin your journey to becoming an interpreter, it is essential that you think about the total of your life experiences. Give serious consideration to your language and interpersonal skills; think about your relationships with your family, friends, and colleagues and reflect on the many qualities that make you who you are: your character, self-confidence, flexibility, sense of adventure, hunger to become more, and curiosity about things unfamiliar to you. All of us have areas in which we may want or need to develop, but it is *unreasonable* to believe you can change your basic personality to be successful in a specific field of work, especially if that work requires more from you than you can give.

For example, if a person wants to become a surgeon, but is unable to function at the sight or smell of blood, it is doubtful they will be successful in this particular area of medicine. Likewise, if a person wants to become an interpreter but is unable to function at a "superior" level in more than one language or has difficulty working closely with people, it is doubtful they will be successful in this particular area of service. As we examine some of the traits found in the life and work of sign language interpreters, it is important to reflect honestly on your own individuality to see if you have what it takes to become a successful interpreter.

COMMON INTERPRETER CHARACTERISTICS

Your individuality is a valuable gift. As you consider becoming an interpreter, recognize that some personality traits are key to being successful in specific fields of study and professional practice. In the field of interpreting, the following characteristics and patterns of interpersonal interactions should be given your consideration:

Self-confidence
Everyone experiences some degree of self-doubt and social discomfort, but interpreters need to have the confidence that allows them to move beyond those feelings and maintain their composure while carrying out their duties, such as:

- Asserting yourself to gather the information needed to accomplish your assignment: details about the type of appointment, time, location, directions, speakers and attendees, obtaining materials needed to prepare, and other relevant information.
- Candid self-reflection regarding your ability to determine if you are qualified to do a specific job: understanding the expectations of an interpreting assignment, able to acknowledge your areas of strength and areas of growth as related the assignment, consider your level of linguistic and cultural competence and comfort, as well as requirements for any specialized vocabulary (lexicons) needed – to name a few.
- Your ability to: (1) relate to a range of participants in a cordial, yet an appropriate professional and multicultural manner; (2) manage introductions, leave-taking, and role clarifications, as needed; and (3) establish rapport with interpreter team members, agreeing on physical placement, co-interpreting norms,[1] turn-taking, and other logistics.

Flexibility
Every appointment has common elements; becoming familiar with those elements is part of an interpreter's preparation. While these norms lend to the reliability and continuity of a given setting, you must have the ability to adapt quickly to the unexpected, which is key to our success as interpreters. When things go in a different direction than what we had predicted and prepared for, it is important that we demonstrate the flexibility to adapt accordingly. This includes being aware of our facial expressions and other nonverbal reactions as well as our signed and spoken communication throughout the interaction, particularly when unexpected demands arise. Our overall *composure* is critical as it may communicate our willingness to accommodate reasonable requests, changes, and challenges.

Respectful
We need to be respectful toward the diversity within the dDeaf community as we deal with individuals from different socioeconomic groups, generations of education and language use. We will encounter a range of personalities and interactional styles. It is important to remember that interpreters are sojourners in the lives of dDeaf individuals – sometimes welcome, while other times tolerated.

---

[1] *Co-interpreter is the colleague with whom we are working, often referred to as our team in the US, but more often referred to as a co-interpreter in Canada.*

Chapter 1

NOTES

These attitudes can be true of hearing people who are involved in some interpreted interactions as well. Interpreters are 'visitors' in the private and public lives of dDeaf individuals, and in the normally private offices of service providers; it is important that interpreters consistently demonstrate respect for those with whom they interact.

One way respect is reflected in our work is in being accountable to the people with whom we work. Evidence of this type of respect will be seen when you:

- Manage your time so you arrive on time, ready to work
- Dress appropriately for the setting that you are working in
- Refuse to engage in gossip or negative side talk about your employer, colleagues or clients
- Speak directly with your employer, supervisor or colleagues if you have concerns, questions or suggestions regarding your performance or how things are going at work

Respect, like trust, is a professional courtesy we extend to the other interpreters we work with simply because we perform the same work. Differences in personality, interpretation, style, and decision-making are all opportunities for growth which, when welcomed, can broaden your professional horizons. This may include situations as minor as encountering new signs or unfamiliar English terms while working or as significant as dealing with subtle cultural distinctions that may impact the interactions. Interpreting is like dancing – it works best when those involved can respect your lead or follow the lead of another.

Committed to Lifelong Learning

Interpreters must be lifelong learners who have an unquenchable thirst to know more. While we should have a *yearning for learning*, our learning must be intentional. We must be confident enough to seek clarification for questions that may arise, assuring that the information conveyed when we interpret is accurate. It is also critical that we make time to seek answers to questions for new terminology, both in spoken and signed languages. Each interpreting assignment is an opportunity to learn, to gain an understanding of the roles and duties of someone new to you, unique jobs or practices, as well as gaining new experiences and learning about different lifestyles.

The need to remain relevant in an ever-changing world necessitates that interpreters live and work on the cutting edge of information and education. Of particular importance is adopting a deep curiosity regarding the language and culture of the particular dDeaf population you work with and relying primarily on resources developed by dDeaf people themselves.[2] Some other practical ways to increase your general knowledge base are to watch television shows like National Geographic, PBS, History Channel, and other documentaries as well as visiting your local cultural centers, museums, zoos, aquariums, or conservatories. When you become an interpreter, you will be expected to meet requirements for ongoing professional development. This does not relieve you of your responsibility for ongoing learning outside of your field of professional practice. Consider attending classes presented through community and continuing education on a wide range of subjects that are unrelated to interpreting.

Staying ahead of the learning curve is reflected in your knowledge of daily news,

---

[2] *The authors encourage you to review resources like these created by the dDeaf community in the US regarding their culture and world view: https://www.youtube.com/watch?v=U1xQaRbWHus&t=23s*

technology, legislation, and the evolution of language and terminology, all of which influence our personal and professional communication preferences and styles. It is essential that interpreters attend trainings, workshops, and seminars on topics directly and indirectly related to interpreting, thus broadening our awareness and sensitivity to people, languages, and cultures outside of our own. We must aim to continually expand our knowledge regarding social, political, spiritual, global, and economic factors. Additional relevant topics for consideration are social justice, intersectionality, gender, role space, and dilemma paradigms.

Education

A formal degree is foundational for anyone seeking to become an interpreter, but a degree is not enough to sustain your career as an interpreter. On the surface, the work of sign language interpreting may appear to be solely about the language and culture of the dDeaf community, however, it is so much more than proficiency in your working spoken and signed languages. In addition to competence in interpreting, interpreters must be able to make ethical decisions at a moment's notice and develop the requisite interpersonal and business skills. As lifelong learners, formal education is only the *beginning;* participation in ongoing professional development is required to maintain and improve your craft. It is critical that you remember that your primary goal as a graduate entering the field of interpreting is to obtain state or national certification, and even that accomplishment is just a beginning.

In the United States, the Registry of Interpreters for the Deaf (RID) offers national certification for sign language interpreters. This certification test is divided into two parts, the written or knowledge portion and the performance portion. The written exam tests an applicant's knowledge of the field, the languages they use, the process of interpreting as well as their ethical reasoning abilities. The performance exam requires applicants to demonstrate accurate interpreting skills, both American Sign Language to English and English to American Sign Language.[3] The written exam can be taken prior to earning a degree, but candidates in the US *must* hold a bachelor's degree in order to apply for the performance portion of the RID certification test. Under the RID testing system, additional tests have historically been offered in various specialty areas such as interpreting in legal settings and performing arts. RID offers ongoing professional development opportunities for its members as well as interpreting students. The organization hosts a biennial national conference, along with regional and state events featuring multiple workshop tracks and major presentations by renowned leaders in the field as well as social networking opportunities.

The Canadian Association of Sign Language Interpreters (CASLI) has different requirements than the Registry of Interpreters for the Deaf. A 2-year degree meets the educational requirement to enter the field of sign language interpretation under CASLI guidelines, which states that their mission is "to advance the profession of interpreting and to support CASLI members" (Vision, Mission, Core Values and Bylaws, n.d., para. 3). Unlike the entry-level certification administered by RID, the Canadian Association of Sign Language Interpreters administers a professional-level certification for American Sign Language – English interpreters, which is intended to accredit seasoned interpreters; the CASLI Certification of Interpretation (COI) is awarded for life. Like the Registry of Interpreters for the Deaf, CASLI supports American Sign Language and English interpreters through a biennial conference featuring national and international presenters as well as and

---

[3]*In both the US and Canada, there are no requirements regarding a specific field of academic study. However, preferred fields of study are: American Sign Language, American Sign Language Interpretation, Deaf Studies, and Linguistics and/or Sociology, to name a few.*

Chapter 1

NOTES

other opportunities for professional development and networking among working sign language interpreters.

Introversion or Extraversion

Extroverts are people who often get their energy from interacting with others. They are comfortable with people, whether in large or small groups, regardless if the people present are friends, acquaintances or total strangers. Introverts, on the other hand, can become stressed by social interactions and often feel exhausted afterwards. Many times they must plan their "people time" thus allowing themselves time to recuperate afterwards. Introverts and extroverts are the poles, but there is a wide range of "comfort" between the extremes of introvert and extrovert. To learn more about where you feel most comfortable, go online and take the following quiz: *https://introvertdear.com/are-you-an-introvert-quiz/*

Realistic

Like everyone else, interpreters are fallible – nobody is perfect! While you want to interpret to the best of your ability, it is critical not to hold the unrealistic expectations of perfectionism. As interpreters, we must take responsibility for our work and the professional choices we make; we must also accept the reality that we will make mistakes. How we handle those errors is what matters. When we realize an error has been made, our response is crucial. It is a matter of *integrity* to take ownership of our work by acknowledging the error(s) and making corrections promptly and judiciously. It is important to know yourself. If you are hesitant to make decisions because you are fearful of making a mistake or if the idea of receiving feedback from your colleagues regarding your work is unnerving, the stress created in your day-to-day work as an interpreter could compromise your overall physical, mental and emotional health. It is important that you think seriously about how you deal with these challenges and whether interpreting is a good fit for you.

MULTILINGUAL AND MULTICULTURAL COMPETENCE

Before beginning the work of interpreting, multilingual and multicultural competence is essential. This is because language and culture are deeply interwoven and language is the way relevant cultural information is conveyed. Interpreters work with a minimum of two languages and the accompanying cultural norms for each language, so it is critical that interpreters consistently exhibit an adept understanding of and sensitivity to the differences that must be mediated between the languages and cultures present.

You might ask yourself how you feel when interacting with people from a culture different than your own. In cross cultural interactions, it is common for people to view their own culture as the *norm* or as the *standard* by which people measure what they consider to be "normal" and "appropriate." This is known as **ethnocentrism** and it is an unconscious behavior which can be an obstacle for the kind of empathy required to effectively communicate cross culturally. *Effective* cross cultural communication requires an understanding of how people from different cultural backgrounds perceive the world around them and how they communicate.

Communication norms are not simple, nor straightforward because each cultural group places different degrees of the value on indirect and direct communication; the divergence found in **high-context** and **low-context** cultures is a prime example.

6

Are You Ready to Begin?

NOTES

Communication norms are *how* people communicate on a daily basis; it is the adherence to informal *internalized* rules that shape the behaviors and actions of the individuals, helping them know how to interact with people inside and outside of their cultural group. These norms help a community create relational bonds and provide boundaries as a means of social control (Hall, 2017).

Edward Hall (1976) explains that communication conveys thoughts and ideas primarily through language, which means using explicit, direct, and overt communication, referred to as *low context*. However, when sharing ideas and information with people from *high context* cultures, politeness dictates that one use implicit, subtle, and nonverbal forms of communication to convey your point. When individuals share information between different cultures, it is imperative that they are aware of these different norms and are able to utilize the appropriate communication norms used by the members of each culture to express their ideas, values and beliefs (Hall, 1976). For example, if a person from a low context culture wants to address a concern they have with a colleague, they are likely to be confrontational and "calling things as they see them." However, a person from a high context culture in this same scenario is likely to avoid a direct expression of their feelings about a concern with a coworker and would most likely address the issue with subtle redirections. "Although no culture exists exclusively at one end of the scale, some are high while others are low" (Wang, 2008, p. 151). If you want to be a sign language interpreter, it is critical that you understand that members of the dDeaf community are generally considered to be high-context communicators, whereas many spoken languages come from low context cultures.

dDeaf culture, by its very nature, may appear to be a low context culture as the members of the dDeaf community are very direct and factual (some may refer to this as "blunt"). However, one of the reasons that dDeaf culture is considered a low context culture is the vastness of *shared* thoughts, feelings and actions; it is the implicit *knowing* of what behavior is appropriate within the group or community. Hall (1989) describes this internal knowing as personal or **tacit culture**, which he says, "*is not experienced as a **culture** but simply as **BEING**!*" (p. 293). By way of clarification, the idea of a tacit culture is that actions and behaviors are understood or implied without being stated. Though the very actions and behaviors may be visible to everyone, they are not understood by outsiders. Hall (1989) explains that this lack of understanding is because, "all cultures are blind to other cultures, and especially so towards those within their own midst" (p. 298). Thus, communicating effectively across cultures requires recognizing and honoring those linguistic and behavioral differences, including:

- Verbal and nonverbal norms
- Interactional expectations such as turn taking, volume of speech, sustained or diverted eye contact while communicating
- Behavioral and social norms reflecting the perceived power status

Take an honest assessment of yourself because interpreters must demonstrate awareness of their own cross-cultural beliefs and attitudes. To get a snapshot of your cross-cultural preparedness, look at the ethnocentrism scale: https://www.midss.org/sites/default/files/ethnocentrism_scale.pdf.

There are various tools available to measure the degree of linguistic and cultural competence of sign language interpreters. According to the Sign Language Proficiency Interview (SLPI) rating scale, candidates with *"superior"* language skills are *able to engage in fully shared and natural conversations, with in-depth elaboration on both social and work topics* (Newell & Caccamise, 2006). This definition reflects the level of language competence you will need as an interpreter. There are significant differences between a *native* user of a language and an individual who acquires, or is acquiring a second or third+ language.[4] Furthermore, an individual who acquires their second language through family and social interactions may initially be more competent in that language than those who learn a second or third language by taking classes in a formal academic setting. This is why community involvement and immersion is such a focus of emphasis in North American interpreter education programs for sign language interpreters. Developing this level of near-native competence in your second and third language and culture requires an intense commitment of time and effort. It should be noted that developing linguistic and cultural competence does not guarantee one's ability to develop competence in generating accurate interpretations – interpreting is another skill altogether.

Linguistic and cultural aspects of a people group are most visible when viewed through community and social interactions. Interpreters must be sensitive to the communicative norms and expectations in various social settings in both their native language and culture and their acquired language and culture. Communicative norms are the accepted and followed practices of a community of people who share the same language and culture; the norms of people who are dDeaf and people who can hear are typically very different. Each culture has rules for how people speak to each other depending on the context of their interaction, their relationship with each other, and the formality of the environment. For example, children do not typically speak to their parents the same way they speak to their siblings. Employees do not speak to their supervisor in the same way they speak to employees they supervise. Interpreters must demonstrate awareness of these communication expectations, in order to utilize the appropriate language features within a range of social situations. The differences in the communicative expectations are subtle and are rooted in the social and cultural norms of each people group. It would benefit interpreters to identify these subtle yet significant differences, which would include being aware of everyday interactions, and the unwritten rules that govern our behavior in those interactions such as:

- How you greet a friend is typically different than how you greet a stranger
- The use of manners, behaviors of "politeness" or "rudeness" vary based on setting
- The degree of intimacy in relationships, the type of interaction, the cultural and linguistic norms, etc.

Cultural norms and customs define which behaviors are socially acceptable or unacceptable in daily interactions. In many cultures, for example, the use of consistent eye contact, facial expressions and physical gestures form the foundation of effective and successful communication. In other cultures, however, these communication norms may be viewed negatively and are discouraged. Because the appropriate application of cultural norms influences interpersonal interactions, interpreters must develop the ability to comfortably incorporate the cultural and linguistic norms of each people group with whom they work.

The phrase, "The Ugly American," was coined in 1958 as a pejorative term used to

---

[4] *"native language refers to the language that a person acquires in early childhood because it is spoken in the family and/or it is the language of the region where the child lives"* (Nordquist, 2019, para. 1).

refer to perceptions of the arrogant, thoughtless, culturally ignorant, and ethnocentric behavior of American citizens visiting abroad (Burdick & Lederer). The term is typically associated with travelers and tourists with limited experience in the international arena. If you want to be an interpreter, your language skills, your cultural and social knowledge must be advanced beyond that of a "tourist." Developing the requisite social and cultural acumen, as well as the communication skills required to become an interpreter, can only be gained by *intensive interaction* and involvement in the various facets of dDeaf community life. It is essential to take frequent and honest assessments of yourself in order to ensure proficient language use, effective communication across a range of language users, social awareness and evolving interpreting knowledge and skills – all of which are marks of a true professional.

Reflective Practitioner

A *reflective practitioner* means thinking about your interpreting work – "how you are doing it, and how you can make it better" (Leal, Martinez, Stockton, & Bose, n.d. para. 4). After each interpreting assignment, you should have ideas about how you can improve your work. An open-mind is required in order to embrace the challenges of consistently improving your skills and decision making. The *vigilance* of a reflective practitioner calls you to be watchful and aware, requiring careful recall and critical thinking. The appropriate use of these skills require the interpreter to *predict, reflect on* and *analyze* their work of interpreting to identify areas where *best practices* need to be applied in future assignments. Reflective practice doesn't focus solely on preventing and correcting errors; it includes questioning both effective and ineffective decisions. This is part of critical self examination in order to consistently make effective decisions in the future. The goal of reflective practice, then, is to consider every interpreting experience and continuously move toward *superior reproducible performance* (Ericsson, 2006).

Reflective practice is different from self-criticism. Reflective practice is productive, leading to the application of self-assessment resulting in improved performance, while self-criticism typically identifies one's errors and weaknesses with no plan for improvement. An effective reflective practitioner is able to consistently maintain healthy, realistic expectations. Entry level interpreters must be able to monitor their comprehension of a source language message while taking responsibility for the target language output, including an awareness of errors, additions or omissions that may occur in their interpretation. The goal of every interpretation is to ensure the intended message is conveyed in an accurate, linguistically and culturally equivalent manner for all participants. Reflective practitioners[5] develop the ability to identify and rectify their own errors, while recognizing that some things happen during the interpreting assignment that are beyond their control.

Self-Care

Any time you deal with people, the work can become "messy" and we need to safeguard our *wholeness,* which can be an indicator of our overall health. The more whole we are, the better our service to others will be. Interpreters have been known to neglect their own care while working to improve the lives of others.

Taking care of ourselves physically, emotionally, psychologically, intellectually,

---

[5]The term participant is used in place of the term client or consumer, as it appears to equalize all persons at an interpreting assignment.

Chapter 1

NOTES

financially, spiritually, and socially is important for us as people, not solely as interpreters. When one or more of these areas are ignored, neglected or inadequately addressed, the result is often burnout, resentment, frustration and even anger. It is in our best interest to spend time in *reflection*, not solely about our interpreted product, but considering our thoughts, feelings, and beliefs about the impact our career is having on us.

We did not all grow up with the tools, language or confidence to give priority to our own needs through self-care. Ask yourself if you grew up recognizing and talking about your feelings, ideas and beliefs. If not, you may need to develop those skills. However, the opposite may also be true. You may have grown up spending an inordinate amount of time pondering your own point of view, to the point that it eclipsed the perspectives of others. The key to self-care and the care of others is finding a genuine balance that enables everyone to feel valued. Wisdom and experience dictate that we do not ignore the principles and priority of self-care.

When we recognize and attend to the various facets of our lives that lead to wholeness, we are supporting healthy habits of self-care. In order to do that, we must give adequate time learning and adopting a lifestyle of self-care because this may involve a steep learning curve with lots of practice; it is highly recommended that you develop these skills *before* becoming an interpreter. Some vivid examples of healthy self-care are provided below:

❏ **Honor Your Identity and Center Yourself:** Embrace your ethnicity, race, religion, orientation, and individuality. Know yourself. Breathe, take time for *you*, make time to do things you enjoy: cook, read, nap. Spend time with those you love. *Do not disguise work as fun.*

❏ **Behave Responsibly:** You have power – each of us does. We need to accept the responsibility that comes with our power and we must use it wisely. Claiming our personal power enables us to help others by using it with love; it can turn our world upside down!

❏ **Forgive Yourself and Others:** Let go of past hurts and move past unproductive blaming. Absolve yourself and others of the guilt and shame from past mistakes. To err is human, to forgive generates hope and second chances.

❏ **Stay Hydrated and Active:** *Get Up, Move, Walk!* Everyday, drink as many ounces of water as you can. Go ahead and have another glass with a slice of lemon or lime. While you are up, get moving! Walk around the office, wander through the house, walk around the block. You don't have to run a marathon – just get out of the chair!

❏ **Learn to Say, 'No':** Think before you agree to do anything. There's nothing wrong with saying no, and not feeling guilty about drawing a line in the sand. You can deflect by saying, "let me think about it" or "I don't know, maybe..." Protect your time.

❏ **Stretch Before and After Interpreting:** Reach high, twist at your waist – stretch out your arms, legs, your back and neck. Developing a habit of stretching before and after every interpretation will increase the years you will be able to work pain free (see handout in Toolbox).

❏ **Sleep, Nap, Rest:** Sleep is one of the most important parts of our lives, but

Are You Ready to Begin?

NOTES

an area we often neglect. Most people need at least 7-8 hours a night. Go lay down without any guilt, it's good for you – take a twenty minute power nap.

❑ **Remain Curious:** Invest in your personal growth. Try to learn a new word every single day or study something you have always been curious about.

❑ **Be Kind to Yourself and Others:** Occasionally shut down all screens – give yourself a break from constant stimulation. It is healthy and good for your brain to have less environmental "noise." Respect yourself and others; say please and thank you. Ask people about themselves...

❑ **Balance Your Books:** Set aside one day every week to take care of your invoices, banking, and receipts...in essence, take care of your financial wellbeing.

❑ **Declutter then Create Something New:** Organize the junk drawer, the pantry, the hall closet. Creating order from disorder is incredibly satisfying. Do something for the first time – paint a picture, learn to crochet, bake bread, try ceramics or pottery. Escape your rut – take a risk!

❑ **Quiet Your Soul/Envision a New You:** Take a wee break! Take time to pray, meditate, go for a walk, call a friend. Drink a glass of tea on the porch and watch the sunset or the sunrise. Write a personal creed based on the truths you want to live by. Allow your creed to shape your life and guide your actions.

❑ **Laugh Often and Laugh Loud:** Remember the old adage "laughter is the best medicine"? It's true. Keep company with people who make you laugh and those who laugh with you. Laughter and deep breathing help release stress.

BECOMING AN INTERPRETER

As we conclude this chapter, we would ask you to start keeping a journal. This text is deliberately designed for you to express your thoughts, feelings, and ideas; please consider writing throughout this book. Jot down meaningful activities of your day, note something you learned today, or identify an area of personal growth and reflect on your overall development. Use this textbook as your journal to help you recognize your characteristics, personality traits, growing knowledge and skills, as well as the areas in your own life where you want and need to grow. Take time to journal about your thoughts and your reflections about your goal to become an American Sign Language interpreter and to outline your path to success.

chapter *Review*

This chapter has provided insightful ways to begin the practice of interpreting. There have been essential tools provided and definitions that student interpreters need to know. Below are some key terms that are important to the field and profession of interpreting as well as tips about areas that can be improved.

Terms to Know:

▪ **Communication norms**: Are *how* people communicate on a daily basis; it is the adherence to informal *internalized* rules that shape the behaviors and actions of individuals, helping them know how to interact with people inside and outside their cultural group. These norms help a community create relational

11

bonds and provide boundaries as a means of social control (Hall, 2017).

- **Tacit culture:** Tacit culture can be described as the actions and behaviors that are understood or implied without being stated. Though the very actions and behaviors may be visible to everyone, they are not likely to be understood by outsiders. E. Hall (1989) explains that this lack of understanding is because, "all cultures are blind to other cultures, and especially so towards those within their own midst" (p. 298).

- **Ethnocentrism**: Typically, an unconscious belief that one's own culture as the "norm" or as the "standard" by which we measure what we consider to be "right." This belief can be a significant obstacle in cross cultural interactions, lacking the kind of empathy required to effectively communicate with people from different cultures and beliefs.

- **Low-Context culture**: The cultural norm of communicating one's thoughts, ideas and information *primarily* through the words of a language, resulting in expressing oneself in explicit and direct ways; typical of low context cultures.

- **High-Context culture**: The cultural norm of communicating one's thoughts, ideas and information using politeness, subtlety, hinting and nonverbal forms of communication; typical of high context cultures.

Your journey to becoming an interpreter requires:

- The ability to use two or more languages at *superior-to-near-native* level of skills
- Know yourself – know where you feel most comfortable when interacting with a variety of people from different cultural and experiential backgrounds
- Flexibility, the ability to gracefully "go with the flow," when things don't go as predicted or hoped; being realistic, committed to lifelong learning, excited about education, and respectful to others.

Becoming a reflective practitioner – developing the ability to regularly think "about your own work, how you are doing it, and how you can make it better" by being "open-minded enough to take on new challenges" (Leal, Martinez, Stockton, & Bose, n.d., para. 4).

- Accept the fact that there will be room to improve every time you interact with people from different language and culture groups, as well as each time you interpret
- Consider areas of growth in your ASL knowledge and fluency; consider getting a Deaf mentor to help you improve
- Fingerspelling clearly and correctly, and knowing when NOT to fingerspell
- Expanding your ASL and English vocabulary across the range of linguistic registers
- Closing knowledge gaps you have identified in dDeaf history, social interaction rules, etc.

Self-Care: *Required to survive the journey!* Develop self-care skills and a self-care routine *before* becoming an interpreter. Do you take care of yourself now? Eating, sleeping, relationships and so much more. Make yourself a priority – no one is going to do that for you. Attend to the facets of your life that lead to *wholeness*; commit to supporting healthy habits of self-care – learn what a lifestyle of self-care looks

Are You Ready to Begin?

NOTES

like. We recommend that you begin to establish self-care habits now.

- Our lives are made up of various people, activities, and expectations. Unfortunately, our society often encourages us to put ourselves as a low priority and instead to value others over ourselves. This mindset is rife for self-neglect rather than self-care!
- The key to being able to care for yourself is learning that you are important, deserving first place now and then. When you are able to find genuine balance that enables you to feel special, valuable, and important, deserving care and self-love, you will be able to begin the path to self-care.
- Wisdom and experience dictate that we must not ignore the principles and priority of self-care.
- One self-care tip to better prepare you for the work of interpreting – stretching beforehand. The Toolbox has a handout that will show you some of the appropriate ways to stretch before and after you interpret.

THOUGHTS

Healthy Habits of Self-Care

13

TERMS TO KNOW:

- Culture (way of being)

- Language Broker

- Ghostwriters

- Gatekeeping

- Transliterating

*In the beginning...people who could hear gave birth to babies who could not hear as well as babies who could hear. Their dDeaf children grew up and gave birth to babies, some of whom were dDeaf like them and some who were babies who could hear. Over time, there were siblings, cousins, aunts and uncles ... some were "**people of sound**" and some were "**people of the eye.**" They didn't need interpreters ... they figured out by trial and error how to communicate through talking, gesturing and perhaps drawing stick figures in the dirt. But one day, these "people of the eye" and "people of sound" who could communicate with each other, came upon people who didn't understand the ways of those who couldn't hear. Recognizing the **chasm of no understanding**, those who could hear and were familiar with the world of the people of the eye, closed the chasm of no understanding – **and interpreting was born!***

2 | In The Beginning...

The folk tale above is based on liberal presumptions flowing from the Genesis story of creation in the Bible and what we know in modern times about chromosomes, inherited forms of deafness and the lives of dDeaf and hearing families. Spoken language interpretation has been documented from ancient history, and recent research tells us that sign language interpreting has been around for a very long time and it was originally provided by people who were dDeaf (Stone, 2009). But how did sign language interpreting evolve?

People in general, whether they are "*people of the eye*" or "*people of sound*" are drawn to other people who share the same language and culture – *ways of being.* This is true of "people of the eye." dDeaf people have their own **way of being** – ways of greeting people and ways of showing appreciation to another person, ways of demonstrating feelings of friendship. These *ways of being* are known today as **culture**. Interpreting evolved naturally within the dDeaf community. When a dDeaf person needed assistance navigating interactions with people in their communities who didn't know sign language, they naturally turned to other dDeaf people – people they trusted, knowing those individuals could mediate communication with people who could hear comfortably. They typically met in the Deaf clubs of the day – a place where dDeaf individuals of all ages and all vocations gathered – enjoying the company of others who shared their *ways of being* (Stone, 2009). When one of them received written correspondence that they struggled to understand, they asked another dDeaf person who had greater skills in the language the letter was written in to help them understand what the document said. This was the beginning of translation and interpreting among "people of the eye."

In dDeaf communities all over the world, there were dDeaf individuals who served as translators and interpreters between members of the dDeaf community and those in the community who did not know sign language. Research has identified one small Australian Irish Deaf community where talented dDeaf **language brokers** provided written, and sometimes spoken, translations at the request of various members of their community, which dates back to the 19th century (Adam, Carty & Stone, 2011; Napier, 2012). "Language brokers facilitate communication between two linguistically and culturally different parties. Unlike formal interpreters and translators, brokers mediate, rather than merely transmit, information" (Tse, 1996, p. 485). In that community, those who were able to facilitate understanding between *"people of the eye"* and *"people of sound"* were referred to as **ghostwriters** (Adam, Carty & Stone, 2011). The ghostwriter would function as the community interpreter/translator and read the document and translate it into sign

In The Beginning...

NOTES

language. If a response was required, the dDeaf interpreter worked between written English, Auslan (the majority sign language of Australia), British Sign Language (BSL) and Australian Irish Sign Language (AISL) to transform information from the recipient's sign language into written English, which would be returned to the sender.

dDeaf individuals who possess proficiency in both written, spoken and signed forms of the local language were a benefit to the entire dDeaf community. They frequently used their ability to explain complicated letters, function as an intermediary between *"people of the eye"* and *"people of sound"*, always striving to assure their dDeaf brothers and sisters understood. These interactions happened in dDeaf communities the world over; those dDeaf individuals who were more skilled in the country's written and spoken language and used the indigenous sign language of the region (Adam, Carty & Stone, 2011). Because *"people of the eye"* cannot hear, it was challenging for them to master the spoken language used in their communities. However, some dDeaf individuals, often by circumstance, developed more advanced skills in the language used by the non-Deaf community. This individual might have been born with the ability to hear but became dDeaf a few years after being born or they may have been born into a multigenerational dDeaf family, learning signed communication from birth and watched how their parents and grandparents navigated communication with people who could hear.

In addition to ghostwriters, family members and close friends of dDeaf individuals who knew sign language and could hear sometimes served as language brokers, but this only happened when the dDeaf community had some level of trust in that chosen individual. This type of **gatekeeping** allowed dDeaf people to monitor who was or was not *acceptable* in the role of an interpreter or translator. Gatekeeping was the vetting process of the dDeaf community, serving "as a protective mechanism to ensure that the interpreters had a significant connection to the community" (Mathers & Witter-Merithew, 2014, p. 158). Typically, this was a person who respected the *ways of being* among members of the dDeaf community and seemed to have the best interest of the dDeaf individual in mind (and heart). Over time, hearing individuals who had dDeaf family members or those who immersed themselves in the dDeaf community, learning the language and respecting dDeaf culture, developed *trusted* relationships with members of the dDeaf community. As a result, they were sometimes called on to interpret for members of the dDeaf community (Fant, 1990). The relationships of interpreters and dDeaf community members were based on the "Deaf way" of showing appreciation by engaging in acts of reciprocity (Philip, 1993). Money rarely, if ever, was exchanged for interpreting the birth of a baby or going to court to deal with a traffic ticket. Rather, the dDeaf individual might take the interpreter out for dinner or offer to mow their lawn for the upcoming summer. However, for those who did not have dDeaf family members, their "payment" for interpreting services was gaining access to the dDeaf community and culture by being welcomed into the dDeaf club, and having dDeaf mentors who would informally tutor the outsider in the "Deaf way."

Eventually, interpreting became more *professional,* leading to formal interpreter education programs – a new avenue of admission into the role of an interpreter. As interpreting students, you need to consider the history, as well as the future of interpreting as a profession by examining the roots of interpreting and where the interpreting profession is heading. In this text, we will introduce you to both the Registry of Interpreters for the Deaf (RID) and the Canadian Association of Sign Language Interpreters (CASLI). Each organization is discussed in some depth,

Chapter 2

NOTES

including their organizational structure, officers, their respective certification systems as well as some of the current issues facing each organization.

Please know that this information is fairly detailed for two reasons:

1. It is essential that you understand the historic evolution of the profession and the continued relevance of specific professional organizations
2. This information will prepare you to take the first part of the written certification test, administered by both the US and Canadian interpreting organizations

THE BEGINNING OF INTERPRETING AS A PROFESSION

The modern practice of interpreting as a *profession* only emerged during the last few decades of the 20th Century. Spoken language interpreting was first formalized during the Nuremberg Trials following World War II. Sign language interpreting in North America was established as a profession when the Registry of Interpreters for the Deaf (RID) was founded on June 16, 1964, at Ball State Teachers College in Evansville, Indiana (Myers, 2013). RID had 66 founding members, one-third were dDeaf and 7 of those founding members identified as Deaf interpreters (Myers, 2013). The remaining 59 founders were non-deaf individuals who provided interpreting services on a voluntary and as needed basis, as was the custom. Most of the founders held full time jobs and, at the founding of the organization, none of them envisioned a day when individuals would earn a living wage as a sign language interpreter.

Fifteen years after the founding of RID, Canada established the Association of Visual Language Interpreters of Canada (AVLIC) in 1979. However, even before AVLIC was officially established, discussions about a national organization were well under way. This is evidenced by regional organizations that formed in the mid-1970's. Both the "Manitoba Registry of Interpreters for the Deaf (MRID), and the Alberta Chapter of the Registry of Interpreters for the Deaf (ACRID) were incorporated provincially in 1976 and 1977 respectively" (Letourneau, 2009, p. 1). These founding RID organizations provided opportunities for networking and professional development among sign language interpreters on both sides of the border. The Association of Visual Language Interpreters of Canada (AVLIC) was founded at the first national interpreting conference held in Winnipeg, November 16-19, 1979. "It was at this first conference of Canadian interpreters that the federal government, Bureau of the Secretary of State Department, made a groundbreaking announcement. Sign language interpretation services, in both French-langue des signes quebecoise (LSQ) and English-American Sign Language (ASL), would now be provided to assist the federal government in its communication with Deaf citizens" (Association of Visual Language Interpreters of Canada, 2011, p. 1). In July, 2018, nearly forty years after its founding, AVLIC changed its name to the Canadian Association of Sign Language Interpreters (Association of Visual Language Interpreters of Canada, 2018). You will see these names often used interchangeably, but the official name of the interpreting association is the Canadian Association of Sign Language Interpreters (CASLI).

The Roots of Our Profession

Sign language interpreters have probably been around since the first dDeaf person desperately needed to communicate something to a person who could hear but did not know sign language. In the early stages of interpreting it was very likely a family member served as an intermediary.

The earliest record of sign language interpreters in Canada and the United States show that those early interpreters were often:

1. Individuals who had dDeaf parents or dDeaf siblings
2. Teachers of the Deaf
3. Members of the clergy

Prior to the late 1950's and early 1960's, there were no formal sign language classes or interpreter preparation programs. Being paid for interpreting services was unheard of into the mid-1960's and early 1970's as interpreters were rarely called upon.

The field of interpreting prior to 1964 was vastly different from what we see and experience today. It would be a strain on your imagination to truly comprehend the difference; people did not *work* as interpreters, rather they *volunteered* their time to interpret. Individuals who could hear and who knew sign language, typically donated their services as their schedules permitted. In the event they received any compensation it was happily accepted, but not expected. Out of the goodness of their hearts, or possible obligation to family members, these individuals interpreted for the occasional medical appointment, wedding, funeral or other significant life events. No one was trained to interpret in legal, medical or mental health settings; individuals did their best to meet communication needs as they arose and their services were accepted gratefully. For that period in our history, the services rendered were likely just adequate.

But the mid-1960's and 1970's were revolutionary in many ways. It was an era of hippies, rock music, civil rights, women's liberation and the Vietnam war. It was also a time of increased social conscience, leading to attempts at including some minority groups who had been disenfranchised from the dream of equality. It was also a critical time in the field of sign language interpreting.

REGISTRY OF INTERPRETERS FOR THE DEAF (RID) ESTABLISHED

The first-ever national "Workshop on Interpreting for Deaf People" was held in 1964, at Ball State Teachers College (now Ball State University). Sixty-three sign language interpreters from across the country convened for this historic event. Dr. Edgar Lowell, a participant at the workshop and Director of the John Tracy Clinic in Los Angeles, made a recommendation to the participants that they establish a national organization of interpreters and suggested an evening meeting to discuss his idea. The interpreters hired to work for that workshop agreed to stay to discuss the increased demand for interpreters and to follow up on the idea of developing a national registry of those who were qualified to interpret.

When the group assembled, Dr. Lowell served as Chair as the National Registry of Professional Interpreters and Translators for the Deaf was established. An election for officers was held and Ken Huff was elected President of the new organization, with Elizabeth Benson as Vice-President (Myers, 2013). The following year, the name was changed to the Registry of Interpreters for the Deaf (RID) and a constitution, bylaws, and Code of Ethics were drafted. The working relationship between RID and the National Association of the Deaf (NAD) can be traced back to the 1966 NAD Convention. However, the Registry of Interpreters for the Deaf was

Chapter 2

NOTES

still only a "paper organization." Though RID did not have an office or staff, their membership had begun to grow. At the 1966 National Association of the Deaf Convention, both NAD and RID agreed that NAD would apply for funding from the Vocational Rehabilitation Administration to fund the provision of office space for RID and establish an operations budget. With financial support from the Vocational Rehabilitation Administration, a national registry of sign language interpreters for the dDeaf was actually established. The organization was incorporated in 1972 and sign language interpreters throughout the US, Canada, Europe, Australia, and New Zealand joined RID – the first such organization in the world.

Historically, the relationship between NAD and RID has been quite amicable and each organization has strived to serve and promote the wellbeing of the dDeaf community, whether through advocacy, education or interpreting services. The preservation of the rights of the dDeaf community has always been a priority. However, as each organization continued to grow and change, their paths diverged and on January 17, 2016, the NAD-RID partnership ceased by a unanimous vote by the NAD board.

The name of the organization, Registry of Interpreters for the Deaf, has been the topic of much discussion since the phrase *for the Deaf*, in the age of equality and disability rights, can be perceived quite negatively, viewing dDeaf individuals in a paternalistic manner. Furthermore, interpreters do not interpret only *for* dDeaf people; interpreters provide interpreting services for all people – whether they can hear or not. We interpret for those who identify as hard of hearing and others who identify as DeafBlind. We provide interpreting services for every person requiring support to bridge communication with others. When asked about this controversy, Lillian Beard, one of the founding members of the Registry of Interpreters for the Deaf replied, "I can't believe there is such a debate about changing our name. When we decided upon the name, I was so proud of the acronym, RID, after all, having professional interpreters would hopefully *rid* the world of barriers for Deaf people!" (Ricks, 1976).

"The Registry of Interpreters for the Deaf is a professional organization for interpreters who use signed and spoken languages" (https://rid.org/about-rid/mission-vision-statements/). The original purposes of RID included:

- Publishing a registry of interpreters
- Investigating evaluation and certification systems
- Educating the public about interpreting services

Today, practitioners in North America commonly refer to themselves as sign language interpreters. However, they may also refer to themselves as ASL/English, Spanish/MSL or LSQ/Canadian French interpreters, rather than interpreters for the dDeaf. The designated mission for the members of RID is to commit to the provision of ethical, quality interpreting services for individuals. In addition, committing to ongoing professional development to provide international, national, regional, state and local forums, as well as structure for the ongoing growth and development of the profession of interpreting and transliterating. RID is also committed to increasing the number and quality of interpreters in the United States, ensuring that they are qualified to practice and that they practice in accordance with the Code of Professional Conduct.

An additional goal of RID is to promote the profession of sign language interpreting

In The Beginning...

NOTES

and **transliterating.** The term transliteration carries with it the expectation that an interpreter will work between spoken "English and one of several contact varieties [PSE, CASE] that incorporate linguistic features from both English and ASL" (Livingston, Singer & Abramson, 1994, p. 2). Robert Ingram (1974) felt that the *process* of rendering the message from spoken English into a form of signed English involved a verbatim translation; thus, he believed the only change was the modality. "On the basis of Ingram's writings, the term transliteration was adopted by the field" (cited in Siple, 1997, p. 85). However, the authors feel much like Locker (1990) "that there is no well defined or standardized description of transliteration (even though the term is used as if there were), since this target form attempts to accommodate both the syntactic order of spoken English and a range of ASL features (including principally the lexicon) in order to convey the message in a signed modality" (pp. 168-169). In other words, Conceptually Accurate Signed English (CASE) and Pidgin Signed English (PSE) "are synonyms for the same method of signing; both combine parts of two languages, thus they do not completely represent the grammar of either one" (Rendel, Bargones, Blake, Luetke & Stryker, 2018, p. 19; Stringham, 2019). For more information about this topic please see the Comparative ASL/English Language Continuum by Doug Stringham in the Toolbox.

Both Conceptually Accurate Signed English and Pidgin Signed English are erroneously labeled as if they were actual languages with genuine grammar and syntax. Furthermore, though both CASE and PSE varieties utilize American Sign Language signs while attempting to adhere to English word order. Neither CASE or PSE add prefixes or suffixes, nor do they utilize verb-noun endings (-ing, -ed, -s, -er). It must also be recognized that Manually Coded English (MCE) and the many varieties of signed coded systems were contrived to create greater English representation in signed communication (SEE 1, SEE 2, LOVE, etc.). Prefixes or suffixes were added to make use of verb tense and related noun endings, (-ing, -ed, -s, -er), yet all were influenced by American Sign Language. One of the purposes of both CASE/PSE is that it served as a bridge, helping people who used American Sign Language and those who use Manually Coded English to better understand each other (*Conceptually Accurate Signed English (CASE),* 2019; Rendel, et al., 2018).

Furthermore, interpreters have an obligation to stay abreast of current trends within the interpreting profession and continue to grow professionally. RID encourages this commitment to professionalism by:

- Providing training for interpreters through the Certification Maintenance Program (CMP)
- Maintaining the Center for Assessment of Sign Language Interpreters (CASLI); ensuring the development and administration of knowledge and performance tests
- Supporting self-regulation, accountability and decision latitude in the field of interpreting through the Ethical Practices System

RID has historically been a member run organization which encourages voting members to vote on organizational business biennially and on certain issues by mail ballot. The various membership categories include:

- **Certified Member:** Members who hold a valid certification accepted by RID, are in good standing, and meet the requirements of the Certification Maintenance Program.
- **Certified Inactive:** Members who hold temporarily inactive certification, are not

Chapter 2

NOTES

currently interpreting and have put their certification on hold. Members in this category are not considered currently certified and do not hold valid credentials.

- **Associate Member:** Members engaged in interpreting or transliterating, full-time and part-time, but do not hold certification accepted by RID. Members in this category are enrolled in the Associate Continuing Education Tracking Program.
- **Student Member:** Members currently enrolled, at least part-time, in an interpreting program. Student members must provide proof of enrollment every year. This proof can be a current copy of a class schedule or a letter from a coordinator/instructor on school letterhead. Student membership does not include eligibility to vote.
- **Supporting Member:** Individuals who support RID but are not engaged in interpreting. Supporting membership does not include eligibility to vote or reduced testing fees.
- **Organizational Member:** Organizations and agencies supporting RID's purposes and activities.

As of 2020, The Registry of Interpreters for the Deaf board was composed of eleven members. The board is comprised of the president, vice president, secretary, treasurer, dDeaf member-at-large, member-at-large as well as five regional representatives (the member-at-large positions can be a certified or associate member). The immediate past president can also serve as the ex-officio member. Their term of office lasts two years, beginning at the conclusion of the RID National Conference and concluding at the end of the following RID National Conference. The board's role is to govern the national organization by determining the course and vision of RID through internal and external stakeholder engagement. Furthermore, the structure of RID allows for affiliate chapters. Generally, there is at least one affiliate chapter per state, some states have multiple regional or affiliate chapters.

There are multiple benefits to RID membership including:

- Eligible for reduced certification testing fees; associate, student or certified members only
- *Journal of Interpretation* – free for associate and certified members only
- Discounts on all RID publications and products
- Subscription to *VIEWS,* RID's quarterly newsletter as well as monthly email updates such as *RID e-NEWS*
- Annual Continuing Education Center discount code for associate, student or certified members who maintain good standing
- Discounts on RID's biennial conference registration
- Voting privileges – associate and certified members only
- Leadership opportunities to help shape RID and the interpreting profession by serving on committees, councils and task forces
- Access to members' only online benefits, including *VIEWS* online, and a searchable, archived article database
- Opportunities to purchase dental and vision, life, disability, and liability insurance

THE CANADIAN ASSOCIATION OF SIGN LANGUAGE INTERPRETERS (CASLI)

In The Beginning...

NOTES

As previously mentioned, the Association of Visual Language Interpreters of Canada changed their name to the Canadian Association of Sign Language Interpreters in 2017. in spite of this transition, the acronym AVLIC will often be associated with the Canadian Association of Sign Language Interpreters. It should also be noted that the acronym for the Canadian Association of Sign Language Interpreters (CASLI) and the Center for Assessment of Sign Language Interpreters (CASLI), a subsidiary of the Registry of Interpreters for the Deaf, are the same.

The evolution of sign language interpreting in Canada followed along the same lines as the United States. Those involved in sign language interpreting were primarily individuals who had dDeaf family members, educators of the dDeaf, hearing individuals who had developed friends within the dDeaf community, or graduates of formal interpreter education programs. The transition from the belief that sign language interpreters were friends, family or clergy changed gradually when people adopted the idea interpreters were professionals with specialized skills and training (Letourneau, 2009; McDermid, 2008). Members of the dDeaf community began to expect more, they demanded quality interpreting services.

The Registry of Interpreters for the Deaf (RID) fell short of meeting the needs of Canadian interpreters. Canadian interpreters longed for a professional association that supported their desire to improve their language and interpreting skills, establish best practices for sign language interpreters and enable Canadian interpreters to affiliate with one another as professionals, while reflecting the needs unique to Canada. Prior to the first conference and the establishment of AVLIC, now CASLI, a letter was sent to individuals and agencies across Canada in fall of 1977 stating that "The increasing demand for interpreting services can no longer be adequately met by the haphazard means we have relied upon for so long" (Letourneau, 2009, p. 4). Furthermore, there was serious concern expressed from the dDeaf community, schools for the dDeaf and sign language interpreters, all sharing the same sentiment – there was a clear need for quality interpreting and ethical competence (Letourneau, 2009). It was during the "inaugural conference a decision was made to establish a Canadian professional association that would go on to draft a constitution, bylaws, a Code of Ethics and certification standards" (AVLIC Policy & Procedure Manual, 2011, p. 1). The involvement of both the dDeaf and interpreting communities in the birth of the organization is a model of community consultation and collaboration which CASLI has sought to maintain in all of its affairs to date.

The founders of CASLI (AVLIC) were fortunate to learn from the trials and errors of RID, its sister organization. The original name of the *visual language interpreters* was adopted with great care as Canadian interpreters were aware of the challenges encountered by RID regarding its name. CASLI (AVLIC) wanted a name that was broad enough to include those practitioners who provided oral and signed transliteration, as well as sign language interpretation. In addition, the Canadian organization needed a name that could cover a variety of working languages, including French and LSQ. CASLI (AVLIC) officially recognizes American Sign Language, La Langue des Signes Quebecoise, English-based sign systems, speechreading, elements of gesture, and spoken French and English.

The Canadian Association of Sign Language Interpreters has been a member run

Chapter 2

NOTES

organization from its inception, and eligible members vote on organizational business biennially. CASLI (AVLIC) has several membership categories:

1. **Class A Members, Active:** Includes working ASL-English interpreters, Deaf interpreters, and LSQ-French interpreters and only active members are allowed to vote on organizational issues.
2. **Class B Members, Students and Deaf interpreters:** Student membership is reserved for those enrolled in a CASLI-recognized interpreter education program (IEP) and who are training to become professional sign language interpreters. Deaf and student interpreters must meet the additional criteria outlined on the AVLIC website; you are not able to vote as a class B member.
3. **Subscription Service:** If you, as an individual or organization, do not meet the eligibility criteria for class A or B membership, you may subscribe to information provided by CASLI; you are not able to vote as a subscription service member.
4. **In Lieu:** This membership option is only open to CASLI members that live in a province or territory that doesn't have an Affiliate Chapter established; in lieu members are allowed to vote only if they are active members.

It is important to note that *dual membership* is required for ALL membership levels of CASLI (AVLIC); meaning you are required to be a member of CASLI and at least one CASLI Affiliate Chapter of your choice. However, if the province or territory does not have an affiliate chapter, members may opt for the *In Lieu* membership. Which means an interpreter with a Class A active membership in good standing, living in a province or territory where there is no CASLI Affiliate Chapter can request that dual membership in an Affiliate Chapter be waived.

CASLI (AVLIC) was established to accomplish several purposes, including:

1. Provide a professional milieu in which the nurturing of positive growth could take place
2. Promote networking
3. Develop personal knowledge, skills and ethical behavior while advancing the profession

The basic premise of CASLI's approach to the tasks above includes the active involvement and frequent consultation with the Canadian Cultural Society of the Deaf (CCSD) and the Canadian Association of the Deaf (CAD). The Canadian Association of Sign Language Interpreters (CASLI) announced in July 2010 "to work in close partnership for the future benefit of Canadian Deaf people who use Sign Languages and the profession of interpreters whose working languages include a Sign Language" (Joint Communication Team, 2010, p. 1).

The Core Value Statement of the Canadian Association of Sign Language Interpreters, states that individuals have the right to interpreting services and that those services should be rendered by persons who demonstrate excellence in ethical conduct, professional behavior and linguistic proficiency.

The Canadian Association of Sign Language Interpreters (CASLI) is guided in all its activities by the beliefs that:

1. Collaboration, cooperation and mutual, transparent communication between the Deaf community and Sign Language interpreters at a local, regional and national level across Canada are essential

In The Beginning...

NOTES

2. The Association and its members will work with each other collegially, respectfully and with professional integrity
3. The Association will be responsive to its members.

The CASLI (AVLIC) Board of Directors is composed of officers and committee coordinators. All individuals hold office for two years following their election or appointment. The nine-member Executive Board includes:

1. President
2. Past President
3. First Vice President
4. Second Vice President
5. Treasurer
6. Secretary
7. Evaluations Officer
8. Director (formerly Member at Large), 2 positions

There are many benefits to CASLI (AVLIC) membership including:

- Eligible to serve on the CASLI board, available for Class A members
- Representation in the Directory of CASLI members, available for Class A members
- Eligible to vote, available for Class A members
- National dispute resolution process, available for Class A members
- Memberships card, letters to your employer and first year membership discount, available for Class A members
- Discounts on national and provincial conferences and additional professional development opportunities, available for Class A & B members
- Opportunity to participate in certification evaluation service (CES), available for class A & B members
- E-mail Buddy introduces two members by email for informal mentoring, available for Class A & B members
- Serve on committees, councils and task forces, available for Class A & B members
- Subscription to the association's quarterly bilingual newsletter, available for all members
- E-mail announcements may include, but are not limited to, news releases, conference advertising, job postings, professional development opportunities, available for all members

The certification of interpreters is currently offered by two national interpreter organizations in North America: the Registry of Interpreters for the Deaf (RID) and the Canadian Association of Sign Language Interpreters (CASLI).

Currently (2020), there are approximately 150 interpreter education programs in the US, ranging from those granting a two year associate degree to one doctoral degree program, teaching American Sign Language/English interpreting skills to dDeaf and non-deaf students. In Canada, there are five American Sign Language/English interpreting programs; four of which offer a 2-year diploma (three of which require American Sign Language (ASL) and Deaf Studies as a prerequisite), and one that offers a 4-year program which offers a bachelor's degree. There is also an infrastructure across the globe, providing interpreting services, and in some countries supporting educational programs for developing interpreters.

Chapter 2

NOTES

As we enter the 21st century, we are embarking in new territory regarding the profession of sign language interpreting and the relationship of interpreters with both dDeaf and non-deaf communities. If you are reading this text, you are probably beginning your education to become an interpreter between the languages of American Sign Language (ASL), Langue des signes du Québec (LSQ), and/or Mexican Sign Language and English, French, and/or Spanish.

As this book goes to press in 2020, all of the testing for certification of sign language interpreters described and being administered by CASLI was on hold. CASLI is working diligently to conduct an in-depth evaluation and revision of the current certification system. They are reviewing by:

1. Maintaining the validity of the test so the rating standards reflect the expectations of dDeaf community members and employers
2. Administering the test, balancing affordability for applicants with the viability of administering the test across the diverse regions of Canada

Canadian sign language interpreters seeking certification should join the provincial interpreting organization where you live and stay in contact with CASLI so you will know when their certification process is reinstated. In the meanwhile, interpreters in Canada seeking certification are taking a national or regional exam in the United States.

As graduates of your interpreting education program, you will play a big part in how the field of interpretation evolves in the years to come. Here are some of the challenges that lie ahead:

- Most hearing graduates from the interpreter education programs in the US or Canada will have learned sign language as a second language. In addition, the majority of those graduates are hoping to become professional practitioners. Unfortunately, the bulk of students graduating from programs will not possess the requisite "superior" level of linguistic fluency in either ASL or LSQ (Newell & Caccamise, 2006). Sadly, this means they will be unqualified linguistically and culturally to work as interpreters in many settings upon graduation. Of even greater concern, very few members of this generation of interpreters will have been vetted by members of the dDeaf community; they may have a book-knowledge of Deaf history and culture, but the majority have little, if any, personal ties to the dDeaf community (Mathers & Witter-Merithew, 2014).

- A new and exciting development is seeing a significant number of dDeaf individuals studying to become interpreters, providing a pool of interpreters who possess native or superior linguistic abilities, as well as internalized Deaf *"ways of being."* The increased numbers of dDeaf students attending interpreter education programs in order to become dDeaf interpreters/ translators is unprecedented and is a much welcomed change in professional practice. dDeaf interpreters work in the same settings as interpreters who can hear, including educational, legal, social services, employment, religious, performing arts, medical, and mental health venues, to name a few.

- If you are a dDeaf student with the goal of becoming a Deaf Interpreter (DI), you are likely already a member of the dDeaf community, fluent in the sign language of your community and comfortable with the dDeaf cultural norms and expectations. However, there are areas where you may need additional focus. These include: (1) Improving your knowledge concerning the written and/or spoken language used in your community, (2) broadening your understanding and ability to communicate across a wide range of visual communication, including the use of academic ASL/LSQ, colloquial community based ASL/LSQ and a visual gestural forms of communication used with individuals who may be unfamiliar with formal signed languages; (3) and finally, one of the biggest challenges you will likely face is navigating your relationship with members of the dDeaf community as an *interpreter*, which is quite different from the relationship you have as a dDeaf person with automatic acceptance into the community.

- If you are a student who can hear and do not have a family member who is dDeaf, becoming an interpreter means you have to make a commitment to immerse yourself into the dDeaf community, soaking up the language and internalizing the norms of dDeaf culture. There is a requisite expectation that you show appreciation for the gift of sign language and access to the dDeaf culture in your community by *reciprocating.* This is done by contributing to the dDeaf community, donating your time and talents where appropriate, and demonstrating the humility of a "foreigner" in their community.

Graduation from your interpreter education program is another *beginning* as you start a lifetime journey and adventure to becoming an interpreter. Your first steps will require:

- Committing yourself to the daily challenge of developing your first and second language to levels of professional competence
- Engaging in regular and deliberate reflection, alone and with your colleagues, concerning the ethical decisions you will make and the subsequent actions required after those decisions are made
- Developing your people skills and your comfort with both dDeaf and non-deaf people
- Remaining curious and open to the ways of dDeaf people (for those of you who can hear) or the ways of hearing people (for those of you who are dDeaf)
- Giving back to the dDeaf community in grateful appreciation for their willingness to share the treasure of their language and culture with you
- Earning the trust, support and approval of dDeaf community members for you as an interpreter (or translator) committed to growing into a responsible professional practitioner

chapter Review

This chapter provides a more in-depth view into the requirements needed to become a certified interpreter in the field. Interpreter certification differs between countries and learning the aspects of your country are essential in your preparation. Below are key terms and important information to know as you continue to learn about becoming an interpreter.

Terms to Know:

- **Culture:** People have their own *way of being* – ways of greeting people and ways of showing appreciation to another person when they show friendship.

Chapter 2

NOTES

- **Gatekeeping:** This term is the vetting process dDeaf people used to decide who was allowed or was not allowed to be an interpreter or translator.

- **Ghostwriter:** dDeaf individuals in the community who were able to facilitate between people who could hear and people who were dDeaf, they would often function as the community interpreter/translator reading documents and translate it into sign language and would often help write a response (Adam, Carty, & Stone, 2011).

- **Language Broker:** This term is used to describe those who provided written, and sometimes spoken, translations. "Language brokers facilitate communication between two linguistically and culturally different parties. Unlike formal interpreters and translators, brokers mediate, rather than merely transmit, information" (Tse, 1996, p. 485).

- **Transliterating:** This refers to the rendering of spoken languages (such as English) and contact languages (such as American Sign Language) in a verbatim manner.

After graduation you should look forward to a lifetime journey which will include:

- Daily development of your language skills
- Engaging in regular and deliberate reflection on your ethical decisions and actions
- Developing your people skills
- Continuing to be curious and open to the ways of dDeaf people (for those of you who can hear) or the ways of people who can hear (for those of you who are dDeaf)
- Giving back to the dDeaf community in appreciation for them allowing you to share their language
- Earning the trust, support and approval of the dDeaf community as an interpreter and/or translator

The earliest documented sign language interpreters in North America were:

- Children of dDeaf parents or siblings
- Teachers of the Deaf
- Members of the clergy

Conceptually Accurate Signed English (CASE) and **Pidgin Signed English** (PSE) "are synonyms for the same method of signing; both combine parts of two languages, thus they do not completely represent the grammar of either one" (Rendel, et al., 2018, p. 19; Stringham, 2019). PSE and CASE are signing structures that blend American Sign Language signs with English syntax. Most signed messages that use PSE/CASE will often include initialized signs, weak adherence to the grammatical structure of English, and though it is the goal of PSE and CASE to be conceptually accurate the signer may not always achieve the goal.

The Registry of Interpreters for the Deaf was founded in 1964. The original purpose was:

- Publish a registry of interpreters
- Investigate evaluation and certification systems
- Educate the public about interpreting services

In The Beginning...

NOTES

CASLI or CASLI? This acronym CASLI is used to refer to two different organizations:

- In Canada, it stands for the **Canadian Association of Sign Language Interpreters**.
- In the US, it represents the **Center for the Assessment of Sign Language Interpretation**, LLC.

KEY POINTS

TERMS TO KNOW:

- Interlocutors
- Metamessages
- Culture
- Minority Group
- Sociolinguistics
- Linguistic Register
- Complementary Schismogenesis
- Deafcentric
- Ingroup Speak
- Deafcentric
- Jargon
- Backchanneling

3 | Communication

Communication requires the finesse of constructing messages to convey our goals and intentions to someone while being sensitive to their nonverbal responses as we hope to have the intended impact on the recipient. Then the person you are attempting to communicate with takes your signed or spoken message and begins to decode it, interpreting the prepositional phrases, noting whether you used direct or indirect speech, giving attention to the forms of politeness you used. All of this while considering the tone of voice, visual and physical markers that help determine how you felt about what you were saying/signing.

As sign language interpreters, we receive messages that are not intended for us and we deliver those messages to the intended recipient with the goal of having understood and conveyed the precise goals and meanings of the sender. Sensitivity to the act and art of communication is at the heart of what we do as we mediate communication between two **interlocutors**. An interlocutor is one of the people involved in a dialogue or conversation. In this process, it is important to recognize that many of the same features that occur in spoken conversations also occur in signed conversations. However, the communication features (e.g., grammar, syntax) likely to be employed in spoken and signed messages are quite different. The way others send and receive messages, and how interpreters convey those messages lends to fluid and meaningful communication while preserving the intention of the sender. Throughout the interpreting process, the interpreter deals with the differences in how the two languages convey content. The way signed languages and spoken languages manage the details of the languages are different; how verb tenses are managed, the use of direct or indirect speech, how the concept of time is communicated, forms of politeness, and the use and meaning of repetition, all of which will be different in each language. Overlaying all of the above, interpreters must identify and convey not the actual signs or words that are used, but the meaning that results from the envelope of nonverbal and affective elements that carry the bulk of the meaning for *all messages*.

This is an example of what you will be doing if you become an interpreter – decipher what a person is communicating when someone says, "I love my brother," while rolling their eyes and delivering the proclamation with an icy tone. You must have the ability to convey that the speaker, in fact, *does not* love their brother. One of the reasons we pay particular attention to nonverbal communication, "is that

Communication

NOTES

nonverbal communication is the predominant means of conveying meaning from person to person" (Guerrero & Floyd, 2006, p. 2). Research indicates that *much* of our daily conversations are conveyed nonverbally, it is estimated "that nonverbal behaviors account for 60 to 65% of the meaning conveyed in an interpersonal exchange"(Birdwhistell, 1970; Burgoon, 1994 cited in Guerrero & Floyd, 2006, p. 2). "Information conveyed by the meanings of words is the message. What is communicated about the relationships – attitudes toward each other, the occasion, and what we are saying – is the **metamessage**. And it's metamessages that we react to most strongly" (Tannen, 1987, p. 29). If in the midst of a heated discussion someone states through gritted teeth, "I'm sorry!", the genuineness of the apology is doubtful. Every time we communicate with those around us, we spend time coding and decoding the *intent* of the messages exchanged based on our personal conversational styles.

CULTURE AND COMMUNICATION

What is Culture?
When groups of people "do life" together over a significant period of time by engaging in common activities, they gradually adopt norms. These *shared* ideas, beliefs, values, and expectations form the foundation of their culture (Useem, Donoghue, & Useem, 1963). **Culture** is the term used to describe the normal "way of life" that is practiced among members of an identified people group. These norms are the habits and values of that people group, which include: customs, beliefs, taboos, attitudes and behaviors. "Culture has been defined in a number of ways, but most simply, as the learned and shared behavior of a community of interacting human beings" (Useem, Donoghue, & Useem, 1963, p. 169). Recognizing that there are numerous components of culture including, but not limited to, language, customs, social behavior, holidays, arts, and ways of expressing group identity.

Most often, the culture of a people group is passed from generation to generation through stories, customs, celebrations, education, and religious institutions. Over time, cultural norms and beliefs are often enforced by religious, legal and social expectations, with consequences for those who fail to conform to cultural expectations. At its core, culture reflects the accepted shared patterns of behaviors and interactions, all of which are learned through a process called *socialization*. These shared beliefs, values and patterns of behavior distinguish the members of one cultural group from members of another group, resulting in unique and differing *cultural identities* (What is Culture?, 2019). "The essence of a culture is not its artifacts, tools, or other tangible cultural elements...it is the values, symbols, interpretations, and perspectives that distinguish one people from another in modernized societies" (Banks & McGee, 1989; cited in Nkomo, 2017, p. 47).

Third Culture
The majority of today's interpreters acquire sign language as a second language. It is imperative that they not only demonstrate native fluency in their own language but also acquire superior to near-native fluency in the language of the dDeaf community, while also demonstrating cultural competence (Newell & Caccamise, 2006). As an interpreter, it is important to remain sensitive to the features unique to the communities where you live and work. Because interpreters possess the ability to communicate with people who use sign language and people who use spoken language, they are in a unique position which enables them to interact in multiple cultures.

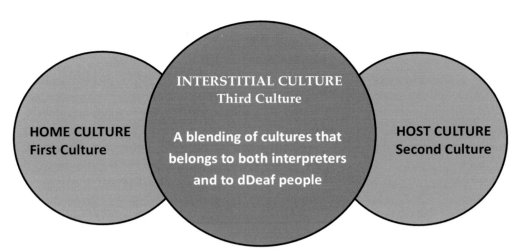

FIGURE 1: This illustration is one way to depict third culture. The Home Culture could be the hearing person's culture/community, the Host Culture would be the dDeaf person's culture/community, the Interstitial or Third Culture would be where the two cultures/communities intersect. It is a place for those who live or work in a culture outside their native or "passport" country.

A "third culture" emerges when two *dissimilar* communities, each with their own unique culture, customs, language, and norms intersect. The intersection of two cultures make it possible for members of each group to experience the cultural practices and behavioral norms practiced in each group. Interpreters and dDeaf people are both members of the third culture because they understand the *"ways of being"* of both groups (Bienvenu, 1987). Interpreters are able to move between both signed and spoken language(s) and are sojourners in both worlds. This familiarity with multiple cultural, behavioral and linguistic norms is foundational to individuals working toward becoming quality sign language interpreters. One goal is that the skill of sign language interpreters would be such that they would be able to move seamlessly between a culture based on sound and a culture based on vision.

Interpreters must make culturally appropriate decisions at every interpreting assignment. Consider attending a *dDeaf event* as the interpreter – you would have to determine which cultural and behavioral norms should be observed while at the interpreting assignment. Norms such as hugging, which is a common physical expression within the dDeaf community, both upon meeting and leaving, whereas, a handshake is the common greeting and leaving norm within the mainstream American community. For example, you are the interpreter for a large group of people who can hear at a dDeaf celebration and when you arrive you are met by several prominent leaders of the dDeaf community, what do you do? Bienvenu (1987) describes third culture clearly and explains that,

> Third culture is neither permanent nor stable. It varies constantly, depending on the immediate reason for the contact. It is a very flexible, changeable, and temporary phenomenon. There is an important distinction to be made between this third culture phenomenon and normal bi-culturalism. People who are bi-cultural have a first culture which they temporarily give up in exchange for a second culture. In the move to the second culture, they take on the language, rules, and values of that second culture. Then they are able to return to their first culture. Being bi-cultural means knowing how to move comfortably between two distinct cultures. Third culture is special in that it represents the possibility of coming to a halfway point, making contact with members of the other culture, but maintaining all the while one's identity as a member of one's first culture (p. 1).

Communication

NOTES

Cultural and Linguistic Minority

Today, ideas and beliefs about dDeaf people, as well as their culture and language are shifting. Historically, dDeaf people were perceived as individuals who had special needs because they lacked the ability to hear. Yet, the more we have come to understand this unique people group, the more we accept that they are "considered a cultural and linguistic minority group, who use a fully formed language—American Sign Language (ASL)—and are members of a distinct minority culture" (Higgins & Lieberman, 2016, p. 9). However, it is worth noting that minority groups may not always be a *numerical minority*; likewise, the majority group in a society may not always be a *numerical majority*. For example, women may outnumber the men in a society, yet they are considered a minority group because they do not hold sufficient societal power or positions. In this illustration, men, though numerically fewer than women, are considered to be in the majority because of their positions of power and privilege "These definitions correlate to the concept that the dominant group holds the most power in a given society, while subordinate groups are those who lack power compared to the dominant group" (Griffiths & Keirns, 2015, para. 7). It is the *lack of power* that is a predominant characteristic of a minority or subordinate group. An example of this reality was seen in South Africa, where the norm of apartheid (a system of legislated racial segregation) resulted in the black numerical majority being exploited and oppressed by the white minority.

Wirth (1945), a sociologist, explains that a **minority group** is often a group of people who are singled out because of their physical, linguistic or cultural characteristics, often because these characteristics are different from those of the dominant group. Minority group members are regarded as objects of collective discrimination receiving unequal treatment and limited opportunities by the dominant (power) majority group in society. Oftentimes because communication between people who can hear and people who are dDeaf does not occur with simplicity, dDeaf people are ostracized. People who are dDeaf have dealt with various forms of oppression and discrimination for years.

It is evident that there is a substantial difference in the way people who can hear communicate from people who are dDeaf. Sign language is a visual, spatial language that includes both non-manual and manual components while spoken language is an auditory, oral communication system. The obvious differences are not simply about mode of delivery, but rather how the users of each language interface with the world. The number of users of spoken languages are considerably greater than the number of people who use sign languages. "It is estimated that for every one thousand children born in the United States approximately two to three are identified with a significant hearing loss, thus, deafness is classified as a *low-incidence* disability" (Higgins & Lieberman, 2016, p. 9). A person who can hear has the ability to learn sign language, but a person who is dDeaf cannot learn to hear. Further, a person who can hear can acquire the language and culture of the dDeaf community, but it is critical to understand that this acquisition does not give them access to the lived experience of a person who has no experience with sound. The *dDeaf experience* can be *inadequately* described as the everyday life and feelings of a person who is dDeaf and how they interface with the world around them. However, the cumulative effort expended to communicate, to understand and be understood – this description is a gross oversimplification of the dDeaf experience. As a cultural and linguistic minority group found in every country, dDeaf people do not simply have a different way of living and communicating. In a world based on sound, they have a unique lived experience that is based primarily on *visually interfacing* with people, places, and things.

Importance of Communication

The importance and value of effective communication cannot be overemphasized. It has been proven that people require both *physical contact* and *communication* with each other to survive (Ross & McLaughlin, 1959; Schachter, 1959; McDaniel & Johnson, 1975; Shattuck, 1980). While communication may be complex at times and imprecise at other times, *meaningful* communication is essential for life, health, and the development of one's sense of self. We know that human interaction is the primary way relationships are formed and maintained. It is also critical to meet our requisite social needs such as, inclusion, control, and affection which afford us opportunities to interact with others, thus allowing us to receive feedback regarding our ideas and behavior (University of Minnesota, 2016).

Some view communication as a linear process in which information and ideas flow one at a time in only one direction – this is rarely the case. Instead, communication is often a lively, interactive and dynamic process in which participants simultaneously send and receive multiple overlapping messages. We must recognize that, "communication isn't as simple as saying what you mean. How you say what you mean is crucial, and differs from one person to the next, because using language is learned social behavior: How we talk and listen are deeply influenced by cultural experience" (Tannen, 1995, p. 5). Many of us believe that our ways of communicating ideas, expressing values, agreeing and disagreeing are natural and shared by those around us. However, that is how most misunderstandings occur, because we mistakenly believe that everyone thinks like we do.

By this point, it should be evident that people who can hear and people who are dDeaf have different "thought worlds," in essence, how dDeaf people think and express their thoughts are not the same as people who can hear (Lawrence, 2003; Kurz & Hill, 2018). It is essential that interpreters gain this understanding in order to use the skills and knowledge they acquire in both language and culture to create meaningful interpretations.

dDeaf people engage in conversations with people who can hear for a variety of reasons, such as their need to talk to a mechanic, doctor, store clerk, restaurant server, colleagues at work as well as with immediate and extended family. In these situations, dDeaf people have found ways to get their needs, wants or desires communicated – writing a note to a store clerk or pointing at the menu to order a meal. However, in other situations – doctor appointments or staff meetings – sign language interpreters are the better option. dDeaf people need and want effective and efficient communication across a variety of social, medical, academic and recreational settings (to name a few) and the services of a qualified sign language interpreter are invaluable.

Sociolinguistics

Language use is a social activity. The use of any language will vary according to the *social* characteristics of the speaker, their social standing, ethnicity, age and gender, as well as the social context in which they find themselves (Sarigül, 2000). For our purposes, we will define **sociolinguistics** as the relationships that exist between a language, culture, and the society where that language is used. However, sociolinguistics not only considers the social characteristics of the speaker, but also the characteristics of language, the variations, the functions and how context

Communication

NOTES

influences language use. This is noteworthy because language use varies according to each social situation and the variations in those settings or contexts are the "most powerful determinant of verbal behavior" (Sarigül, 2000, p. 415).

To put it another way, sociolinguistics helps us understand how conversations work in a wide range of situations. How we speak, who we are speaking to and the degree of formality have to do with styles of **linguistic register**. Register refers to the variations of language use based on "specific social situations, such as advertising, political journalism, shopping, or academic discussion" (Sarigül, 2000, p. 415). Most of us gain our knowledge about the formality and informality of language from our many life experiences, attending weddings, funerals, a court appearance, doctor appointments, conversations with teachers, friends and siblings, to name a few. From each life event we learn how to use different stylistic variations of language, which is known as linguistic register. There are a variety of ways to define or describe language formality; these variations of register are evidenced in both writing and speaking. Our preference will focus on the approach that depicts five distinct registers, as listed below (Nordquist, 2019).

Frozen: Language that is considered static and is always rendered the same. Frozen register is often associated with a location or specific event. Examples: The Lord's Prayer or Psalms 23 are often read at funerals; the Pledge of Allegiance to the Flag is recited at a little league game. While the interpretation into sign language of a frozen text may vary as there does not appear to be a single or "frozen" way in which to always interpret these texts. However, they should be rendered using "formal or platform" rules of sign formation reflecting the fact that these texts are typically signed to large groups of people, including: larger signing space, use of two-handed signs where such exist, and limited fingerspelling. In addition, if they are being signed and being accompanied by a spoken interpretation, the interpreter should have a copy of the text to read verbatim with the signed rendition.

Formal: Communication is typically moving in one direction, from the speaker to the audience. Most often the language used is more precise, utilizing complete sentences and subject specific terminology. This is often the expectation for a graduation address, church sermons, and inaugural speeches. There is not typically an opportunity for dialogue or questions from the audience.

Consultative: Very often in a consultative setting one of the speakers is a *content area expert,* possessing specialist knowledge that the patient or client does not possess, such as a doctor or lawyer. The doctor will provide consultation to the patient; the patient is free to ask the doctor questions, and the doctor will often employ medical terms that they will explain to the patient. Because there are multiple participants present, the degree of formality depends on each speaker.

Casual (Informal): The language in the casual register tends to be more conversational or colloquial and is frequently used among friends and family. Word choices are generally familiar to all users, and conversations are often dependent on prior dialogues. Gestures are often used in the discussions. Casual language is often peppered with slang, profanity and humor.

Intimate: This language is exclusively shared between close acquaintances and typically cannot be fully understood by anyone outside the communication circle. These individuals often have a greater degree of intimacy, such as siblings, spouses, lovers and close friends. By way of clarification, if an interpreter observes a conversation between a set of twins who are dDeaf, the interpreter may recognize some of the signs, but may not know the genuine meaning *intended* by the users. For example, if one of twins signs 'dog' to his brother while looking at his sister, he may mean referring to her loyalty, instead of her appearance (Joos, 1967; Payne, 1995; Nordquist, 2019).

There are identifying features that can help us to determine the register being employed by the speaker or participants, which will likely influence our sign and fingerspelling choices. The following questions identified by Sarigül (2000) noted that all linguistic choices, regardless of the situation, are typically influenced by one or more of the following features:

- The Participants: The person or people speaking and who they are speaking to?
- The Setting: Where the interaction is taking place?
- The Topic: What is being talked about?
- The Purpose: Why are they speaking?
- The Relationships: Among those present or involved are the relationships casual, formal, social or business, family, friends or strangers?

The information above forms the basic sociolinguistic components which explains "why all people don't speak the same way, and why they don't all speak the same way all of the time" (Sarigül, 2000, p. 415). Most of us learn the unwritten social rules related to language use as we learn the language. For example, you don't speak the same way at a funeral as you speak at a wedding, nor would you speak to the president of a university the same way you speak to your roommate. It is worth examining why we speak to each person differently and how we know the difference. Awareness of these innate differences is invaluable in the work of interpreting.

The Communication Process

Communication occurs in stages – it unfolds when we use our language combined with the knowledge and skills to construct statements, questions, and sentences to convey our thoughts, feelings and ideas to another person. Communication is rarely perfect since what is said doesn't always have the impact on those we intend, especially when the speakers do not share the same gender, culture, thought worlds or life journey. In our efforts to communicate we give voice to our beliefs, questions, attitudes, and opinions as we seek to know, and be known. Communication is also composed of *metamessages* which are conveyed through facial expressions, body language, gestures, tone, and other elements unrelated to the actual signs or words used to deliver the message. Metamessages can convey sarcasm, anger, joy, relief, sadness, frustration, etc.

- You are a person who can hear and your sibling, friend, or cousin, has broken your favorite gadget. Feeling guilty or fearing retribution, they hid it. Later, you discover the broken gadget – one of your favorites – in anger, you call their name by speaking slowly and using a low, growling tone. The tone of your voice is the *metamessage,* conveying your anger toward the miscreant.
- Likewise, if a Deaf person signed, "We wrote back and forth to communicate" followed by furrowing their brow and rolling eyes, it would likely communicate that they were annoyed by the experience being described. Their facial expression is the *metamessage.*

Communication

NOTES

When individuals have difficulty communicating, due to different linguistic signals, communication styles or dissimilar cultural norms – these exaggerated differences are known as **complementary schismogenesis**. This term, coined by Gregory Bateson (1935), is used to describe what happens when people with different cultural norms come into contact – when each person reacts to the other's differing patterns of behavior by increasing the opposing behavior (Tannan, 2013). An example of complementary schismogenesis is when an individual who is accustomed and comfortable standing close to those with whom they are talking, but the person they are speaking with feels more comfortable with a larger physical space between them. The first person will likely keep moving closer to the person they are talking with while the second person will continue to back away. This example of proxemics (the study of how people use space) demonstrates complementary schismogenesis. Consider the difference in the dDeaf and hearing communities and how complementary schismogenesis may be seen.

Interpreters must be prepared to recognize and deal with possible challenges in communication. One example of a common difficulty is when the recognized or accepted meaning of certain words is not shared by everyone who uses the term. *Mainstreamed*, for example, is a word used in dDeaf education, referring to placing children with special needs in the regular education classroom. Because of their lived experience, this term is often viewed negatively by members of the dDeaf community, whereas people in general view it positively. These differing views and uses of certain terms must be considered by interpreters. For example, if a dDeaf person was describing their educational experience and signed, "I was mainstreamed in high school," accompanied by the signer's facial affect indicating that the experience was negative, in order to convey the actual message being communicated, an interpreter would need to give voice to the clearly *implied*, but not signed component of the message. Hence, if the interpretation was rendered verbatim, though it conveyed the signed content, it would *fail* to communicate the unfavorable emotions associated with the experience of being mainstreamed. Though the term mainstreamed is shared by both communities, the *meaning* is different in each community.

Ingroup speak refers to an interaction where members of any community, group or organization use common terms that have a unique or different meaning from society in general. Ingroup speak are terms often used by a social group such as a gang, club, or religious affiliations. This can likely result in a breakdown in communication among individuals of differing cultures and communication norms; this is not exclusive to interactions between people who are dDeaf and those who can hear. However, as seen in the illustration above, there are a number of common terms used by members of the dDeaf community that carry significant emotional weight, such as mainstreamed, hearing, and residential school. These terms have a **Deafcentric** meaning. Deafcentric refers to the deeper meaning, or *semantic intent* of specific lexical terms that have a unique meaning or intent because of the lived experience of members of the dDeaf culture and community. Interpreters must be aware of such terms and the lived experience informing the Deafcentric meaning. This is critical because it allows interpreters to convey the intended meaning of the signer, which is not typically *transparent* to outsiders. Thus, it is important to note when interpreters render these Deafcentric terms literally, the intended message of the dDeaf person has not been successfully communicated.

Ingroup speak is slightly different from **jargon**, which refers to distinctive terminology used within professional circles. When jargon is used by members of a particular profession, it usually connotes an *atypical* meaning known specifically by members of that profession. Jargon is challenging because it is unclear to outsiders and can often be misunderstood and confusing to members of the dDeaf community if not interpreted in a way that conveys the intended meaning of the term. Likewise, it is worth considering whether jargon used by members of the interpreting community should be replaced or avoided altogether; instead, consider terms that are more accessible to individuals outside of the interpreting community. Some examples of interpreter jargon include such words as "feed," "voice," and "team."

Backchanneling, (also known as listener's feedback), is a term coined by Victor Yngve (1970). It refers to the subtle responses of a listener during a dialogue or interpretation, including verbal utterances (uh-huh, mmm, right, etc.) or non-verbal responses (nodding, smiling, frowning, etc.) indicating that the listener is understanding or following what the other person is saying. Whether these responses are verbal or nonverbal, backchanneling responses occur simultaneously throughout the communication. Backchanneling is an essential element of signed communications. For example, suppose a dDeaf person is having a conversation with a student learning sign language, the concentrated blank stare of the student (striving to understand) often leads the dDeaf person to ask the student if they understand what is being said. However, if the student employed backchanneling, such as nodding, the dDeaf person would receive the nonverbal feedback that the student understood.

Communicating with others is *essential* for our wellbeing. This is true whether you speak the same language or different languages. There are several keys that aid in communication. The first key is active listening. Listening to those talking to you instead of attending to the differences in language, culture, and the way you may communicate – focus on the message. The second key is to learn. Learn from one another, recognize that sharing our lives is one of most meaningful ways to learn and grow; purposefully choose to be around people unlike you. Finally, be open to change, suspend your judgment long enough to consider another's perspective and ponder long enough on their view to recognize its worth.

chapter Review

The chapter provides a look into more of the details related to the profession of interpreting. As an interpreter, the aspects mentioned are essential to know because they directly apply to your life now, as well as to the life you will develop as you continue on your journey to becoming an interpreter.

Terms to Know:

- **Backchanneling:** Is when someone shows active participation by using verbal utterances (hmm, right, uh-huh, etc.) or non-verbal responses (nodding, frowning, smiling, etc.).

- **Complementary Schismogenesis:** This is what happens when people with different social and cultural norms interact using their *normal* differing patterns of behavior. When this happens and their individual norms are significantly different, there is often a response of "opposing behavior" – resisting or objecting to the other person's way of interacting socially.

- **Culture:** Is the normal way of life that is practiced among people of an identified group, such norms are: customs, beliefs, taboos, attitudes, and behaviors.

- **Deafcentric:** Refers to the semantic intent of specific lexical terms that are different or unique because they relate to the culture or community of Deaf people.

- **Ingroup Speak:** Is encountered when members of any community, group, or organization use terms that have a unique or different meaning compared to those held by society in general.

- **Interlocutors:** Is one of the people involved in a dialogue or conversation.

- **Jargon**: Refers to distinctive terminology used within professional circles and when it is used by members of a particular profession, it usually connotes an *atypical* meaning known specifically by members of that profession. Jargon is challenging because it is unclear to outsiders.

- **Metamessage:** "What is communicated about the relationships – attitudes toward each other, the occasion, and what we are saying" (Tannen, 1987. p. 29).

- **Minority Group:** Is often a group of people who are singled out because of their physical, linguistic or cultural characteristics, often because these characteristics are different from those of the dominant group (Lumen - Introduction to Sociology, n.d.).

- **Register:** Refers to the variations of language use based on the "specific social situations, such as advertising, political journalism, shopping, or academic discussion" (Sarigül, 2000, p. 415).

- **Social:** Language varies depending on the characteristics of each user, reflecting things such as traits, social standing, ethnicity, age, gender, and the social context that the individual identifies with (Sarigül, 2000).

- **Sociolinguistics:** Examines the variations observed in how language is used in diverse settings or contexts. Specifically, sociolinguistics considers how factors such as the participants, setting, topics of discussion, purpose of interactions and relationships among the interlocutors influence communication (Sarigül, 2000).

- **Third Culture:** When two *dissimilar* communities, each with their own unique culture, customs, language, and norms intersect with each other. This happens when one's "home culture" intersects with one's "host culture," which is their second (or more) languages/cultures. Being a member of a third culture makes it possible for members of each group to experience the cultural practices and *"ways of being"* of each group.

Sociolinguistics

Language use and register varies according to each social situation and the variations in those settings or contexts in those situations. Sociolinguistics helps us understand how conversations work in a wide range of situations. Sarigül (2000) noted that linguistic choices are often influenced by one or more of the following features:

Chapter 3

NOTES

- The Participants
- The Setting
- The Topic
- The Purpose
- The Relationships

Sociolinguistics helps us understand by explaining why people communicate in different ways.

Ingroup Speak

Ingroup speak is when members of any community, group or organization use common terms that have a unique or different meaning from society in general.

The word *mainstream* has different meanings depending on the community that uses it. Though it refers to placing children with special needs in the regular education classroom, both cultures attach different meanings. For example:

- **Deaf culture** views the term negatively
- **Society in general (especially people who work in special education)** view it positively

The variations in meaning can be based on perception, experience, familiarity and exposure.

Jargon refers to words, terms, or expressions that are used by a profession (like sign language interpreting) that have different meanings that are known by members of that profession. Below are some examples of interpreter jargon and ways to substitute or explain the words:

- Feed = Providing linguistic or language support
- Voice = Rendering interpretation through spoken word (English, Spanish, etc.)
- Team = when two or more interpreters are supporting one another or are taking turns interpreting the message
- Consumer = Participant
- Hearing = Person who can hear
- Terp = Interpreter

Jargon, not to be confused by **ingroup** speak, has created words to fit their profession.

- These terms are not proper meanings nor share a cultural background.
- These terms were developed to fit the profession, opposed to gaining meaning through experience.
- They separate the profession of interpreting from those interpreters work for.

Be mindful of the words you use and the way you describe what you do.

Metamessages:

- Are conveyed through expressions, body language, gestures, tone, and other ways unrelated to the words spoken.
- Convey sarcasm, anger, sadness, frustration, etc.

38

Communication

NOTES

Examples of Metamessages:

- A sibling, friend, cousin, etc. broke one of your toys and hid it. When you found the toy, in anger, you would (likely) call their name by lowering your voice. The tone of your voice is the **metamessage**.
- If a Deaf person signed, "We wrote back and forth to communicate" followed by the Deaf person furrowing their brow, it would tell you they were annoyed by the experience. Their facial expression is the **metamessage**.

An example of cultural **complementary schismogenesis** is:

A process by which two speakers drive one another to more and more extreme expressions of divergent ways of speaking in an ever-widening spiral. What begins as a small difference becomes a big one, as each speaker tries harder to do more of what seems obviously appropriate. Here is a hypothetical example. An American man asks a Japanese woman directly if she'd like to go to lunch. She does not want to, so she declines the invitation by saying, *That's a very nice idea, maybe we could have lunch one day.* Because she has left the door open, he asks again. This time she replies even more indirectly: *That's an idea . . . lunch is nice . . .* Befuddled by this ambiguous response, he tries to pin her down: *Are you trying to tell me you never want to have lunch with me, or should I keep asking?* He regards this as the best way to cut through the ambiguity. However, given her conviction that it would be unacceptable to reply directly (Tannen, 2013, p. 365).

Register:

- **Frozen:** Language that is unchanged regardless of how much time has passed. The information relayed should be rendered verbatim. An example of frozen text would be the Preamble to the Constitution or the national anthem of Canada "O Canada".
- **Formal:** Language that is used academically or in settings where a high level of professionalism is required.
- **Consultative:** The participants in this setting make use of dialogue to share information. There is ample opportunity for questions and answers. The language utilized can vary between participants; at least one person involved in the interaction is an *expert,* and has knowledge the participant needs.
- **Casual (Informal):** Relaxed language that is used every day between majority people.
- **Intimate:** Language that is shared between close individuals. This language can include inside jokes, personal information, and nicknames.

Deafcentric is a mindset that expresses the collectivist community of Deaf people. The term below is an example of a word associated with Deafcentricism:

- *Hearing:* It is not recognized as an identity marker by people who can hear because hearing is what they do and not who they are.

Deafcentric:

- This term refers to the semantic intent of specific lexical terms/signs used by members of the dDeaf community that have a unique or non-standard meaning within dDeaf culture based on the collective experiences and *ways of being*

39

shared among these individuals. Examples include terms such as: hearing, Deaf (signed in a way to indicate a person's reflection of "hard core" commitment to Deaf cultural norms, and public or residential schools for the deaf). While people who can hear may use some of these terms, their understanding of the meaning is not the same as those understood by dDeaf individuals. Use of Deafcentric terminology presents challenges to interpreters who are required to communicate the meaning of such vocabulary to uninitiated members of the hearing community.

In the boxes below, write the differences between the dDeaf culture and the hearing culture. In the box where the two meet, write the similarities between the two cultures.

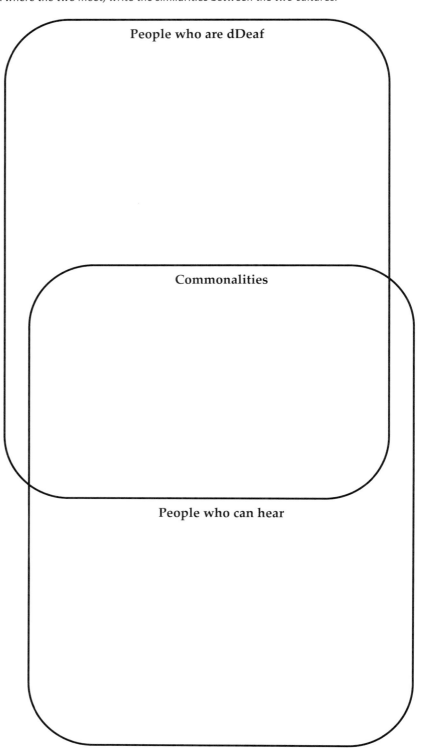

4 | Identity, Family, & Culture

There are literally hundreds of definitions for culture. It is not a concept that can be contained in one definition as it is largely amorphous – impossible to capture, put into a container, measure, or otherwise get our hands on (Hofstede, 1997). The United Nations Educational, Scientific and Cultural Organization (UNESCO) defines culture as "a dynamic value system of learned attitudes with assumptions, conventions, beliefs and rules that permit members of a group to relate to one another and the world" (Meusburger, Freytag, & Suarsana, 2016, p. 4). In this chapter we will provide a framework for the idea of culture and human existence. Little (2016) explains that our shared human experiences have *meaning,* and culture is the source of that meaning. Culture is the term used to describe the significant dimensions of our collective lives. Human life – relational, political, spiritual, familial, etc. – is conducted through various life events and experiences to which we attribute *meaning*. "Culture provides the ongoing stability that enables human existence. Living together, people developed forms of cooperation which created the common habits, behaviours, and ways of life known as culture" (Little, 2016, p. 99). It is our goal to generate discussion. We hope this text using the following definition of culture, and many more, will create a more robust explanation. Culture is "a system of meanings and values that shape one's behavior" (Lane, 1999, p.5).

The culture in which we are reared shapes the concept of who we are and the utilization of language is the primary instrument of that shaping. Culture defines the meaning and value we attribute to:

- Family and our place in it (e.g., birth order)
- Gender
- Social and sexual experiences
- Economic status
- Educational experiences
- Physical, mental, emotional and spiritual development
- Temperament or personality type

"This means that within a community, cultural behavior is constrained not just by individual beliefs, but also by the (perceived) beliefs and actions of others in one's cultural group, and in particular by those with whom one interacts frequently" (Akkus, Postmes, & Stroebe, 2017, p. 2). The individuals with whom we share language, beliefs and ideals are typically the people who "do" life with us,

TERMS TO KNOW:

- Cultural Frames
- Subculture
- Stereotyping
- Institutionalized Oppression
- Cultural Duality
- Intersectionality
- Individualistic Culture
- Collectivistic Culture
- Oral Traditions/Oral Lore
- Microaggressions

thus the social dynamics of a community shape and regulate our cultural behavior, as well as that of the community (Akkus et al., 2017).

dDeaf Distinction

The specific identity adopted by people who are dDeaf is as unique as each dDeaf person you are likely to encounter. It is essential to respect each person's choice of community, where they choose to "make their home" and how they define and demonstrate their "dDeaf identity." A common convention utilized today, as previously mentioned in chapter 1, that helps distinguish between identities and affiliations is explained here:

- **Uppercase "D" Deaf:** This identification is typically used to denote those individuals who use sign language and share the values, beliefs and *ways of being* followed by members of the core Deaf Community. These individuals actively and regularly engage with other members of the Deaf community. Deaf individuals in this group typically display *attitudinal deafness* in their daily interactions, which refers to the degree an individual subscribes to the norms, beliefs and ideals of the Deaf culture community in their day-to-day lives.

- **Lowercase "d" deaf:** This designation refers to individuals with an identified medical condition of having a significant hearing loss, but prefer to communicate by speaking, making the most of their residual hearing, and occasionally using sign language. However, some of the individuals in this group who experience a significant hearing loss early in life frequently interact with the Deaf community, typically using anglicized signs in English grammatical order and often choosing to speak as they sign.

It is important to recognize these differences, however, it is impossible to "deny that there is a gray area between the two; for example, some hard-of-hearing people are active in the American Deaf-World; others are not" (Lane, 2005, p. 1). It is important to remember that each individual's core identity is unique, and has some fluidity based on the other people present in the environment. Whether a person identifies as deaf, Deaf, hard of hearing, or DeafBlind, it is critical to demonstrate respect and positive regard for the ways in which they communicate and seek to be understood. Because one's identity is partially shaped by the community with whom they share a common language, culture, values and experiences, their hearing loss does not necessarily correlate with their identity or "cultural home." For that reason, an individual can refer to themself as "Deaf" while having enough residual hearing to converse on the telephone. Likewise, someone who has a profound hearing loss may refer to themself as "hard of hearing." The irony is that degree of hearing loss does not necessarily define their identity, which is again, partially shaped by the community with whom the individual shares a *common* language, culture, norms, values and experiences. The authors caution you not to stereotype individuals based on these terms or labels, but to engage with each dDeaf or DeafBlind person you meet as a unique human being – someone to be respected.

The dDeaf community is culturally and linguistically complex. In this diverse community there are those individuals who did not lose their ability to hear until some point during their early childhood/youth or in early adulthood. If you want to be an interpreter, it is important that you become familiar with the range of ways dDeaf individuals identify themselves and the variety of signing methods used across this spectrum of people. It is important to be sensitive to the subtle

Identity, Family, & Culture

NOTES

distinctions of personal identity within the dDeaf community. As mentioned previously, the authors are *purposely* using two new conventions; *dDeaf* and *dDDb* (DeafBlind) both of which recognize the differences and abilities within the community of dDeaf-dDDb people and we choose to honor the ways people identify their "home" within the dDeaf-dDDb community.

Common Language?

The idea that the dDeaf community has a *common* language is a bit incongruous as sign language interpreters will likely work with dDeaf people who use a variety of communication methods and modes. Some individuals who are dDeaf speak for themselves and do not use sign language at all, while on the other end of the continuum, there are dDeaf individuals who use one of many recognized sign languages. This could be American Sign Language or one of the Hispanic-based sign languages used in various Spanish-speaking countries. A point of interest, the sign language used in each Spanish speaking country is unique to that country and the sign language used in French speaking Quebec is totally different from the sign language used in France. The range of communication options can sometimes be confusing. As previously stated, this text focuses on interpreting for members of the dDeaf-dDDb communities that use signed communication in one form or another. Language is fluid and much like a rainbow, it does not have hard lines where one color ends and another begins, rather the gradual shades blend from one color to the next, indicating the lack of rigid divisions between the various forms of communication.[1] Like all languages, sign language is used by members of the dDeaf-dDDb communities for the purposes of social interaction, communication of ideas, sharing of emotions, and for the transmission of the group's culture to next generations (Baker & Cokely, 1980; Wilcox & Wilcox, 1997).

All languages have supporting structural rules that make meaningful communication a reality. "The five main components of language are phonemes, morphemes, lexemes, syntax, and context. Along with grammar, semantics, and pragmatics, these components work together to create meaningful communication among individuals" (Introduction to Language, n.d., para. 12). According to the Linguistic Society of America (2020), language is in constant motion, it does not remain the same, it evolves and adapts to the emerging needs of its users. As a living language, American Sign Language is no different. It is adapting, developing and changing over time to reflect each generation of users. American Sign Language is used by a majority of dDeaf people in Canada and the US, though it is not the only sign language in North America. In Quebec, most dDeaf people use La Langue de Signes Quebecoise, or LSQ. Similarly, in the far northeastern provinces of Canada, members of the dDeaf community use Maritime Sign Language (MSL), a critically endangered sign language also known as Nova Scotian Sign Language (Yoel, 2009; Carbin & Smith, 1996).

As world citizens, we live among multicultural communities and it is our responsibility to become aware of the cultural norms, values and traditions of people groups that surround us. Striving to understand the communities that we interact with enables us to gain an appreciation for the various **cultural frames** in which communication and meaning occur. A cultural frame is the way in which we understand the world, through the lens of our values, language, beliefs, and norms. Some people identify the dDeaf community as a **subculture**; "a subculture is just as it sounds—a smaller cultural group within a larger culture. People of a subculture are part of the larger culture, but also share a specific identity within a smaller group" (Little, 2016, p.128). However, after preliminary research, it is unsure if

---

[1]*This topic is addressed further on the Comparative ASL/English Continuum by Dough Stringham in the Toolbox.*

members of the culturally Deaf community consider themselves as members of a subculture, this is worthy of future study (K. Cagle, personal communications, July 3, 2020; T. Polstra, personal communications, May 8, 2020).

THE RELATIONSHIP OF CULTURE AND LANGUAGE

Language and culture are so deeply entwined that it makes no sense to talk about one without the other (Erting, 1990, as cited by de Garcia in Christensen & Delgado, p. 72). Our ability to understand the meaning of words or signs is based on having a shared cultural frame. Miscommunication often occurs when individuals trying to communicate do not share the same frame. Cultural frames are not universal. Indo-Canadians have a different "script" (norm or expectation) for holiday foods, celebrations, and traditions than Puerto Ricans or African Americans. Everyone has a unique *frame of view* which is heavily influenced by contextual settings and, as a result, each word or sign can be interpreted in different ways (Isenhath, 1990). Given a person's cultural frame of reference, individuals may struggle to assign *meaning* to the words or signs used, even if they are recognized. In the same way, it is one thing to be familiar with American Sign Language and it is another thing to know how to use the language with the subtle, yet meaningful nuances conveyed by a fluent user of the language. Furthermore, the intent of the signed message can be modified on different levels, depending on how the user produces the utterance and corresponding non-manual signals. For both signed and spoken messages, the *literal* or surface level of meaning, known as *denotative* is often referred to as the dictionary definition. Whereas the *implied* or deeper level of meaning known as *connotative* is often inferred or figurative in nature. We must have a shared **schema** to be able to understand and utilize a language competently, especially when the speaker subtlety implies or infers meaning to words or ideas.

Your *schema* is a cognitive framework that helps you make sense of the world around you. Most often our schemas[2] are rooted in our personal experiences and help us understand and organize the information in our environment. Centered around our experiential knowledge, schemas include the setting, vocabulary used, ways of behaving, and the people typically found in specific contexts, which are all drawn from our personal experience. We all hold a mental schema for each setting, event and situation in our lives. For example, we all have a *restaurant schema,* which is based on our experiences of going out to eat. Because of our restaurant schema, we know what is expected when we go for fast food, casual dining or make reservations at a fine dining establishment. Upon entering a family restaurant in the US or Canada, we can predict that someone will lead us to a table to be seated and give us menus to order our food. We can further predict that after ordering, someone will bring our meal to the table and afterward present us with a bill. Our schema informs us that we are not free to enter the kitchen or wash our own dishes after eating. Schemas are helpful, but our North American restaurant schema would not likely prepare us to know how things would unfold or what would be expected of us in a restaurant in Spain or Japan. Schemas are beneficial because each schema enables us to take *shortcuts* in understanding and information that we encounter in each setting, event or situation (Cherry, 2019). Our schemas, then, shape our *expectations* about what will occur in a given situation, based on prior experience and cultural background (Schemas in Psychology, 2015).

It is important to note, however, that none of us possess a schema or life script for events and experiences we have never encountered. People who can hear, for

---

[2]*The plural of schema is technically schemata but the authors have chosen to use a non-standard form for readability.*

Identity, Family, & Culture

NOTES

instance, rarely have a life script or schema for dDeaf clubs, residential schools for the dDeaf, or even the concept of being unable to hear the doorbell or their alarm clock. In the same way, people who are dDeaf may not have a life script or schema for community choirs or talk radio. The frame of reference held by people who can hear in Canada and the United States will likely include sounds, such as a soprano voice, birds singing or a police siren. Among those who can hear, decisions and beliefs are shaped from sound-based sources. The same can be said about visual stimuli for people who are dDeaf. For example, when a police officer is trying to pass vehicles on the road, for people who can hear, the siren may be the first indicator that an emergency vehicle needs to pass. Whereas, flashing lights will alert drivers who are dDeaf that a police officer is heading to an emergency. Though the results are the same, the frame of reference held by the drivers is vastly different.

The world we live in is based on sound; as a result the world around us is an environment rich in auditory *communication* sources – radio, television, cellphones, as well as conversations with family, friends, and co-workers. People who can hear often inaccurately assume that dDeaf people have the same experiential, linguistic and cultural frame as they do. There are many similarities between people who can hear and people who are dDeaf, including the desire for community, relationships and a sense of belonging, to name a few. However, in spite of the many similarities there are also numerous differences resulting in innumerable misunderstandings between members of the differing communities. This is not a new issue nor is it limited to our current interpersonal experiences. Edwin Smith's work addressed this very concern in 1946, stating, it is "our tendency to think that the other fellow has the same view about essential things that we have; or that, even if the other fellow does not think and act as we do, at least he knows what are our point of view and our customs" (p. 36).

While schemas help you determine how to act in particular settings, it is important to realize that your schema may be different from the person beside you. Examples include such things as, your schema for school which will vary depending on whether you attended public school, private school or if you were homeschooled. You likely have a schema or frame of reference for different types of relationships, as well: a friend schema, a family schema, a domestic partner schema and so forth (Wilcox & Wilcox, 1985; Alcorn & Humphrey, 1989). Life scripts and schemas are useful tools that members of all cultures use to make sense of their world. However, members of differing cultural groups typically have different experiences which shaped how their scripts evolve. "We typically select, organize and interpret behavior in ways that fit our pre-existing concepts about people's motives" (Adler & Towne, 1998, p. 100). Many of these notions or constructs are transmitted to us through cultural institutions such as family, religion, schools, and the media. Sometimes our mental framework makes overgeneralizations about individuals or people groups which may not reflect the truth or their reality; this misbelief is often the basis of **stereotyping** (McLeod, 2018). Stereotyping is faulty thinking regarding a person or people group that leads to negative views, destructive behaviors, and sweeping generalizations. These unhealthy attitudes can be powerful, leading to individual, group and even **institutionalized oppression**. Institutional oppression is known to create invisible barriers, which limit individuals because of their membership in groups that are viewed negatively by society. The irony is that these barriers are only *invisible* to those unaffected by them (Kelly & Varghese, 2018). Furthermore, institutional oppression takes place when the practices or customs of an organization, whether they are educational, religious, medical, financial, or

Chapter 4

NOTES

social, creates inequities for individuals because of their personal identification with a minority group; in addition, these oppressive practices do not have to be purposefully discriminatory to be considered oppressive.

Some of the following features or characteristics are most commonly utilized when organizing our schema:

- **Physical:** Classifying individuals based on their appearance, gender, physique, age, etc.
- **Role:** We have certain expectations of others based on their social position: neighbors, doctors, students, athletes, etc. and what we might expect of them
- **Interaction:** The way people behave in various situations (social, academic, legal) all influences our sense of who they are and how we will interact with them; whether we consider them aloof, friendly, judgmental, etc.
- **Psychological:** We tend to group individuals based on our uninformed, personal psychological assessments of them: curious, nervous, insecure, etc.
- **Membership:** We also categorize others according to their group affiliation: refugee, Baptist, member of the Rotary club, LGBTQI/straight, etc.

Returning to the schema of the restaurant, you can confidently predict the actions of the server, cashier, host, and fellow customers. In the same way, your life script enables you to recognize when a person is being helpful, flirtatious, indifferent, entertaining or sarcastic. Likewise, we use our restaurant script to *classify* people in the restaurant based on their appearance and dress, whether or not they are wearing a uniform and a name tag. We often make psychological judgments about the people we encounter based on whether we think they are jittery, jumpy, creepy or rude. Some people in the restaurant may have group memberships you can identify (e.g., senior citizen) and sometimes the restaurant itself might be affiliated with membership groups (e.g., a Japanese restaurant, health food, food truck, or veggie delicatessen). Oddly enough, "our understanding of the world is formed by a network of abstract mental structures" (Cherry, 2019).

The ability to interact respectfully with persons who live, act and perceive the world from a "different center" is a quality required of every interpreter. Since culture is a system of meanings and values – and language is the primary medium through which culture is communicated – the ability to recognize and name your personal perceptions, attitudes, beliefs and subsequent values is essential. Every interpreter must have the ability to interact comfortably among people with a wide variety of cultural frames, which requires being aware and sensitive to diverse perspectives. It is imperative that you acknowledge and distinguish your own cultural frame from those with whom you are communicating and for whom you are interpreting. We should also be aware that culture is always present as an invisible guest at every interaction.

Identity

Some members of these diverse communities adhere to the norms and values of their home culture, while others pursue **cultural duality**, meaning they attempt to live with one foot in mainstream society and the other foot in their familial culture (Christensen & Delgado, 1993). Some individuals have assimilated into the mainstream culture, while others retain a strong separate ethnic identity. On the other hand, others may be alienated from their ethnic identity, familial culture and the mainstream culture of the country in which they live. For some individuals coming from cultural minority groups,

Identity, Family, & Culture

NOTES

the only explicit knowledge they possess about their ethnic heritage is likely to be limited to stock phrases and food names. They may carry values from their ethnic communities but be unaware of the origins of those values, because these families are often physically integrated into suburban neighborhoods, their lifestyles reflect the ambiance of the neighborhood rather than anything noticeably ethnic (Akamatsu, 1993, p. 135).

The descriptions of the various cultural norms presented throughout this chapter are intended to increase your awareness of significant characteristics you may encounter as an interpreter, particularly when living and working in cultural settings that may be different from your own. Student interpreters are reminded that the actions, beliefs, norms and values of one culture should not be compared to another cultural group for the purposes of deciding which is more or less correct; each group stands independent of each other.

Intersectionality

Cultural identification is a very personal, yet fluid decision that is both individual and collective, while also being central to the core of who we are as people. Everyone is *multi-definitional,* particularly in regard to race, ethnicity, cultural identification and group membership. However, our cultural identity can also encompass other identities such as being southerners, northerners, gay, lesbian, bisexual, transgender, as well as people with physical, emotional and mental disabilities, etc. (Bowleg, 2012). Suppose a dDeaf woman recognizes, honors and identifies with the culture of her First Nation Canadian origins. Must she make a choice of identifying as one or the other identity, being exclusively dDeaf or First Nations? No, she is a woman, who is dDeaf of First Nation Canadian heritage; she is *all* of these, yet she is *each* of them. It is the place where these identities converge that forms her **intersectionality**.

> Intersectionality is a theoretical framework for understanding how multiple social identities such as race, gender, sexual orientation, SES [socioeconomic status], and disability intersect at the micro level of individual experience to reflect interlocking systems of privilege and oppression (i.e., racism, sexism, heterosexism, classism) at the macro social structural level (Bowleg, 2012, p. 1267, bracketed information inserted by author).

Individual identity is fluid rather than static. It may change over time and can be shaped by the context of one's life. Some dDeaf and hard of hearing individuals become members of the dDeaf cultural community while others do not. One person might see themself as a dDeaf African American – identifying primarily with African American culture and secondarily with dDeaf culture. Another person might see himself or herself as an African American dDeaf person – a dDeaf person who happens to be African American. Furthermore, depending on the context in which they find themselves, one element of their identity, culture, language or values may be more pronounced. For example, suppose a person is invited to a celebration of Black history month and happens to be the only dDeaf person present or they attend a dDeaf community celebration and they are the only person of color. These generalizations can be applied to various ethnic heritages, European, African American, Hispanic/Latinx,[3] Native, or First Nation Canadian. People can be different *like* you, and not different *from* you.

---

[3]*The term Latinx is a gender-neutral version of Latino/a/. It has been adopted by various individuals and groups, including those who are part of Council de Manos, an organization of Latinx Deaf, Hard of Hearing, and DeafBlind individuals in the US. Quinto-Pozos, D., Martinez, M., Suarez, A., & Zech, R. (2018). Beyond Bilingual Programming: Interpreter Education in the U.S. Amidst Increasing Linguistic Diversity. International Journal of Interpreter Education, 10(1), 46-59. Retrieved May 28, 2020, from https://www.cit-asl.org/new/wp-content/uploads/2018/07/f-IJIE-10-1-quinto-pozos.pdf*

Chapter 4

NOTES

Familial Identification

Sometimes the first dDeaf person that parents meet is their own child. Oftentimes the sense of belonging and the feeling of being part of a family comes from the ability to communicate with one's significant caregivers. Can the members of the family who can hear, sign or communicate *effectively* with their dDeaf child? "Decision making regarding communication and language choices for children often weighs heavily on parents. This is true for both medical decisions – in the case of cochlear implantation—and/or nonmedical decisions, such as incorporating the use of sign language" (DesGeorges, 2016, p. 443). Each generation of dDeaf children has grown up with slightly different familial and educational experiences. Among the baby boomer generation (1945-1964) and their predecessors, it was common for families to send their children away to residential schools for the dDeaf and see their children only during holidays and summers. Communication between hearing family members and the dDeaf child was usually limited to gestures, some lip-reading and perhaps fingerspelling or home signs (Wallis, Musselman & MacKay, 2004). However, subsequent generations (1975-today) have more educational options, such as early interventions programs, mainstreaming, residential day programs, residential dDeaf school (dorm) programs, or a combination of various programs, etc. "In recent years, experts' views have evolved to include the idea that parents don't need to make a 'choice' between spoken or signed language but can incorporate both—some form of bilingualism—into a child's development" (Napoli, et al., 2015, as cited in DesGeorges, 2016, p. 444). More programs have emerged offering family members the opportunity to learn sign language and Deaf culture. This increased communication has made it possible for dDeaf children to learn about their family history, traditions and ethnic heritage. Likewise, hearing members of the family are more likely to attend dDeaf community events and to communicate with the dDeaf family member's friends and peers.

However, we do not want to give the misimpression that open, natural and fluent conversations are typical between dDeaf children and their parents. Most often, parents who can hear have to learn sign language to communicate with their dDeaf children, to model language for them and build active living relationships with them. "Ninety percent of deaf children are said to have hearing parents and ninety percent of the children of deaf parents are hearing" (Mitchell & Karchmer, 2002, p. 5). Language and culture are often communicated from parents to their children. However, when the language of parents and siblings is significantly different from that of the dDeaf child, the essence of culture and language is difficult to convey. This is especially true when most parents of dDeaf children perceive their child's deafness as a disability, as a deficit, and not as a difference. It is common practice today to refer to anyone who has some type of hearing loss as *hearing impaired,* in an attempt to be politically correct. This term is often perceived by people who can hear as courteous, respectful and acceptable.

However, culturally dDeaf individuals typically view the term *hearing impaired* as negative and stigmatizing, as they do not view themselves as impaired individuals. They proudly see their deafness as a difference, not as a disability which infers that the term *hearing impaired* is fundamentally inaccurate. However, culturally dDeaf people are not the only individuals who object to the label of hearing impaired. Several chapters of Hearing Loss Association of America (HLAA), a national organization for late-deafened individuals, and provincial chapters of the Canadian Hard of Hearing Association have stated that they do not want the term hearing impaired used to reference them for similar reasons (Babcock, 1992).

Identity, Family, & Culture

NOTES

When a dDeaf child is born into a family, the dynamics within the family change; language, getting one another's attention, simple and complex communication, cultural norms, and so much more. Fortunately, family dynamics can continue to evolve and become more capable of communicating, often using a combination of American Sign Language, English-like signs, fingerspelling, gestures and home signs. As an interpreter coming into this communication environment to provide interpreting services for dDeaf children, youth, and adults, you can expect to see a variety of communication techniques, each with different degrees of proficiency from hearing family members. It is imperative to *respect* these bonds and family interactions. Be sensitive to family dynamics, the parents of the dDeaf child may want to actively clarify by signing to their child – respect the family's involvement. In essence, the "idea of culture as a shared, stable living space, supported equally by all members of the group, which passes it onto the next generation, is becoming less and less a reality" (United Nations Educational, Scientific and Cultural Organization, 2013, p.7).

Furthermore, some of the ideals held by the family may no longer be common or shared. As stated previously, it is common for dDeaf people to perceive and experience the world around them differently from people who can hear. These differences shape how they define the world. Specific words and ideas will often have definitions that represent the perspective and values of dDeaf people. Because of that, these Deafcentric definitions may be different for members of the family who can hear. By way of explanation, the word *hearing* is a good example. If you were to ask a person who can hear to describe themselves, making sure to include their identity and their roles, they would likely list multiple facets of who they are: woman, mother, sister, manager, and likely included would be ethnicity and other aspects of their life. But rarely would a person who can hear self-identify as 'hearing,' because their ability to hear is what they do, not who they are. Historically, however, members of the dDeaf community use the sign 'hearing' as a Deafcentric mark of identification. For dDeaf people the word 'hearing' identifies a different people group, not simply people who have the ability to hear.

Two World Views

Communication takes place between people – individuals who bring with them cultural and group memberships, both visible and invisible. These memberships infuse each person with expectations regarding roles, behavior, communication, politeness and much more. However, most of us are not consciously aware that we harbor or act upon these invisible norms and expectations, nor are we sufficiently aware of the expectations we brought to the interactions that we have with members of other cultural groups. This awareness recognizes that not everyone thinks, behaves or interfaces with the world as you do. Awareness of variations in culture and interpersonal relationships is often related to **individualistic** and **collectivistic** cultures. "Individualism is defined as a situation in which people are concerned with themselves and close family members only, while collectivism is defined as a situation in which people feel they belong to larger in-groups or collectives which care for them in exchange for loyalty—and vice versa" (Hofstede & Bond, 1984 cited in Darwish & Huber, 2003, p. 47). Individualistic cultures infer a degree of independence and self-reliance with limited relational reliance, whereas collectivism suggests interdependence as related to self and community relationships (Rodriguez Mosquera, 2015).

Historically, beliefs concerning individualism and collectivism were ideas that existed at the poles of a continuum. It was assumed that the cultures and people

49

who adhered to these identities, were on polar opposites – either individualistic or collectivistic. However, it is clear that elements of both individualism and collectivism can coexist within the same culture (Rodriguez Mosquera, 2015). Of these two cultural frames, collectivist cultures are quite prominent, with approximately 70% of the world cultures fitting into a collectivist frame (Mindess, 2006). The American mainstream community operates as an individualistic culture; whereas, the Deaf community demonstrates values, norms and behaviors of a collectivist culture. Harlan Lane (2005) explains that ethnic groups have distinct properties and these groups are characterized by certain internal criteria. The dDeaf community possesses the following criteria which identifies them as an ethnic group. The internal properties of the dDeaf culture community include:

- Collective name
- Customs
- Feeling of community
- Social structure
- Norms for behavior
- Language

- Values
- Art forms
- Knowledge
- History
- Kinship (p. 292)

"Cultural differences are undeniable: people from different cultural backgrounds act differently in a wide range of situations" (Akkus, Postmes, & Stroebe, 2017, p. 1). It must be remembered that high context cultures are usually collectivist cultures. Please note that high-context and low-context cultures often "refer to the value cultures place on indirect and direct communication" (Intercultural Communication, 2020 para. 2). Simply put, the dDeaf community is considered a collectivist culture and such cultures

> emphasize loyalty to the group (while the group in turn cares for the well-being of the individual), emotional dependence on groups and organizations, less personal privacy, the belief that group decisions are superior to individual decisions, interdependence, an understanding of personal identity as knowing one's place within the group, and concern about the needs and interests of others (Darwish & Huber, 2003, p. 49).

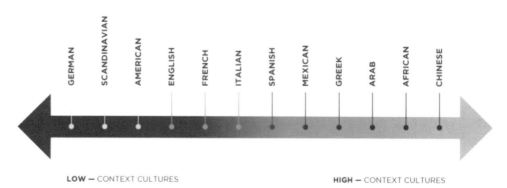

SOURCE: https://online.seu.edu/articles/high-and-low-context-cultures/

In general, people who can hear are considered to be representative of low context, individualistic cultures.[4] Furthermore, individualistic groups "do not feel as attached to an in-group when there are numerous in-groups to which they can belong and when each in-group provides only a small part of their material and emotional security" (Darwish & Huber, 2003, p. 48).

---

[4]*For more information regarding high and low context, please see chapter 1.*

Identity, Family, & Culture

NOTES

Culture helps us determine if it is more desirable to stand out or to blend in and it influences how strongly individuals choose to identify with a group. Mainstream American culture, for example, typically encourages people to be outspoken and assertive at home, work and school. This includes discussing and expressing our thoughts and feelings about events and people. These characteristics fit individualist behaviors. "In contrast, Canadian culture is said to be more collectivist, meaning the welfare of the group and group relationships are primary values" (Little, 2016, p. 115). Similar to the dDeaf community, "Canadians are less individualistic and more collectivistic than [mainstream] Americans, especially in instances where personal liberties conflict with the collective good" (Little, 2016, p. 136, bracketed information added by author).

There are other features and factors that unify dDeaf people into a tight knit collectivist community. One of the central features is the language of interaction, American Sign Language. Currently, there is no single agreed upon written form for most signed languages, including American Sign Language (ASL), but pockets of interest exist. William Stokoe was the first to propose a way to write ASL in 1960, using the *Stokoe notation system*. Stokoe's (1960) article, *Sign Language Structure: An Outline of the Visual Communication Systems of the American Deaf* captured elements of the manual aspects of American Sign Language yet did not identify the non-manual elements of the language well. In the late 1970's, SignWriting, derived from an extensive system for describing dance and movement, was introduced. Its capacity for detail gave it the ability to be used as a transcription or an everyday writing system. Feedback from dDeaf readers and writers in the United States, Brazil, and around the world have greatly influenced the current form of that writing system. In 2003, Robert Arnold introduced his system called *si5s* which aimed to be more of a phonemic writing system that intended to cover enough details that an ASL signer could fill in the gaps with their knowledge of the language. The proprietary nature of *si5s* led to a variant – called ASLWrite led by Adrean Clark which has been building a small but loyal group of readers and writers who use this system. Competition between writing systems and negative perceptions of writing ASL have inhibited widespread adoption of any specific writing system for ASL in the United States.

Among dDeaf people, the most commonly utilized genre of expression is the *narrative*. American Sign Language narratives make use of numerous details describing the characters, setting and experiences in an elaborate, visual manner. The dDeaf community tends to share their experiences and events from one generation to the next generation in the form of *narrative traditions*. In numerous cultures, narrative traditions are known as **oral traditions** (Bauman, Nelson, & Rose, 2006). **Oral traditions** or **oral lore** is a way in which knowledge, history, art, ideas and cultural roots are conveyed *orally (narratively)* from one generation to the next (Miles, 2019). Narrative traditions are often how dDeaf people share information, memories and experiences that are held in common – like the many cultures that value narrative histories, storytelling is a highly prized art form. Technology has been a boon for dDeaf people. Video recording, digital cameras, YouTube, and the internet have enhanced the ability of dDeaf individuals, and the community as a whole, to preserve the beliefs, values and ideals of the dDeaf community. For the first time, the dDeaf community has been afforded an opportunity to record, save and share the history and traditions of the wider dDeaf community.

It is important, more than this, it is essential to become familiar with the history of the dDeaf community and the narrative traditions passed down from each generation. For anyone who hopes to become an interpreter it is necessary to demonstrate bilingual competence in American Sign Language and English. As you develop your interpreting skills, it is imperative that you become skilled at conveying information in a detailed and visual manner. You must also develop the ability to interpret these elaborate signed narratives for people who do not know sign language in such a way that the audience is engaged and can appreciate the often graphic visual descriptions.

Recognizing the dDeaf community as a collectivist linguistic minority that utilizes sign language within the larger society that surrounds them is essential to understanding dDeaf culture (Lane, 2005). As a collectivist group,

> there are norms for relating to the Deaf-World: for decision making, consensus is the rule, not individual initiative; for managing information; for constructing discourse; for gaining status; for managing indebtedness; and many more such rules. Cultural rules are not honored all the time by everyone any more than are linguistic rules. Such rules tell what you must know as a member of a particular linguistic and cultural group; what one actually does or says depends on a host of intervening factors, including other rules that have priority (Lane, 2005, p. 292).

Although we recognize that social environments are influenced by many factors, it is clear that the social relationships of individuals within those social environments are relatively stable (Akkus, Postmes, & Stroebe, 2017).

Attention-getting and Signaling Devices

The visual norms of the dDeaf community often necessitate that the world they live in be adapted to alert them with visual or other sensory stimuli. Many of the devices that alert us – fire alarms, alarm clocks and ringing cell phones have alternative alert signals such as the use of flashing lights and vibration which are effective for dDeaf individuals. Attention-getting between people who are dDeaf is also based on visual or physical signals. Most often getting the attention of another person who is dDeaf falls into several typical approaches, including:

- If you are in close proximity to the person, gently tap the person on the shoulder
- If you are a short distance away from them, gently wave your hand, making use of the dDeaf person's peripheral vision
- If you are in relative proximity to the person, you may stomp your foot on the floor (if it will transmit vibration) or if you are seated at a table, gently pound on the table – however this approach may be misunderstood by people who can hear
- If you need the attention of a group of people, or the individuals are a fair distance away, you may turn the lights on and off several times to get everyone's attention

There are actually unwritten rules about appropriate light-flashing etiquette in various contexts. It is important for interpreters to develop the sensitivity to the appropriate use of these various attention-getting and attention-maintenance behaviors, which are critical for starting and maintaining personal and interpreted interactions.

Identity, Family, & Culture

NOTES

Eye Contact and Physical Presence

For dDeaf community members the significance of the eyes and the hands in the culture and in communication with people who are dDeaf cannot be emphasized strongly enough. The intricacies, nuances and richness of American Sign Language enables signers to visually convey detailed thoughts, feelings, beliefs, values and so much more. This avenue of communication is dependent on the ability to see, sufficient light and clear sight lines are a must. Interpreters are expected to demonstrate sensitivity to this valued norm by ensuring there is proper lighting and an appropriate background when interpreting, as well as wearing solid colors that contrast with the interpreter's skin tone in order to reduce the potential for eye strain during interpreting assignments.

When communicating with a dDeaf person in sign language, sustained eye contact is mandatory. For example, if you can hear and while you are talking with a person who is dDeaf and another person calls your name, it is considered extremely rude to break eye contact and look toward the person who called your name. In such a situation, it is best to respond to the person calling your name by holding up an index finger which indicates you heard them, but you are engaged and temporarily unable to respond. When there is a natural break in the conversation you are having with the dDeaf individual, it is socially acceptable for you look away, but breaking eye contact before a natural pause and responding to an auditory call of your name sends a powerful nonverbal message to any dDeaf person that you value sound, over sight. Members of the dDeaf community share information about such rude behavior with others, so failing to respect this and other subtle dDeaf cultural norms can tarnish your reputation within the dDeaf community.

The following information may seem like common sense, but it is worth spelling out. The nature of a visual language and culture requires that people be present in the same visual and physical area to communicate. You can't communicate with someone from another room or through the bathroom door when they can't hear you. Cultures that are based on sound allow indirect forms of communication, such as speaking to a person without actually looking at them or talking to someone who is not physically present in the room. This is not to say that all members of hearing communities like or accept the norm of calling to someone from another room or talking from behind a newspaper but what is acceptable in one community may not be in another.

It is wise to examine your communication norms when it comes to eye contact and physical touch to get someone's attention. As a person who hears, do you typically talk to people while doing something else? For example, having conversations with people in the room, while washing dishes or preparing a meal, or maybe talking while cooking but not actually looking at the person you are talking to. The valued norm of sustained eye contact when interacting with people who are dDeaf may be a challenge for those who have ingrained habits of multitasking while talking. It is important to become more aware of and sensitive to these habits now. Hopefully, this early awareness coupled with your intentional efforts will modify these behaviors and better prepare you to interact with dDeaf and hard of hearing individuals in respectful ways.

Effective communication requires that each of us identify our own cultural and group identity. We must also identify and understand the cultural and group norms of those with whom we will work. The more we understand cultures, languages and people who live differently than we do, the greater the likelihood

53

Chapter 4

NOTES

that we will minimize unintentional **microaggressions**. Merriam-Webster defines microaggressions as "a comment or action that subtly and often unconsciously or unintentionally expresses a prejudiced attitude toward a member of a marginalized group" (Merriam-Webster, 2020). Awareness of the biases and behaviors that result in microaggressions will hopefully minimize insensitive comments or judgmental reactions toward those who have a different cultural frame and group identity.

It is difficult for you as a student interpreter to be fully cognizant of the personal expectations, beliefs, values and ideas you hold based on your *subconscious allegiances.* However, the influences from a lifetime of internalized beliefs and habits will likely impact your interpreting choices and behaviors. Furthermore, you carry the influence of your first language, culture and group memberships into every interpreted event – all of which influence how you will view the interaction. As an interpreter, you will need to identify and accurately represent the multiple cultural frames that are influencing the content being interpreted. It is important to become aware of how these factors influence our work as interpreters as well as our interpersonal relationships. We need to develop positive relationships with our colleagues. This means we need to identify and reduce the potential for cultural and communicative misunderstandings and develop the ability to mitigate cross-cultural dynamics influencing our interpreting as well as our interactions with our colleagues.

It is essential that interpreters demonstrate intercultural competencies – the abilities to adeptly navigate complex environments marked by diverse people, cultures and lifestyles, which means we must consistently conduct ourselves "effectively and appropriately when interacting with others who are linguistically and culturally different from oneself" (Hurwitz-Leeds & Stenou, 2013, p. 5).

chapter *Review*

This chapter expands on the definition of dDeaf culture, the meaning of culture, the inner workings of culture and the unique differences that must be respected. Learning the language and terms of the profession are essential when working in this field. This review defines terms you will use as you become an interpreter and delves into ways to successfully communicate with dDeaf people (such as attention getting techniques).

Terms to Know:

- **Collectivistic:** This term refers to those individuals who are foundationally supported by people from the same culture, and share similar bonds. They are group oriented and dependent on community.

- **Cultural Frames:** This is the way in which we understand or make sense of the world, through our values, language, beliefs, and norms.

- **Deaf:** This term is used to define a person or a group of people who share sign language, culture, values, beliefs and are actively involved in their community.

- **deaf:** This term refers to a medical condition that signifies a significant hearing loss.

- **Individualistic:** This term is defined by people who are more focused on themselves and their immediate family opposed to society at large.

- **Intersectionality:** Is the term use to explain the multiple converging identities (i.e., being both dDeaf and First Nation Canadian).

- **Institutionalized Oppression:** This term that describes the systemic mistreatment, destructive actions, words, and views of minority people because of their membership with a social identity group

- **Microaggressions:** This term refers to comments or actions that can unintentionally convey prejudices toward groups or people that are marginalized.

- **Oral traditions or oral lore:** This is a way in which knowledge, history, art, ideas and cultural roots are conveyed "orally" from one generation to the next (Miles, 2019). The dDeaf community tends to share their experiences and events from one generation to the next generation in the form of *narrative traditions.*

- **Schema:** This term is the cognitive framework that helps us make sense of the world around us (vocabulary, questions, setting, our knowledge of social settings, interactions, etc.).

- **Stereotyping:** Is faulty thinking and subsequent beliefs regarding a person or people group that leads to negative views, destructive behaviors, and sweeping generalizations.

- **Subculture:** This term refers to people who reside within a larger cultural group, but shares a specific commonality related to their identity with a smaller group.

Culture defines the meaning and value we attribute to:

- Family and our place in it (e.g., birth order)
- Gender
- Social experiences
- Economic status
- Educational experiences
- Physical, mental, emotional and spiritual development
- Temperament or personality type

Deaf or deaf, what's the difference?

- Uppercase "D" Deaf is not focused on the audiological condition that enables people to hear. The uppercase "D" embodies the Deaf culture, language, behavioral norms, and other aspects about the people group.

- Lowercase "d" deaf is focused on the audiological condition of hearing loss. However, these individuals sometimes associate with the Deaf community but often prefer to communicate by speaking and rarely use sign language. Often, the individuals in this group have a significant hearing loss early in life.

It is essential to understand how the Deaf culture functions as a whole. Learning a language does not provide all the rich cultural heritage or unique behaviors that encompass a culture.

Sign Language: Not all dDeaf people exclusively use one mode of communication.

- Some speak and sign
- Some only sign
- Some only speak (which is often used by people who have gone deaf later in life)

Cultural Distinctions:

An essential aspect to know is the mindset of the Deaf culture. Deaf people are a **collectivist** culture and information is readily shared and accessible, which differs from (most, but not all) interpreters' upbringing. American culture has been identified as an **individualistic** culture, focusing primarily on themselves or immediate family.

- **Collectivistic culture** can be compared to a herd or pack. A pack of wolves, for example, provides for one another. Wolves hunt, share their food, and bring back food to their young. They fight, eat, and drink as a community.

- **Individualistic culture** is more focused on themselves and their immediate group of family and friends. This characteristic could be compared to tigers. Tigers are solitary animals and provide for themselves or their young, but they do not live as a community and only come together when necessary.

High-context cultures are usually collectivist cultures. The dDeaf culture is a high-context collectivist culture.

Ethnic Group:

The dDeaf community possess the following criteria which identifies them as an ethnic group. According to Harlan Lane (2005), the internal properties of the dDeaf culture community are:

- Collective name
- Customs
- Feeling of community
- Social structure
- Norms for behavior
- Language

- Values
- Art forms
- Knowledge
- History
- Kinship (p. 292)

Attention Getting:

Every culture or family has their own way of getting someone's attention. Some call their name, snap their fingers, or clear their throat. However, the dDeaf culture has their own ways of getting the attention of another person. Learning them will help you know when to use them.

- Tapping: Is a technique used by dDeaf and people who can hear. This technique is hardly ever disrespectful to use. Be mindful of the cultural differences between tapping location for dDeaf and for people who can hear.

- Waving: This technique should not be used when a dDeaf person is engaged in a conversation, unless there is a direct need (emergency, or when someone is leaving, etc.).

Identity, Family, & Culture

NOTES

- Lights flashing: This one is often best used in a group setting (if you're trying to get everyone's attention) or when an individual is across the room from you (the room should be empty or nearly empty).

- Stomping/pounding: Be mindful of where you are and what you are stomping on. Stomping will not work on tile or concrete. Using this method is best for getting the attention of a single person or for getting the attention of a small group (such as pounding on the table).

Each method is based on situational need. Some examples of things to **avoid** are listed below.

- Do not flash the lights in a group when you are seeking the attention of one person
- Do not wave when you are in a large group and are standing a distance away from the person you are trying to reach
- Do not tap an uninitiated hearing person on the leg when you are sitting beside them (it is not culturally appropriate)

Appropriate conversation cues:

Unlike people who can hear, dDeaf people require:

- Sustained eye contact
- Backchanneling (nodding, shaking your head, inquiry, etc.)

If you continually look away, they will likely follow your eye gaze, or they may ask what you're looking at and they will likely feel **disrespected** by your lack of attention.

Common untrue **stereotypes** about the Deaf community:

- Deaf people can't drive
- Deaf culture isn't a real culture
- American Sign Language isn't a real language

Intersectionality covers a wide range and diversity which overlap in different ways and degrees for each individual, including such identities as:

- Race, ethnicity
- Cultural identification: group membership, southerners, northerners, etc.
- Disabilities (physical, emotional, etc.)
- Sexual/gender identity

It is essential to be respectful to others because we don't know how they choose to identify themselves.

Microaggressions: This idea and term can apply to a vast range of people groups or individuals who have experienced prejudiced actions or words. Some words or actions would be:

- When women are told to smile more
- "I don't see color"
- Men shouldn't cry
- "Some of my best friends are dDeaf"

57

Recognizing when these microaggressions occur will enable you to be mindful of your own tendencies, and therefore, minimize the incidents.

Schema: Some of the following features or characteristics are most commonly utilized when organizing our schema:

- **Physical:** Classifying individuals based on their appearance, gender, physique, age, etc.
- **Role:** expectations of others based on their social position: neighbors, doctors, students, etc.
- **Interaction:** how people behave in social situations influence our sense of who they are and what we might expect of them (whether they are aloof, friendly, judgmental, etc.)
- **Psychological:** tendency to group individuals based on our personal psychological assessments of them (curious, nervous, insecure, etc.)
- **Membership:** categorize others according to their group affiliation (refugee, Baptist, member of the Rotary club, female, etc.)

Schema helps you determine how to interact appropriately in a particular setting.

- **Denotative:** The **literal** or **surface** level of meaning or what is often referred to as the dictionary definition
- **Connotative:** The **implied** or **deeper** level of meaning or what is often inferred or figurative in nature

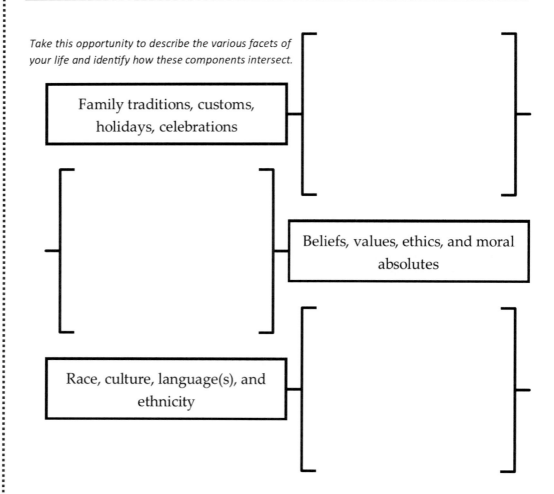

Take this opportunity to describe the various facets of your life and identify how these components intersect.

Family traditions, customs, holidays, celebrations

Beliefs, values, ethics, and moral absolutes

Race, culture, language(s), and ethnicity

5 | Power, Privilege, & Oppression
THE INFLUENCE OF AUDISM

Members of the dDeaf community – like members of many minority groups – have unfortunately been the target of oppression and **marginalization** for centuries in almost every country in the world. According to the World Fair Trade Organization, marginalization "is both a condition and a process that prevents individuals and groups from full participation in the social, economic, and political life enjoyed by the wider society" (Alakhunova, Diallo, Martin del Campo, & Tallarico, 2015, p. 2) Furthermore, *marginalization* describes some intentional behaviors or inclinations of societies, "where people who they perceive to be undesirable, or without useful function are excluded, i.e., marginalized. The people who are marginalized are outside the existing systems of protection and integration. This limits their opportunities and means for survival" (Sadanand, 2017, p. 66).

Many of the dDeaf individuals you will work with as an interpreter carry with them the scars of ongoing marginalization and **disenfranchisement**. The idea of disenfranchisement is to deprive an individual of a legitimate right, or some privilege or immunity. There are still a disproportionate number of dDeaf people who are unemployed or underemployed (Allerton, 2016; Baker-Shenk, 1986). Our thoughts often gravitate to race or gender when we think of the words, *discrimination* or *prejudice*. This is because minority groups and those who are considered "less than" are being singled out because of their *distinctions,* whether it is language, skin color, beliefs or behavior, any of which could differ from members of the majority group. It is not uncommon for minority groups to experience (or feel as though) they are the target of oppression or unfair treatment. They are often denied access to education, employment and opportunities that are available to members of the power or majority groups in society. dDeaf and hard of hearing people experience discrimination or encounter prejudice from people who can hear these people are referred to as **audists**. Tom Humphries coined the term audism in his 1975 dissertation, as a way to describe oppressive attitudes demonstrated by some individuals, businesses, and organizations towards people who are dDeaf or hard of

TERMS TO KNOW:

- Marginalization
- Disenfranchisement
- Audist
- Lipread
- Privilege
- Sense of Entitlement
- Social Inequality
- Uninitiated
- Medical Model
- Ally
- Normalize
- Oral Program
- Ethnocultural Identity
- Benefactors
- Learned Helplessness

NOTES

hearing. Humphries (1975) defined audism as "the notion that one is superior based on one's ability to hear or behave in the manner of one who hears" (Coltrane, 2012, para. 3). Within the dDeaf community, referring to someone as an audist is equivalent to calling someone a racist – not a term to be taken lightly. Furthermore, audism is an attitude that views deafness through a single lens, judging people who are dDeaf as disabled, as if no other reality could exist.

Much like racism, sexism, ageism – the people who hold these ideologies maintain the belief that certain people are inherently inferior, while also believing that other individuals or groups are superior. Sadly, this attitude can be held by anyone, regardless whether the individual can or cannot hear. A person with an audist belief system makes numerous assumptions about the capability and capacity of people who are dDeaf and their ability to manage daily life. Audistic beliefs often subjugate dDeaf people by making unrealistic, unfair and unilateral demands of them, rather than making any accommodations to communicate. The focus of dDeaf-hearing relationships should be about a *genuine* effort to communicate productively, while making every effort to understand each other, rather than, centering on an individual's inability to hear. Whether intentional or not, audists oppress dDeaf people by asking, expecting or requiring them to conform to the hearing majority population norms and *ways of being*.

Ways of Being
Mainstream American culture actively encourages people to limit or control their visual displays of emotion. Children who can hear are taught at an early age not to make faces, not to point, and to avoid overt gestures. They are taught that if emotions are going to be conveyed, they should be communicated through vocal intonation and volume, refraining from visual or physical expressions. In contrast, visual emotion is *embedded* into the very language used by the dDeaf community and thus is always on display (Smith, 2014). In addition, ASL conveys adjectives, adverbs and verb conjugation visually, so grammatical facial expressions and affect are a critical component of the language and therefore the message being communicated. This explicit visual and physical display of emotion is a frequent cause of *misunderstanding* between dDeaf and hearing people. People who can hear often negatively misinterpret the overt facial expressions, the speed and size of signs being produced, the associated vocalizations, and the visible display of emotions as threatening. The demonstrative nature of American Sign Language can be misperceived as an expression of frustration and even agitation due to the overt display of facial expressions and upper body movement, which is often more intense than typically expressed in mainstream culture. Most individuals from North America are socialized to suppress visible emotions by channeling them into vocal intonation. Oftentimes, this results in sign language students struggling to adequately display emotions with enough strength to satisfy the level of affect and facial expression required when communicating in sign language. If you want to be an interpreter, you need to be aware of your facial expressions and how certain words in English will need to evoke additional facial and physical expression. As an interpreter, you must recognize that *all behavior is communicative* and a dDeaf person may be sending *metamessages* with each gesture, facial expression and vocalization. It is our responsibility, as interpreters, to recognize and respond to such messages in an appropriate manner (for more information on metamessages see chapter three).

As previously mentioned, audism is the belief that the ability to hear is superior and people who hold to such beliefs often make assumptions regarding the value of

Power, Privilege & Oppression

NOTES

being able to speak or talk. People also often presume that intelligence is equivalent to clarity or intelligibility of one's speech; the more understandable a person's speech is, the more intelligent they must be. Closely related to that is the idea that one's clarity of speech is necessarily associated with one's ability to hear – the more *typical* sounding a dDeaf person's speech is, the more residual hearing the dDeaf person must have, this is not always the case. Along those same lines of faulty reasoning, dDeaf people are deemed smarter and more "successful" if they can **lipread** (speechread) and talk. Unfortunately, people who can hear often assume that a dDeaf person who has some speech and lipreading abilities requires no additional accommodations to support their inclusion in a classroom or on the job. "Lipreading is the task of decoding text from the movement of a speaker's mouth. Lipreading is a notoriously difficult task for humans, especially in the absence of context" (Assael, Shillingford, Whiteson, & de Freitas, 2016, p. 1). The research regarding lipreading (speechreading) states that the ability to identify and distinguish between words is difficult and accuracy rarely exceeds 10-30 percent of what is being spoken (Bernstein, Demorest, & Tucker, 2000). Simply put, the ability to read people's lips is extremely limited. It is not uncommon to sacrifice academic achievement by focusing an excessive amount of time learning how to pronounce words and phrases. Heather Whitestone, the first dDeaf woman to become Miss America (1995) stated that "she spent six years learning to pronounce her last name alone" (Witchel, 1994, p. 1). Oftentimes, parents of dDeaf children dream their child will talk like a person who can hear. Miss Whitestone explained in her interview with The New York Times, "My mother fought all her life for me to achieve my dreams" (Witchel, 1994, p. 1).

Audism perpetuates the belief that dDeaf people should act, speak and function like people who can hear. Frequently, people who are dDeaf encounter situations where decisions have been made for and about them that are counterintuitive to their needs. For example, when a dDeaf person makes an appointment with a doctor, lawyer, realtor or other professional and requests an interpreter, often the hiring entity resists hiring an interpreter, insisting instead that writing back and forth will be adequate. Meanwhile, the dDeaf individual is often silently judged for their imperfect use of written English. Another related form of audism is arbitrarily stripping dDeaf people of their autonomy by not allowing them to decide what *is* or *is not* important to them. For instance, when a dDeaf employee asks their colleague at a staff meeting why everyone seems so angry, the fellow employee decides the dDeaf individual might not understand and responds, "Ahh, it's not important, no big deal!" denying their fellow employee the power to decide for themself whether or not that information is important. Even worse, when a dDeaf family member asks a sibling or parent why everyone is laughing during a dinner meal – oftentimes, the dDeaf family member is told, "I will tell you later," or "You wouldn't understand," so an explanation sadly never comes.

Audism often appears to be benevolent with a rationale of trying to help the dDeaf person "fit in" and become like everyone else. However, it is a mask of hypocrisy perpetuating the false belief that dDeaf people are inferior because of their hearing loss and are unable to communicate by conventional means – speaking. Marginalized people groups are typically oppressed in every society – subjected to unjust treatment or unneeded and uninvited control by others. Oppression is basically "a cruel or unjust exercise of power imposed on members of minority populations or groups of people viewed as less valuable or influential by those who hold the power in a community or country" (Merriam-Webster, 2020). Ideas triggered by the word *oppression* include concepts, such as abuse, maltreatment, subjugation, enslavement, exploitation, and hardship. Historically, oppression has been experienced by people groups who have a different ethnicity, culture, and language from that of the majority, power population in a community. Oppressive behavior and treatment is not solely reserved for those with a different ethnicity, culture, and language but often perpetrated against those who have a physical or mental disability. Unfortunately, women and children often experience mistreatment even though they are from the same ethnic, cultural and linguistic group as the population holding power in a society.

Much of the history regarding dDeaf people in the US and Canada reflects that they were denied access to quality education, employment and numerous other benefits granted to those who could hear and speak (Humphrey & Alcorn, 2007). The goal of most parents of dDeaf children was for their children to learn to speak and lipread. Often children who were born dDeaf were forced to spend enormous amounts of energy trying to develop clear articulation of the family's primary language and to read the lips of teachers, parents, siblings and people in the public arena. Educators lacked a genuine understanding or empathy concerning the difficulties in learning to speak and read lips, which often resulted in cruel physical and mental abuse toward the dDeaf students and their family members (Vidor, 2020; Christenson, 2020). Frequently, the majority of dDeaf individuals lived a life dependent on others, with little or no control over their own lives. Those who were "fortunate" enough to go to a school that used sign language for communication were taught almost exclusively by people who could hear and speak, most of whom had no understanding of what it was like to be marginalized simply because you could not hear.

Privilege, Entitlement and Social Inequality

There were, however, those who recognize that the ability to hear did not make them better than those who do not hear and, in turn, use their **privilege** to level the playing field. The term *privilege* can be traced to the 1930's when William Edward Burghardt DuBois, better known as W.E.B. DuBois, an American sociologist and civil rights activist who wrote about Caucasians who felt superior to African Americans, claiming biological white superiority which DuBois *adamantly opposed* (Biobliography.com, 2020). He spent much of his life debunking the fallacy of such claims. Nearly sixty years later, Peggy McIntosh (1988) built on the idea of privilege in her work entitled, *White Privilege and Male Privilege: A Personal Account of Coming to See Correspondences through Work in Women's Studies*, in which she challenged access to an array of unearned opportunities available to men and denied to women based simply on gender (Ferguson, 2014). As a result of these founding leaders, we define "privilege as a set of unearned benefits given to people who fit into a specific social group" (Ferguson, 2014, para. 7). Privilege allows members of the majority group to have access to resources that they did not work for, pay for, or earn, but simply because of their social membership they are able to enjoy freedoms above and beyond those from different social groups (NCCJ, 2020). In fact, privilege is so pervasive that attorney Dale Boam (2019) has declared that,

> Privilege is a parasite. It feeds on unearned opportunity and excretes undeserved power, and though obvious to everyone around, it attempts to convince its host it doesn't exist. In other words, I have to work hard at all times to see it, because it doesn't want me to (p. 25).

It is possible for individuals to hold audist, racist, and/or sexist beliefs and attitudes, particularly if those persons possess influence and power in society. This is because those who hold political, economic, and social power are typically *privileged.* Privilege often results in *personal advantage* and often fosters a **sense of entitlement**, which typically results in **social inequality**. Sadly, a sense of "entitlement is essentially a personality trait, based on the belief that someone deserves resources that other people don't deserve" (Porter, 2020, para. 3). This feeds directly into *social inequality.* Privileged individuals, who hold power, have the ability to prevent individuals they feel are not deserving from accessing resources. Social inequality is evidenced by unequal opportunities, limited employment, and fewer rewards for those individuals from a different social position or status within a group or society. Such inequality demonstrates regular patterns of unfair distributions of goods, services, benefits, consequences and available employment (Crossman, 2020). All of these unequal realities result in a type of *immunity* which appears to be granted to or enjoyed by certain societal groups to a greater degree than other groups; which is often invisible to those who have it. Those who are privileged often have economic stability and financial resources to take care of the cost of college, they have an expectation that they will receive a new car or maybe a down payment for a home from their parents or grandparents when the need arises. Others, who are less privileged, may have to work two (or more) part time jobs to pay for college tuition and books; they know that they will have to work and save their money if they are going to own a car and that home ownership may be a distant reality.

Take a moment to think about the privilege or advantages you carry with you each day. Before continuing your reading, consider the following quote.

> In the end, whether racism, sexism, ableism, audism, genderism or any other "ism" you can think of, I have the responsibility to pay attention and work past each layer of privilege that clouds my vision, to purposely see when my privilege is smoothing my path and to actively make sure it is not blocking the paths of others. Most important of all I must now and forever be bothered by privilege when I see it, even if it's my own, because for so very long I failed to look, let alone to see (Boam, 2019, p. 25).

Look at the list below and consider additional areas of privileges you enjoy but have never thought about:

- **Social Status:** Do you live in a safe area of town? Do you have more than 2 credit cards? Do you have easy access to a car? Can you pick between at least 4 different clothing choices when you dress each day? Do you have a bank account with a typical balance of $100 or more?
- **Age:** Are you between 18-24 years old? 25-35 years old? 36-45? 46-60? 60+?
- **Education:** Did you finish high school? Did you attend special, regular or gifted classes? Are you able to go to almost any postsecondary institution to learn a trade or get a degree?
- **Ethnic and Racial Identity:** Are you white/light skin tone? Do you speak "standard English" (the kind used by English teachers and politicians) without a noticeable accent?
- **Gender Identity:** Do you identify as a male or female? Were you born with the physical characteristics that match the gender you identify with?
- **Marital Status:** Married? Living together? Divorced? Divorced more than once? Are you a single parent – how many children do you have?
- **Sexual Identity:** Are you gay, straight, bi, lesbian, other?

Chapter 5

NOTES

- **Religion:** Do you identify as Atheist? Baha'i? Buddist? Christian? Hindu? Confucian? Jewish? Wicken?
- **Physical and Mental Fitness:** Do you have a cognitive, developmental, intellectual, physical or sensory challenge/disability? Do you deal with ongoing mental health issue(s)?

Think about additional categories that could be added to the above list. Consider your cumulative life experience as you reflect on each of these categories and list additional questions, ideas or thoughts that come to your mind. In your opinion or life experience, do any of the categories listed come with *immediate* or *eventual* advantages or disadvantages? If so, can you *discuss* your perspective concerning the positives and negatives with your friends, family, colleagues or with anyone who identifies with any of the above categories?

The Privilege of Interpreters

It is hoped that you have begun to consider how this will impact you. You will likely be a sign language interpreter in the US, Canada, Australia, Puerto Rico or other 21st century countries. Interpreters – dDeaf and hearing – carry privileged status. The things we have learned over our lifetime that we consider *normal and acceptable* or *unusual and unacceptable,* influence our actions and reactions every day. If you have lived a life able to hear, much of your life has been based on sound and the ability to hear that sound. You get up each morning – waking to the sound of an alarm clock, or knowing it is raining by the sound on the roof. Overhearing side conversations about what is happening in the media, making decisions based on incidental learning – all of this amounts to *hearing privilege,* the privilege you have simply because you can hear and communicate by talking. If you are a dDeaf interpreter you have gained additional education regarding language, culture, ethics and interpreting which are not commonly available to all members of the dDeaf community – that background will likely give you access to jobs and income a majority of dDeaf individuals may not experience. You are identified as the linguistic and cultural *expert* that affords you an additional degree of privilege.

Our beliefs about what is polite or rude, appropriate or inappropriate, good or bad influence us as we move through the world interacting with others. When others have different norms of behavior than our own, we are sometimes puzzled, perhaps even uncomfortable. Whether you are a person who is dDeaf or a person who can hear, your expectations of others frequently reflects the degree of privilege you have experienced in your life. Evidence of your privilege can be seen in numerous parts of your life, from socioeconomic status to personal hygiene, views on dental and health care, beliefs regarding education and employment.

THE IMPACT OF OPPRESSION FROM INTERPRETERS

As briefly mentioned, interpreters – dDeaf or hearing – carry degrees of privilege that some of the participants[1] present at an interpreting assignment may not possess; it is our *responsibility* to use our privilege to benefit the less privileged. We are to do everything we can as benefactors of the dDeaf community to leverage our privilege to *benefit* the dDeaf community. Interpreters are exposed daily to the encounters of the privileged and the disenfranchised – to the conflict of cultures, norms and expectations (Humphrey & Alcorn, 2007). The presence of an interpreter ameliorates the lack of access to some degree but in other ways our presence exacerbates the situation.

---

[1]*The term participant is used in place of the term client or consumer, as it appears to equalize all persons at an interpreting assignment.*

Power, Privilege & Oppression

NOTES

Interpreters see the subtle ways dDeaf individuals are regularly disregarded and mistreated. The ignorance and arrogance of some educators and medical practitioners, who believe they know what is best for people who are dDeaf, and they are determined to "fix" dDeaf people. Interpreters work in situations where they see disrespect and the denigration of dDeaf people on a daily basis (Harvey, 2015). Furthermore, interpreters encounter people who can hear who are wholly **uninitiated** about the needs, wants and daily experiences of dDeaf people. For our purposes, the term *uninitiated* refers to those individuals who have limited or no prior experience, knowledge or understanding of the dDeaf culture, community or communication norms. Furthermore, what information they have is typically from the **medical model**. The Canadian Hearing Services explains the medical model as focusing on the,

> medical/pathological condition of the individual – a functional loss, handicap or impairment that needs medical intervention and rehabilitation to increase one's quality of life. Common terms used in...this model include 'disabled,' 'hearing impaired,' and 'deafness.' Nowadays, such terms are considered antiquated and offensive in the Deaf community (Models of deafness, 2015, para. 3).

This ideology comes from a place of privilege and superiority, which believes that the inability to hear means that one's quality of life is somehow less. This kind of thinking is evidenced in big and small ways. For example, those employers who ignore a dDeaf employee's requests for minor accommodations, such as an interpreter for the monthly staff meeting or captioned training videos. It is not uncommon to resist, if not reject, what we do not understand; such as patrons in a restaurant making rude gestures and offensive comments regarding the dDeaf people sitting at a nearby table, unaware someone sitting at the table can hear. Even distraught parents, in denial about their child's deafness, bringing their child to every doctor hoping for a cure.

Another form of oppression comes from those who appear to have allied themselves with the dDeaf community. The behavior of interpreters, for example, who work alongside dDeaf community activists fighting against the closure of state and provincial schools for the dDeaf, but who accept work as interpreters in the local school districts where children are being mainstreamed (Alcorn, 1986). Interpreters also see the plight of qualified dDeaf individuals seeking employment and repeatedly being overlooked. However, interpreters who earn a respectable living and benefit from interpreting also take work from dDeaf people by teaching sign language classes – robbing members of the dDeaf community of viable employment for which they are more likely to be qualified than a person who can hear. It is hoped that the number of interpreters who make use of their privilege as an ally, then turn around and oppress the community are very few. All of this puts interpreters in an awkward position – dDeaf people view interpreters as friends and allies and often struggle to separate these very interpreters from the majority culture of people who can hear. Further, interpreters are often the target of the backlash of the oppressed members of the dDeaf community, which manifests itself in (Alcorn, 1986):

- Frequent comments about uninitiated, ignorant hearing people
- Laughing at and telling interpreting jokes that make fun of interpreters and people who can hear
- Interpreting the comments of a dDeaf person who is condemning or criticizing

65

the very person who is interpreting those comments

When these things happen, interpreters labor to separate their feelings of hurt, disappointment and irritation resulting from the insult and from what they know to be justified statements based on the dDeaf experience. In addition, there is a certain amount of testing and teasing from the dDeaf community as a type of *initiation* that interpreters will experience as they establish ties with the dDeaf community; this may involve being the brunt of interpreter jokes (Alcorn, 1986). This reality sometimes creates a personal-professional dilemma for the interpreters, who are typically drawn to the field of interpreting because they care about people, communication and access. But seeing oppression in action day after day stirs up empathy in them that results in feelings of rage, shame or a sense of powerlessness. Harvey (2015) clarifies that, "those who bear witness to trauma, such as interpreters, may experience vicarious trauma: the transformation of one's inner experience as a result of empathetic engagement with another's distress...Simply put, when we open our hearts to someone in emotional pain, we are changed" (p. 6). It is important that interpreters are aware of vicarious trauma; this phenomenon occurs when an individual witnesses or is exposed to harmful behaviors that are directed at another person. In the case of interpreters, vicarious trauma often refers to witnessing implicit and explicit oppression, abuse or cruelty that is experienced by a dDeaf person for whom they are interpreting. Again, though the attack was not aimed at the interpreter, they often feel like they personally have experienced the trauma. Prolonged or repeated exposure to vicarious trauma can lead to caregiver burnout, which "is a state of physical, emotional, and mental exhaustion that may be accompanied by a change in attitude – from positive and caring to negative and unconcerned" (Beckerman, 2018, para. 1). Numbing one's emotions as a method to manage the negative emotions and thoughts is not a healthy solution as it may result in anxiety, stress and depression (Beckerman, 2018).

A recommended solution is finding someone to talk about your experiences, whether with a professional or a good friend – it is essential to express what you have been through. Harvey (2015) explains, "articulating and examining one's experience with another person who seeks to understand one's reactions and validate one's feelings often renders the detrimental effects of the vicarious trauma less emotionally toxic" (p. 11). However, remember it is necessary to respect the confidentiality of those you interpreted for while you are working through your own pain. Finally to begin to find a place of wholeness and

> to transform vicarious trauma, you must love your work or some important aspect of your work.... This work is too difficult and too personally demanding to do without a sense of mission or conviction.....[sic] The work must be meaningful to you. Then, paradoxically, your work itself is part of your antidote to vicarious trauma (Saakvitne & Pearlman, 1996, p.72; cited in Harvey, 2015, p. 13).

It is evident that sign language interpreters work alongside members of the dDeaf community; our work can impact the lives of dDeaf people in both positive and negative ways. However, our work also has the power to influence our lives in potentially challenging ways. In light of such potential influences, it is important that, as student interpreters, you develop the necessary strategies that will support your overall emotional health as you begin your professional practice.

Power, Privilege & Oppression

NOTES

On a personal level – the authors would like to encourage you to guard your emotional and mental health. A few suggestions that may enable you to process your experiences – you may want to include:

- Regular self-reflective journaling – write what you are thinking and feeling, and ask yourself why what you witnessed is bothering you
- Possibly include quiet times of meditation or prayer – striving to "let go" of the negative feelings and energy
- Find a *confidential* colleague (or therapist) who can support you as you develop appropriate coping strategies

Power Implications for Interpreters

When you become an interpreter, you may be surprised to find yourself in a very powerful position (Baker-Shenk, 1992). In many situations, you are the only person in an interaction who knows what is happening in both languages and cultural frames. Further, as a student of interpretation, you will be developing your own values and belief systems related to the dDeaf community, American Sign Language, Deaf education, interpreting and numerous related areas. Denying that you have influence will not make it so. Abdicating your power is fruitless because the authority is inherent in your role and ascribed to you by the people present in each situation. Rather, you must learn how to *leverage* your authority in a judicious and prudent manner to ensure that the truth in every situation and circumstance prevails.

However, this may require that you spend some time in self-reflection to identify your personal history with power, marginalization and oppression. Consider your experiences over the course of your life, both personally and professionally; were you oppressed or an oppressor, the victim or victimizer? Many of us have assumed both roles – at home we may be bullied and mistreated but at school we might be the bully. We may be in an abusive relationship, living in fear, but as the supervisor we create a working environment of fear. All of us have varying degrees of power and privilege and it is critical we examine our ideas, beliefs and values concerning this essential topic. Why is spending time in introspection important? "If you don't make the time and effort to refocus your mind on the positive through introspection, you won't give yourself the opportunity to grow and develop" (Ackerman, 2020, para. 10). Introspection, the informal reflection process enables you to stop and consider your inner *thoughts* and *feelings* (Ackerman, 2020). All of us must *examine* how we make use of the influence we are afforded. Contemplate your use of power and how closely related it is to privilege. If you want to be an interpreter, you must begin a lifetime practice of reflecting on your history, attitudes, beliefs and behaviors to identify any oppressive tendencies present in your life and take steps to change them.

It is also important to avoid the error of early anthropologists who made brief sojourns into foreign territories, observed and interpreted what they saw from their own *experiential frame*. They became immediate "experts" on the customs and traditions of the culture they visited, without considering that their frame of reference was contaminated by their native culture. This prevented them from accurately interpreting the information they gathered, nor did they give ample consideration to the subsequent ramifications of their "interpretations." It is vital, as interpreters that we are lifelong learners, eternal students, inquisitive, observant – and ever humbled by the reality of how much we do not know or understand about the culture and norms of each dDeaf culture and community with which we

67

come in contact. Step back and consider what your current beliefs and practices imply – this act of self-reflection can be "transformative because it focuses on dominant assumptions which may influence…[your] practice unwittingly" (Dymoke & Harrison, 2008, p. 35, bracketed information added by author).

Advocate or Ally?

Charlotte Baker-Shenk was one of the first to challenge sign language interpreters to consider their role in light of the historic oppression experienced by the dDeaf community. She asked interpreters to think about what we could do to foster equality by refusing to perpetuate the systemic oppression of members of the dDeaf community. Our awareness of the ongoing oppression of the dDeaf community compelled many (well-intentioned) individuals, who can hear, to work toward ending the injustice. One of the most notable ways to stem the oppression was to become an advocate on behalf of dDeaf individuals. Yet, there is a subtle but discernible difference between becoming an advocate *for* dDeaf people and becoming an advocate *of* dDeaf people. When people who can hear assume the role of advocate, they often become the *expert* regarding all things dDeaf, while not being dDeaf themselves.

Advocacy work provides the advocate with potential feelings of value, importance, and being an irreplaceable member of the dDeaf community. This position can be a slippery slope because an advocate is one who speaks out on issues on behalf of others. As the expert, they often will be invited to speak to the press, a group of employers, or other members of the majority group. This results in advocates who can hear – rather than those who are dDeaf – taking a position of leadership in the fight for equality, stepping into the light and unintentionally pushing capable dDeaf individuals aside. This subtle form of oppression is often invisible because the oppressor is veiled in good deeds.

The cycle of oppression can be broken but each and everyone of us has a role to play. Interpreters, both dDeaf and hearing, by virtue of our position carry historic power and our role is not to *rescue* people who are dDeaf. We are service providers whose obligation is to provide equal language access. A special word of caution for dDeaf interpreters, as a member of the dDeaf community and a service provider with advanced education, you need to be careful not to use the power afforded you to gain leadership positions or roles. The role which we can most appropriately play is that of an **ally** – one who supports dDeaf individuals on their journey of liberation. Consider this, if you are standing with the dDeaf community, but you are not standing close enough to get "hit," then you are not standing close enough.

Author Anne Bishop (1994) has outlined some strategies for becoming an ally. Bishop has worked for nearly thirty years supported many groups striving to achieve social justice. A small sampling of her ideas that will help us to understand the position of an ally:

- Learn about oppression – identify it in your own life and begin a journey toward personal liberation
- Help members of your own social groups, professional circle and colleagues understand oppression
- Recognize that you may be part of the problem – we have all grown up in a society surrounded by oppressive, "power-over other people" attitudes and can easily become oppressors ourselves
- Remember that as a member of the majority group, you cannot see reality as

Power, Privilege & Oppression

NOTES

clearly as members of oppressed groups; listen to and believe dDeaf people when they tell you about the discrimination and pain they have experienced and are still experiencing
- Do not take on a leadership role; work with and support members of oppressed groups but do not make the mistake of assuming leadership in their community
- Develop and maintain friendships with members of oppressed groups outside of your professional involvement with them

It is important to remember that if you are a person who can hear, you cannot fully comprehend the *dDeaf experience*, nor should you lay claim to the roots and interconnectedness of a community that has endured a lifetime of oppression. Baker-Shenk (1992) provides an excellent discussion on this subject in her article entitled *The Interpreter: Machine, Advocate or Ally?* We urge you to read her article and to discuss it with your instructor, classmates, and members of the larger dDeaf community.

Becoming an interpreter, you must be prepared to struggle with conflicting and sometimes confusing feelings regarding your role in relation to the dDeaf community. At the same time, some interpreters may feel attacked or become defensive when they perceive some of the comments, jokes and insults are indirectly aimed at them. The role of an ally is challenging and living with one foot in the world of people who are dDeaf and people who can hear is no easy task. One of the most underrated tools you can use is a good sense of humor. More than you realize, it can help you in your journey into the culture and community of dDeaf people (Bienvenu, 1992). As a member of the majority hearing culture, it is easy to take offense at jokes aimed at your language, culture and behaviors. Don't, just don't. Try instead to gain insight by taking a glimpse into the world of dDeaf people – you have a chance to learn something from a member of the minority. Learning to laugh at yourself and your inevitable cultural faux pas is one tool that will help you on your journey.

As an interpreter, it is also important to realize that when you see dDeaf individuals talking about "hearing people" in humorous or critical ways, they are typically speaking of the doctor, school administrator, psychologist or some other person who can hear that does not understand the thoughts and feelings of the dDeaf community. They are likely not talking about those people who can hear whom they view as friends and allies. As you learn to respect and observe the cultural norms of the dDeaf community, you have the potential of becoming accepted as a member of the larger dDeaf community. As such, these comments typically refer to uninitiated people who can hear and who have not yet demonstrated an awareness or sensitivity to the needs, wants and day-to-day life experiences of members of the dDeaf culture and community.

STEREOTYPING, OPPRESSION AND THE DEAF COMMUNITY

For some time there have been two perspectives that are in stark contrast to one another related to how society perceives people who are dDeaf. One view identifies dDeaf people from a pathological perspective of being broken or defective, while the second regards dDeaf people as members of a cultural and linguistic minority. However, for years, dDeaf individuals have been categorized as disabled, impaired, and less-than solely because their worldview is significantly different from the "normal" view of a world based on sound. Different is not defective, nor are those individuals who embrace the world from that perspective. Living a life based on vision instead of one based on sound, does not make one broken. Historically, the medical community has influenced how people view and categorize deafness, perceiving it as a disability. Thus, the general population has adopted a pathological view of dDeaf people, which has further reinforced the drive to fix dDeaf people rather than accept them. This has led to systemic oppression of dDeaf children, teens and young adults.

dDeaf people cannot simply be "cured," rather medical professionals attempt to **normalize** dDeaf people through professional *intervention*. *Normalization* by medical or educational professionals takes several forms, but often begins with the overt elimination of sign languages as a means of viable communication (Lane, 2005). This is almost always followed by maximizing the use of residual hearing and increasing the environmental sound through amplification and technology (e.g., hearing aids, cochlear implants). In addition, the utilization of lipreading and speaking to aid in two-way communication is typically the final step taken to normalize dDeaf individuals.

Often, these students are educated in academic programs that focus on listening with their residual hearing, speaking and lipreading, these programs are referred to as **oral programs**. It is essential to note that oral education, also known as oralism, was a radical form of *colonization*, which had "policies actively intending to eradicate or marginalize sign languages and deaf cultures" (Ladd, 2005, p. 13). However, if parents choose not to educate their children in oral programs, they may be included in the mainstream classroom with age appropriate peers for educational and socialization opportunities (Lane, 2005). Mainstream or inclusive environments are concerning because it means placing a dDeaf child in a classroom with other children who can hear and a teacher who most likely does not have the educational background or experience to effectively communicate, educate and understand the needs of the dDeaf child (Lane, 2005). Sadly, residential schools for the dDeaf, rich with dDeaf language models, are rarely the first choice for parents who have dDeaf children. "The percentage of children enrolled in mainstream schools, as opposed to schools for the Deaf, has increased by 55% since the 1950s" (Burke, 2019, p. 19). Because dDeaf children of hearing, non-signing parents often cannot understand or participate in spoken-voice conversations, they are often excluded from family discussions. "Familial exclusion is so common, in fact, that dDeaf people colloquially use the term 'dinner table syndrome' to describe the isolation one feels when eating dinner with hearing family members" (Mousley & Chaudoir, 2018, p. 342).

Dr. Harlan Lane (2005) goes one step further and explains that parents of children who are dDeaf typically do not share the same **ethnocultural identity** of their children and thus lack a *shared language.* Furthermore, the differences in language and culture of their parents means that cultural characteristics and traits cannot be passed on to their children. "Moreover, they commonly do not advocate in the schools, community, courts, and so on for their Deaf child's primary language. Minority languages without parental and community support are normally endangered" (Lane, 2005, p. 294). Ethnocultural identity is a phrase used to discuss the behavioral elements of ethnic identity (language, attitudes, values and behavioral factors). Furthermore, ethnocultural identity focuses on the degree to which a person approves and practices a *way of life* that is rooted in particular cultural traditions. In addition, ethnocultural identity tends to be only identified and labeled as such when two or more cultures (for example, dDeaf and hearing) come into contact (Yamada, Marsella, & Yamada, 1998). People who are dDeaf often spend much of their lives working "against the system" by seeking to understand and be understood.

The exhaustion of consistently educating and defending the values, beliefs and ideals of the dDeaf community to people who can hear often causes dDeaf people to feel powerless; this is not uncommon for marginalized people groups (Baker-Shenk, 1986). dDeaf people often feel there is no value in fighting the system, as the system never seems to change. Some of the systems that require *unending* education are medical, educational, spiritual and social systems, especially as it relates to *quality* interpreting services. Some dDeaf individuals have fought so long that they have become jaded and now accept whatever injustice befalls them, believing there is absolutely nothing they can do to effect positive, *lasting* change. Charlotte Baker-Shenk (1986), explains that the dDeaf "oppressed person becomes docile and passive toward their oppressive situation, feeling 'I can't do anything about it.' The person simply adapts" (p. 47).

This "what's the use" attitude may be reflected in the failure of those who struggle with the English language to register to vote. Or it can be observed in the hesitancy of any Indigenous Person to file a lawsuit regarding the discrimination they experience. It is important to note that while "prejudice refers to biased *thinking*, discrimination consists of *actions* against a group of people" (Little, 2016, p. 433).

Fatalism or Passivity

North American culture has historically been a white man's culture (David Boaz, 2015). Boaz explains that those who were Black in the US – from its founding until the civil rights movement – had to learn about White people, while those who were White went about their lives knowing almost nothing about those who were Black.[2] In the same way, advertisements, movies, magazines or books glorified healthy, tan, able bodied young people. Until recently, the media has not positively represented a person in a wheelchair or a dDeaf person using sign language in their messages. Furthermore, members of numerous minority groups (disabled, LGBTQI, minority people groups, etc.) rarely have equal opportunities to advance in school or work and achieve the financial freedom of the dominant culture. These conditions are evidence of institutionalized oppression in which the dominant group devalues individuals in marginalized or minority groups minimizing their personal worth, abilities, intelligence, and right to be different. For those in minority or marginalized groups, this means having no power to influence the very agencies and institutions that impact their life (Jung Young Lee, 1995). As a result, those members of marginalized groups, which may include linguistic and ethnic minorities, women, the unemployed/underemployed, the homeless, and so many more who are oppressed, powerless, and rejected by the power group in a society (Jung Young Lee, 1995). Charlotte Baker-Shenk (1986) explains her perspective about oppression saying she feels that everyone

> has experienced being oppressed, that is, hurt by someone putting you down, making you feel inferior, or unfairly denying some opportunity to you. I also assume that all of us have oppressed other people, that we have made others feel inferior, perhaps taking advantage of someone else's problems, or trying to make ourselves look good at the expense of others. In

---

[2]*The authors have decided to standardize the capitalization of the "B" in Black in our writing, when referring to people of African descent, it is common to see "Black" in lower case, even though other racial and ethnic groups like Asian, Latinx, and Indigenous Peoples, are routinely capitalized; as cited Nguyen, A. T., & Pendleton, M. (2020, March 23). Recognizing Race in Language: Why We Capitalize "Black" and "White". Retrieved June 24, 2020, from Center for the Study of Social Policy: https://cssp.org/2020/03/recognizing-race-in-language-why-we-capitalize-black-and-white/*

both cases, we may not use the language of oppression to describe our experience, but we have experienced what oppression is (p. 43-44).

Historically, Caucasians in the US and Canada possess the greatest political power, while people of color, typically belong to marginalized groups. Privilege is not automatically guaranteed to Caucasians; factors that influence status are education, profession status (e.g., banker compared to janitor), language, socioeconomic status, and gender to name a few. Opportunities for self-determination can be truly limited for oppressed persons because they are often not permitted to exercise the right to use their native language or to observe their customs and beliefs in educational and business settings. *Personnel Today*, a leading human resources website based in the United Kingdom, explains that one in four dDeaf employees has quit a job because of discrimination – including being passed over for a promotion and an increase in pay (Allerton, 2016). Furthermore, this oppressive behavior is not limited to their professional life, it spills over into other areas of their lives, dDeaf people are frequently asked to bring their own sign language interpreter to meetings or appointments at facilities that are unaccustomed to communicating with dDeaf patrons.

Mousley and Chaudoir (2018), explain that the quality of life for dDeaf people may be less than optimal "because experiences of past discrimination, expectations of future discrimination, and residual feelings of shame have each been linked to poor well-being" (p. 342). Understanding that the experiences of dDeaf people are consistent with other marginalized populations and those negative experiences are evidenced in the disparity in the mental and physical wellbeing of dDeaf and hearing people (Mousley & Chaudoir, 2018). In addition, the dominant culture continues to subjugate the language and culture of dDeaf individuals by compelling them to access resources in the written language of their country. Forms, applications and other official documents are often denied when submitted incomplete or inaccurately which inadvertently results in discrimination in housing, bank loans, and other services. Harlan Lane (1984) reviewed professional literature from 1970-1980 and confirmed the stereotyping and institutionalized oppression that results from pathological thinking, reflected in negative labels ascribed by audists.

CHARACTERISTICS OF OPPRESSIVE "BENEFACTORS"

Most people do not consciously hurt, malign, or oppress others. In their own minds, the people we will describe believe themselves to be benefactors – doing "what is best for those poor folks." Showing kindness, improving the quality of their lives, helping those individuals who are likely a different race, ethnic background, culture, economic status or observe different group norms (Lane, 1992). However, members of the majority culture react to members of the minority culture in *predictable ways*. **"Benefactors"**[3] repeatedly oppress minority group members in an effort to shape them into something or someone they are not, rather than accepting their unique differences. The genuine definition of benefactors is – those individuals who typically give money or other forms of aid to help those in need. However, in this case, benefactors are those individuals who perceive the dDeaf community as being in need and the benefactors foist/impose their help on the dDeaf community. Below are some of the ideals that will describe the many faces of the benefactors: oralism, audism, hearing privilege and the power of the majority community. It is not possible to address every topic thoroughly, but we will strive to do our best with our limited space.

[3]See "The Mask of Benevolence" by Harlan Lane (1992) for an in-depth look at this concept.

Power, Privilege & Oppression

NOTES

Benefactors Are All Knowing

A common characteristic of the marginalized people groups is the idea that the benefactors are somehow "super-beings." Baker-Shenk (1986) refers to this as 'magical thinking' and notes that somehow the benefactors know everything, rarely make mistakes, live a life overflowing with success, winning every battle. Further they are invulnerable, thus making them smarter than the minorities who just "survive" (Freire & Ramos, 1970). There are dDeaf adults who have been conditioned to believe that the lives of people who can hear are better, that they all have mastery of English, rarely struggle to get jobs or promotions, they can hear everything regardless of the conditions, and that somehow they 'know things' simply because their ears work (W. Ross, personal communication, 1992).

This phenomenon is evidence of the powerful effects of colonization in the global dDeaf community. Oralism was the tool of colonization, disguised as a benevolent caretaker and teacher, beginning its takeover in the 1880's, and it has lasted more than 120 years. The proponents of oralism slowly denounced and condemned the utilization of "sign language in deaf education, and removed deaf teachers and deaf adults from the education system in order to try and prevent them from passing down deaf culture to the next generations of deaf children" (Ladd, 2005, p. 13). The destructive philosophy of oral education began in France and spread across the globe, still continuing in most countries today (Ladd, 2005). The voices of many authors recognize oralism as one of the most powerful oppressors of dDeaf people, stating:

> Inevitably, oralism has also seriously affected the quality of deaf individuals' collective lives in their signing communities. This has been manifested in damage to their traditional cultures and artforms, and in their ability to run their own clubs and Deafhood organizations, which were subsequently taken over by non-deaf peoples and administered, in effect, as deaf colonies, with subsequent community divisions which are characteristic of the colonization process (Ladd, 2005, pp. 13-14).

Normalcy and the Misguided Child

The majority population defines *normalcy* according to *their* group experience, financial standing and worldview, then subconsciously imposes their norms on minority group members, often labeling any difference as unusual, a problem and a departure from their standards. Thus, the majority group establishes the ways in which minorities should think, believe and live. Minority group members are further stigmatized by the dominant cultural group when they fail to comply with the dominant expectations. The stigmatized group is systematically prevented from seizing opportunities for growth and change (Mousley & Chaudoir, 2018). Oftentimes this leads the majority group to feel that persons who are dDeaf may need a deliberate intervention to live a *normal life*. In addition, members of the power group struggle to believe that a rational person would reject attempts to help *them* become *normal*. When this occurs, they assume dDeaf people – like children – do not know what is best for them (Freire, 1970; Freire & Vasconcillos, 1989). With sweeping benevolence, people who can hear make decisions that determine the course of the lives of people who are dDeaf. There is no place to argue logic, research or experience, for their minds are made up. Thus, audists dictate what is best for members of the dDeaf community – educational options, methods of communication and professional capabilities (Ladd, 2015). Of course, benefactors expect a measure of gratitude for "pouring their hearts and souls" into the lives of dDeaf people. They believe gratitude is in order for their investment of

73

time, energy, and concern which has helped to improve the quality of the lives of dDeaf people. This repeated intervention has created an unhealthy cycle of oppression and dependence.

Reliance on the Benefactor

Members of a marginalized group are often perpetually victimized by the majority culture members. These well meaning individuals may be family, friends, neighbors and coworkers who desire to *rescue* the dDeaf person from the "hardships" of deafness. The desire to *protect* and *prevent* dDeaf people from making mistakes inadvertently creates a detrimental environment of **learned helplessness**. Mathews (2015) explains that "learned helplessness is a psychological phenomenon...whereby individuals become cognitively programmed to believe they are helpless – a state which is, for them, 'personal, pervasive and permanent' [and the] reversal of learned helplessness is a laborious process" (Mathews, 2015, p. 4). "[D]eaf people have been viewed as disabled in their childhood families and, consequently, as helpless people in serious need of assistance" (Harvey, 1984 cited in de Bruin & Brugmans, 2006, p. 367). In addition, some dDeaf people have learned that others can solve their problems for them and, as an oppressed people group, some have come to accept the 'helpless role' (de Bruin & Brugmans, 2006). There are additional contributing factors that perpetuate the cycle of oppression. When caregivers, parents, teachers, and other professionals circumvent the journey to adulthood by removing or lowering the normal responsibilities, they delay or preclude the growing up process. "Acquisition of life skills can be compromised by a number of factors including: lower expectations during their school years, barriers to incidental learning opportunities, poor communication at home, learned helplessness, and poor literacy and numeracy skills" (Mathews, 2015, p. 1). Sadly, this learned helplessness can be so deeply ingrained that some dDeaf people have redefined what is normal and part of the definition involves heavy reliance on the majority group (de Bruin & Brugmans, 2006).

The Faces of Oppression

As sign language interpreters, we need to do more than simply work in the dDeaf community; we should make our presence known through visible and ongoing support. When the dDeaf community faces persecution related to state or provincial school closures, lack of or substandard provision of interpreting services, or overt discrimination against dDeaf individuals, it is important for interpreters to use their privilege in support of the community and culture of dDeaf people. Alexander Graham Bell is known for his numerous inventions, most notable among them was the telephone. However, he had a much darker side; Bell is historically the "most famous advocate of regulating Deaf marriage to reduce Deaf childbirth" (Lane, 2005, p. 302). As one of the original founders of oral education in the United States, Bell believed that, "residential schools, where most Deaf children acquired language, identity, and a life partner, should be closed and Deaf people educated in small day schools" (Lane, 2005, p. 302). Bell encouraged the sterilization of dDeaf people to prevent the creation of a dDeaf community of sign language users (Lane, 2005). Randy Alcorn (1996), in his work *Dominion,* warns that we should not fear those who are blatantly, overtly and obviously evil, but rather be worried about those "normal folk." Those who neither stand up or speak up when evil occurs but quietly turn their back and walk away in the face of unspeakable horror (Alcorn, 1996). As interpreters, we must ally ourselves with the oppressed, be they young or old, male or female, dark or fair skinned. We are to resist the oppression of those around us. Martin Luther King Jr. in his fight for equality, justice and peace penned a letter from Birmingham City Jail, in 1963 declaring,

Power, Privilege & Oppression

NOTES

in a real sense, all life is interrelated. All men are caught in an inescapable network of mutuality, tied in a single garment of destiny. Whatever affects one directly, affects all indirectly. I can never be what I ought to be until you are what you ought to be, and you can never be what you ought to be until I am what I ought to be (para. 4).

Oppression does not only come from the outside of the dDeaf community; it also exists within the dDeaf community. There is a phenomenon that occurs within Aboriginal people groups, ethnic populations and Indigenous Peoples and it is known by several names – horizontal or lateral violence, internalized colonialism and it is also known within the dDeaf community as *crab theory*.

Mick Gooda (2011) the Social Justice Commissioner for the Australian Aboriginal and Torres Strait Islander communities states that the Aboriginal and Torres Strait Islander peoples face many difficulties but sadly "some of the divisive and damaging harms come from within our own communities" (p. 50). The community struggles with backstabbing, gossiping, bullying and overt cruelty toward one another. "When we already have so many of the odds stacked against us, it is tragic to see us inflict such destruction on ourselves" (Gooda, 2011, p. 50). It is obvious that people all over the globe deal with similar problems and struggles. However, within ethnic, Aboriginal and Indigenous communities lateral violence "stems from the sense of powerlessness that comes from oppression" (Goode, 2011, p. 54).

Matthew S. Moore (1993), refers to the destructive practice of crab theory as dDeaf people pulling and putting down accomplished dDeaf people. Several well-known dDeaf people who have publicly experienced disparaging remarks, ridicule and backstabbing from members of the Deaf community including: Marlee Matlin, Heather Whitestone, former President Gallaudet University Dr. I. King Jordan, and most recently Nyle DiMarco. Baker-Shenk (1986) explains that dDeaf individuals often struggle with a sense of *ambivalence* concerning their overt self-identification as a cultural and linguistic minority. This struggle results from a society that stigmatizes them for living proudly as dDeaf individuals in a "society that labels deafness an impairment and operates in ways that exclude and devalue deaf people" (Mousley & Chaudoir, 2018, p. 341). Subsequently, "stigmatized people tend to both embrace the feature that makes them different, viewing it as an essential part of their identity, and also to degrade themselves and other group members because of the feature that makes them different" (Goffman cited in Baker-Shenk, 1986, p. 46). People who can hear hold an overwhelming position of power, coupled with their historic oppression of the language, values, ideals and *ways of being* among members of the dDeaf community, fostering an environment rife with internalized negative beliefs. Gooda (2011) explains that because of situations like this the oppressed feel "safer and more able to attack [the people] closest to us who do not represent the potent threat of the colonisers" (p. 56).

Change the Narrative

How we generate change is no easy task, rather it is accomplished through the laborious task of education. Yet, it is imperative that we are a partner in generating change, not the instigator of change. Encouraging the adoption of new views, beliefs and ideas must be propagated through a *partnership* with the dDeaf community. It is essential we be an *avenue of access*[4] for dDeaf individuals to educate people who can hear about their language, culture and community. Up to

_____

[4]*Avenue to access means that we recognize the issue with deafness is not the absence of sound, rather is the absence of ACCESS; we, as interpreters, provide access to understand what is being communicated to them and provide them with the opportunity to respond clearly and accurately to that communication.*

Chapter 5

NOTES

this point, the narrative about the lives and wellbeing of those who are dDeaf has been rather dismal. If the perceptions of hearing people can be reframed concerning the dDeaf community it will go a long way toward improving the lives of the dDeaf people. When people who can hear begin to accept, believe and view the dDeaf experience as a *difference,* instead of a *disability* they will understand that dDeaf people and hearing people are *equal,* nothing more, nothing less.

As interpreters, you have the opportunity to make a notable contribution to changing the narrative about dDeaf people. Simply shape the way people think about people who are dDeaf. One small thing you can do as an interpreter, as often as the opportunity allows, when asked about the dDeaf community, sign language or the culture of dDeaf people, direct the question toward a person who is dDeaf. Offer to interpret the questions instead of answering the question yourself. We know this cannot always be done, but it is the small things that change the perspectives of people who can hear, one such thing is hearing the story directly from a dDeaf person.

In addition, we challenge dDeaf community members to attempt to reframe their negative life experiences. Szarkowski and Brice (2018) encourage dDeaf people to adopt alternative ways of thinking about their lives – start by asking a simple yet powerful question, "What makes life worth living?" (p. 112). In addition, begin to change the focus of their lives from hardship to human potential and aspirations, considering what it means to live a "life well lived" (Szarkowski & Brice, 2018, p. 112). Leaders within the dDeaf community have been trying to reinvent the way people who are dDeaf look at their worth. "Many scholars have written about the Deaf Gain concept. A consistent theme has been the contributions to our larger world from the Deaf community" (Szarkowski & Brice, 2018, p. 113). Mousley and Chaudoir (2018) explain that another benefit of the Deaf Gain perspective is that dDeaf "people celebrate being deaf as a social and cultural identity rather than a disability or impairment" (p. 342). Chris Wixstrom (1988) in her outline entitled, *The Two Views of Deafness* drew a powerful comparison between *deaf* people, those who view their deafness as a pathology and *Deaf* people, those who view their deafness as social and cultural identity. The "views of deafness" are gentle reminders that dDeaf people positively shape the world with their linguistic and cultural diversity. Wixstrom encourages each of us to

- Respect, value and support the language and culture of Deaf people; believe the best role models for Deaf children are successful Deaf adults
- Emphasize the use of visual communication as a positive, efficient alternative to the auditory channel of communication
- View sign language as equal to spoken languages and the most natural communication tool for people who are Deaf (Adapted from Wixstrom, 1988, p. 21)

One of the greatest ways to change the narrative of the dDeaf community is to show the members of that community respect. One of the most powerful, meaningful and genuine demonstrations of respect is to *always* sign when dDeaf people are present. Do not give into the temptation to cheat, to whisper, to talk. Understand the moment a dDeaf person enters the space, *all* of the space becomes dDeaf space. Demonstrations of respect (or the lack thereof) will be remembered – consider how you want to be remembered. As we close this chapter we wanted to encourage every student interpreter – dDeaf and hearing – to alleviate oppression when it is within your power to do so, and to leverage your privilege for the underprivileged.

Do not forget the words of Martin Luther King Jr. (1963) written from a jail in Birmingham, Alabama, *"Injustice anywhere is a threat to justice everywhere"* (para. 4).

chapter
Review

This chapter discussed difficult realities faced by people as we live and grow together. This review will help solidify your knowledge related to important aspects discussed in the chapter and draw your attention to key points worth mentioning again.

Terms to Know:

- **Ally:** One who supports dDeaf individuals on their journey of liberation and equality.

- **Audists:** Refers to the oppressive attitudes demonstrated by some individuals, organizations, or businesses towards people who are dDeaf or hard of hearing. An attitude based on pathological thinking resulting in a negative stigma toward anyone who does not hear. Often associated with hearing privilege.

- **Benefactors:** Individuals who typically give money or other forms of aid to help those in need. However, in this case, benefactors are those individuals who perceive the dDeaf community as needing to be rescued and benefactors foist their help on the dDeaf community.

- **Disenfranchisement:** Is to deprive an individual of a legitimate right, or some privilege or immunity.

- **Ethnocultural Identity:** Refers to the absence of a shared language, cultural norms and identity that will not be passed down from hearing parents to their dDeaf child (especially those who do not share a language with their deaf child).

- **Learned Helplessness:** Is the desire to *protect* and *prevent* dDeaf people from making mistakes inadvertently creating a detrimental environment and the dDeaf person's overreliance on others for help.

- **Lipread:** "Lipreading is the task of decoding text from the movement of a speaker's mouth. Lipreading is a notoriously difficult task...especially in the absence of context" (Assael, Shillingford, Whiteson, & de Freitas, 2016, p. 1).

- **Marginalization:** The systematic exclusion of minority group members from quality social services, economic opportunities, health care, and meaningful education; the absence of power or voice (Alakhunova et al., 2015).

- **Medical Model:** This is the term used by medical professionals to define dDeaf people.

- **Normalize/Normalization:** Is done by the medical or education profession to "assimilate" dDeaf people into the rest of society. They strive to eliminate sign language as a viable communication and maximize the use of residual hearing through amplification and technology (hearing aids, cochlear implants). Often, the final step is utilizing lipreading and speaking to aid in two-way communication.

- **Oral Programs:** Refers to students who are educated in programs that focus on residual hearing, speaking and lipreading.

- **Privilege:** Is a set of unearned benefits given to people who fit into a specific social group (Ferguson, 2014).

- **Sense of Entitlement:** Is the belief that someone deserves resources that others do not (Porter, 2020).

- **Social Inequality:** Is evidenced by unequal opportunities, limited employment, and fewer rewards for those individuals not from the majority group.

- **Uninitiated:** Refers to individuals who have limited or no prior experience, knowledge, or understanding of the dDeaf community/culture.

Critical Components:

Mainstream American culture misunderstands and misinterprets these elements of American Sign Language and the dDeaf community as anger or frustration:

- Facial Expressions
- Vocalization
- Speed of signs

Ethnocultural identity: Without a shared language, dDeaf children cannot learn about or participate in multiple aspects of their family's culture.

Cultural View of Deaf People: Deaf individuals are normal, capable human beings encountering life in a different – yet acceptable way, conforming with norms and behaviors based on visual/non-hearing norms.

Pathological View of Deaf People: Deaf individuals are viewed as disabled and imperfect needing to be fixed.

Audist: Individuals who support the idea that the ability to hear is superior. These attitudes are:

- Oppressive
- Uninformed
- Prejudiced

How **Audism** Affects Deaf People

- **Institutionalized oppression** – subtle, long-term conditioning of the public to view the minority group and its members as less than others that continues over an extended period of time until the marginalization is normalized and accepted
- **Ambivalence** – mixed negative and positive feelings about oneself based on society's view of being deficient
- **Fatalism or passivity** – passively taking whatever happens, sensing that you can do nothing to change things
- **Horizontal violence** – hostility that members of an oppressed group take out on one another as a result of frustration at the disenfranchisement they experience
- **Benefactors are perfect** – mistaking privilege for perfection
- **Emotional dependence on the oppressor** – feeling powerless and believing only members of the majority group can change things (learned helplessness)

- **Fear of freedom** – wanting to be free of the benefactor's help, but simultaneously fearing equality and empowerment

Uninitiated People: Those who have limited, or no prior experience or knowledge related to the dDeaf culture or community, whose false assumptions and beliefs are often made up of and supported by the medical model. They believe dDeaf people are:

- Disabled
- Handicap
- Impaired
- Unable to effectively participate in society
- Unequal

Privilege is based on these categories:

- Social status
- Age
- Education
- Ethnic and racial identity
- Gender identity
- Marital status
- Sexual identity
- Religion
- Physical and mental fitness

Sense of entitlement & ascribed social inequality:

These are not always given or earned, but each person has one, oftentimes:

- Those who do not experience it, do not see it.
- Provides a sense of *immunity*

Becoming an Ally:

- **Learn about oppression** – by identifying it in your own life and beginning a journey toward personal liberation
- **Help people understand oppression** – help members of your own social groups, professional circle and colleagues understand oppression
- **Recognize that you may be part of the problem** – we have all grown up in a society surrounded by oppressive, power over other people attitudes and can easily become oppressors ourselves
- **Listen to and believe** – when dDeaf people tell you about the discrimination and pain they have experienced and are still experiencing
- **Do not take on a leadership role** – instead, work with and support members of oppressed groups
- **Develop and maintain friendships** – with members of oppressed groups outside of professional involvement (Anne Bishop, 1994)

Practicing Self-Care, take time to regularly:

- Self-reflection – write what you are thinking and feeling, and ask yourself why what you witnessed is bothering you
- Regularly, planned quiet times of meditation or prayer – striving to "let go" of the negative feelings and energy
- Confide in a confidential colleague (or therapist) who can support you as you develop appropriate coping strategies

Chapter 5

NOTES

Oppression: The unjust or excessive exercise of power or position that hurts, maligns, or disempowers others. Types of oppression: Individual, Group, and Institutional

Characteristics Benefactors or Oppressors:

- **Pejorative view of the minority group** – feel that being different than the ideal (fat, poor, blind, etc.) is bad
- **Paternalism** – desire to take members of the minority group under their wing assuming a know- it-all or take-charge stance
- **Need for approval** – expectation that minority group members should make regular expressions of appreciation and gratitude for all of the help given

---

To become an interpreter, you must begin thinking about your history, attitudes, beliefs and behaviors to identify any oppressive tendencies present in your life. This may require you to spend time self-reflecting to identify your personal history with power, marginalization and oppression – please express your thoughts below.

6 | People of Color

The field of sign language interpreting in North America has historically been dominated by white women and men using English/ASL in the US, and in Canada using French/LSQ. Populations of both countries are increasingly multicultural and multilingual, made up of a beautiful blend of skin tones, eye colors, and a range of physical height and body shapes. While the official language in the US is English, the population is increasingly multilingual with 20.6% of the population speaking languages other than English at home (US Census Bureau, 2015).

Canada is a multicultural country with a total population of around 35 million, or around 0.5% of the world's population. Ontario, the most populated province, has 13 million people, followed by Quebec with 8 million, and British Columbia with 4.6 million. The largest city in Canada is Toronto, followed by Montreal. Canada is one of the most multicultural countries in the world, and responses to ethnic origin surveys are incredibly diverse. "Canada was the first officially declared multicultural society in which, as Prime Minister Pierre Trudeau declared in 1971, no culture would take precedence over any other. Multiculturalism refers to both the fact of the existence of a diversity of cultures within one territory and to a way of conceptualizing and managing cultural diversity" (Little, 2016, p. 113).

Though the bulk of Canadians self identify as Canadian, many have not forgotten their ethnic roots; in 2016, over 250 ethnic origins or ancestries were reported by the Canadian population (see figure 1). Canada's growth has been driven by immigration since 1990, accounting for as much as 82% of the population growth. "Canada's population growth rate is the highest among G7 countries.* It is more than twice that of the United States and the United

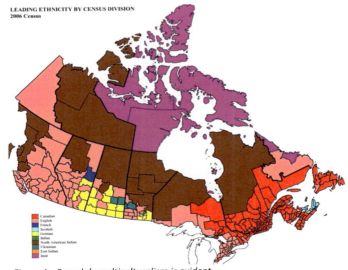

Figure 1: Canada's multiculturalism is evident.

TERMS TO KNOW:

- Language Broker
- Minority
- Race
- Ethnicity
- Aboriginal/Aborigine
- Deafhood
- Colonialism
- Acculturation
- Indigenous Peoples
- Collectivist Norms
- Individualism
- Trilingual Interpreters
- Heritage Speakers

---

*The Group of Seven is an international intergovernmental economic organization consisting of seven major countries: Canada, France, Germany, Italy, Japan, the United Kingdom and the United States.

Kingdom" (Statistics Canada, 2019, p. 1).

The increase in other languages in Canada is mostly due to the increase in immigrant languages with international migration being the main driver of population growth in the country. "Linguistic diversity is on the rise in Canada. More and more Canadians are reporting a mother tongue or language spoken at home other than English or French" (Census in Brief, 2016, p. 1). In 2016, nearly twenty percent of the Canadian population reported speaking more than one language at home. This multicultural reality is reflected among students who are studying to become sign language interpreters, dDeaf individuals, and sign language interpreters across Canada. The focus of this chapter will be about recognizing and honoring our colleagues of color, as well as the dDeaf people of color we serve.

Heritage Culture and Languages

According to the 2017 US Census, "nearly one-fourth of school age children growing up in the US speak a language other than English at home" (p. 9). "Indeed, some of these multilingual...students are currently enrolled in educational programs for American Sign Language (ASL)–English interpretation in the U.S, and over time they will likely become working interpreters in settings where languages other than ASL and English are used" (Quinto-Pozos, Martinez, Suarez & Zech, 2018, p. 47). If you grew up in a home with dDeaf family members, you may have served as a **language broker** for your parents, siblings or extended family, and perhaps other community members who were not fluent in English. Antonini (2015) explains that child *language brokering* is defined as the

> interpreting and translation activities carried out by children who mediate linguistically and culturally in formal and informal contexts and domains between their family, friends and the members of the linguistic community they belong to and the institutions and society of the country where their families reside or have migrated to (p. 97).

As it fits the dDeaf cultural context, Antonini (2015) states that language brokering is most common within immigrant communities, however, "it is a practice that is also performed by children who belong to specific minority language groups, such as children of deaf adults (CODAs) who have grown up learning and using a signed and a spoken language" (p. 97). "These language brokers may be well suited to become professional interpreters as adults, with continued development of linguistic skills and the learning of interpretation techniques" (Quinto-Pozos, et.al., 2018, p. 47). For example, if you grew up in a home where French was a primary language, you may want to look at interpreter education in Quebec where they teach French/Quebecois Sign Language (LSQ). Whereas, if you grew up in a home where Spanish was spoken, you may want to focus on trilingual interpreting using Spanish-English-ASL (Quinto-Pozos, et.al., 2018).

An Overview of Diverse Cultures

While definitions of culture abound, Naomi Kipuri (2009) defines *culture* as a "patterned way of life shared by a group of people...agreed-upon principles of human existence (values, norms and sanctions), as well as techniques of survival" (Department of Economic and Social Affairs, p. 52). Culture incorporates every aspect of our lives and includes how people relate to one another; culture is the "aspect of our existence which makes us similar to some people, yet different from the majority of the people in the world" (Department of Economic and Social Affairs, 2009, p. 52). We know culture to be the shared *way of life* represented by

People of Color

NOTES

the beliefs, values and ideals held by a group of people. This chapter will discuss three cultural groups found in the United States and Canada in some depth, while briefly mentioning two other cultural groups. The authors acknowledge that with the multitude of ethnic groups, we are only able to scratch the surface in this brief overview. We hope to spark your interest, curiosity and respect for the diverse beliefs, norms and values of each of these ethnic groups – and hopefully spur your desire to dig deeper on your own. It is our goal to increase your understanding of the history, cultural norms, and values held by members of each of these groups: Black/African Americans, Hispanics/Latinx groups, and Indigenous people groups (Nguyen & Pendleton, 2020).

As sign language interpreters, you will work with members of these and many other minority groups as you interface with dDeaf individuals and with fellow sign language interpreters. It is important to note that the word **minority** is a misnomer because by the,

> middle of the 21st century, non-Hispanic whites will make up a slim and fading majority of Americans, because Hispanics will be nearly one-fourth of the U.S. population. Further, Blacks, Asians, and American Indians together will make up close to one-fourth of the population (Pollard & O'Hare, 1999, p. 3).

The reality is that people of color will not likely be the minority in the 21st century. In North America, those who are Caucasian already appear to be in the numerical *minority*.

> Minority Americans are found in every U.S. region, state, and metropolitan area, but they are highly concentrated in a few states and areas. More than one-half of America's minority population lives in just five states: California, Texas, New York, Florida, and Illinois (Pollard & O'Hare, 1999, p. 23).

According to the Population Reference Bureau, in 2018, over 63% of the population of California self-identified as a racial or ethnic minority (Population Reference Bureau, 2020). This is evidence that our world is rapidly changing and we are an increasingly diverse planet.

Before going further, it is imperative that we remember that members of any cultural group are not all cast from a single mold, rather each racial and ethnic group incorporates a great deal of diversity. Consider the Hispanics/Latinx communities, which include Dominicans, Colombians, Cubans, Spaniards, Mexicans, Puerto Ricans and a host of others. There are twenty-three countries speaking numerous dialects of Spanish, and while they may appear to share a common language, there are significant dialectic, grammatical and vocabulary variations making it challenging for people who reside in different countries to understand one another (Annarino, Aponte-Samalot & Quinto-Pozos, 2014). This is represented in the fact that virtually every Spanish speaking country has a distinct form of Spanish sign language. Furthermore, in spite of having some common cultural values, behaviors and celebrations, there are also cultural elements that are equally as unique from one group to the next. Though we are all people with a shared sense of humanity, we are also unique and vary in beliefs and culture. Elements of our existence make us the same and different from others in the world (Department of Economic and Social Affairs, 2009). This fact is true for all people, African Americans, Asians, Pacific Islanders and members of all culture groups.

Race vs. Ethnicity

Frequently the words **race** and **ethnicity** are used interchangeably and, to compound matters, there is not consensus regarding the definitions in the public arena. We are choosing to utilize the definitions offered by the American Sociological Association. The American Sociological Association (2020) distinguishes between race and ethnicity, explaining that *race* most often refers to the physical characteristics of the individual – skin color, physical features, hair type, eye color, and other features that are considered socially significant. This translates into races most commonly recognized in the United States: Black, Caucasian, Asian, Hispanic/ Latinx and Native American, etc. However, it is important to note that there are no biological determinants of race. "Sociologists recognize that our idea of race and racial categories are social constructs that are not fixed but fluid and shifting" (Crossman, 2020, para. 7). Whereas *ethnicity* speaks to elements held in common by such people groups – culture, language, ancestry, practices, and beliefs (American Sociological Association, 2020). Equally relevant is how sociology examines the structure and the workings of human society, using and critiquing "the concepts of race and ethnicity, connecting them to the idea of majority and minority groups and social structures of inequality, power, and stratification" (American Sociological Association, 2020, para. 1).

"Immigrants from each immigration wave in Canada, as well as their Canadian-born descendants, have contributed to the ethnocultural diversity of the country's population" (Minister of Industry, 2017, p. 3). Furthermore, 41.1% of the total population of Canada reported multiple ethnic origins. However, the largest populations that self-identify as having a single ethnic background in Canada are the Chinese, English, East Indian and French (Minister of Industry, 2017). In addition, Canada has "more than 2 million people of Aboriginal ancestry; Aboriginal people in Canada contribute to the richness and diversity of Canadian cultural heritage. In 2016, 6.2% of the total Canadian population, reported Aboriginal ancestry" (Minister of Industry, 2017, p. 1). The First Nations (North American Indians) are comprised of multiple native groups, the three largest are the Cree, Mi'kmaq, and Ojibway but also included are those of Métis and Inuit ancestry (Minister of Industry, 2017). "The term **Aboriginal** has been in the English language since at least the 19th century, formed from the 16th century term, **Aborigine**, which means *original inhabitants*. It derives from the Latin words 'ab' (from) and 'origine' (origin, beginning)" (Online Etymology Dictionary, 2020, para. 1). In simple terms, aboriginal people are *typically* the first or original people of the land prior to colonists arriving (Commonground, n.d.).

As previously mentioned, ethnicity refers to a shared culture and a *way of life*, material evidenced is often seen in clothes and cuisine. "Ethnicity is often a major source of social cohesion as well as social conflict" (Crossman, 2020, para. 1). The dDeaf community fits within the parameters of ethnicity, which recognizes numerous elements, but our focus is on some of the most prominent elements, "history, language, and culture, all of which provide group members with a common identity" (Crossman, 2020, para. 2). The norms of ethnic groups are not inherited – but taught and group boundaries are somewhat fluid (Crossman, 2020). Race is not typically a criteria for one's ethnic identity, although some ethnic groups do require certain traits for membership, thus in these particular cases, race can be a factor. Each ethnic group typically has several defining elements or traits that are representative aspects of that ethnic group, such as the language of French Canadians, which is a critical element because it distinguishes them from English Canadians, Scottish Canadians, and Irish Canadians. In addition, Jewish people are characteristically associated with their religion which is a valuable aspect of their ethnic identity (Crossman, 2020). "Because ethnic groups are self-defined, it is important to remember that no single aspect of group identity (language, religion, etc.) can be used to sort people into one group or another" (Crossman, 2020, para. 10). "Race and ethnicity are defined by society, not by science" (Population Reference Bureau, 2020, p. 8).

Deafhood

Dr. Paddy Ladd coined the term **deafhood** in 1993, and he further developed the idea while writing his doctoral dissertation on Deaf Culture; his studies culminated in 2003 when he published *Understanding Deaf Culture – In Search of Deafhood.* One of the aims of his text was to increase cultural awareness and gain a greater understanding of the ideal of **colonialism** (Loeffler, 2016). "It seems generally, if not universally, agreed that colonialism is a form of domination – the control by individuals or groups over the...behavior of other individuals or groups" (Horvath, 1972, p. 46). It is apparent that Colonialism has been seen as a form of exploitation and as a method to powerfully shape culture and language (Horvath, 1972). The dDeaf community has long been subjected to marginalization and mistreatment by people who can hear and deafhood is one way to reclaim and reframe the knowledge, history, beliefs and values of dDeaf culture. Furthermore, it is the unrelenting effort to throw off the limitations of Colonialism that have been repeatedly imposed upon Sign Language Peoples (Loeffler, 2016). Ladd (2005) proffered a new culturo-linguistic model which impugns the medical model of deafness. Moreover, his model offers the term *deafhood,* as a means to share the value systems of deaf peoples, as a unique people who are "'visuo-gesturo-tactile' biological entities, [that] believe they offer a different and positive perspective on what it means to be human" (p. 13). Sign Language Peoples have been oppressed for more than 120 years in North America resulting in longstanding and pervasive internalized oppression and self-shame, so much so that the dDeaf community no longer knows much about the elements of their pre-colonized culture(s) or recognize that a "larger" deaf self ever existed (Ladd, 2005).

Another key term is **acculturation**, which often describes the varied *experiences* which African Americans, Hispanics/Latinx, Indigenous Peoples and many other people of color experience when they interact with the majority culture. "Acculturation refers to the process that occurs when groups of individuals of different cultures come into continuous first-hand contact, which changes the original culture patterns of either or both groups" (Rothe, Tzuang & Pumariega, 2010, p. 681). The ongoing cross-cultural encounters elicit responses of varying degrees and these responses may have one of three possible outcomes: "(1) acceptance, when there is assimilation of one group into the other; (2) adaptation, when there is a merger of the two cultures; and (3) reaction, which results in antagonistic contra-acculturative movements" (Rothe, Tzuang & Pumariega, 2010, p. 681).

Power and Privilege

We will conclude this chapter with a brief discussion of power and privilege within the context of relationships, both personal and professional. As interpreters we must give ample consideration to the issue of power. Interpreters, by virtue of their position, exert power in every interpreting assignment because we manage communication between two or more persons. As these people work to communicate with one another, their interactions are navigated by a sign language interpreter. Interpreters must respect the role and responsibilities that their position embodies, being especially mindful to consider and honor the perspectives of each participant.

Acknowledgements: We recognize that this chapter could in no way fully address people of color, the authors also acknowledge that we are only touching the surface of the realities that make each people group different from one another. Furthermore, there is not *one lived experience* rather there are many experiences that shape and form the culture and language of each person of color.

INTERPRETING WITH INDIGENOUS dDeaf PEOPLE

Indigenous peoples are defined primarily as the "original peoples of the land who lost their land and were displaced and marginalized by colonizers or by a group of people who arrived at some later date" (Department of Economic and Social Affairs, 2009, p. 54). Two of the strong identifying characteristics of indigenous people are land and language, both create a sense of belonging, a sense of community and to lose one or the other damages the sense of community (Department of Economic and Social Affairs, 2009).

Some indigenous groups were not the original people in each country. For example, the Tuareg of the Sahara and Sahel regions of Africa, both are nomadic peoples, are inhabiting that region in Africa but they arrived within recent history. "Their claim to indigenous identity status (endorsed by the African Commission on Human and Peoples' Rights) is based on their marginalization as nomadic peoples in states and territories dominated by sedentary agricultural peoples" (Department of Economic and Social Affairs, 2009, p. 54). They have built their identity through and with the land – which has sustained them for several generations, and has shaped their culture. Further, they have become spiritually attached to the land because it is where their ancestors are buried (Department of Economic and Social Affairs, 2009).

Colonialism has not simply impacted the life of dDeaf people, it's reach has been felt far and wide. "Since the colonial period, Indigenous Peoples have been dispossessed of their lands or faced the threat of dispossession and forced removal, leading to increased poverty, erosion of cultures and even outright extinction or complete assimilation" (Department of Economic and Social Affairs, 2009, p. 54). According to the United Nations (2009) a document entitled, *State of the World's Indigenous Peoples,* explains, "Indigenous Peoples today continue to face the threat of dispossession of lands, a great deal of progress has been made in recent years in terms of legislative reforms and policy making. Nevertheless, there is a persistent implementation gap between the laws passed and daily reality for indigenous peoples" (Department of Economic and Social Affairs, p. 54).

Many terms have been used to refer to these original inhabitants in countries around the world, including: First Peoples, American Indian, Natives, First Nations,

People of Cclor

NOTES

Aboriginals, and Indigenous Peoples.

> The terms "Indigenous Peoples" and "First Nations Peoples" are used...to refer to the descendants of the first inhabitants of the Americas (those misnamed American Indians, Native Americans, and Alaska Natives). "Indigenous Peoples" and "First Nations People" are capitalized because they are used as proper nouns (particular persons) and signify the cultural heterogeneity and political sovereignty of these groups (Yellow Bird, 1999, p. 2).

Even though European colonizers considered the Indigenous Peoples as if they were a single racial group, Indigenous Peoples in the United States represent more than 550 distinct tribes, including 223 Alaska Native villages (Yellow Bird, 1999).

> Under colonial rule Indigenous People in the United States and Canada were systemically subjugated and oppressed because Europeans and Europeans Americans considered them to be an inferior race. Because colonizers regarded Indigenous Peoples as inferior, they felt justified in ignoring individual tribal identities and labeling Indigenous Peoples as one racial group: Indians (Yellow Bird, 1999, p. 3).

The mindset of conquering Indigenous Peoples was not limited to attempts at colonization – *forced assimilation* continued for years. This was evidenced when the United States government removed thousands of children from Northern Arapaho, Rosebud Sioux and native people of Alaska, forcing them to be separated from their families, culture and language and placing them in boarding schools in the late 19th century under the Indian Removal Act (Swenson, 2017; Little, 2016). Forced assimilation was reflected in the motto of the school, established by former U.S. cavalry officer, Captain Richard Henry Pratt, "Kill the Indian in Him and Save the Man" (Little, 2016, para 1). At the Indian Schools, children were not allowed to maintain their Indigenous names or wear their native clothes; speaking their home language or celebrating centuries old traditions and holidays were banned. Susceptible to the diseases of their non-native teachers and "care-takers," many of the children died, while many others endured brutal physical and mental abuse (Little, 2016). The truth of history shows that Indigenous populations in virtually every country in the world have faced forced assimilation.

This was the experience in the Americas, Russia, Australia, New Zealand, and the Arctic, however, the experience in most parts of Asia and Africa were different. In those regions, there were no large scale settlements from European colonial powers; as a result, no foreign entity displaced whole populations of Indigenous Peoples and replaced them with settlers of European descent (Department of Economic and Social Affairs, 2009). Some argue that in these regions there should be no distinction made between the original inhabitants and newcomers. However, the UN has taken the stand that we should identify the initial inhabitants of traditional lands whose ancestral land and territory have

> a fundamental importance for their collective physical and cultural survival as peoples; on an experience of subjugation, marginalization, dispossession, exclusion or discrimination because they have different cultures, ways of life or modes of production than the national hegemonic and dominant model (Department of Economic and Social Affairs, 2009, p. 6).

Chapter 6

NOTES

The "United Nations has recognized that these people groups have basic rights of self-determination by adopting the *Declaration on the Rights of Persons Belonging to National or Ethnic, Religious and Linguistic Minorities*" (Department of Economic and Social Affairs, 2009, p. 6). Further, they have promoted the protection and monitoring of the rights accorded to these groups.

Mr. Sha Zukang (2009), Under-Secretary-General for Economic and Social Affairs, wrote the foreword in the United Nations report entitled, *State of the World's Indigenous Peoples.* The United Nations is committed to its unwavering support to a future where all indigenous peoples will enjoy peace, human rights and well-being.

> Indigenous Peoples are custodians of some of the most biologically diverse territories in the world. They are also responsible for a great deal of the world's linguistic and cultural diversity, and their traditional knowledge has been and continues to be an invaluable resource that benefits all of mankind. Yet, indigenous peoples continue to suffer discrimination, marginalization, extreme poverty and conflict. Some are being dispossessed of their traditional lands as their livelihoods are being undermined. Meanwhile, their belief systems, cultures, languages and ways of life continue to be threatened, sometimes even by extinction (p. v).

Indigenous communities keep their cultures alive by *passing on* their worldview, their knowledge and know-how, their arts, rituals and performances from one generation to the next. Preservation of their cultural heritage includes teaching and speaking their native languages, as well as protecting their sacred and significant sites and relics (Department of Economic and Social Affairs, 2009). Indigenous Peoples maintain a strong commitment to defending and holding onto their lands and territories, since these are fundamental for sustaining them as peoples and cultures (Department of Economic and Social Affairs, 2009). Although global statistics on the situation of Indigenous Peoples are not readily available, it is clear that Indigenous Peoples continue to suffer disproportionately from poverty, marginalization, lack of adequate housing and income inequality (Stavenhagen, 2004).

THE TRANSMISSION OF TRADITIONAL KNOWLEDGE

Historic traditional knowledge was routinely passed from generation to generation through songs and stories. Tom Mexsis Happynook belongs to what he calls a hereditary whaling family that comes from Cha-cha-tsi-us, which is part of the Huu-ay-aht First Nation on the west coast of Vancouver Island, British Columbia, Canada. He recalls the following:

> As a child, I was fortunate to be raised and taught by my grandfather, 2 great grandmothers and 2 great aunts. I am still being taught by my grandmother who turned eighty-five on December 7, 1999. She was taught by her grandmother, who died in 1958 at the age of 108. I am still receiving the teachings from the mid-1800s. I was taught that there is a natural law of nature which we must live by; that we are only one component in the web of life; that we are not dominant over the environment but if fact related; that we take only what we need and utilize all that we take; that everything is inter-connected and when one component in the environment or ecosystem is over exploited and then protected, the balance is lost (Happynook, 2000, p. 65).

People of Color

NOTES

Interpreting with Indigenous Individuals

Before working with Indigenous dDeaf Individuals, interpreters must come to understand their history. Dr. Melanie McKay-Cody, an Indigenous dDeaf Person from the United States, shares some advice. She stresses the importance of becoming familiar with and gaining an understanding of the indigenous approach to life, developing an awareness of their cultural norms, expectations, and worldview (McKay-Cody, 2020). We are sharing some of her knowledge and experience to better prepare non-indigenous interpreters to work as interpreters with Indigenous dDeaf People and groups.

The authors urge you to make an effort to read her detailed and informative work which provides detailed guidelines and cautions for interpreters called to interpret in gatherings of Indigenous Peoples: McKay-Cody, M. (2020). *Protocol for Sign Language Interpreters Working in North American Indigenous Settings.* (J. Wardle, Ed.) VIEWS, 1(37), retrieved May 20, 2020.

- Without the knowledge and sensitivity to the culture of Indigenous Peoples, interpreting will be challenging and cross-cultural communication may not succeed. Without the proper understanding of Indigenous cultures, the interpreter will likely be confused or uncertain regarding the meaning/intent of things being discussed or some of the norms observed, such as greetings and how respect is shown between Indigenous Peoples.
- When interpreting for Indigenous dDeaf Peoples, Dr. McKay-Cody encourages us to, "go with the flow," allow the circumstances to shape your interpretation as far as is possible. The best approach is to communicate what is being said, even when you don't fully understand the exact meaning. Your choice actually empowers the Indigenous dDeaf Person to respond in a culturally appropriate manner. They may ask for clarification when and if it is culturally appropriate to do so.

Dr. McKay-Cody expresses genuine concern because Indigenous dDeaf People feel that interpreter training programs were not meeting the communal needs of Indigenous Peoples. Most non-indigenous interpreters graduate from interpreter training programs do not represent their way of knowing, being, and doing. She urges interpreters to follow an indigenous approach or philosophy when working with Indigenous dDeaf Individuals and their families and tribes. Dr. McKay-Cody has suggested the following protocol for non-indigenous interpreters working in indigenous settings/events.

1. If you are asked to interpret for an indigenous event or ceremony, you must enter the event with an understanding that it is an *honor* to be present at special events involving Indigenous Peoples. It is truly a rare privilege for you, as an outsider, to be present at such sacred and celebratory events. As an interpreter it is your responsibility to facilitate the event with courtesy and respect, and build a bridge so that both the dDeaf and the hearing individuals can intersect on their life journeys.
2. Be keenly aware that the mere presence of an interpreter will impact the setting and the individuals involved, both in positive and/or negative ways. Be open to, and respectful of, indigenous values and customs, which are likely different from those your own culture and upbringing. For example, in the indigenous culture, eye contact is acceptable between the interpreter and the dDeaf individual but shouldn't be expected between non-dDeaf members of the tribe.

89

3. When you, as the interpreter, need support to understand the interaction, require clarification regarding what is being said, or need additional understanding of the cultural norms surrounding an interaction, seek assistance from the *designated* indigenous coordinator or appropriate contact person. It is not appropriate to ask other attendees present at the event for assistance.
4. Interpreters must be aware that it is not uncommon for many dDeaf tribal members to have their own indigenous way of signing. As the interpreter, you must make it a *priority* to demonstrate respect by incorporating those signs into your interpretation.
5. When interpreting in some sacred indigenous spiritual event settings, consent to be present to interpret must be obtained. This is because some sacred prayers are not to be interpreted. For example, some dancers are to stay silent and are not to be touched. Know your boundaries, and theirs, within the culture.
6. Appropriate clothing in indigenous settings is flexible, and interpreters need to inquire prior to the interpreted event what attire is appropriate. In some cases, black clothing is not appropriate. For example, if colorful regalia or traditional clothes are being worn, it would be wise for the interpreter to select a solid colorful shirt/blouse that allows the dDeaf individuals present to see your hands.

Please note the authors have selected only six of the many protocols for sign language interpreters interpreting in North American indigenous settings listed in the February 2020, VIEWS. Again, we recommend you take the time to become familiar with the forty plus protocols provided if it is your intention to be available to interpret for Indigenous Peoples of North America.

INTERPRETING WITH AFRICAN AMERICAN dDeaf PEOPLE AND COLLEAGUES

Today's racial and relational climate makes the history of African American people more difficult to share, yet it is in the telling that the truth can be brought to light and we, as people, can actively work toward reconciliation.

> For many Americans, blended ancestry is an integral part of their identity. The mosaic of hyphenated heritages preserves cultural connections beyond the United States, lineages that build pride and a sense of belonging. But for Americans descended from enslaved Africans, the roots of their ancestry are often a mystery. Family trees go dark after five or six generations, a reminder that 150 years ago, Black people weren't considered people (Ellis, 2020, para. 1).

White European settlers of the 17th century, who had historically utilized the labor of indentured servants (most often poor Europeans), capitalized on a cheaper and more plentiful laborers, African slaves (History Editors, 2018).

It is widely accepted that African Americans are primarily the descendants of slaves — their lives are a testament to the "migration histories of Africans forcibly carried on slave ships into the Atlantic" (Emory University, 2009, para. 1) to be the work force in the New

People of Color

NOTES

World. It should be evident that their rights were nearly nonexistent as they were "long denied a rightful share in the economic, social, and political progress of the United States. Nevertheless, African Americans have made basic and lasting contributions to American history and culture" (Lynch, 2020, para. 2).

Each person taken from their African homeland and compelled to become slaves, refugees and members of the New World are part of the great African Diaspora. The atrocity of slavery began in the United States roughly around 1619, when 20 Africans landed in Virginia as indentured servants. Today, African Americans make up one of the largest minority groups in the US. Black people in America have been victimized and oppressed for years and the trail of brokenness has been overtly *conspicuous.* The Population Reference Bureau (1999) states that the

> legal oppression of African Americans has been the most blatant and well documented. The ancestors of most African Americans were brought to the United States as slaves. After slavery was abolished in 1865, blacks could own land and vote, and some held public office. But their social position deteriorated when post-Civil War Reconstruction ended and the Southern states began to pass "Jim Crow" laws, which required the segregation of blacks from whites in schools, public transportation, restaurants, and other public places. Whites justified these laws with the theory that intimate social contact between blacks and whites would harm both races (p. 5).

It is unfair to assume every African American individual is truly from Africa. Numerous Black Americans have deep roots back to the continent of Africa, while other Black individuals can trace their heritage to the Caribbean, Haiti, Dominican Republic, Jamaica, Trinidad and Tobago (Population Reference Bureau, 1999). People from each island have unique linguistic and cultural backgrounds. We recognize that each people group, regardless of overt and subtle similarities, are not the same and each should receive the respect they deserve.

The move toward fair and equitable treatment must begin and be continued as individuals who are not people of color work alongside, become friends with and advocate on behalf of all the dDeaf and hearing people of color. In spite of the diversity among members of the Black community in the US, they often share some common negative experiences – that of disenfranchisement and oppression. In the eyes of most Black community members, genuine access to social justice and inclusion in the majority culture is still an uphill battle that few African Americans seem to achieve; yet the positive news is that some do *achieve* it. Regarding African Americans in the US,

> At the turn of the 21st century, more than half the country's more than 36 million African Americans lived in the South; 10 Southern states had black populations exceeding 1 million. African Americans were also concentrated in the largest cities, with more than 2 million living in New York City and more than 1 million in Chicago, Detroit, Philadelphia, and Houston each had a black population between 500,000 and 1 million (Lynch, 2020, para. 3).

The evident theme being conveyed in this chapter concerning all persons of color is that they will likely experience discrimination, oppression and overt racism during the course of their lives. As friends, and colleagues of individuals experiencing such bias may need our support and we should provide affirmation during these sensitive situations. As an interpreter working alongside these colleagues, as well as dDeaf and hearing members of the African American community, you may be witness to hurt, frustration and anger. Some individuals of color may be politically active in the on-going quest for genuine inclusion and social justice, and your respect and support would be invaluable. It is important to leverage our privilege in support of those around us.

If you are of European-American descent and find yourself feeling personally attacked or blamed for the history of injustices, remember that this anger is rarely directed at you as the interpreter, but at the generic majority white culture. Similarly, you might encounter dDeaf people from a range of ethnicities whose anger about oppression and lack of access may be directed at all people who can hear.

Family and Community

The African American culture has been suppressed by the majority culture for hundreds of years, and it is worth noting that the majority culture is extremely individualistic, whereas the African American culture has managed to retain many elements of its collectivist nature. One example is the strong familial ties, elderly family members are respected and cared for; extended family plays an important role in resources, sharing, supporting one another while teaching children survival strategies. Family is a powerful influence within the African American community, and the role of the extended family caregivers is critical as they provide monitoring, correcting and instructing for the younger upcoming generations – this resource is frequently under examined and under utilized within African American communities (American Psychological Association, 2008). "Identity for African Americans is not an individual or autonomous sense of functioning as is often reflected in European culture. Rather, *positive identity* [emphasis added] is an extended sense of self embedded within the African collective" (Allen & Bagozzi, 2001, p. 3).

Family members typically share quality time together and extend hospitality to all visitors. Strong bonds of kinship are evident within the family and community; respect and care are expected and evidenced through a display of manners (Boyd-Franklin, 1989). Interpreters working with members of this community would do well to be aware of and respect these norms, as well as reflecting similar values and behaviors. In settings that involve a dDeaf African American individual and family members, interpreters can expect most often there will be hearing parents, siblings, aunts, uncles and grandparents. Robert Hill (1999) identified several key strengths and life coping skills that are evident in African American families. Hill identified five strengths of African American families:

- Strong achievement orientation
- Flexible family roles
- Strong work orientation
- Strong kinship bonds
- Strong religious orientation (p. 43).

You will likely observe the strong bond of parent child relationships demonstrated in open expressions of unconditional love.

To understand emotional development and its relation to resilience and strength in African American children and adolescents, one must understand cultural expressions of emotions. Identified strengths included a sense of

People of Color

NOTES

spirituality, cooperation, respect for others, and a sense of humor (American Psychological Association, 2008, p. 45).

The Role of Elders: Keepers of the African American Legacy

Family has been the bedrock of African American culture from times of slavery through the tumultuous days of mandated racial segregation. Slavery attempted to weaken and distort the family institution by separating family members from one another. Fortunately, those attempts were unsuccessful. In fact, the structure of the African American families are still well grounded in **collectivist norms**. Collectivist norms are most concerned with the welfare of the group and the group relationships (Little, 2016). They also focus on the importance of social bonds and duties, which emphasizes the *interdependence* and supremacy of the collective well-being, and the need for connection within the family and community (American Psychological Association, 2008). "Family reunions surfaced as vehicles through which cohesiveness could be restored and culture revitalized. They emerged as rituals capable of strengthening and stabilizing the African American family, and as tools for building strong and viable foundations for future generations" (McCoy, 2011, p. 16). These rituals enabled the family to survive many painful and difficult times – slavery, Jim Crow laws and the horrors of white supremacy. However, while the trials of the civil rights movement yielded positive results by increasing equal opportunities, it also resulted in dramatic shifts in cultural patterns and processes of family life among Black American families. Furthermore, global changes in communication and the transient nature of our world have made the world a 'smaller' place but in the process "family cohesiveness and identity became diluted and less essential for survival, making families more American and less African" (McCoy, 2011, p. 16). As many of us are aware, the civil rights movement did not end the practice of racism, nor did it resolve issues related to poverty, underemployment, poor education and disproportionately high numbers of incarcerated Black men and women. All of these obstacles impede the preservation of the culture and values of Black families, resulting in the adoption of **individualism** by the Black community. Individualism is the belief that the needs, preferences and desires of the one are stressed over the needs of the whole; "people are considered 'good' if they are strong, self-reliant, assertive, and independent" (Schoeneman, 1997 cited in Cherry, 2020, para 5). The American Psychological Association (2008) addresses the concept of self preservation among African youth by reframing how they perceive themselves. Encouraging youth to consider "theoretical perspectives on the African self, which include a sense of *we* instead of *I* and take into account the collective nature of African societies" (p. 30).

Spirituality and Religion

It is known that spiritual beliefs have been identified as a strength for African American families. However, family faith and spirituality is clearly a personal matter; this is particularly true if families believe that their faith can enable their family to weather painful crises (Rockymore, 2006). "The church has been a source of social support for African Americans historically, and spirituality has served as a source of cultural transmission (Dancy & Wynn-Dancy, 1994 cited in *Task Force on Resilience and Strength in Black Children and Adolescents*, 2008, p. 39). Family and spirituality are closely tied together, it is evident that many

African American family reunions include attending one or more Sunday worship services: this provides a way to reconnect with spiritual traditions and invite the participation of a higher power in the health and welfare of the family. Typically, religious affiliation is not important. What matters is a

93

Chapter 6

NOTES

common belief in and communion with a supreme being (p. 20).

Today the church continues to play a central role in the Black community. Church attendance is strongly encouraged, the responsibilities of leadership in the church are valued and songs termed "spirituals" are highly prized as powerful historical markers. Families will make almost any accommodation necessary to be sure their dDeaf and hard of hearing children have access to religious training.

The authors encourage interpreters to visit a church several times before offering to interpret. It is essential to know your place – you can observe the interpreters working, which will give you the feel of church in the Black community. Your reputation, experience and humility needs to be established. It is best to be *invited* to interpret in a Black church and it is unwise to take it upon yourself to begin interpreting. Should you be fortunate to be invited to interpret in a Black church, it is essential you have a strong grounding in the doctrine and theological beliefs (whether they are Protestant or Catholic). The music is an essential part of worship and is composed of gospel, hymns, pop, and rap (to name a few), which typically involves solos and congregation participation is commonly found in this setting. Further, the sermon will typically be delivered using a dramatic and unique style of speech, which is actually a cultural form or expression of worship. Interpreting in African American churches will always *require* preparation; religious interpreters must be prepared to work with a colleague since church services typically last for 2-4 hours and interpreters must do as much preparation as possible because of the unique styles of music and exceptional style of sermon delivery found in Black culture.

Language
When interpreting in settings steeped in African American culture and language, you may encounter numerous literary forms, such as folk tales, proverbs, aphorisms, verbal games and oral "narrative" poems that have been handed down from one generation to the next. Further, distinct styles of speech and dialects are used by some participants, partly as an indication of community membership and unity. If you are not a member of this community and take work interpreting in African American church services, family reunions, and similar events, you must make time to become familiar with these speaking styles and dialects and they should always be done with a co-interpreter who is a member of this community. Better yet, refer a request for interpreting to interpreters from the Black community. Seize this time to learn, go observe and benefit from their interpreting choices. *Community norms* and expectations around time and status vary across this population, often reflecting the individualist cultural norms in today's American culture. However, historically Black culture, like Deaf culture, values time with group members. Beginning and ending times for events (church, parties, and social gatherings) in these cultures tends to be more flexible.

INTERPRETING WITH dDEAF PEOPLE AND COLLEAGUES WHO ARE HISPANIC/LATINX

The terminology referring to individuals of Spanish heritage is still evolving at the date this book was published. Formerly identified as "Hispanic, Latino, or Spanish origin" the current term (used since the 2010 US Census) is "Hispanic/Latinx," however, that term is still under debate by people who are members of this community. This community represents a diverse population of people from a host of other countries. In spite of this diversity, there are some underlying commonalities, all of which fit the collectivist categorization.

Insights into Hispanic/Latinx Cultural Norms of People Living in the US

In 2011, nearly one in six people living in the United States were of Hispanic/Latinx origin (Selig Center for Economic Growth, 2006). A few years later, in 2017 there "were nearly 60 million Latinos in the United States, accounting for approximately 18% of the total U.S. population" (Noe-Bustamante & Flores, 2019, para. 1). More than 30% of dDeaf and hard of hearing children throughout the US are from Latino/Hispanic backgrounds, with some states, such as California, Texas and Florida combined reporting figures nearing fifty-five percent of the Latino population (Gallaudet Research Institute, 2011, 2013; Pew Research Center, Noe-Bustamante & Flores, 2019).

Of the 10.4 million Hispanic family households in the US: 62% included children younger than 18 years; 66% consisted of a married couple; 43% included a married couple with children younger than 18 years; and 70% of Hispanic children lived with two married parents (U.S. Census, 2008a). The Hispanic/Latinx population in the US are younger than the non-Hispanic population, with a median age in 2006 of 27.5 years compared with that of the U.S. population at 36.9 years of age. In fact, 62.7% of Hispanics/Latinx individuals are ages 34 years or younger (American Community Survey, 2008). In spite of the younger population, income levels are rising. Yes, the median income is lower than the U.S. average, but data suggests that more Hispanics/Latinx individuals are moving into the middle class (earning at least $40,000) more than any other ethnic group. Further, they are an increasing proportion of the total affluent market (defined as adults with household incomes of $100,000 or more). From 1991 through 2000, the growth of affluent Hispanics/Latinx rose 126% (U.S. Census, 2008b).

Language Use

The Latinx community is a collectivistic culture where group activities are priority, responsibility is shared among group members, and accountability is shared. Because of the emphasis on collectivity, harmony and cooperation, the group tends to be the focus rather than the individual (Gudykunst, 1998). Children are a big part of family households among Hispanic/Latinx families. dDeaf individuals and interpreters from "Spanish influenced" backgrounds often come from a home where Spanish is spoken and Hispanic/Latinx cultural norms are followed. As this population continues to grow in Canada and the US, it is common that some family members do not speak English fluently. Families may not be overly concerned when a family member is found to be dDeaf or hard of hearing. Furthermore, "children from non-English-speaking homes in the US often serve as translators and interpreters for members of their family and community who are not fluent in English" (Quinto-Pozos, Martinez, Suarez & Zech, 2018, p. 47). As previously mentioned, these multilingual children may be the next wave of professional interpreters since their life circumstances have prepared them through informal educational avenues. Should they become interpreters, they will indeed help meet the growing need for trilingual interpreters (Quinto-Pozos et al., 2018).

In addition to these challenges, the varieties of Spanish and where each is spoken in the US are varied: *Mexican Spanish* is more common in California, *Salvadoran Spanish* is more common in Washington, DC, while *Cuban Spanish* is more frequently found in Florida (Quinto-Pozos et al., 2018). Non-heritage or non-native Spanish speakers face the greatest challenges in becoming a trilingual interpreter because they typically do not have a command of the various linguistic registers in their spoken language. They often "lack fluency in the intimate and informal registers," (Quinto-Pozos et al., 2018, p. 4) which means they require additional language development in Spanish before being qualified to consider working as a trilingual interpreter. Another challenge is knowledge and skill when dealing with ambiguities arising in Spanish, English or American Sign Language (Navarez, 2009).

Robert R. Davilla, Vice President Emeritus of the Rochester Institute of Technology and President Emeritus of Gallaudet University, shares his experience as the child of migrant parents who followed the crops across Southwestern United States. His parents spoke no English when he was entered into the California School for the Deaf at the age of five. He explained that California School for the Deaf did not have any Spanish-speaking interpreters to aid communication between his mother and the school officials. As a result, "my mother neither visited the school nor spoke to anyone who had any involvement with class work, social concerns or plans for after graduation. My mother's lack of communication with school personnel lasted her lifetime" (Annarino, et al., 2014, p. v). We ask the reader to stop and consider the *impact* on the family dynamics: emotional, relational, spiritual, psychological and familial.

Learning Styles and Values

Hispanic people generally thrive in cooperative learning environments rather than in competitive ones (Triandis, Martin, Lisansky & Bettencourt, 1985; Bird, 1990). They often flourish in student-centered, cooperative and hands-on educational settings. This is summarized by one Hispanic woman who said, "We are taught to listen, not to speak out; to work, to do our best; to do anything for a friend and to work in a cooperative mode" (Delgado-Gaitan, 1987, p. 93).

When confronted with competitive, negative or critical situations regarding cultural traditions, a culturally Hispanic/Latinx person may "freeze" or be unable to respond (Suzrez-Orozco, 1987; Walker, 1987, p. 94). The context in which this feedback is received is important as respect for parents, teachers and elders has a powerful influence in how Hispanic/Latinx individuals handle criticism. An interpreter's awareness of these familial and cultural aspects will provide insight into common schema and places where cultural mediation may be required to understand the intent of the speaker or signer.

Family

Family is the primary cultural structure in Hispanic/Latinx cultures. The father is almost always seen as an authority figure. Extended family members often live together or nearby, and elders always hold a position of respect. Historically, children rarely, if ever, rebel, talk back or openly disobey their parents or teachers, who are to be respected. The Spanish language embeds formal linguistic structures which are the requisite linguistic forms utilized when young people address their elders. Thus, their language reflects the *mandatory* cultural respect for elders and those in authority. It is important for interpreters to be aware of these culturally required forms of formal address when providing sign language interpreting. It is important to include spoken, signed and visual indicators of respect toward elders and those in positions of honor.

People of Color

NOTES

Spirituality and Religion

Hispanic countries have a traditional multigenerational connection with the Roman Catholic Church. Though many Hispanic/Latinx people living in the US are exposed to various Protestant faiths and some appear to be drawn to evangelical denominations. According to Pew Research Center (2007),

> Religious expressions associated with the Pentecostal and charismatic movements are a key attribute of worship for Hispanics in all the major religious traditions. More than two-thirds of Hispanics (68%) identify themselves as Roman Catholics. The next largest category, at 15%, is made up of born-again or evangelical Protestants (para. 2).

The impact of their faith on their view of the afterlife is significant. Reasonable efforts are made regarding wellness, but extreme precautions are not the norm because there is generally an acceptance that health problems cannot always be avoided or solved. While death is viewed as a natural part of life and sorrow is inevitably felt at the loss of a loved one. However, time and resources are not spent trying to avoid an inevitable because of the religious belief in a life after death – the afterlife is not approached with fear. It is important that interpreters be aware of their own beliefs, values and ideas concerning death and dying. Interpreters need to 'check' their schemas and filters to assure their own beliefs regarding death, illness and the afterlife are not intruding on the beliefs of the Hispanic/Latinx dDeaf individuals and their family members.

The Work of Trilingual Interpreters

> Defining what is meant by "Trilingual Interpreting: American Sign Language-Spanish-English" is complicated. It does not refer to any one particular kind of translational act, nor does "trilingual interpreter" currently refer to one particular kind of practitioner. Just as the word "deaf" is often used in a broad sense and refers to people who may be deaf, hard of hearing or deafblind, "trilingual" alludes to more than its surface definition of English, Spanish, and ASL (Annarino, et al., 2014, p. 1).

Defining Trilingual Interpreting and Its Practitioners (2014) explains that **trilingual interpreters** must possess the skills and knowledge required to accomplish the work of interpreting, including competency in American Sign Language, Spanish, and English as well as sensitivity to participants, background knowledge, interpreting skills and language(s) beyond the assumed proficiency in American Sign Language, English, Spanish with a *lived* understanding of U.S. majority culture and American Deaf Culture, necessary to provide equal communication and cultural access, both in content and affect, receptively and expressively, for all participants present (Annarino, et al., 2014). In addition, these practitioners need to be able to read and write in English and Spanish because written or print documents are often referred to during interpreted interactions. Consideration should be given to **heritage speakers** of Spanish, who are quite capable in comprehending spoken Spanish, but often struggle to express themselves clearly in spoken Spanish. In addition, some native speakers "will not be able to read it, and many will not be able to write it" (Annarino et al, 2014, p. 3). Much like children of dDeaf adults (CODAs),

> who have been using ASL since childhood, heritage speakers of Spanish have an ease of use in their two languages, but their Spanish competency must

97

be further developed for the purposes of professional interpreting. One effective solution to this challenge is for heritage speakers to enroll in formal Spanish classes at a local university or college (Annarino et al, 2014, p. 3).

When we talk about *heritage speakers*, we're usually referring to a person who has learned a language informally by being exposed to it at home as opposed to having learned it formally in a school setting. It may be their native tongue – the language they identify as being their primary language – but more often than not, their heritage language becomes secondary to English (Language Testing International, 2020, para. 1).

Needless to say, the need for Spanish-English-American Sign Language interpreters "is becoming more visible and more critical than ever before as Spanish-speaking populations continue to grow in the United States and the demand for services increases" (Casanova de Canales & Trevino, 2014, p. 171). The work is quite challenging because of the numerous linguistic demands; such as the ability to manage linguistic nuances represented by twenty-three "different Spanish speaking countries who are using a variety of formal or informal Spanish, along with differing accents, dialects and linguistic nuances" (Annarino, et al., 2014, p. 7). Casanova de Canales and Trevino (2014), suggest that one "means of addressing the shortage of qualified trilingual interpreters, was...that Latino Codas be recruited as potential trilingual interpreters" (p. 101).

COMPLEXITIES of TRILINGUAL INTERPRETING

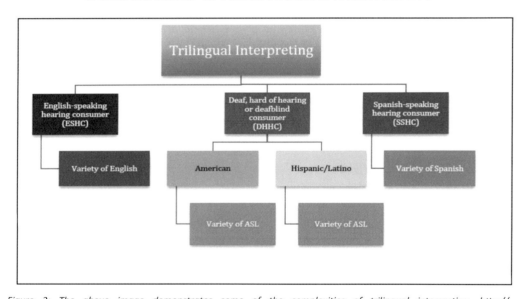

Figure 2: The above image demonstrates some of the complexities of trilingual interpreting. http://www.interpretereducation.org/wp-content/uploads/2015/06/complextril2large.jpg

Erica Alley (2014) conducted a survey focused on determining the various competencies and skills needed to be an effective trilingual interpreter. Alley made several recommendations based on the results of the study,

> aside from fundamental interpreting coursework, trilingual interpreters would benefit from activities that focus on Spanish-English interpreting. Time would be wisely spent on the exploration of Latin American cultures, United States government and policy, as well as interpersonal skills and ethical scenarios, as opposed to devoting extensive time to the goal of

People of Color

NOTES

"sounding native." The majority of hiring entities look toward RID certification when hiring trilingual interpreters. Trilingual interpreting curricula should be sure to include practicing materials from the RID National Interpreter Certification test (p. 133).

Certification Status	Performance Test Eligibility
Not certified	Not eligible
BEI Level I, Level II, Level III, Level IV, Level V, Basic, Advanced, or Master	Trilingual Advanced
*RID CI, CT ,or CI/CT, CSC, **NAD-RID NIC, NIC Advanced, NIC Master	
BEI Level III, Level IV, Level V, Advanced, or Master, Trilingual Advanced	Trilingual Master
RID CSC, CI/CT, NIC Advanced, or NIC Master	

Figure 3: It is important to note that holders of RID/NAD certification from another state who are applying for the Advanced or Master Trilingual Performance Tests must submit a copy of their valid certification for verification purposes.

Trilingual Interpreting Certification

At the date this text was published only the Texas Office of Deaf and Hard of Hearing Services (DHHS) provided certification for trilingual sign language interpreters through the Texas Board for Evaluation of Interpreters (BEI). They offer Advanced and Mastery level certifications for trilingual interpreters. For additional information concerning trilingual interpreting certification please visit their website at: *https://hhs.texas.gov/laws-regulations/handbooks/bei/chapter-6-trilingual-certification*

The Texas Board for Evaluation of Interpreters (BEI) has specific eligibility requirements to take the Trilingual Advanced and the Trilingual Master test, see figure 3.

OTHER ETHNIC/RACIAL GROUPS IN THE UNITED STATES

Indo-Americans

Immigrants from India first arrived in the United States in small numbers during the early 19th century, primarily seeking any type of employment but often settling for farm labor. In 2000, there were less than two million Indian immigrants living in the US. At the time this book went to press (June 2020), the population of Indo-Americans (including East Indians, Asian Indians, and American Indians) was 3.9 million, one of the largest immigrant populations (Pew Research Center, 2017). Today, the majority of Indian immigrants are young and well educated. Many work in science, technology, engineering, and math (STEM) fields.

Asian Americans

The Asian population in the United States is incredibly diverse; "A record 20 million Asian Americans trace their roots to more than 20 countries in East and Southeast Asia and the Indian subcontinent, each with unique histories, cultures, languages and other characteristics" (Lopez, Ruiz, & Patten, 2017, para. 1). With that in mind, it would be nearly impossible to try to describe the diverse cultures, languages and peoples of the numerous countries. Nearly three-quarters (74%) of Asian American

---

*Registry of Interpreters for the Deaf |**National Association of the Deaf-Registry of Interpreters for the Deaf National Interpreter Certification

adults were born abroad; of that number, about half feel they have a mastery of English while the other half feel that they do not utilize English well. According to the 2012 Pew Research Center report, entitled *The Rise of Asian Americans,* "Asian Americans are the highest-income, best-educated and fastest-growing racial group in the United States" (p. v). It appears that many of "today's Asian Americans do not feel the sting of racial discrimination or the burden of culturally imposed 'otherness' that was so much a part of the experience of their predecessors who came in the 19th and early 20th centuries" (Pew Research Center, 2013, p. 12). Hispanics/Latinx and Blacks/African Americans (two of the larger minorities) feel that discrimination is of greater significance. Lastly, some of the largest Asian origin groups residing in the United States are Chinese Americans, Filipino Americans, Indian Americans, Vietnamese Americans, Korean Americans and Japanese Americans (Pew Research Center, 2013).

Power and Privilege

In this chapter, the authors have attempted to paint a picture of key populations within the US and Canada. As an interpreter, you will likely work with dDeaf children, youth, adults and elders from every race and ethnic group in North America. It is important that you look carefully at your beliefs, biases, and attitudes you have acquired on your life's journey. As an interpreter, those perceptions may negatively influence your ability to provide high-quality interpreting and access to communication across a range of settings. Our job, as interpreters, can be challenging on many levels:

- Having adequate English and American Sign Language vocabulary
- Possessing the mental processing skills and speed required to convey the meaning of messages being communicated between people who are dDeaf and those who can hear
- Sometimes experiencing vicarious trauma because of the injustice and unkind treatment some human beings impose on others...and the list can go on and on

It is critical that you take a good look at your status and give ample consideration to your privilege before you enter the professional interpreting world. We must recognize that those of us who are privileged rarely recognize it. Everyone has a degree of privilege, even among the oppressed some have greater status while others have less. Most of us likely did not work for it; our privilege was inherited.

Power often has invisible and unacknowledged presence in human interactions, making it urgent that we recognize its presence and how interpreters can function as a source of balancing that power or supporting an unequal sharing of the power dynamics present in interpersonal interactions, especially when one or more of the participants are dDeaf.

Jonathan Webb, the first Black President of RID, talked about *making space* in the President's Column in the Views (February, 2020). In his article, Webb explained that making space is an idea related to empowerment, but it does not stop there and it moves beyond the idea that the dominant culture has the power to empower others. "Unfortunately, we know from history that when a group has the ability to empower another community, the same group conversely has the ability to disempower that community" (Webb, 2020, p. 6). Jonathan goes on to propose the concept of *resistance.* He states that resistance is a "powerful notion, an act that asserts our objection to being swallowed up by the system. It demonstrates an unwillingness to go with the status quo of being exploited by a system made to benefit only a few" (Webb, 2020, p. 6). We *must* acknowledge that we live in a society where opportunities are greater for those with lighter skin tones, who speak articulately, those who are well-dressed, with the nice car and the right address – the privileged minority. Even though we may not have given it much thought, interpreters are privileged by this unequal system because of the inherent power of the interpreting position. Our biggest task, as holders of intentional or unintentional power and privilege, is to get out of the way. Failing to do that limits our ability to evolve, grow and become whole (Webb, 2020).

One of the most effective ways we make space is by continuing to engage in the discussions at hand. But rather than doing all the talking, we instead engage in questioning and deep listening. This is a way to *make space* for others from different backgrounds and cultures to share their thoughts, ideas, and experiences, opening opportunities to change the system into something that is more fair and beneficial to all. For more information on power and privilege please see chapter 5, Power, Privilege and Oppression.

chapter Review

This chapter hopefully deepened your understanding of the rich cultural differences between every culture and race you encounter. As your cultural awareness and etiquette grows, these skills should be applied to your knowledge of interpreting and toward mediating language/culture.

Terms to Know:

- **Aboriginal:** Original inhabitants.

- **Acculturation:** Is a process where two cultures come into contact, which changes one or both cultural groups (Rothe, E. M., Tzuang, D., & Pumariega, A. J., 2010, p. 681).

- **Collectivist Norms:** Are most concerned with the welfare of the group and the group relationships (Little, 2016).

- **Colonialism:** Is a form of domination by controlling groups/individuals which demonstrated through the exploitation of that group's culture and language.

- **Deafhood:** Dr. Paddy Ladd's (2005) model offers the term *deafhood*, as a means to share the value systems of deaf peoples, as a unique people who are "'visuo-gesturo-tactile' biological entities, [that] believe they offer a different and positive perspective on what it means to be human" (p. 13).

- **Ethnicity:** Refers to the culture, language, history, etc. of a people group.

- **Heritage Speakers:** Defined as people who excel at comprehending their native tongue, but can still struggle articulating themselves through spoken or written word.

- **Indigenous Peoples:** Defined as people who originally resided in the land but were removed forcibly.

- **Individualism:** Is the belief that the needs, preferences and desires of the one are stressed over the needs of the whole.

Chapter 6

NOTES

- **Minority:** Refers to a small group of people that are often discriminated against in a community, either by society or on a national level because their language, race, beliefs, etc. differ.

- **Race:** Is defined as the physical characteristics of people, which are considered significant on a social scale.

- **Trilingual Interpreter:** Possess fluency in three unique and separate languages and cultures. They must possess knowledge related to the unique aspects that create distinctions between the cultures as well as the ability to successfully interpret these differences.

Cultures and Races have aspects that make them different and unique, such as:

- Language use
- Learning styles and values
- Family
- Spirituality and religion

Races and Ethnicities

There are no biological determinants of races nor distinctions between these words. These races are commonly recognized in the United States:

- Black
- Caucasian
- Asian
- Hispanic/Latinx
- Native American

Cultural sharing is how family members pass culture, traditions, experience, etc. to their children.

Acculturation experiences vary depending how the minority culture interacts with the majority culture

Indigenous Peoples identifying characteristics are land and language, which create a sense of community and to lose either hurts the sense of community (Department of Economic and Social Affairs, 2009).

Trilingual Interpreters must also be able to read and write in all of their languages.

Dr. Melanie McKay-Cody, an Indigenous dDeaf Person from the United States, shares some advice. McKay-Cody, M. (2020). *Protocol for Sign Language Interpreters Working in North American Indigenous Settings.* (J. Wardle, Ed.) VIEWS, 1(37), retrieved May 20, 2020.

- Without the knowledge and sensitivity to the culture of Indigenous Peoples, interpreting will be challenging and cross-cultural communication may not succeed.
- Without the proper understanding of Indigenous cultures, the interpreter will likely be confused or uncertain regarding the meaning/intent of things being discussed or some of the norms observed, such as greetings and how respect is shown between Indigenous Peoples.
- When interpreting for Indigenous dDeaf Peoples, "go with the flow," allow the circumstances to shape your interpretation as far as is possible.
- The best approach is to communicate what is being said, even when you don't fully understand the exact meaning.

- Your choices may actually empower the Indigenous dDeaf Person to respond in a culturally appropriate manner. They may ask for clarification when and if it is culturally appropriate to do so.

Dr. McKay-Cody has suggested the following protocol for non-indigenous interpreters working in indigenous settings/events.

- If you are asked to interpret for an indigenous event or ceremony, you must enter the event with an understanding that it is an *honor* to be present at special events involving Indigenous Peoples.
- Be keenly aware that the mere presence of an interpreter will impact the setting and the individuals involved, both in positive and/or negative ways.
- When you, as the interpreter, need support to understand the interaction, require clarification regarding what is being said, or need additional understanding of the cultural norms surrounding an interaction, seek assistance from the *designated* indigenous coordinator or appropriate contact person.
- Interpreters must be aware that it is not uncommon for many dDeaf tribal members to have their own indigenous way of signing. As the interpreter, you must make it a *priority* to demonstrate respect by incorporating those signs into your interpretation.
- When interpreting in some sacred indigenous spiritual event settings, consent to be present to interpret must be obtained.
- Appropriate clothing in indigenous settings is flexible, and interpreters need to inquire prior to the interpreted event what attire is appropriate.

Equality

The move toward fair and equitable treatment *must* begin and be continued as those who are not people of color work alongside one another, become friends with and advocate on behalf of all the dDeaf and hearing people of color.

Reflect on your home, school, and work life. Where have you observed or experienced positive and negative situations that involved people of color, racism, equal treatment, discrimination, etc. Briefly describe the event, but more importantly, how it made you feel and why.

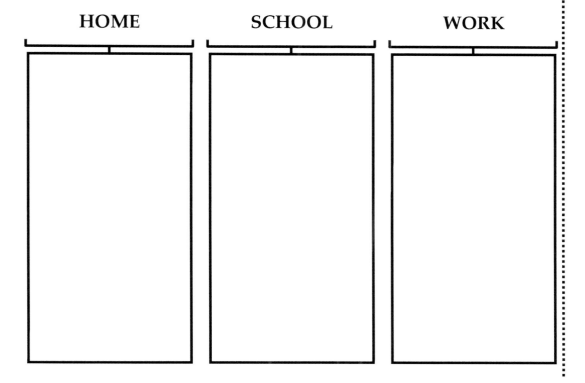

TERMS TO KNOW:

- Tandem of Interpreters
- Tactile Interpreting

Photo credit: Steve Brown, WBUR

7 | The Deaf Journey

To the reader...the information in this chapter is a departure from the approach the authors have taken thus far; we will move away from our emphasis on research and academic study. Instead, we will be listening to the heartbeat of the dDeaf community. It is well known that "Deaf storytellers have been passing on their stories, culture, and identity through a tradition that has been kept alive through face-to-face events" (Bauman, Nelson, & Rose, 2006, p. 23). The *dDeaf narrative* is an essential element of the dDeaf community and culture, conveying the lived experience of dDeaf people (Bauman, Nelson, & Rose, 2006). This chapter was drafted from group discussions, interviews and candid dialogues that will be retold in the form of numerous mini-narratives. The focus of this chapter will be about the journey of five dDeaf people, each on their own journey to become interpreters: *this is their story*.

Joseph Featherstone was the primary interviewer. He interviewed the four dDeaf interpreters who you will *meet* as the chapter unfolds. You will see that this narrative often reflects the first person experience. Much of this chapter is told from Joseph's perspective and represents his thoughts, feelings and ideas, which are presented in first person narrative unless noted otherwise. Enjoy!

Meet Joseph Featherstone
Lives and Works in Utah

This chapter is intended to give aspiring dDeaf people an idea of what it takes to become a professional interpreter. It will also explain why dDeaf interpreters are needed and a few things every dDeaf interpreter should know. Additionally, it will give insight to people who can hear, helping them better understand how to work with dDeaf interpreters. It is impossible to cover every aspect of dDeaf interpreting in one chapter, however, we will cover the basics. If you want to learn the skills needed to become a professional dDeaf interpreter, I strongly recommend going to the *Deaf Interpreter Institute* website. Complete the various activities, work with the faculty in your interpreter training program or find a mentor. To write this section, I interviewed four Deaf interpreters and gathered their insights along with mine. I strongly recommend that you research other materials written by professionals in the field because there are many who have contributed to the interpreting profession, and the more you learn, the more efficient and professional you will become.

Why dDeaf Interpreters are Needed

I remember a time when I was involved with an internship program that was hosted twice a year by an interpreting company. We held a prestigious interpreter boot camp that was guaranteed to enable almost anyone to get certified at the conclusion of our program. That meant we had a lot of applicants and my team would go through a long, rigorous, three day process where we would screen over 100 applicants and narrow it down to 12 finalists. There were a lot of heated discussions on why an applicant should be considered or removed, analyzing language skills, processing skills, reviewing their reasons why they wanted to be an interpreter, and basically just analyzing every detail of these 100 applicants. In the end, we had 12 of the most qualified candidates.

I was with this team for three years, and went through this boot camp six times. During the 6th bout, I knew what to expect, and had stocked up on my peanut M&M's and was ready for another bout of wrestling with my teammates – honestly, I enjoyed the process. However, this time, it was different. We had a dDeaf interpreter apply for our program. I remember very vividly watching her video, explaining why she wanted to be an interpreter and then she interpreted the stimulus that was given and it was like watching a master violinist give us a masterpiece compared to watching the other applicants fumbling with their violins. She easily got the highest marks from me, but of course, it was part of the process that we had to wrestle as a team and decide if she was qualified for our program. Being a Certified Deaf Interpreter myself, I was already dreaming about having my first dDeaf interpreter in the program, about paving the way for a new generation and starting a new track for future dDeaf interpreters. In my mind, she was already in. She was already worthy. She blew everyone else out of the water. She had work to do, she had a lot of room for improvement, but I was ready to start teaching her.

Sadly, not everyone on my team agreed. One argued that we were not ready to have dDeaf interpreters, that the applicant would be bored and not learn anything since we were geared and designed for hearing interpreters. I argued that if we didn't start now, learning with her, we would never learn. We went back and forth, and the conclusion was that she was "overqualified" and thereby not accepted to the program but to ease the blow, our program invited her for a couple of weeks, here and there to learn specific skills and that was it.

At that moment, I realized something – the dDeaf interpreter applicant was so easy for me to understand, so easy for me to interact with, so easy for me to digest the information that she was interpreting and was obviously someone that we needed working out there. As a profession, sadly, we brush dDeaf interpreters aside and focus on the development of hearing interpreters while ignoring the fact that there are interpreters that are already multicultural and multilingual experts. We are missing out on the opportunity to make the interpreting profession more dDeaf centric. If we truly want to offer quality interpreting services, we will bring in the dDeaf community; dDeaf interpreters are the bridge. We must be more intentional about increasing the number and availability of dDeaf interpreters. They need to be given greater consideration, in education, in hiring and in decision-making. They should not be considered as an *afterthought*. In a perfect world, decisions concerning every appointment would have the consideration of two interpreters; a dDeaf and hearing team. They would collaborate to determine whether the dDeaf interpreter should accompany the hearing interpreter; that decision should be made at the *beginning* of every assignment, not at the end.

You may be wondering, what is a Deaf interpreter? According to the *Deaf Interpreter Institute* website:

> A Deaf Interpreter is a specialist who provides interpreting, translation, and transliteration services in American Sign Language and other visual and tactual communication forms used by individuals who are Deaf, hard-of-hearing, and Deaf-Blind. As a Deaf person, the Deaf Interpreter starts with a distinct set of formative linguistic, cultural, and life experiences that enables nuanced comprehension and interaction in a wide range of visual language and communication forms influenced by region, culture, age, literacy, education, class, and physical, cognitive, and mental health. These experiences coupled with professional training give the Deaf interpreter the ability to successfully communicate across all types of interpreted interactions, both routine and high risk. NCIEC studies indicate that in many situations, use of a Deaf Interpreter enables a level of linguistic and cultural bridging that is often not possible when hearing ASL-English interpreters work alone (National Consortium of Interpreter Education Centers, 2016, para. 1).

Where Did We Start?

Many dDeaf interpreters discovered they already had translating and interpreting skills because when they were younger they helped their friends and family with written texts, so they chose interpreting as their career path. Any way, being an interpreter is not for the faint of heart. There are many unspoken and unwritten skills that you will need to acquire, in addition to your interpreting skills. But here are some of the most important things that you should always be working on:

- Flexibility & Fluidity
- Assertiveness & Aggressiveness (maybe once in awhile)
- Facilitating effective communication with your team and between all the involved parties of the interaction

One skill that is pertinent in being an effective interpreter is the ability to work with your team. There cannot be any ego or power play while working with a team. Patrick Lencioni explains that,

> the kind of people that all teams need are people who are humble, hungry, and smart. Humble being little ego; focusing more on their teammates than on themselves. Hungry, meaning they have a strong work ethic, are determined to get things done and contribute any way they can. Smart, meaning not intellectually smart but interpersonally smart. They understand the dynamics of a group of people and how to say and do things and have a positive outcome on those around them (Lencioni, 2016 quoted by Schawbel, 2016, para. 6).

The process of becoming certified is outlined in chapter two and additional information is located in the Toolbox. Please refer to the requirements and certifications in becoming a nationally certified dDeaf interpreter. There are several states that offer state certification. There is one state test that is recognized and often accepted in several states and that is the Texas Board for Evaluation of Interpreters (BEI).

The Deaf Journey

NOTES

As a certified DI, I have heard some comments about how the written test is a barrier to many prospective dDeaf interpreters with developing English skills. I feel like if you want to be a multicultural and multilingual interpreter, you need to know English and be able to have the skills to pass the written test if you are going to be translating documents for your dDeaf clients. The performance test addresses your sign language skills in different settings and that is another area you should demonstrate fluency. I guess what I am trying to say there is a healthy balance between education and community knowledge and membership – we must have both.

Mathis: "I want to share a buzzword, *elitism.* Is it possible to separate the Deaf interpreter from the Deaf client? Where I am right now, I'm not advocating for Deaf interpreters to have advanced degrees. I'd rather we use another method of skill assessment to determine if the Deaf interpreter is ready. I prefer we look at things like experience, native language, and skills like that, rather than advanced degrees. I have a college degree, I see that it seems to separate me from people. They are in awe of me and look up to me, that separates me from them. They are intimidated by my education. I don't want that. I want to interact with them on the same level and sometimes my college degree prevents that. I'm not an advocate of requiring college degrees" (Mathis, 2020).

Ethical Challenges, Dilemmas and Common Sense

As an interpreter that comes from the dDeaf community, there might be times where you will find yourself in a situation that is not ideal. For example, if you interpret for a client at a regular job and then you are called to interpret for a job interview and it is the same client, it can be a little unsettling to be looking at someone across the table knowing their history from their previous job and comparing their answers against what you have seen.

dDeaf interpreters are more likely to be much more involved in the dDeaf community and will have a greater likelihood of working with clients that we may know personally. There will be some situations where it would be very appropriate for you to be their interpreter and other times it will be very inappropriate to interpret for them. For example, I am a male and called to OB-GYN appointments. I know for a fact that many of my female dDeaf friends wouldn't want me to interpret for them. Anytime I get a request for those appointments, I refer them to female interpreters.

Other times, you will be asked to interpret for occasions that will conflict with your personal beliefs, morals or just flat out not what you signed up for. How do you move forward? You will have to do your best to keep your bias, preferences and opinion in check, and if you cannot, communicate your struggles with the client and call the agency and request a replacement. On one such occasion, I attended a conference and the speaker started to speak strongly about a controversial issue and the interpreter also had strong opinions about the issue. The interpreter showed his feelings on his face, folded his arms and refused to continue interpreting, leaving all of us – dDeaf people – without access. I found myself really angry at the interpreter for robbing us of our right to access because of his personal opinions, and he made it all about him and not about providing access. I found out later that interpreter *knew* what the topic was and *still* accepted the assignment. I became livid.

Know your limits. My point is – know *yourself,* know your *boundaries*, know your *triggers*, and interpret within your boundaries. If you have experienced trauma,

107

avoid places that might trigger you. If you know you have some unresolved history, and the assignment could put you at risk, decline the appointment (for more information on self-care see chapter 1). If you have no knowledge of the subject matter and you know that another interpreter would be more qualified for the job, make the referral. If you find out that this is a job that involves a specific ethnic group, refer and find someone from their community.

Be careful of vicarious trauma. You will be interpreting some situations that are hard to see, such as court hearings, rape stories, recounting domestic violence stories, death – these are difficult to handle. Find a counselor or a therapeutic means to keep yourself grounded and balanced and know that you are not alone.

Accepting Assignments – What to Expect
Now you're a working dDeaf interpreter. When a person or company is requesting interpreters, money is always in the forefront of their mind. It seems like one of the biggest issues when requesting a second interpreter, they often assume that the second interpreter is able to hear. Yet, when they find out it is a dDeaf interpreter, they balk. This issue must be addressed – one way is to negotiate with the person requesting the services is by explaining that a **tandem** (or team) of interpreters has been assigned to provide communication access. Trenton Marsh, a dDeaf interpreter in Utah, and Laurie Monell, a case manager at the community center in Utah, utilize the term *tandem* as a way to request a dDeaf/hearing team. From their experience, when they are talking to a hiring entity that is requesting interpreting services for their dDeaf staff, patients or participants, they instruct the hiring client to call an agency and request a tandem. The agency, in turn, knows that a tandem means a dDeaf/hearing team and it saves everyone the headache of trying to explain what is needed or why a dDeaf interpreter is being requested. For this to be a reality in more places, you may need to work with your local agencies and educate them on the term "tandem," and once that term is something everyone understands, it makes hiring dDeaf/hearing teams a lot more easier.

Meet Stephanie Mathis
Lives and Works in Utah

"I arrived at a medical appointment and the hearing interpreter told the Deaf patient that her team had arrived. Not that the CDI interpreter had arrived. But her team arrived. She spoke about me as an equal. If she had disrespected me, then the Deaf patient would also disrespect me. Because of years of oppression, some Deaf patients would automatically turn to the hearing interpreter as the expert. I see that. In my experience, the best team is the hearing interpreter who views me as equal, we support each other, and we work together as a team for the benefit and success of the appointment" (S. Mathis, personal communication, March 21, 2020).

Mathis: As a dDeaf interpreter, you need to reach out to local, state, or national interpreting agencies. Some agencies might have experience in working with dDeaf interpreting professionals and others might not. Do your part to educate the agencies if they need some help, and advocate for yourself. "Sometimes you will never develop the skills you need if you don't take assignments that push your skill set. But, of course, the guiding principle is always – *do no harm*. Two things I ask myself:

1. Are there any conflicts of interest for me because I'm an active member of the Deaf community?
2. Does my skill set match the job requirements?" (Mathis, 2020)

Meet Topher González Ávila
Lives and Works in Texas

"Agency owners tend to value people who are fast to respond to their email or text, who show up early for appointments, and communicate everything back to them. González Ávila (2020) explained, 'When going into the interpreting field, it is important to understand what privileges you have and to start unpacking those privileges. This will support both you and the consumer in navigating all kinds of possible barriers while facilitating communication. And sometimes, your team will point out something that is bothering them or something, explore the concerns with further conversation instead of just brushing it off" (T. González Ávila, personal communication, March 27, 2020).

González Ávila: Be sure to always be professional, be prepared by talking with your team beforehand, do your part to be on time (at least 15 minutes early) and dress appropriately for the job. Dressing appropriately for the job means to dress one level above the expected dress code. For example, if you are working at a college and the professor dresses business casual, dress business casual that is slightly a little higher than them. How you dress for the job is reflected in how people treat you. Court interpreters will dress formally. Religious interpreters will look out of place if they dress too casually. Avoid the trap of *self-expression* when you are working as a professional interpreter (González Ávila, 2020).

dDeaf people have seen interpreters do all kinds of things. For example, a female interpreter showed up to an appointment with a tight, revealing outfit because she knew there would be single men in the room. After the appointment was over, many men started talking to the dDeaf participant to ask if they could have get the interpreter's phone number. This interpreter made the appointment all about her and not about facilitating communication.

Another time, a male interpreter arrived to interpret a job interview. He was not dressed up, had visible tattoos, and unkempt facial hair. The dDeaf person didn't get the job. We cannot help but wonder, was it because of how the interviewer perceived the interpreter and connected the interpreter's sloppiness to the dDeaf applicant? Sure, it's illegal to discriminate but it doesn't stop some companies from doing so. These two examples show how the interpreter's need for *self-expression* was likely detrimental or at least contributed in a negative way to the outcome, preventing the dDeaf person from achieving their goal. Do your best to make the interpreting assignment about the communication and interactions between the parties and not about yourself.

González Ávila: "Agency owners don't know you and your skill sets as well as you do. As a result, you will sometimes have to communicate with the agency. I am often asked to do LSM (Mexican Sign Language) assignments. Because I am a native LSM user, it is easy for agencies to assume I am qualified for any and all LSM assignments and for any and all Latinx consumers. This is not true at all. There are a lot of factors to consider. I am not always a good fit. No interpreter is a perfect fit for everyone. I always advocate for multicultural and multilingual aspects of working as an interpreter. Look beyond ASL. Talk to the consumer and consider what factors will make access to communication truly effective" (González Ávila, 2020).

Before accepting any job, ask the hiring agency for the job details and begin to consider what the demands are, what will the assignment require of you – do you have what they need? What do you already know about the setting? What more information do you need? Do you know who you will be interpreting with – what is your relationship with your colleague? If the agency is vague on the details, ask for more. Once you know the details, accept the job or refer them to the right interpreter to interpret for the clients more effectively.

Meet Regina Daniels
Lives and Works in Minnesota

"People accept jobs mostly because of the money, the goal of improving their skills and to provide continuity of service (which I totally understand and agree with), but there is limited representation of people of color. For example, if a speaker happens to be Black, Hispanic, or another ethnicity, why not have an interpreter of similar ethnic background to represent the speaker? For example, I interpreted the play *The Color Purple*. The play is based on the 1982 novel by the same name, written by Alice Walker. It was later made into a movie, the movie follows the journey of Celie, an African American woman in the American South from the early to mid-20th century. My Black male team and I really had to fight to get this gig. We explained our rationale about the play, our work and about the likely response from the Deaf community. And we totally understood their concerns about customer service and patrons coming to the theatre. But I went to talk with someone I knew who was a regular patron of this theatre (he is Deaf) and I pointed out that the play was *The Color Purple*. A play based on the history of Black culture and way of life. This person understood my point and asked about the issues we were facing. When I told him that the theatre was worried that people may not come to the theatre if we were the interpreters. He was shocked! I mean, we had been fighting with the theatre for 3 months and if I never talked to this regular patron, what would have happened? But as soon as I contacted him, he went straight to the theatre and vouched for us and they hired us. That's great, but why did it have to go down like this? Why did we have to work harder than our white colleagues who typically do not have to go through things like this? So, there are a lot of things like this...if there is a job that you feel would be better represented by a different person, refer them to that professional" (R. Daniels, personal communication, March 24, 2020).

Daniels: As for the issue of equal representation, "I feel one of the problems is that there isn't a community, there aren't enough people of color in the interpreting profession. Not enough at all! I'm one of the few interpreters of color and they use me often. I am one of the only Black Deaf interpreters. They know my skills. They see my work. They see how I'm motivated to do the job BUT I want them to use me for good reasons. Not simply because they have access to a Black interpreter. There is definitely an issue of *tokenism!* I know that this is happening and I find it disturbing and off-putting. But at the same time, I want to represent the Black Deaf community, especially to young kids. Without me, the only role models that they have are all White and they've seen it all before, then I come along and change things up!" (Daniels, 2020).

Different Types of Interpreting
In the field of interpreting there are different types of work and the logistics and dynamics can be different when a dDeaf interpreter is involved. We have several solutions to manage the environment, sight lines and the needs of the participants.

Some of the most common types of interpreting are:

- Platform
- Mirroring
- Consecutive
- Simultaneous
- Tactile or Close-vision

There are many other job types and other roles that you will have the opportunity to fill. Here are some thoughts from other interpreters and their feelings regarding these jobs:

Daniels: "I prefer working platform assignments. I do not have stage fright and don't mind standing in front of a crowd of people even when the audience is in the dark and the stage is brightly lit. Actually, if I can't see the people in the audience I look at my team and we just do the work. This suits me fine. On the other hand, I steer clear of interpreting for one-to-one assignments...literally, I run in the opposite direction. These kinds of assignments aren't for me because if something doesn't go well, I lose my cool. I am a protector of rights and one of my personality traits is to fight back. And I know that I'm not supposed to react that way as an interpreter but I can't stop it. It's safer for me to interpret on the platform or at conferences because I'm not in the middle of any of the conversations that take place during a presentation. I like it that way!" (Daniels, 2020)

Platform: Platform interpreting means you're interpreting in front of a large audience, most often in a formal setting where the speaker does most of the talking. During platform interpreting, you should do your very best to get the script. When you get the script beforehand, you have ample time to prepare for the job. In many cases, the platform interpreting team set up looks like this (see figure 1).

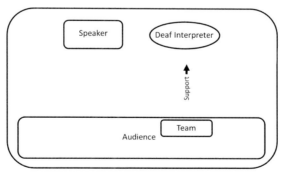

Figure 1: Platform interpreting

As the speaker addresses the audience or camera, the dDeaf interpreter will be next to the speaker and the co-interpreter or team will be sitting directly in front of the dDeaf interpreter and providing the informational support to the platform interpreter.

Mirroring: The purpose of mirroring is when there is a large number of people attending a gathering, such as a workshop, or a presentation and members of the audience use American Sign Language. The concern is that the sightlines may be hampered by members in the audience. Because not everyone can see when audience members are making comments or asking questions (see figure 2). The dDeaf interpreter will be on stage with the speaker and will follow the speaker's cue. It is important to be sensitive to the speaker (do not point or assume the speaker's role) once the speaker points at a person, the dDeaf interpreter will mirror, or copy what the signer from the audience is saying. The set up is the same as the platform approach, without the team (see figure 2).

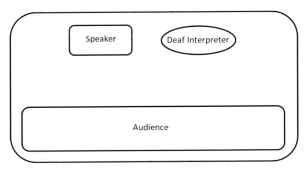
Figure 2: Mirroring

Consecutive: This is the most common approach employed by dDeaf interpreters. This happens in medical, legal, educational and numerous other settings. Consecutive interpreting usually has a unique set up – the dDeaf interpreter sits next to the hearing participant and the co-interpreter sits or stands either right next to the dDeaf participant or slightly behind (see figure 3).

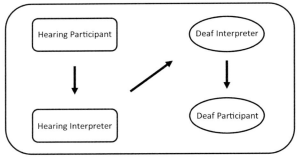
Figure 3: Consecutive interpreting

González Ávila: "I love teams that show up early before the assignment, and we come up with a system because I always tell my team to be in view of the client so the client can see them as well, and they have the choice of either watching the team or me. It's up to them. Some CDI's I know will make their team go in the back and not in view and that's their choice, but mine is that the team is in view. The reason why I do that is that it builds trust in CDI's and it builds trust in me and that I am relaying the right information" (González Ávila, 2020).

Simultaneous: There are times when it may feel like you're interpreting simultaneously but it is often consecutive. You will be working with a team, and you will often be supporting each other and working together. The information that is being relayed will often come in chunks, hence the reason it is more consecutive. "One thing that makes simultaneous interpreting challenging is that if I had it my way every time, consecutive jobs are the best. I MUST have eye contact with my client and I must make sure I am catching all the nuances of the language and their facial expressions so I ask interpreters to hold the information until I look at them and then they will fill me in and then I will look back at the client and the interpreter can work with the hearing client to make sure they are not rambling on and not impeding the process. It takes time (4 people) so they need to understand that" (González Ávila, 2020).

Close-Vision and Tactile: Oftentimes, the dDeaf interpreter will be assigned to a DeafBlind client or a low-vision client, in this case, it really is up to the DeafBlind participant and how they like to receive the information. Some like to sit side by side, some like to sit directly across from each other. Some prefer one and others prefer two. Work with the dDeaf participant and figure out what works best for both of you because if you are craning your neck, trying to relay the information while interpreting, you *will* get a neck cramp fast, so work together. While interpreting as a dDeaf interpreter, it becomes easy to watch the signing presenter and never have any form of check in with the client because you are busy receiving the content. Practice the skill of checking in and making sure that the client is tracking what is going on and make adjustments as needed. **Tactile interpreting** is when some participants "have little to no vision and need to receive linguistic information by feeling the interpreter's hands while the interpreter signs or fingerspells, this is called tactile interpreting" (Western Interpreting Network, 2020, para. 4). It is also important to note that the sign language interpreter may add "visual descriptions along with the interpreted message. Depending on the consumer's preference, tactile interpreters may either be a CDI or a hearing ASL interpreter" (Western Interpreting Network, 2020, para. 4), (see figure 4).

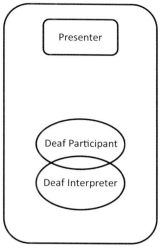

Figure 4: Close-Vision and Tactile interpreting

The Interpreting Process

Refer to chapter 9 in this text that discusses the various interpreting processes. dDeaf interpreters and hearing interpreters have very similar interpreting processes and the only exceptions are that you are watching the information instead of hearing it. Something to keep in mind – do not sacrifice eye contact with the dDeaf participant to receive information, especially in consecutive appointments.

dDeaf-Hearing Interpreter Team

As an interpreter, you will work with many other interpreters. You will need to develop an arsenal of tools that you can employ on demand. When working with your colleagues, you will have the opportunity to work with experienced interpreters, new interpreters and everyone in between. For every situation you encounter, you will need to assess the situation, determine the best course of action and work with your team to implement your strategy. Several things to consider:

- What kind of teaming/co-interpreting approach do you want to use?
- What are the goals of each client?
- Where should we be standing/sitting to be most efficient?
- What are some potential obstacles or difficulties that might arise and how to address them?

Meet Aleksandr Riabinin
Lives and Works in Oregon

"I prefer the hearing interpreter sign to PSE so they will include more original and accurate information. I mean – I want the hearing interpreter to use ASL signs in English word order. That way I can understand the full message and then interpret it accurately. If the hearing interpreter gives me the source message in ASL, *they have already unpacked the meaning of the message* and by the time I get the message, I may interpret into the target language incorrectly. I'd rather do this my own way" (A. Riabinin, personal communication, March 21, 2020).

While working, make sure you remain very aware of how you are affecting the situation and do your best to keep your bias in check. It is impossible to be *neutral* but you can do your best to keep your bias in check and do your best to facilitate communication to the best of your ability. You will start to develop your own preference as it relates to teaming.

González Ávila: "I love teams that have a real, raw debrief after every appointment. I hate it when they just leave (unless they have an appointment they need to run to) but there needs to be 15 minutes after every appointment and we go through the appointment and discuss what went well, what didn't, what we missed, what we did well, and it's sometimes hard (especially when you're new and learning) but those were my favorite teams. I could tell who cared about the job, who really strived to get the best out of every appointment than those who just would say see ya, and moved on. Felt like they saw the job as a 'clock in, clock out' mentality" (González Ávila, 2020).

There is No "I" in TEAM

When working as a team, you must truly be a team. You need to work together and avoid any power plays. It's interesting because I now have my favorite teams, having worked with many interpreters. Something I would really like to stress – *I like working with hearing interpreters who really value working with CDIs and understand how the CDI can positively impact the work.* However, the downside is that there are other hearing team members that still try to do *all* the work themselves and take over the interpretation. For some situations that might work, especially if the hearing interpreter and dDeaf client already have a relationship but it makes my work harder. I think it's best if the hearing interpreter steps back and supports the interpretation by having full confidence in the dDeaf interpreter so we can work together. We will work *better together.* If the hearing interpreter doesn't have *full* confidence in the CDI, we won't be a good team.

I hate to say this, but I see this attitude most common from CODA interpreters. Many CODA interpreters feel they are qualified and don't need to work with a CDI. But the point is not about needing a CDI; it's about providing the dDeaf person with a dDeaf interpreter (who has the shared life and language experience). And that the dDeaf person feels empowered, that is what it is all about. It's not about the hearing interpreter. It's not about me either. It's about the process of teaming and producing an interpretation that makes the dDeaf person feel supported. That's what I've noticed with teaming – relative to the value of CDIs.

Mathis: "I find I do my best work when the hearing interpreter wants to work together with me as a team, being willing to engage in conversation, and respecting me as an equal" (Mathis, 2020). If you are asked to work with a dDeaf interpreter, it does *not* reflect negatively on your skills. It is *not* a reflection on your experience. It is an opportunity to give the clients the best in team interpreting. It is about successfully facilitating the message from one person to the other and it's a great opportunity to learn from each other.

I have a message to hearing interpreters, you are our biggest ally, advocate and accomplices, please continue to advocate for us and promote us daily in the work we do. We are not here to take your jobs, but to work alongside you. Please spread the word and if you know dDeaf people who would make good interpreters, nudge them to start the process of becoming one. Also, when you see a situation that could benefit from having a dDeaf interpreter, speak up, make recommendations that support the dDeaf interpreting community.

Mathis: "A thought I have is that sometimes there is this misconception that Deaf interpreters are automatically experts in every category and should be the one that should answer all the questions, let me reiterate: we still are learning our ways, we

The Deaf Journey

NOTES

are still acquiring our skills, and preferences, so when we say we are not all ready or qualified, we mean it. Also when you're working in a team, you're a team, you should answer as a team, and both members make the team even better, and you can back each other up and have each other's backs. I hate hearing stories where either party (deaf or hearing) think they are better, or more qualified, or more experienced, and won't trust each other. That is plain stupidity and ego is getting in the way. Work together for the sake of the clients. Don't be afraid to mess up, you will mess up, and often. Don't be afraid to accept assignments that are just out of your comfort circle, and keep expanding your circle" (Mathis, 2020).

Cultural Considerations

While working in the interpreting community, there are some cultural nuances that need to be addressed. Something we refer to as dDeaf Standard Time (DST) does not apply to interpreters. You must be on time and by "on time," I mean 15 minutes *early*. When the appointment is over, be professional and take your leave because you are working. It is very likely you will see family, friends, and other familiar people while you are working. Remember it is work first, behave like an interpreter.

Confidentiality will determine how far you will go as a dDeaf interpreter. The dDeaf community is a very tight knit community and people will know if you are a professional interpreter or not by how you take care of their information; the key is confidentiality. Sometimes I will see a friend who I previously interpreted for that day and I have to catch myself from asking, "Are you doing better now?" It is important to make conversation based on the last time you had a conversation with them – outside of interpreting.

While working as a dDeaf interpreter, you will have a special role as a native member of the community. You will have the advantage of watching little nuances and behavioral cues from the dDeaf participants to really make sure that they are understanding what is being interpreted. As a dDeaf interpreter, you will also have opportunities to determine if the playing field is uneven because of privilege during interpreting appointments. You can work with your team to try to make the interaction more balanced and give the dDeaf person more equal footing in a world where they will often be at a disadvantage.

dDeaf Interpreter Mentoring and Networking

Mathis: "Most CDIs don't work with each other. Most of the time we are working with hearing interpreters. I would like to see more regular CDI training where we can learn together. I don't want us to have to wait until the next CDI conference. I would like regular local training, workshops, or cohort discussions. Many hearing interpreters get together at RID events but CDIs don't tend to go. I don't know why they don't. Maybe because the hearing interpreters talk to each other, rather than signing, even though they welcome us. But I don't see Deaf interpreters going there much. I remember when I became a CDI I was so excited to go to RID and when I did, I realized there were not many Deaf interpreters there, to my surprise. Also my community wasn't there. I think we need more regular training for those of us who are post-certification (who are already working interpreters) and also pre-certification (those who are preparing to become interpreters) so we can hone our skills and be better prepared to do our work. We need more mentoring experiences" (Mathis, 2020). The Deaf Interpreter Conference (DIC) is a wonderful way to meet other aspiring interpreters and learn from professional Deaf interpreters.

115

Once you become a working professional, I implore you to find ways to help those around you to become better professionals. Collaborate with your colleagues – build working and learning relationships.

What Makes a Great dDeaf Interpreter

A good CDI is comfortable with themselves and their language skills. And what I mean by *comfortable* is being able to accept areas where improvements are needed and being aware of their areas of strength. Understanding yourself – knowing your strengths and limitations. Having the ability to connect with the people that you are working alongside – the hearing interpreter team, the participants, both dDeaf and hearing. A good CDI is one who can relate to all the parties in the interaction and be a team player. It is so important to be a team player.

Mathis: No one can afford to have an arrogant attitude in the interaction, not the CDI, not the hearing interpreter – no one. CDIs must recognize they are only one person, they do not decide who should deal with the dDeaf person directly, cutting the hearing interpreter out, without a role in the interaction, or that the provider doesn't know how to provide the best service. A good CDI *must* respect the roles of everyone in the situation. "The CDI also needs to have the ability to adapt to different situations especially when unexpected things happen or new information comes up that throws things off in the interaction. S/he must be able to go with the flow. I think that's important" (Mathis, 2020).

Final Thoughts

Becoming a dDeaf interpreter is a lot of work, it requires knowledge and skills. There is a great deal of pressure trying to find the *perfect balance* between living in the dDeaf community and interpreting for them. At the same time, it is one of the most rewarding jobs. If you are considering becoming an interpreter, please spend the time needed to see if interpreting is a good fit for you. Once you figure out what you want to do, get the education you need before you get the necessary certifications or credentials. Just because you are dDeaf does not mean you do not need to network – get your name out there. As you begin working, unpack your privileges and bias – get to know yourself well. Each and every time you interpret, do it to the best of your ability. Once the assignment is finished, assess the job and see how it went, how it could have been better and how to improve the teamwork. Be humble, honest and do your best – never be satisfied.

Author's note: We chose not to follow the APA 6th edition formatting for personal communication in this chapter.

After reading Daniel's comments about the play and representation for people of color; how will you advocate for representation? Write your thoughts.

The Deaf Journey

NOTES

You have accepted an interpreting assignment with a dDeaf interpreter. What are the areas of strength and areas of growth you will bring to the assignment? Please name three of each and describe why you feel they are your areas of strength and areas of growth.

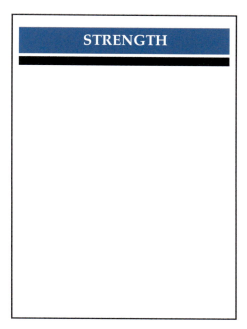

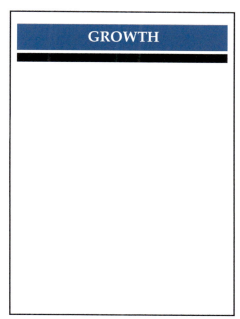

On page 109, González Ávila concludes his comments with a word on self expression, followed by two examples of overt self expression. Where is the line between self expression and professionalism?

117

TERMS TO KNOW:

- Mediate/Mediation
- Contextualized/Context
- Emotive Value
- Worldview

8 | Mediating Ways of Being

"It is widely recognized that language plays a key role in the transmission of human culture, but relatively little is known about the mechanisms by which language simultaneously encourages both cultural stability and cultural innovation" (Gelman, & Roberts, 2017, p. 1). The intricate relationship between language and culture is seen in the ways that language users adhere to differing cultural rules. Language is embedded in the culture where it evolved and is consistently used. "Interpreters have always occupied a unique social and cultural position relative to the communities within which they work...they who are positioned 'between worlds' and who make possible communication with 'outsiders'" (Cokely, 2008, p. 1). Thus it is essential that sign language interpreters have a rich, full and thorough understanding of the linguistic and cultural *boundaries* between the dDeaf-World and the world of people who can hear (Lane, Hoffmeister, & Bahan, 1996). Interpreters who have dDeaf parents are typically reared in dDeaf culture and the signed language used by their parents. Whereas, individuals who have grown up in the language and culture of people who can hear and who have chosen to become sign language interpreters are expected to become sojourners in dDeaf culture. Most interpreter education programs typically require that students meet certain prerequisites in American Sign Language, dDeaf Culture and minimal experiences interacting within the dDeaf community. They likely will require you to engage in advanced cultural learning and community involvement as you study to become an interpreter. It is essential to recognize that "sign language interpreters are positioned between sign language and spoken language worlds, there are critical aspects of their social and cultural positionality that have no counterpart among interpreters who are positioned between two spoken language worlds" (Cokely, 2008, p. 1). Along those lines, this chapter will share the ideas and concepts necessary for you to **mediate** culture, as well as language. Mediation enables citizens from differing cultural and linguistic communities to come together to foster personal interaction, communication and understanding; mediation can help dissolve psychological and social barriers that exclude certain people groups (Pronovost, & Harrison-Boisvert, 2015). However, interpreters who adhere to antiquated philosophies of interpreting (helper philosophy, conduit philosophy, etc.) may not have the experience required, nor the comfort with cultural and linguistic mediation.

Unique dDeaf cultures have emerged in every country based on the signed language of the country and the *ways of being* of the dDeaf community in that country. dDeaf

Mediating Ways of Being

NOTES

culture in the US and most of Canada, centers on the use of American Sign Language and unity with other people who are dDeaf based in the culture of the dDeaf population in each country. Although the focus of this text is on interpreters in the United States and Canada, Cokely (2008) explains "the observations developed here [in the US] will...hold relevance for Deaf Communities and sign language interpreters/transliterators in other countries" (p. 1).

George W. Veditz (1913), then president of the National Association of the Deaf, recognized the powerful sense of *identity* American Sign Language gives dDeaf individuals in the film *Preservation of the Sign Language*.

> As long as we have deaf people on Earth, we will have signs, and as long as we have our films, we can preserve our beautiful sign language in its original purity. It is our hope that we all will love and guard our beautiful sign language as the noblest gift God has given to deaf people (00:10:13 - 00:11:07).

Years later, Dr. Barbara Kannapel, a Deaf sociolinguist, defined American Deaf culture as including "a set of learned behaviors of a group of people who are deaf and who have their own language (ASL), values, rules, and traditions" (*American Deaf Culture*, 2015, para. 2). It is the language, values, behaviors, and traditions that will form the foundation of your ability to understand and efficiently mediate between the dominant hearing culture and dDeaf culture. As an interpreter, you might ask, why do you need to mediate cultures? Maybe you thought once you gained superior skills in your working languages and developed the skills that convey meaning between spoken and signed languages you would be fully prepared to be an interpreter. Language does not exist in a vacuum; it only has meaning when it is **contextualized**; reflecting and encompassing the beliefs, traditions, and values of the people who use that language. Because of that, it is not possible to determine the *meaning* of things in any language unless you have an understanding of the culture in which language wraps meaning. It is essential that consideration be given to the *context* of each and every signed message – we know that context is comprised of the various "parts of a written or spoken statement that precede or follow a specific word or passage, usually *influencing* its meaning or effect. [Or] the set of circumstances or facts that surround a particular event, situation" (Dictionary.com, 2020, bracketed and italics information added by author). Another very simple way to remember context is this: people, place and purpose.

How Deaf Culture Evolved

From the moment we are born, human beings are learning, first by looking around, imitating the smiles and gestures, later by mimicking the language we hear/see. dDeaf communities and sign languages were no different – they were the foundation to the formation of the Deaf-World. Historic and geographic conditions often isolated communities which resulted in distinct communities, this was especially true in rural locations. "It has become widely known that there is a Deaf-World in the United States, as in other nations, citizens whose primary language is...Sign Language...and who identify as members of that minority culture" (Lane, 2005, p. 291). Today, there are

> hundreds of sign languages are in use around the world today. While each is distinct, all use the shape, orientation, position, and movement of the hands, combined with subtle uses of facial expression and movement of the head and body (Schwartz, 2007, para. 2).

119

Chapter 8

NOTES

Residential schools throughout the United States and Canada were the places where North American dDeaf culture was born. Like the experiences and struggles of other minority groups, the dDeaf community evolved, along with their ways of communicating and interacting with each other – which is what we recognize as culture. The first dDeaf school in America opened in Hartford, Connecticut in 1817 and within 40 years of the opening, twenty other schools for the dDeaf had been established. By the turn of the century, more than fifty schools were operating in the US. These schools were complete communities with children sleeping in dormitories, taking meals together, attending classes and engaging in sports, social and religious activities outside of class. "As long as Deaf people have congregated in schools, clubs, and homes, they have passed down cultural patterns, values, and beliefs in the DEAF WORLD[1] from one generation to the next in something very much like an oral tradition" (Bauman, Nelson, & Rose, 2006, p. 21). Having come from scattered farms and small towns, they were immersed in the language and visual ways of turn-taking and interacting with other dDeaf children and adults. Deep, long-lasting friendships were formed and former students stayed in close contact with each other. It was fairly common for students who graduated from school to return to the same school as an employee, filling a variety of roles. Others returned to their schools as teachers after completing their education. By the 1860's, dDeaf teachers made up nearly 40 percent of the total number of teachers throughout the country.

Over the years, thousands of deaf children and youth came to these schools, spending years living and studying together. In the process, a new language was formed and the countless hours of interactions living in this intimate community resulted in the emergence of dDeaf culture, which has evolved over the years, enriched by each generation of students and the influence of dDeaf the communities that emerged in cities around the country. Over time, American dDeaf culture had produced folklore, poetry, storytelling and oratory; as well as games, jokes, naming customs, rituals of romance, and rules of etiquette and proper conduct – all enacted in a language fit for *people of the eye.* They have also organized politically to protect and promote their interests, formed local, state and national organizations, established newspapers and magazines, founded schools and gathered in churches where ASL was the language of song and sermon alike. The majority also found their spouses within the Deaf community.

This same experience can be found in the history of dDeaf people in countries around the world – clusters of people in India, China, Africa, South America, Australia who could not hear, found each other and over the years a culture and language evolved based on their *ways of being.*

The civil rights movement emerged in the US during the 1960's with marches, sit-ins and protests as tools for change, inspiring many minority groups, including members of the dDeaf community, to press for greater self-determination and economic opportunity. As the US population began to recognize and embrace cultural diversity, dDeaf people began to explore and express their cultural and linguistic identity more openly, as well as asserting their right to access information. A pivotal moment in dDeaf history occurred in 1988 when the Board of Trustees of Gallaudet University (composed entirely of individuals who could hear) appointed a hearing person as President. At the time, Gallaudet was 124 years old and of the six presidents who had served since its founding in 1864, none had been dDeaf. Not surprisingly, many people felt that it was long past time for a dDeaf person to be

---

[1] *The capitalized DEAF WORLD is used to reflect how it is signed in ASL. As used in Lane et al. (1996), it roughly translates as a way of life for those who are oriented visually.*

Mediating Ways of Being

NOTES

the chief administrator of the world's only liberal arts university for dDeaf students and overnight, hundreds of protesters challenged their decision. The protest, known Deaf President Now (DPN), was radical and revolutionary. After a week of protests that garnered unprecedented media attention and captured the imagination of millions of people in the US and around the world, the hearing presidential designate resigned, along with the Chair of the Board of Trustees, who was also a person who could hear. The Board then selected a dDeaf person to become the President of Gallaudet University and simultaneously selected another dDeaf person to become the Chair of the University's Board of Trustees.

A few weeks after the DPN revolution at Gallaudet University, hearings in the US legislature to discuss the Americans with Disabilities Acts (ADA) began. dDeaf people joined forces with the disability rights movement to push for passage of the 1990 civil rights law which resulted in their access to telecommunications, public events and interpreting services (Holcomb, 2013).

UNDERSTANDING dDEAF and NON-DEAF WAYS OF BEING

It is essential for interpreters to understand the _ways of being_ among those for whom they will interpret. Of course, this requires bilingual fluency in the languages used by each people group, which demands that interpreters understand rules that determine how that language is used, as well as the unwritten rules defining acceptable behavior. This includes, among a myriad of other elements how members of that culture interact with each other, take turns in conversations, interrupt, and change the ways they use language based on where they are or who is present. It also includes how they confirm understanding, and how they express emotions when communicating with others who share their communication norms. Furthermore, given the ever increasing multicultural reality in Canada and the US, interpreters will no doubt find themselves mediating communication with individuals whose roots can be found in East India, China, South America, or Africa. Because interpreters mediate cultural elements of interactions, in addition to the languages of those involved, they must continually be learning about the way members of various people groups express themselves. Almost all communication is contextualized, which requires we consider the various elements of communication – every setting and situation, including how loudly or softly people speak to one another, dynamics of power or lack of power between participants, accurate and appropriate sign choices, all of which influence the outcome of each communication.

In this text, we are focusing on communication between dDeaf and hearing individuals as it is mediated by a sign language interpreter. The tool that we use to communicate our cultural norms to each other is language (Mahadi, & Jafari, 2012). Armed with fluency in at least two languages and growing multicultural awareness, an interpreter must be able to "unwrap" the _intention_ of each question or comment expressed in one language and culture, and then re-wrap that message in the language and culture held by the person receiving the interpreted message. If done correctly the individuals communicating will understand one another and the _intended_ meaning of the questions, comments, and ideas will successfully be conveyed. The only way this type of mediation is possible is for interpreters to immerse themselves in the primary languages and cultures encountered in their work.

It is necessary that sign language interpreters become experts in communicating

121

Chapter 8

NOTES

the *mundane*. Learning how to *ask, say* and *tell* simple things in both of their working languages is essential; like asking for a phone number and address, giving directions or describing a person, building or location well enough for it to be recognized. Mastery of such things may seem ridiculous but these foundational skills pave the way for interpreting about sensitive and complex matters. The above language skills are noted areas of concern in the bulk of interpreting students. The authors have identified specific areas of concern in student interpreters, specifically, expressive and receptive fingerspelling, accurate production of the sign language number systems (e.g., height, age, ranking, etc.), use of space, classifier production, and correct depiction production which effectively communicates size, shape and amount, which in turn, aids in the identification of the details of the people or objects being described. As a student interpreter your cultural and language learning must be *intentional*. Simply because you are able to have effective conversations with people who are dDeaf does not mean you are adequately prepared to manage conversations that are infused with linguistic and cultural nuances, subtleties, and intimations. Often, the language skill of student interpreters or recent graduates has not reached the level of complexity to be called *superior* or *native-like*. As described in chapter 1, superior language skills enable an individual to have a rich, in-depth conversation that is full and natural with the ability to elaborate on a variety of topics (Newell & Caccamise, 2006).

Interpreters must learn how members of each people group extend condolences at the unexpected death of a child, seek advice about dating or marriage, ask the costs of one's car or home, warn others regarding the character of someone both parties know and hundreds of other types of messages. This knowledge is gained *intentionally*, it comes from watching, observing, and analyzing the details of how the language is used at such events as funerals, weddings, family and community gatherings. Such things are sacred and are difficult to teach in the classroom. Communication is not complete unless the very words and signs are wrapped in the fabric of culture – the *ways of being* – used by each people group. The interpretation must embody all of the nonverbal cues, such as the facial expression or tone of voice that conveys the *genuine meaning* behind the signs and words. As an interpreter, you cannot understand what another person really means unless you can correctly identify the attitude, thoughts and emotions behind each word or sign. Consider the look on someone's face, the angle of their body and the volume of their speech/size of the signs – all of which can convey heartache, concern, suspicion, or disinterest. It is important to be attentive to details, such as when someone signs very small or extremely large, interpreters must strive to determine the meaning and the intention of the signer's message. Is it the dDeaf person's desire to express anger, strong conviction, or maybe a sense of being threatened? The signed message likely has **emotive value** that will influence the meaning of the signs, which can indicate any range of emotional meaning, such as loss, sarcasm, pain, love, and so much more. *Emotive value* refers to the array of emotions visible in the communication, whether signed or spoken, it is most typically a nonverbal expression that influences the message meaning – it can be identified in a raised voice, pronounced facial expressions, or obvious posture change, etc.

It should be evident that cultural mediation is complex and multilayered. It is also important to recognize your limitations; even when people who share the same *ways of being* try to communicate, they sometimes need another member of their community to mediate the communication. Most often all participants have the same goals, the desire to communicate effectively and to understand each other's intentions.

Mediating Ways of Being

NOTES

In addition to learning and using each language (spoken and signed) accurately, interpreters must be able to recognize and apply the interactional norms or signals of those involved as they strive to correctly identify the *intended meaning* within each utterance. The formation of each expression may contain an embedded hesitation or a forthright delivery, whether it is overt or implied it is a manifestation of one's feelings. Often it is our *delivery* that carries the bulk of the meaning being communicated, the words are simply the avenue by which meaning is conveyed (Tannen, 1986). Linguists refer to the way people express meaning in a manner that is vague or non specific as *indirectness* (Tannen, 1986). Sapir (1956) insists that "every cultural pattern and every single act of social behaviour involves communication in either an explicit or implicit sense" (p. 104).

It is worth remembering that all behavior is communicative. We are consistently responding to the stimuli around us – reacting to our environment, to those around us, to messages we are receiving (blatant and subtle). Even choosing not to react is a response. All communication, whether expressed through words or nonverbal behavior, such as shrugging, refusing to make eye contact, or any number of other behaviors, communicates information. It is not uncommon for people to say one thing and mean something completely different. For example, a couple arguing because the husband forgot an important milestone in their relationship and he screams, "I'm sorry!" as he throws down the book he was holding to the floor. It is apparent that he is anything but sorry. You likely have already internalized many of these communication behaviors, it is important to intentionally consider them. Interpreters must learn all of these cultural and linguistic elements and what they mean in context. As a beginning interpreter, you *must* start your journey now, learning how each language and cultural group conveys and accomplishes their communication goals. Furthermore, Chase (1969) explains that the purposes of language involve communicating with others, thinking and shaping our personal point of view, as well as our outlook on life. In other words – to influence your view of the world (as cited in Mahadi, & Jafari, 2012).

A person's **worldview** contains everything they know about the world around them. Funk (2001) explains that worldview is fairly self-evident, and can be defined as, "an intellectual perspective on the world or universe" (para. 1). Some of the most powerful factors that shape our worldview is our ability to see, smell, hear, taste, and feel stimuli from the world and from ourselves (Funk, 2001). For a moment consider how your worldview would be shaped if you were visually focused, instead of being stimulated by sound; if manual communication was your norm, not speech. Following that logic, each communicative behavior, including getting another's attention, interrupting, commenting, questioning as well as the use of nonverbal behaviors used to communicate would likely all be different from those who did not share the same worldview. It should be evident that Sign Language Peoples, "worldview is implicit...and can be at least partially inferred from...[their] behavior" (Funk, 2001, para. 15). Consider the behavioral norms of the dDeaf community (especially as related communication), and how each of those behaviors demonstrates that the dDeaf community assuredly holds a different worldview.

Once you understand that people who are dDeaf think differently than people who can hear, you must take a deep dive to master the art of interpreting. Gaining an understanding of the cognitive processes and prerequisites for moving messages between cultures and languages will foster unhindered communication between members of the dDeaf and non-deaf community. In the discussion below, the authors will delineate some of the characteristics and features of each language

123

and the cultural knowledge required to mediate understanding between two or more individuals who have different *ways of being*.

Developing Your Mediation Skills

We have repeatedly talked about *people of the eye* and *people of sound* having different *ways of being*. On your journey to becoming an interpreter, you will take several classes to learn about dDeaf Culture, likely taught by members of the dDeaf community. Your educational program will also require you to spend a number of hours volunteering in the dDeaf community, attending dDeaf events, and encourage you to develop genuine friendships that will make it possible for you to ask the "tough questions." The authors suggest that you not limit yourself only to meeting those requirements but that you double or triple the hours required; consider it an investment in your future. Build relationships with some of the dDeaf individuals you meet and spend quality time with them which will also provide you with opportunities to seek clarification about things you are experiencing, as well as the meaning of some interactional norms.

A foundational requirement for every interpreter is knowing the differences in how dDeaf and hearing people *behave* and how those differences can be mediated. In the table below you will find multiple elements of cultural variation between dDeaf individuals and non-deaf individuals (see table 1). Your goal is to develop numerous ways in which an interpreter might mediate the cultural and linguistic variations during an interpreted interaction. Below you will be presented with several scenarios demonstrating interactional differences between people who are dDeaf and people who can hear, all of which you will likely encounter in your first few interpreting jobs

Use of names: inserted throughout the conversation; call each other by name to get attention [**low context**]	**Use of names**: shared the first time you meet, accompanied by one's name sign – of more interest is the other person's background. It is important to note that the *additional information is more important* than the person's actual name. Such as, where each grew up, went to school; determine if they have mutual friends and if either has other deaf people in their family, etc. [**high context**] Rarely use another person's name in conversation; instead indicate who they are talking about by pointing at them or if not present, in a space set up to represent that person, possibly followed by their sign name
Eye contact: a type of "glancing" eye contact is required throughout a conversation; prolonged, sustained eye contact often makes people feel uncomfortable – such staring can be interpreted as intimidating, flirtatious or may be perceived as a threat (or many other ways depending on context and participants) [**auditory**]	**Eye contact**: required throughout an interaction, not just looking at the signer, the person receiving the message will follow spatial indicators, such as signs, indexing, eye gaze; some responses are made by the type of eye movement used. The eye gaze of the signer will often follows in the direction the signer indicates (indexes) [**visual**]
Indication of engagement: minimal head nods, consistent vocalizing ("uh huh, right, wow", etc.) [**auditory**]	**Indication of engagement**: backchanneling,[2] nodding, occasional signs, affirmation of comprehension, other head movements to indicate questioning and clarifying, soliciting more detail, etc. is expected *(required)* throughout the interaction. If one person keeps breaking eye contact without explaining why, others will be suspicious of them [**visual**]

Table 1

[2] **Backchanneling** *refers to the subtle, yet deliberate responses from a listener during a dialogue (or interpretation), including but not limited to non-verbal responses (affirmation, negation, comprehension, inquiry, etc.). Such behaviors indicate that the listener is understanding, backchanneling also indicates when participants do not understand (frowning, shaking their head, etc.).*

Mediating Ways of Being

NOTES

Now, let's consider several interpreting scenarios in light of the above norms and behaviors. You are the interpreter who will interpret in various settings between the dDeaf person and a person who can hear (the hearing person has some degree of status. This is their first meeting and first impressions are important on both sides; as the interpreter, you have considerable responsibility to mediate the dialogue and cultural elements to generate a positive communication environment. The following examples could be any one-on-one meeting, perhaps a parent-teacher conference, meeting with the realtor to find a home, talking with a lawyer about a legal matter, etc.

Scenario One: A dDeaf individual has made an appointment with a realtor to inquire about buying a home. The appointment was made through a video relay service (VRS). The dDeaf individual (named Charles) arrives at Keith's realtor office, accompanied by a female interpreter – who begins interpreting immediately.

Charles: *"Hello, I'm Charles White, but you can call me Charlie…I'm here for my 2:30 appointment."* The real estate agent looks from Mr. White to the young woman and back again. He is puzzled, as she just introduced herself as Charles White.*

Keith: *"Yes…umm I'm Keith Jones, happy to meet you," putting his hand out toward the interpreter, since she introduced herself as Charlie. Rather than shake the realtor's hand, the interpreter gestures toward Charlie who extends his hand.**

Confused, the realtor gestures toward his desk and the three of them move in that direction. Without asking or explaining why, the interpreter grabs one of the chairs in front of the desk and moves it to the side of the desk, closest to Keith.* Once again, Keith is uncertain why this is happening.

Keith: *"How can I help you?" With the interpreter giving words to his response, Charlie responds with a 5-minute history of his life* – the states and cities where he has lived, the kinds of homes he has owned, what has brought him to this city and finally signs,*

Charles: *"I want to buy a condo near the beach." Keith, relieved to finally get an answer to his question, says,*

Keith: *"I can help with that. How much of a down payment do you have and what's your range on monthly payments?"* Charlie doesn't respond – he is suddenly suspicious of this stranger who has asked several personal questions without sharing anything about himself or his background before jumping right to business.*

In the scenario there are several asterisks (*), each asterisk represents a decision the interpreter made, which could have been handled differently – please discuss what the interpreter could have done and identify your main concern(s).

What went wrong? Tannen (1986) explains that the "danger of misinterpretation is greatest, of course, among speakers who actually speak different native tongues, or come from different cultural backgrounds, because cultural differences necessarily implies different assumptions about natural and obvious ways to be polite" (p. 41). The previous scenario is an example of cross cultural conflict; both the dDeaf and hearing person have the same goal, but significantly different communication expectations about how to achieve them. Without appropriate mediation, the goals and expectations remain unmet causing an unnecessary breakdown in

125

communication and possible negative perceptions of each other. All of which could have been avoided had the interpreter received proper training.

It is evident that, as the interpreter, our presence and purpose in the real estate meeting as the interpreter is very different from the other participants. Yet, when interpreters adopt behaviors that are unique and different from the other participants present, we hinder communication rather than foster it (Lee & Llewellyn-Jones, 2011). It must be understood that "the 'role of [the] interpreter' as a discrete rigid construct has been used historically in ways that actually inhibit (rather than facilitate) interaction amongst participants" (Lee & Llewellyn-Jones, 2011, p. 1). Let's examine the scenario, and consider what the interpreter could have done differently:

Concerns in Scenario One:

- Lack of introductions. Introductions are key – they enable everyone to know *who* is present and *why* they are there. Since this appointment was made through VRS, Keith probably had no real understanding of what *interpreting services* meant. Again, because there were limited introductions, the realtor knew who Charlie was, but not who the interpreter was or why she was there (introductions can also include a brief description of her responsibilities as the interpreter).
- The interpreter attempted to be "invisible," further hindered genuine communication. Instead of avoiding that handshake, she could have used it as a way to introduce herself and the dDeaf participant. Instead her avoidance of Keith's extended hand is interpreted as a rude and dismissive behavior in the American hearing culture.
- Moving the furniture in a person's personal workspace is only acceptable with permission. She assumed it was her prerogative to do so, however her action was likely viewed as disrespectful and rude. If the interpreter felt it necessary to move the chair, she could simply have asked for permission.
- High context cultures are information rich; which is not typical in low context cultures like mainstream hearing culture in the US and Canada. A potential solution to manage Charlie's "history" would be to begin interpreting with a transition such as, "Allow me to give you a little background before we get down to business…"

Let's examine additional differences interpreters may encounter when mediating meaning, culture and behaviors between Deaf and non-deaf individuals.

Turn Taking

Turn-taking rules and expectations are dictated by one's culture. Those norms govern how and when turns are to be taken, they include verbal or nonverbal indicators which function as the *transitional rules* of communication signaling when to take turns. The rules are often influenced by location, participants, status, as well as the various roles held by the participants.

People of Sound

Turn taking is often based on sound, or sometimes lack of sound. In an interaction with just 2 or 3 people, in a doctor's office for example, when a person has finished asking their question or making their comment, there is a pause – silence, signaling the others in the room that this is their opportunity to say or ask something, should they choose. If the silence is more than a few seconds, the doctor or lawyer will begin talking.

Mediating Ways of Being

NOTES

In a larger gathering, perhaps 6-12 people, a physical indication is given by the person who wants to make a comment – they may slide to the front of their chair, slightly raise their hand, or make a guttural sound. As a result, the others present will turn their attention to that individual. This may include verbal recognition (e.g., "Dave, did you want to say something?") or may include making a sound to break the silence (a cough or clearing the throat). When that happens, the message conveyed is, "It's your turn to speak." In a conversation between two or more people, if there are a few seconds of silence, the person in the conversation who has more status or seniority will often use that opportunity to claim the floor and start talking. People who can hear typically have little tolerance for a lull in the conversation.

In a large meeting where people who can hear have gathered, they will often raise their hands to indicate a desire to speak. The moderator will typically call the name of the person to whom the "turn" is being given. If they don't know that person's name, the person leading the meeting will make a gesture – perhaps a head nod or pointing in the direction of the person being acknowledged, In a large venue, microphones may be required, sometimes the speaker will move to a mic or the mic is handed to the speaker.

People of the Eye

Turn taking is based on visual signals, regardless of the number of people present. Since dDeaf culture demands fairly sustained eye contact when communicating, the person who has been commenting will likely break eye contact, which is a pronounced signal that they are finished with their comment. In a small group of 3-5 people, this could be as simple as an eye blink or a shift in eye gaze, accompanied by a short pause. When others see that signal, the next speaker will get the attention of the others in the room, adding something to the topic that was just being addressed or changing the topic altogether.

When a group ranges in size from 10-15 people, the shift of turns requires a visual gesture indicating that someone wants a turn to share their ideas or perspective on what is being discussed. In a group of this size, people who are dDeaf will typically gather in a circle or in a way that allows everyone to see what is being signed without straining. Since they are more or less able to see each other, they may wave to indicate the desire to add something to the discussion. If someone is particularly *eager* to jump into the interaction, they may move their raised arms and hands for others to see. Once all eyes have turned to them, they will start signing their comments.

However, in formal meetings people who are dDeaf would likely raise their hand to indicate they want to speak and, to assure everyone can see, they would walk to the place where everyone is focused (e.g., a stage or raised platform). If the room or group is medium sized and room is set up so it is easy to shift your gaze to see all participants, the dDeaf person wanting to add something may simply stand at their seat, turning their body so everyone can see what they are saying. This process may actually take a bit longer because the person who is taking a turn to address those present is required to position themselves in a place where everybody can see them before they start signing, which could mean moving to the front of the room or walk up on the stage/platform.

Mediating Non-Verbal Signals and Turn Taking

Turn taking can be quite awkward, especially in a mixed group of dDeaf and hearing

127

people. This is especially true when the person who can hear has little or no experience interacting with people who are dDeaf. This is quite evident in one-on-one or small group interactions. When a doctor or accountant finishes asking a question, they are expecting the dDeaf individual to respond. It is very possible that in the absence of a visual cue, the dDeaf patient or client may not realize they are expected to respond, resulting in an award pause.

However, when an interpreter in present and mediates turn taking with facial expressions, a head nod indicating, "your turn" or by overtly signing "it's your turn" all of which will keep the interaction flowing smoothly. Similarly, when the dDeaf individual asks a question, the interpreter needs to use the appropriate vocal intonations to indicate a response is expected. Sometimes one participant makes a statement and pauses without indicating a question, but from a cultural stance is waiting for the other person to agree or add their perspective. In that case, the interpreter needs to convey, whether through speaking or signing, a cue for the other person to respond. For example, the hearing individual may respond, "Hmm, I guess that could be one option." If the dDeaf participant doesn't respond, the interpreter may "interpret" the pondering or inquiry with facial expressions and sign, "What do you think?" or "Would that work for you?"

It is also common for cultures to use non-verbal signals, gestures or facial expressions to communicate. One such example – in some formal settings standing and clapping hands (hearing) or waving hands (dDeaf). In most settings, participants can indicate nonverbally (1) understanding and comprehension, (2) agreement, or (3) disagreement. This can be particularly challenging when dDeaf and non-deaf interact. People who are dDeaf and people who can hear both use the nodding to indicate agreement and the shaking of the head to indicate disagreement. Those head nods and shakes are sometimes slight and at other times, quite pronounced – depending on the setting. The addition of facial expressions and body language can exacerbate the nonverbal message being delivered.

However, when indicating understanding or comprehension, people who can hear typically make verbal utterances (mmm, uh-huh, hmmm) that coincide with the nodding. Furthermore, hearing people may not always attend to the person speaking; they may be writing notes or looking at their computer. Head nodding or shaking seems to occur more often in one-on-one interactions, such as counseling, legal consultation or medical appointments.

Whereas dDeaf people are more likely to use the *same* intentional or overt head nods and shakes to confirm understanding and comprehension as they do to indicate agreement or disagreement. This can be quite deceptive, and confusing especially for uninitiated hearing people. In moments like this it is important to rely on a competent sign language interpreter to accurately mediate meaning. It is not uncommon for a dDeaf individual to momentarily break eye contact and make a pensive side-to-side head shake – indicating a lack of clarity or small up and down head nods to indicate comprehension. These indicators typically grow in size the more a person understands or does not understand what is said or if they want to add a comment or opinion on the topic.

Scenario Two: As the interpreter, your interpreting choices will be influenced by the number of participants. Imagine that you are in a doctor's office and the physician is explaining some test results to the dDeaf patient, using a mix of lay language and professional verbiage – the patient is maintaining steady eye contact while shaking

Mediating Ways of Being

NOTES

their head slowly with a pensive look on their face, brows slightly furrowed. As you look at the dDeaf patient, would you assume they were stunned at the results, doubting what they were hearing, not understanding the complex explanation of the doctor, or possibly more than one of these options? You need to be careful before putting voice to that reaction, yet the physician is reading meaning into those head movements.

Considerations for Scenario Two:

- You might wait, hoping the professional will ask what the dDeaf patient is thinking or feeling. You may choose to pose a side comment or question to the dDeaf individual to clarify the meaning of this nonverbal response. For example, shifting your upper body and head movement while signing in a small space, "ME CLEAR? DOCTOR TALK, MY SIGNS CLEAR – MAKE SENSE?"[3] The dDeaf patient may or may not respond, but your desire to confirm comprehension might give them the opportunity to say what is happening. It may be wise to inform the doctor that you sought clarification regarding *your interpretation.*

- The dDeaf individual may respond directly to you. They may start signing clearly, using normal signing space, addressing you as the interpreter but due to the *conversational size* of the signs, you need to interpret what is being signed to the doctor. If you did not inform the doctor that you asked the patient about the clarity of your interpretation, you may need to couch the interpretation by informing the physician, "I just asked if my signs were clear and made sense." Then offer the interpretation, even if it is directed to you.

- It is worth noting that if they received bad news, their utterances may not be clear, rather their signs may be jumbled and difficult to comprehend. This will not surprise the doctor; they deal with these kinds of conversations every day. As the interpreter, this is not a time to stop the dDeaf patient and ask them to spell a word again or repeat something because you didn't understand it. In that event, it may be best to transition into third person or the role of a *narrator*; describing to the best of your ability what they are signing, and narrating his message "he is talking about his daughter, something about she warned him…" he appears to be trailing off. This will convey critical information to the physician regarding the mental and emotional state of the patient

Scenario Three: *In another case, you might be interpreting a business meeting between three or four supervisors, one of whom is dDeaf. The boss is discussing the financial situation the company is facing and the likelihood of layoffs. The dDeaf supervisor is nodding his head emphatically, indicating his comprehension. When the boss turns to him and says,*

Boss: *"So you agree then. We are laying off the five dDeaf employees tomorrow,"* to which the dDeaf participant reacts strongly,

dDeaf Supervisor: *"NO! No, that isn't right. There has to be another way. At the very least you should lay off some of the hearing employees as well!"* The boss is caught off guard, because he had been interpreting the head nods as an expression of agreement and the meeting turns into unpredicted chaos.

Considerations for Scenario Three:

Perhaps, if the interpreter had been voicing utterances of comprehension, such as "Oh…uh, really? I see…yeah…" as the boss was explaining the company concerns.

---

[3] When writing one language (ASL) in another language (English), it is referred to as gloss. It is not an attempt to interpret the language. Rather it is an attempt to write it down, to represent the signs in text form, this is typically done in all capital letters.

The boss would not have been blindsided, nor would he have misinterpreted the head nods as affirmation and support. The resulting cultural conflict likely could have been avoided with a few well-timed expressions of concern, rather than unintentional passive agreement. Then the employer would not have been taken by surprise at the dDeaf employee's reaction to the decision to lay off the dDeaf employees. What are additional ways that the interpreter could have managed the above situation? Take the time to consider all possible options, both good and bad.

The various scenarios presented here are only a few examples where an interpreter's ability to recognize potential cultural misunderstandings and finding appropriate ways to mediate those cultural differences can build cross cultural understanding. The authors encourage you to journal your thoughts, ideas and feelings about the numerous cultural realities you will learn about, but more importantly those situations you experience as you interact at large and small dDeaf events. We anticipate you will see interactions and reactions that may puzzle you. Those could be due to interpersonal relationships, rather than cultural norms, but a majority of those instances that confound you are likely to have a cultural component. Learning a new culture – the habits, norms, prohibitions and celebrations, takes years. Enjoy the journey!

chapter *Review*

This chapter addresses some of the deeper elements of the interpreting process and provides essential scenarios to help broaden your ability to mediate cultures. Armed with the knowledge of this chapter, the review below will continue to reinforce what you have gleaned.

Terms to Know

- **Contextualized/Context:** People, place and purpose, it is not possible to determine the *meaning* of things in any language unless you have an understanding of the culture and the language because together they give words and signs their meaning. Remember that words and signs occur in a specific time and place with certain people, that would be the context.

- **Emotive Value:** Refers to the array of emotions visible in the communication, whether signed or spoken, it can be identified in a raised voice, pronounced facial expressions, or obvious posture.

- **Mediate/Mediation:** Enables citizens from differing cultural and linguistic communities to come together to foster personal interaction, communication and understanding; mediation can help dissolve psychological and social barriers that exclude certain people groups (Pronovost, & Harrison-Boisvert, 2015).

- **Worldview:** contains everything they know about the world around them. Funk (2001) explains that worldview is fairly self-evident, and can be defined as, "an intellectual perspective on the world or universe" (para. 1).

Mediation for sign language interpreters addresses both:

- Culture
- Language

Emotive Value is visible during most communication, such as:

- Sarcasm
- Loss
- Love
- Pain
- Facial expressions

Scenario – interpreters impact situations. Don't forget to:

- Introduce yourself (be polite)
- Provide a brief explanation if the participant hasn't worked with an interpreter before
- Recognize your impact (you're not invisible)
- Ask before touching/moving/rearranging things to belong to someone else
- Recognize cultural differences (e.g., explanation and details)

Writing Prompt: Funk (2001) explains that *"one's worldview is also referred to as one's philosophy, philosophy of life, mindset, outlook on life, formula for life, ideology, faith, or even religion. [Furthermore,] the elements of your worldview are highly interrelated; it is almost impossible to speak of one element independently of the others"* (para. 13 & 15). *Spend time considering your worldview – "very few people take the time to thoroughly think out, much less articulate, their worldview"* (para 15).

In the space below, please take the time to write about your worldview and the various elements that have shaped your view of the world. Consider the impact that your senses (taste, hear, see, feel and smell) have had on your life. Consider things like art, plays, music, a delicious meal, the color and smell of roses, and the nature all around you – these elements are all related to your senses. Spend time thinking about the value you place on your spiritual, mental, physical and familial parts of your life.

Mediating Ways of Being

NOTES

TERMS TO KNOW:

- Stakeholders
- Dynamic Equivalence
- Linguistic Fluency
- Second Language, L2, or B-language
- Bilingualism
- C-language
- Paralinguistics
- Processing Time
- Transliteration
- Interpretation
- Translation
- Sight Translation
- Modality
- Simultaneous Interpretation
- Consecutive Interpretation
- Sign-To-Voice
- Voice-To-Sign
- ASL Modality
- Prosodic Features
- Prelinguistic Formulation
- Miscue

9 | Interpreting Process Models

Interpreters are professional communicators, which means they must possess the ability to understand each person they work alongside and the subtle differences unique to their personal communication styles. There are additional elements under the umbrella term *professional communicator,* referring "to the various forms of speaking, listening, writing, and responding carried out both in and beyond the workplace, whether in person or electronically" (Nordquist, 2018, para. 1). It is evident that sign language interpreters need expertise in two or more languages, which also includes the multiple modes of language expression, (i.e., writing, reading, signing and speaking).

The term *professional,* as applied to sign language interpreters, has been thoroughly examined and the following list will "delineate the major skills, fields of knowledge and attributes that underlie competent professional interpreting practice" (Johnson, Witter-Merithew, & Taylor, 2004, p. 2). The process of identifying these requirements involved numerous **stakeholders**[1] and the engagement of multiple perspectives in order to develop a reliable and inclusive description of a *professional* sign language interpreter. *Stakeholders* can include any "individual or group that has an interest in any decision or activity of an organization" (ISO 26000 cited in American Society for Quality, 2020, para 1). Due to space, the major areas of competence identified for interpreters are listed below (without subheadings) and the link to the complete document is cited in the chapter review. As professionals, we expect standards to reflect an appropriate level of competency for those who want to enter the interpreting profession. "These competency-based standards are driven by a vision of what is required for competent interpreting practice and grounded in the day-to-day experience of practitioners" (Johnson, et al., 2004, p. 2). Though it does not have to be said, it shall be said to remove any doubt – the work of sign language interpreting is so much more than exchanging messages between people who are dDeaf and people who can hear. This is a complex linguistic and cultural approach to message comprehension and production which includes "a million little decisions," (B. Colonomos, personal communications, Fall 2014).

The identified list of competencies below, if incorporated into the life of an individual, will provide a quality foundation for anyone who wants to become a sign

---

[1] *Stakeholders in the sign language community would include anyone who has a vested interest in the topic, activity, or service of the profession; in this case, it would include students of interpreting, interpreters, members of the dDeaf, dDDb communities, those who employ interpreters, policy makers, organizational leaders, parents, institutions that teach interpreter education, etc.*

Interpreting Process Models

NOTES

language interpreter. It is essential to have a well rounded education, an understanding of the world, effective people skills, knowledge of the languages being used (ASL/English-Spanish, etc.), and possessing the skills to proficiently interpret in those languages. Johnson, et al., (2004) provides student interpreters with a quality resource which is focused on developing identified competency-based standards:

- **Domain 1: Theory and Knowledge Competencies:** Identifies competencies which embody the academic foundation and world knowledge essential to effective interpretation (p. 4).
- **Domain 2: Human Relations Competencies:** Identifies competencies which foster effective communication and productive collaboration with colleagues, consumers, and employers (p. 5).
- **Domain 3: Language Skills Competencies:** Identifies competencies that relate to the use of American Sign Language and English (p. 6).
- **Domain 4: Interpreting Skills Competencies:** Identifies competencies related to effective ASL-English interpretation in a range of subject matter in a variety of settings (p. 7).
- **Domain 5: Professionalism Competencies:** Identifies competencies are related to required professional standards and practices (p. 8).

Historically, students, recent graduates (and some seasoned interpreters) have struggled with the above listed competencies. As practitioners we need to look at ourselves holistically; examining our beliefs about what it means to be a professional and the values associated with having that status. Simply put, to be a professional means that (1) you are worthy of the trust that participants give you, (2) you possess knowledge and skills worthy of hire, and (3) you are responsible for maintaining the standard of professional and moral behavior (Humphrey, 1999). Understanding your professional values will help guide you as you learn about the various approaches to the interpreting process, something we refer to as Process Models. [2]

In this chapter we will look at the nuts and bolts of communication that is mediated by an interpreter, because the people attempting to exchange ideas and information not only have different ways of communicating – but they also have different *ways of being.* Communication is not solely about the signs or words used to construct sentences, paragraphs or stories. Genuine communication requires understanding the *spirit* or *intention* behind each question or comment – understanding the implications carried by the signs and words. Interpreting is about mediating communication between people using different ways of conveying respect, doubt, curiosity, excitement and hurt. An interpreter is a bridge between different individuals sharing ideas, feelings and information wrapped in their unique *ways of being* (Cokely, 2008). Effective interpreters are able to look beyond both the signs used, and words spoken, to convey the message, uncovering the intention being expressed, and then presenting the intended meaning to the doctor, teacher, or police officer, in such a way that conveys an *equivalent* message to the individual coming from a different language and culture. It is important to note that accuracy and equivalency are closely related but not synonymous. Interpreters can render a message that is accurate but not equivalent. The idea of **dynamic equivalence** has been defined as,

---

[2]*The authors of this text are designating a new convention, the capitalization of "Process Models" to address them as an entity created by professionals (Colonomos, Cokely, etc.) in the field of interpreting. The use of "Process Models" informs the readers that the act of interpreting should be done in accordance with one of the designated models.*

Chapter 9

NOTES

maintaining the speaker's intended interaction with an impact on the audience; when accomplished in an interpretation, the speaker's goals and level of audience involvement is the same for both the audience who received the message in its original form and the audience who received the message through an interpreter (Humphrey & Alcorn, 2007).

You may have noticed that some of these ideas and concepts have been introduced in previous chapters and will be used in this chapter. The authors assume there is no reason to repeat those terms here however there are additional terms directly related to the work of interpreting that will be addressed.

TERMINOLOGY

Linguistic Fluency: These terms refer to an individual's strongest language and includes, *native language, first language, mother tongue, L1* or *A-language.* This is almost always the language in which one is most fluent, capable of discussing a variety of topics for numerous purposes and across various social interactions. It is *usually* the language used by one's parents, although this is not always the case. One's native language is usually the language they feel most comfortable playing with, bending the rules and in which they have little, if any, trouble deciphering subtle nuances and degrees of meaning. Of course, the way most individuals speak their A-language will be influenced by a regional or geographic accent: a Tennessee twang, a New York accent, etc.

For dDeaf individuals in the US, American Sign Language (ASL) is usually the language of preference but *technically* only those children born dDeaf into a family with dDeaf lineage whose home language is ASL can claim ASL as their *native language.* Children born deaf to families whose home language is a spoken language, like English, Chinese, Japanese or Spanish, are not *typically* exposed to naturally occurring visual language or to fluent signed language users until they are 2 or 3 years old. The same is true of dDeaf children in Quebec where the native sign language is Langue de Signes Quebecoise, or LSQ. Like individuals who can hear who develop a regional accent, dDeaf children who grow up in the US will encounter regionally distinct signing patterns and signed vocabulary. Those who acquire ASL in one region can testify to the underlying similarity of signs and grammatical structure of ASL in those regions, yet specific terminology (signs) will vary. The authors encourage interpreting students to include entries in your student journals recording those variations as you come across them.

Second language, L2 or B-language: These terms refer to acquisition of a second language, typically acquired by living in another country for several years or by having an immersive experience with a language other than your mother tongue. Second language users often have a noticeable accent when they use a second language (McDermid, 2014). On the other hand, if you have acquired a B-language by interacting frequently with a community of people using that language, you will most likely be able to carry on conversations in a variety of settings on various topics, although you will probably be challenged by subject-specific terminology, like auto mechanics, linguistics, or nursing, for example. Second language learners are usually a stranger to some of the subtleties and nuances of meaning in their second language, as well as some forms of humor – particularly playing with the language (Bell, 2007). Bilingual competency is a must for sign language interpreters and developing superior or near native skills in both of your working languages is essential.

Interpreting Process Models

NOTES

Bilingualism: Maftoon, & Shakibafar, (2011) define bilingualism as "the native-like control of two languages" (p. 80). Haugen (1953) goes further and explains that bilingualism is the "ability to produce 'complete meaningful utterances in the other language'" (cited in Mackey, 2000, p. 22). The key word in the definition is *meaningful* – is the utterance comprehensible and is it produced with native elements? However to make matters more confusing, "defining exactly who is or is not bilingual is essentially elusive" (Baker cited in Maftoon, & Shakibafar, 2011, p. 79). Defining bilingualism may be difficult and it may have more to do with determining the essential linguistic criteria of bilingualism which likely include fluency, grammar and overall production.

C-language: This term refers to one who has "picked up" some phrases and simple utterances in a language other than their first or second language. Often, one can comprehend some of what is being spoken or signed in their C-language, but they typically have great difficulty making themselves understood in that third language. Attempts to communicate are often "heavily accented" and the grammar rarely follows their third language. However, those who are truly multilingual demonstrate obvious competence in each of their languages.

Paralinguistics: The auditory, visual or physical elements associated with signed or spoken messages, which convey additional information above and beyond the words spoken. In spoken languages, one might express affect or emotion by raising their voice and frowning to show anger or a soft and loving facial expression to show affection, In signed language, one might express those emotions by signing larger and with more force to show anger; they might produce the signs in a softer, more gentle manner with facial affect showing affection to accompany loving words. Other paralinguistic information could be used to communicate status, frustration, curiosity, or power, to name a few.

Processing Time: The time used by an interpreter to complete an analysis of the source language (SL) utterance and to search for cultural and linguistic equivalents before producing a message in the target language (TL).

Transliteration: The result of taking a SL message, identifying the meaning, goal and intent of the speaker by analyzing the linguistic and paralinguistic elements of the message, and expressing that message in a different form or mode of the same language (e.g. PSE or Signed English to spoken English). In essence the SL and TL are the same, but the mode of transmission is different (this explanation refers to how the term is used in the field of sign language interpretation).

Interpretation: The result of taking a SL message, identifying the meaning of the affective layer, words or signs used, as well as the signer's/speaker's intent by analyzing the linguistic and paralinguistic elements of the message, then presenting a cultural and linguistic equivalent of the original text produced in the intended TL. *Quality interpreting* is not possible if the interpreter does not possess bilingual competence in both of their working languages.

Translation: This is generally done over time and typically with 2 or more persons involved in the development of a translation of a frozen text (written or video) into another language. This is currently an emerging field for dDeaf individuals (e.g. videotaped translations of textbooks, plays and poems) (Forestal & Cole, 2018). Deaf Missions of Iowa, for example, has recently completed a 40-year project of the translation of the Bible into American Sign Language, referred to as the ASLV

135

(American Sign Language Version). Multiple translation teams were used over those years, always with a dDeaf individual with expertise in American Sign Language and Deaf culture working with experts in Hebrew, Greek and Aramaic languages. After each book was translated it was reviewed by a broad selection of dDeaf community members to confirm that the translation was clear, accurate, natural and acceptable.

Sight Translation: Unlike genuine translation, sight translation happens in the moment. Sight translation usually renders a written document into signed language but at times, an interpreter might be asked to write in English a signed text. Sight translation is typically done "on the spot" with little-to-no advanced notice or preparation. This happens when a dDeaf individual asks an interpreter to "explain" a written text whether in English, Spanish or another language. It is not uncommon for an interpreter to be asked to do a sight translation of medical history forms at a doctors office, directions for taking medication, maybe even a personal letter. There may be times when a dDeaf individual may ask the interpreter to write their signed utterances in English to give to their boss or neighbor. The dDeaf person is asking for an "interpretation" of a printed document into the signed language they understand or a written version of something they need to communicate to a person who can hear.

Modality: The physical aspects required to produce each language; often referred to as the method or channel through which a message is expressed, specifically English is auditory/oral while American Sign Language is visual/spatial.

Simultaneous Interpretation: "Is defined as the process of interpreting into the target language at the same time as the source language is being delivered" (Russell, 2005, p. 136).

Consecutive Interpretation: "Is defined as the process of interpreting after the speaker or signer has completed one or more ideas in the source language and pauses while the interpreter transmits that information into the target language" (Russell, 2005, p. 136).

Sign-To-Voice: Interpreting signed messages from the source language into a spoken target language.

Voice-To-Sign: Interpreting from a spoken source language into a signed target language.

THE WORK OF INTERPRETERS

The goal of an interpreter is to support communication between individuals who have different languages and come from different cultural backgrounds; oftentimes the person providing these services is referred to as an interpreter regardless of whether they are providing interpretation or transliteration services.

One-on-One Interactions: This refers to a dDeaf individual meeting with a person who can hear. This designation identifies the number of people in the interaction, but it is a bit of a misnomer since these interactions often involve two-on-one and three-on-one situations. Examples include: an appointment with a real estate agent, a consultation with a doctor, dentist, potential employer, a minister – there is no end to the list. Typically, these encounters involve dialogue, back-and-forth

Interpreting Process Models

NOTES

communication, often with one person having special knowledge or experience of some kind. The purpose of a one-on-one encounter can range from an attempt to comfort, confront, inquire, scold, or discipline, among unlimited other possibilities.

Small Groups: This term also includes many types of interactions and may involve between three to twelve individuals. This could be a group counseling session, a staff meeting, a small training or seminar. Typically, there will be more hearing than Deaf clients in such a setting, although this is not always the case. The goals are quite varied, including informing, advising, teaching, explaining, and planning, among others. In a small group setting, the turn-taking is often more rapid than one-on-one events, making interpretation more challenging. As in other settings, the interpreter must deal with intake and analysis of the SL utterances and production of a linguistic and cultural equivalent into the target language. In addition, in small group settings the interpreter must indicate who is speaking, convey the emotional overlay of utterances, shift back and forth between sign-to-voice and voice-to-sign interpretation – and do all of this within the constraints of sometimes rapid-fire turn-taking. This is probably one of the more difficult settings in which to interpret due to the rapid and overlapping turn-taking, thus more experienced interpreters, rather than beginning level interpreters, are encouraged to work in this type of setting. For this reason, the use of a team of interpreters is more effective than a single interpreter. This allows interpreters to share the work, allowing overlapping comments to be interpreted unless the leader or moderator chooses to enforce a contributor be recognized before sharing their comment.

Group Settings: Medium-to-large groups can range from 20 to 50, or even more participants. In this setting, you will typically find one person leading the event, often standing in front of those attending. The type of language used and the role of the interpreter is different than in one-on-one or small group events. This could be an annual meeting for all employees at a large company or a large parent-teacher conference. Due to the size of the audience, the speaker typically stands on a platform or stage, makes use of a microphone, large screen video in order to be seen and/or heard. This type of interchange often follows the linguistic and turn-taking rules for consultative or formal interactions. Interaction between the speaker and the audience is structured, following a typical question and answer format. If interaction is allowed, people are likely to raise their hand and wait until they are called on. The language used in this setting often has more complex syntactic structures and specific vocabulary. The purpose of these events ranges from educating, entertaining, informing, inspiring, and/or convincing.

Preparation is critical at all times, but in this type of setting preparation can be more crucial because of the high probability of specialized terminology. Gathering the information may take time but needs to be a priority. For example, an interpreter is often able to get a program or agenda some time before the event is scheduled. However, getting the notes, PowerPoint or outline from the speaker should be done in advance of the event as it may be more difficult to get the speaker to share their notes. Such events typically have someone responsible for the program and they may have a summary of the presentation which they can share or they can reach out to the presenter on behalf of the interpreters. It is highly recommended that you conduct a search for the presenter online. This may provide you with an idea of the presenter's style, language and general demeanor – you may also locate a previous presentation made by the same individual that may be on a similar topic. If you are fortunate, you may be able to secure a copy of the speech, sermon, text or presentation prior to the event. Even if this advanced

137

Chapter 9

NOTES

preparation is not possible, the interpreter can sometimes meet with the presenter before the start of the presentation, during which time the speaker's goal can be identified, along with a verbal outline of the presentation to come. New interpreters should be cautious about accepting this type of job unless you are teamed with an experienced co-interpreter. This is the type of setting where hearing interpreters should be promoting the use of a dDeaf Interpreter.

MEDIATED LANGUAGE

It is important to understand that each language and culture has specific ways to manage communication and to accomplish specific linguistic goals or tasks. For that reason, we will look at communication in action.

ASL Modality: As a visual and spatial language, American Sign Language is time-oriented, based on visual perception and the physical conveyance of ideas, information and *feeling concepts* (Humphrey and Acorn, 2007). ASL uses the arms, wrists, hands, face, eyes, head and the torso of the signer to physically produce messages, which are articulated in the space in front of the signer (approximately from shoulder to shoulder width during one-on-one interactions), and is easily perceived visually by the individuals to whom the message is being sent (Klima, & Bellugi, 1979). More specifically, ASL uses *movement* as the medium of communication, producing a series of rule-based hand signals (signs), accompanied by **prosodic features**, such as rule-governed facial and physical markers (non-manual signals), with requisite eye contact and eye-indexing norms (Winston, 2000).

> Prosody is the combination of features in any language that produces the rhythm, accent, and "feel" of the language. In ASL, prosody is a visual spatial image, created by several features. These features include head and body movements, eyebrow movement, mouth movement, speed of signing, sign formation, pacing, and pausing (Winston, 2000, p. 1).

The linguistic rules of American Sign Language, and other signed languages, use visual-spatial elements to create messages expressed with a type of fluency allowing ASL articulation to flow in a manner that maintains clarity, and fosters comprehension by those receiving signed messages while, allowing a timely delivery, thereby avoiding undue visual fatigue. Since the physical articulators of ASL are larger than those used for vocal articulation, the production of signs has longer production time in comparison to the time required for the utterance of English words (Wilber, 2009). In spite of these differences, ASL transmits the same *amount* of information as English in the same length of time (Isenhath, 1990). This is particularly important when considering the significance of receiving information visually, as opposed to auditorily. Unlike the ears, the eyes are operated by muscles that tire with extended use. This is significant because eyes can perceive and process numerous linguistic elements – which enables competent American Sign Language users to identify and convey subtle, nuanced elements simultaneously.

It is important to realize that every sentence is made of various elements, some are overt while others are far more subtle. The signs used in a sentence are more explicit while eye gaze or affect are often (though not always) more implicit. For example if an individual emphatically signs "SATISFIED," while simultaneously shaking their head from side-to-side and rolling their eyes and concluding the sentence by exhaling loudly to indicate their complete dissatisfaction, this utterance

Interpreting Process Models

NOTES

could be interpreted in several ways, including *"I am not satisfied in any way!"*

In the above example, the dDeaf individual used an utterance composed of only one *content element* (SATISFIED) combined with *prosodic elements* – shaking his head from side-to-side, rolling their eyes and a loud exhalation. This message was conveyed in ways that took advantage of the *multifaceted* nature of American Sign Language (Cokely, 1985). Some of the facets we see in typical signed communication are emphasized pauses, physical movement (stepping forward or backward), exaggerated eye movement, signs or facial expressions – all conveying information about how the signer felt about his experience which is conveyed through a single content element and prosodic features.

By comparison, the spoken interpretation of that single-sign-sentence would require multiple words (seven in our example) to convey the same meaning. The robust nature of prosody allows people to communicate so much more than the words *(functional elements),* alone. Winston (2000) explains that there has been much research into the prosodic features in spoken language and that there are apparent distinctions made between words and sounds. Words and sounds are separated into three distinct categories:

> 1) linguistically relevant sounds (words, utterances, etc) and features that co-occur with the linguistic features...such as intonation, accent, rhythm, tempo, speed; 2) paralinguistic: [including]...sounds like sighs or whistles, that add meaning but are not linguistic. 3) Other features (anything non-vocal) are labeled extralinguistic and are not studied as part of linguistics; generally facial expression and body movement, as well as hand gestures have been excluded from spoken language linguistic study (Winston, 2000, p. 2).

It is apparent that spoken English allows for latitude with how users can "play" with the language. However, English is still somewhat restricted by the fact that the mouth can only produce one comprehensible word at a time. As indicated in the example above, seven words were required (*"I am not satisfied in any way!"*) to convey one sign accompanied by a head shake, rolling eyes and an exasperated sigh. The spoken interpretation likely used prosody, including intonation, speed, rhythm, tone, affect and volume all provide emphasis to the words in an effort to deliver the same meaning and impact of that being conveyed in American Sign Language.

It is important to note that in ASL such distinctions between grammar and prosody cannot be made because it "is essential to consider any visual feature as a possible component of prosody" (Winston, 2000, p. 2). Yet the speed of production in each modality varies based on the content being communicated and the linguistic competence of the user. American Sign Language can convey a complex idea in seconds, depending on their language choices. But the inverse can be true, it may take considerably more signs to convey a thought or idea that is easy to convey in a figure of speech in spoken English.

MESSAGE FORMULATION

Before we dive into a discussion of how an interpreter interprets information from one language and culture into another, it needs to be understood there are multiple factors that influence how messages are formulated. When two or more

139

individuals engage in an extemporaneous (non-scripted) spoken or signed interactions, a number of ideas are formulated from the initial impressions; this is referred to as **prelinguistic formulation**. The initial impressions of the participants help shape the preliminary ideas of the interpretation. General concepts will begin forming as you determine the goals of the participants, as well as how you want the interpretation to be expressed. This includes the ideas and thoughts you may want to communicate and how to say what you want to say – including such decisions as selecting the degree of formality to use, whether to include humor, and a thousand other considerations. The impressions, thoughts and feelings about the participants are part of what we attempt to understand. Isham (1985) explains that these abstract ideas and views are referred to as

> Metanotative qualities of the message which are what let us internally answer such questions as "What is the speaker like as an individual? Is he educated or uneducated? Is she friendly? Is she knowledgeable about her topic? Can I trust him?" and so on. Whenever we listen to...[a speaker] we are forming completely subjective opinions based, in part, on the verbal behavior of the speaker (p. 119).

POCHHACKER'S INTERACTANT MODEL

In his 2004 text, *Introducing Interpreting Studies,* Franz Pochhacker, Associate Professor of Interpreting Studies at the University of Vienna, and a conference and media interpreter, proposed the model below in an effort to help us visualize how messages are formulated, whether they are intended for formal or informal interactions. There are many factors which influence why one chooses to formulate a message as they do and the various factors that influence how they will structure that message, the major consideration being the perspective of the person formulating the message and what they believe they know about the person or people with whom they wish to communicate. While it is true that we often plan what we want to say, particularly when it is an important message or the response to the message may be significant. Examples of these types of pre-rehearsed messages include such things as asking someone on a first date, proposing to your parents why you should have the car on Saturday evening or asking your employer

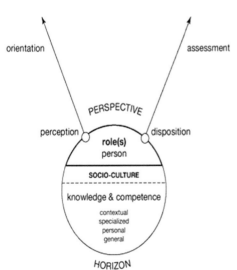

- An interpersonal interaction is basically determined by what each individual brings to the event in terms of (a) their socio-cultural background and (b) the types of cognitive competence and experiences they have had in previous social interactions.

- Because each participant brings her/his personal perspectives and expectations to a social interaction, each makes decisions (or assumptions) regarding the motivation, emotional attitude, expectations and intentions of others in the interaction. This influences how each person interprets the interaction, as well as how they will respond to the other participant(s). An event involving two or more individuals, then, hinges on how each person participates and whether they are open to what the others have to say.

- The level of engagement of each participant is based on an ongoing "assessment" of the interaction of others, the content of what they sign/say, their communication style, and their overt and covert behaviors.

for a raise. In truth, however, most of us think about what we are going to sign/say even in minor, extemporaneous situations, albeit in our subconscious. At conscious

Interpreting Process Models

NOTES

or subconscious levels of awareness, we care about what others will think of us, we want them to like us, or at least to think of us in a positive way.

In advance of an interaction, we often think about the role of the person we want to speak with, especially in terms of their role or position of authority compared to our own. We hope they will listen and think about what we share with them and for those reasons, we often select the *people, place,* and *purpose* (context) when we want to bring up a particular subject. When we are involved in extended conversations, we find ourselves assessing how others are "reading" us by analyzing their responsiveness which may indicate their attention level and whether or not they are agreeing with us. Based on how we interpret those behaviors, we may modify our approach or our plan for addressing the topic.

How an individual utilizes language will vary based on their age, gender, ethnicity, education, social affiliations, etc. In addition, their primary culture and affiliation with groups or organizations may influence their behaviors, norms and values. For these reasons, a person's language and culture often shape how they construct messages in order to accomplish their interactional goals. There are, of course, other factors that influence how one chooses to express their thoughts or ideas, including such things as personality, how they feel about the topic, and the actual content of what they are attempting to communicate, in addition to their relationship or connection to others in the setting.

CONSTRUCTING A MESSAGE

Unless a person is reading a speech, sermon, or notes, most message construction is a spontaneous and dynamic process, typically occurring extemporaneously and influenced by the contextual factors shown on the following page. Using the graphic, consider how you would apply the various facets to the below scenario. How would you manage the facets in the graphic in terms of what you might say.

- **Scenario:** Consider how you might respond to a mall security guard accusing you of taking something from a store without paying, utilizing the information from the graphic. Identify *every* aspect of the scenario: Your language and culture, feelings, style of communication and personality, in addition, to the setting and participants. Consider the aspects of the individual(s) with whom you are interacting – how might they be responding. It may be wise to make a few notes as you consider your responses.

- Video record what you would say, use the language you are most comfortable using. Then, working with another student in your class, role play this event with each of you playing the role of the guard and the role of the accused.

- Debrief with your classmate. Were your renditions similar or significantly different from those imagined by your partner? Why or why not? After this experience, journal your reflections on the experience, noting how this might be similar or different when you interpret – stepping into the shoes of dDeaf or hearing individuals and trying to convey all of the elements included in such an interaction. Consider the perspective of a dDeaf person facing their accuser without an interpreter.

An interpreter's job includes predicting what *themes, ideas* and *language* you may encounter during an interaction where you will bridge communication between two or more participants who are rooted in different linguistic and cultural frames of reference. As the interpreter, you must remember that many things will influence

141

each interaction you interpret, including the people who will be involved and the relationship they have with one another. Stop to consider what a doctor, teacher, or employer might say in the type of interaction you will be interpreting – what is the purpose or goal of the meeting/appointment and what does each person hope will result from this encounter? As an interpreter who can hear, you might think you can draw on your personal experience in appointments or interactions like the one you are about to enter. However, it is important to remember that while you may have gone to similar types of appointments, you have never had to rely on someone to mediate communication between you and the person or people you will meet in this event. It is good to remember that there are some settings where it is possible for you to obtain information in advance of the appointment which can help you mentally prepare for the interpretation. For example, when you check in at the reception desk of the medical facility, you could ask about the type of

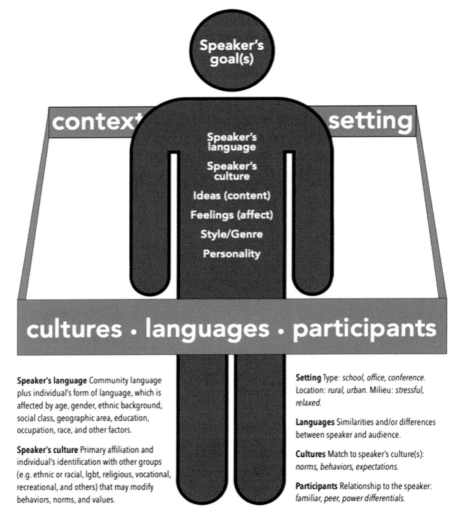

appointment and if this is the dDeaf patient's first time seeing the medical professional.

If you are interpreting for a meeting, you can ask the person leading the event to meet with you briefly ahead of time in order to inquire as to the gist of what they are planning on saying and their goals for this meeting. Contemplate your interpreting approach – could you interpret consecutively, rather than simultaneous? In addition, ask yourself some important questions, "Are you familiar with this topic? Have you interpreted for the dDeaf person before?" Once the appointment begins, you will make use of everything that you used to prepare as you listen attentively, identifying the *intention* and *meaning* of each "chunk" of information being shared. Then, as the speakers pause momentarily, you will begin the process of moving those messages into the target language and culture, communicating the articulated message in linguistically and culturally accessible ways, while conveying the underlying emotive envelope in which message is being communicated.

The goal of all interpreters is to convey the meaning and intention of communications to and from each party during an interaction. Like other language interpreters, American Sign Language/English interpreters are required to ensure that communication exchanged by individuals who can hear and those who are dDeaf are understood by all parties. However, interpreters who can hear and who are interpreting with a person who is DeafBlind has additional responsibilities – that is to convey any auditory information coming from a non-visual source, such as an announcement made through a speaker system or an auditory signal like the class bell at school. Information communicated through an auditory source is, unfortunately, *only accessible* to those who can hear. A sign language interpreter would be expected to convey that information to the participant(s), in addition to any spoken communication directed specifically at these participants. When working with DeafBlind individuals, interpreters must also convey any visual information that is relevant to the interaction. If, for example the DeafBlind individual is meeting with the manager of the apartment where they live, the interpreter would be expected to include in their interpretation the unspoken visual reaction made by the manager to what the dDDb individual has asked or said. These non-verbal responses carry the majority of the communication, but a questioning look on the manager's face, a smile, or the "OK" gesture on their hand – if not interpreted – fails to provide the DeafBlind individual access to all of the information. Just as each person has preferences regarding interpreted communication, dDDb individuals are no different. Some prefer additional information about their surroundings, the number of people, what they look like, where they are in the room and so on, while others prefer just enough information to make them comfortable.

Comprehending a source language utterance and transmitting the communication into the target language requires the same mental tasks and processes no matter where the work takes place or what languages are being used. It is the same process whether one is interpreting between spoken languages or between signed languages and spoken languages. An interpreter is required to analyze linguistically complex source language utterances as quickly and efficiently as possible (Patrie, 2000). One of the greatest challenges in the journey toward becoming an interpreter is discovering, understanding and applying the steps required to convey equivalent messages between two distinct, separate languages and cultures while maintaining dynamic equivalence

PROCESS MODELS

Several Process Models have been proposed in the fields of both spoken and sign language interpretation from as early as the 1950's. While each model is unique, they all attempt to portray the largely invisible cognitive processes required to take an utterance from the initial source language (SL) utterance to the conveyance of an equivalent message expressed in the target language (TL). Attempting to describe the various steps or processes involved in moving a spoken or signed message

Chapter 9

NOTES

through a Process Model includes the auditory and visible conveyance of affective information from one language to the other, while maintaining the spirit and integrity of the messages being communicated. Being sensitive to the details, the minutiae of the language, includes the ability to understand the source language with all nuances and the ability to express yourself fluently and clearly and with the appropriate cadence in the target language (Kelly, 1979). In fact, this is one of the greatest challenges in the journey toward becoming an interpreter – discovering and understanding the steps required to convey *equivalent messages* between two distinct, separate languages and cultures.

Some Process Models are substantiated by formal data collection and research; others are based on the application of emerging field research and each developer's experiences as an interpreter and interpreter educator. Humphrey and Alcorn (1995) summarize the common features of numerous interpreting models, including those we will introduce in this chapter. This summary applies to simultaneous and consecutive interpreting:

A. The interpreter takes in the source utterance;
B. Lexical and semantic units are strung together and held until the interpreter has sufficient units to determine the meaning of what is being said or signed;
C. A string of lexical and semantic units (referred to as a chunk) is analyzed to identify the speaker's or signer's intent and communication goal(s), explicit and implicit ideas, and a multitude of sociolinguistic features that impact upon the meaning of the source utterance. This could include gender. power distance between the speakers, setting, and contextual factors such as the impact or significance of the message on the receiver;
D. A search is made for cultural and linguistic equivalents as well as observing cultural norms and the cultural overlays of meaning;
E. Then a search is made of the target language to identify the lexical and semantic units and communication behaviors that can be used to produce an utterance in the target language with an equivalent meaning;
F. The interpretation is expressed in the target language; and
G. The interpreter monitors internal and external feedback to check for errors or needed corrections (Russell, 2005, pp. 136-137).

It is important that as interpreters are receiving the source message, they are attentive to environmental or paralinguistic factors. The simple phrase, "How are you?" can have very different meanings depending on the environment or setting. In a counselor's office it is often the way for the counselor to get the patient to begin sharing their thoughts, whereas in a coffee shop between two friends it can be taken as a greeting. However, while drinking coffee if the question is asked again, with a pensive tone it is usually understood that this is the time to open up. The words alone do not convey the message, rather *how* those words are delivered typically give the words their meaning. The flexibility of language and language use must be realized before student interpreters begin the work of interpreting. Interpreters should not begin their interpretations after the first or second words have been uttered. It is necessary to possess *enough* of the source message to begin rendering an interpretation, which includes: analyzing the implied and inferred information so we can effectively unpack the intent or goal of the speaker, and in doing so we can accurately deliver a string of lexical and semantic "chunks" (Paneth, 1957). We must also consider the schema and cultural frames of both the signer/speaker and receiver of the source language and target language utterances and search for equivalent ways to express the messages into the appropriate language with the corresponding cultural norms.

Below, you will find the Process Models proposed by three practitioners in the field of interpretation, whose pioneering work in research and interpreter education has laid a strong foundation for the practice of ASL/English interpretation in the 21st Century. Some were developed to describe the numerous processes involved when

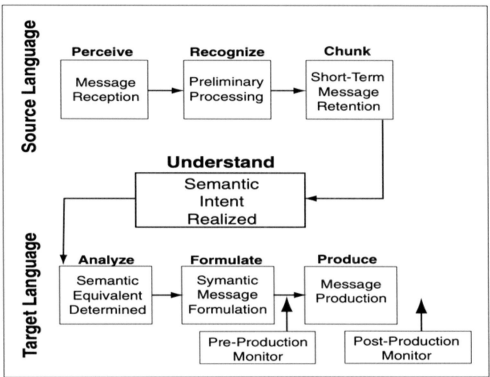

Figure 2. Modified Cokely model

Lee, R. G. (2005). *From Theory to Practice: Making the Interpreting Process Come Alive in the Classroom.* In Advances in Teaching Sign Language Interpreters. C. Roy (ed.) Gallaudet University Press. Pp 138-150

interpreting information from one language to another, regardless of whether the languages involved are spoken or signed. Others were generated for use when teaching students the cognitive sequences required to move equivalent information from the SL to the TL. All of them attempt to capture the cognitive processes taking place in a *dynamic transactional environment* where *message revision* is inherent.

DENNIS COKELY | A SOCIOLINGUISTIC MODEL

Cokely, an ASL/English interpreter and researcher, presented his model, *"Interpretation: A Sociolinguistic Model",* which went beyond the previous "information processing models" proposed by Ingram (1974), Gerver (1976), Moser (1978), and Ford (1981). Rather, Cokely identified seven major stages in the process of interpreting from the viewpoint of cognitive processing. After analyzing simultaneous ASL/English interpretation in a conference setting, he concluded that interpreters could minimize the occurrence of errors or miscues in their interpretations by identifying the stage where the miscues occurred, and determined the cause of those error(s), thus the interpreter would stop making those types of errors.

Chapter 9

NOTES

Cokely's research identified the following taxonomy of miscues: omissions, additions, substitutions, intrusions, and anomalies. He noted that an interpreter's processing time, which is influenced by each interpreter's ability to retain the SL information received, often influences the total number of anomalies/errors that occurred in their interpretations. Specifically, Cokely concluded that the *shorter an interpreter's processing time:* (1) the more the interpretation tended to follow the grammatical structure used to convey the SL, (2) the more frequently errors were made in the use of nonmanual signals (NMS), (3) the greater the number of SL intrusions with (4) an increase in the total number of anomalies. Cokely's model also provides a taxonomy of the errors typically made in interpretations and where those errors were most likely to occur. He defines a **miscue** as "a lack of equivalence between the source language (SL) message and its interpretation or, more specifically, between the information in an interpretation and the information in the SL message it is supposed to convey" (Cokely, 1992, p. 74).

Cokely (1992) explains that interpreting is, "probably more accurately described as serialized parallel processes, because they are undoubtedly several processes functioning simultaneously in an ordered, dependent relationship to each other" (Cokely cited in Witter-Merithew, 2002, p. 5).

Cokely's research noted that the more energy expended by an interpreter at the beginning of the interpreting process, the less energy will be available later in the process. Conversely, using less energy at the beginning of an interpretation leaves more energy for later stages of the process. Therefore, using energy wisely is one of the most important skills an interpreter can acquire. Cokely utilized the terms "resource allocation" and "process management," which included such things as self-talk which can drain an interpreter's store of energy. Furthermore, Cokely taught that interpreters should not focus their energy on whether a choice was "right or wrong;" rather they should develop skills in identifying: (a) where errors were made in the model, (b) which type of miscue was made, and (c) develop the ability of channeling energy to each stage of the process in order to reduce the number of miscues.

BETTY M. COLONOMOS | IMI MODEL

The *Integrated Model of Interpreting* (IMI) is rooted in the work of Danica Seleskovitch, who focused on the need for *message equivalence* in interpretations, because she believed that equivalence is the only way to ensure a correct and complete interpretation that focuses on finding the meaning *beyond form* (Seleskovitch, 1978). The pedagogy underlying this theory is found in Vygotsky's work which focuses on the *learning* of a skill, rather being *taught* a skill. This is a critical point of view and one that students of ASL/English interpreting must understand. Specifically, that you cannot master all of the knowledge and skill required to be an interpreter within a 2 year or 4 year academic program. Your academic education is a launching pad to a lifetime journey to build greater bilingual and bicultural knowledge, as well as interpreting skills, in addition to building on the foundation of your formal education.

The IMI is the only Process Model to date that represents the *simultaneity of the interpreting process* which is conveyed through the use of three graphic arrows incorporated at various stages in the interpreting process. Looking at the image on the next page you will see that Colonomos[3] identifies multiple points at which an

---

[3]*The authors are unable to add explanatory comments to the work of Colonomos because of its proprietary nature. Please study the notes developed by Colonomos regarding her model in the Toolbox.*

interpreter may choose to exit the process in order to return to one of the previous steps in the model. This may be done so the interpreter can (1) confirm

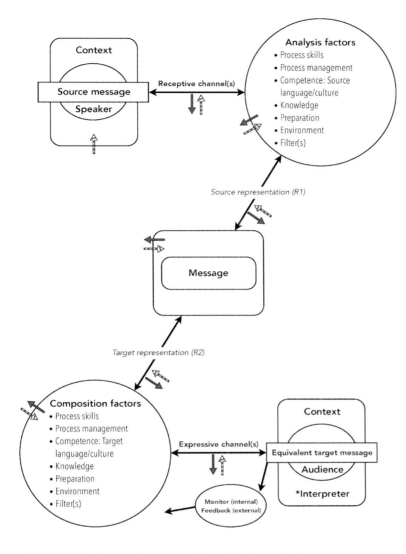

Copyright © 1989, 2016 by Betty M. Colonomos, Bilingual Mediation Center, Inc.

understanding, (2) elicit additional information needed in order to produce an equivalent and/or (3) once aware of an error, to make a correction.

INTEGRATED MODEL OF INTERPRETING (IMI)

This model reflects the foundational reality that a competent interpreter must be truly bilingual with a deep understanding of the *ways of being* among the dDeaf, dDDb and the hearing communities with whom interpreters work. Colonomos also emphasizes a foundational belief that the authors of this text support: *a deep understanding of what is being communicated* is a *prerequisite* to considering how to reconstruct that SL message into the target language and culture. This is a complex model; the creator's notes are in the Toolbox, but they are challenging to understand as first year interpreting students. The authors encourage you to work with your classmates in an effort to understand this Process Model to the best of your ability now. Then carry it with you through your formal study, discuss it with various instructors and working interpreters. Using the supplemental notes and

Chapter 9

NOTES

diagrams to guide you, take a good look at your growing knowledge and ability to actually perform each step in this model as you work with instructors and after graduation with mentors. Your goal is to be the best interpreter you are capable of becoming.

SANDRA GISH | THE GISH APPROACH

Sandra Gish, affectionately known as "Gish," developed this approach to interpreting after attending an event with another interpreter educator who happened to be Deaf.[4] At the event, her colleague was relying on an interpretation from English to American Sign Language to receive the presented content. Afterward, Gish asked her friend and colleague, whether she had enjoyed the presentation. "To my surprise, she said that she had experienced difficulty in following the interpreter. When I asked for details, she replied, 'I understood all the words, but I missed the point'" (Gish, 1987, p. 125). It seemed that the "difference between an effective and ineffective interpreting performance often seemed to lie in the use of appropriate pauses, connections and inflections, as well as in the specific grouping of information for presentation" (Gish, 1987, p. 125). Gish realized that interpreters appeared to struggle to create a clear and articulate interpretation, whether spoken or signed.

It was not necessarily about "accuracy" in content, rather it was about the presentation of the content that seemed to cause concern. Instead of cohesion and fluency, the dDeaf and hearing participants often receive "a jumble of run-on words and signs. The individual phrase seemed to lack any relationship with previously interpreted information and seemed disconnected from the messages that followed" (Gish, 1987, p. 125). In spite of the *content elements* being present, the message lacked flow, structure and organization that lends itself to cohesiveness and comprehensibility. However, a competent interpreter seems able to effectively manage the flow of information by containing it within a logical, organized system. However, without the logical framework, the audience, who is dependent on the interpretation often "missed the point" (Gish, 1987, p. 125).

When student interpreters face moments when they feel overwhelmed, there is often a temptation on the part for the interpreter to "keep up" with the person speaking by throwing out signs or spoken words as fast as they can. Sad to say, those words or signs don't make sense because the interpreter does not appear to understand the point and is unable to connect the message to the presenter's goal of the interaction. Gish (1987) goes on to explain that student interpreters *seemed* able to keep up with the speaker and *seemed* able to convey the content, yet the words/signs seemed unrelated and disconnected. In describing the interpreting work of the students she said,

> In sign-to-voice, the students were guilty of "word salad" interpreting: a run of words that almost made sense, but not quite. In voice-to-sign, it was hard to determine when one idea or sentence ended and when another began. As [the] "audience," I had to work as much at interpreting the interpretation as the students had to with the original message (p. 125).

The goal of this approach reflects a foundational truth – interpreters must *identify* the critical elements of what is being conveyed and *extract* the meaning and purpose of the communication in order to *construct* the interpretation into a *meaningful whole*. The Gish approach identifies and defines those critical elements

[4]Many interpreter educators feel that the Gish approach is a teaching tool in how to apply the IMI of Colonomos.

Interpreting Process Models

NOTES

which are the "glue" of signed or spoken interactions, conveying the goal(s) and objectives of the participants by using linguistic elements and details to create *meaning.*

GOALS: The goal of an individual who is attempting to communicate with others often gives the recipients a *framework* about the forthcoming communication. Sometimes it is simple and direct, while other times it is more elusive. For example, a supervisor may call a meeting with an employee and open the discussion by telling them they want to talk about their job performance – this is more evasive and likely would give the employee a sense of dread, yet the meeting could end with the employee earning a promotion. Whereas calling a meeting with a different employee and starting the dialogue with the statement that they have *concerns* about their overall job performance would be much more direct. Each *framework* should help guide the interpreter enabling them to identify the driving purpose behind the information being shared or comments being made. Knowing the goal, allows the interpreter to understand the point of the interaction, which will in turn aid them in their sign choices. There is always a reason for sharing information before people engage in an exchange of ideas of information. The goals of each participant direct the vocabulary selected, the linguistic register used, the affect displayed or withheld by participants and their reactions to the interactions. Ironically, Gish (1987) points out that student interpreters "demonstrated little ability to tap into their existing knowledge of subject content, participant relationships or discourse norms. In the most predictable of interactions, they demonstrated no confidence in assessing what consumers were likely to discuss" (p. 126).

An interpreter needs to know the purpose or goals of each participant in an interaction, but they are rarely overtly stated. For example, when interpreting for a presenter at a large conference, interpreters should try to arrange brief pre-meeting with the presenter to ask what the speaker hopes to accomplish in their presentation. As the interpreter it would be wise to ask the speaker, for example, to state one or two things they hope everyone in the audience will take away from the event. Likewise, should an attorney call to set up a meeting with a dDeaf client and an interpreter, it is appropriate and *necessary* for the interpreter to ask the purpose of the appointment. Interpreters must also be sensitive to the way interactions evolve during an interpreted event; as this enables the interpreter to identify the goals of the participants, which sometimes change, as the interaction unfolds. Of course, some events utilize specific texts, passages or songs that have implied meaning and sentiment when utilized. For example, reading a biblical passage at a funeral, traditional vows shared at a wedding, the singing of the national anthem at the World Series, etc., each text has a goal and as the interpreter we should give that ample consideration; is it to comfort, celebrate or honor and are we capable of accomplishing that purpose?

OBJECTIVES: Like goals, objectives are seldom overtly stated, objectives influence how information is organized. The organization of information is rarely, if ever, spontaneous and unplanned. Whether it is how a doctor enters an exam room or a politician speaking at a rally, they typically have a plan that will let them accomplish the goal in the time allotted. The more experience they possess the more comfortable they will be with the "routine" of their speeches, appointments or conversations. In a medical office, information is typically divided into four or five segments: (a) basic information is confirmed or updated at the receptionist desk; (b) on the way to the exam room, your weight and height are checked; (c) once you

149

are in the exam room, an assistant will check your temperature, blood pressure and complete other routine activities; and (d) when the doctor enters the exam room, they will likely give a short greeting before tending to whatever brought you in. You can guess what the objectives might be: to get you in and out as expediently as possible while ensuring your medical concern has been addressed and you feel welcomed enough to come back to the same doctor next time. If the interpreter knows the objective of the interaction they are interpreting, it allows them to predict whether to sit or stand, how to position themselves in a room, and what type of dialogue or monologue might take place. Some settings have a singular purpose, and as such only have one goal. For example, the emergency room at the hospital has one purpose the urgent care of patients; you would never have a banquet in an emergency room.

UNITS: The smallest segments of information being shared are the units. The units of a *speech act,* "divide the whole into pieces small enough to handle" (Gish, 1987, p. 132). This element carries the bulk of *overtly stated* propositions, ideas, specific bits of information that must be conveyed before being able to move forward to accomplish the goals of speaker and audience – doctor and patient, parent and their child's teacher. "It is at this level that the most active analysis takes place, for message comprehension and for the determination of the information that needs to be relayed into the target language" (Gish, 1987, p. 132). The interpreter is required to analyze the intended meaning of each utterance, signed or spoken, while also attending to nonverbal communication of the participants. Units are what Isham (1986) calls propositions and these propositions can "be expressed in a discourse in the form of a new:

- Fact
- Idea
- Thought
- Opinion
- Action
- Event
- Time
- Place
- Person" (cited in Gish, 1987, p. 132).

A single sentence can be made up of several propositions requiring the interpreter to separate those units of meaning and grouping similar units of meaning which will be held in the interpreter's active short term memory until a mental search reveals an equivalent word, phrase, idea or concept in the target language and culture, allowing the interpreter to convey the content and affect of each utterance.

DETAILS: This element focuses on specific lexical elements – words, signs, phrases, and other linguistic choices made by the presenter to enable those receiving the message to understand the *intentions* being communicated. The goal of interpreting is never to analyze a message on a word-by-word basis, devoid of context. Rather, interpreters need to understand the overarching message being expressed, relying primarily on their own previous experiences and prior knowledge regarding how discourse works in certain settings and with specified relationships.

Gish noted that this approach to interpretation seems to interface with the way the mind searches for and organizes meaning, providing a framework for identifying and extracting the meaning being conveyed, as well as a system for managing information without "getting lost and not knowing where to begin again" (Gish, 1987, p. 136). Models which describe the cognitive processing, like those above, are critical for you to understand in order to produce an accurate interpretation.

DANIEL GILE | THE EFFORT MODEL

Gile's work focused on the practice of simultaneous interpreting in monologic conference settings, whereas the models introduced previously were applicable to dialogic interpreting. Gile proposes four "efforts" or *ways the brain focuses its energy* while working through simultaneous interpretation between two cultures and languages from reception of the SL information through the delivery of the interpreted TL equivalent (Gumul, 2018). The initial versions of The Effort Model (1983, 1985) only identified three operations and Gile stressed that the three efforts should not exceed the interpreter's total processing capabilities. However, in later refinements of the Effort Model, he stressed that the coordination function or executive function "also consumes attentional resources and that coordinating the efforts is an important prerequisite for satisfactory [interpretation]" (Gumul, 2018, p. 19).

- **L – Listening and analysis:** *comprehension operations from receipt of SL*
  - analysis of SL auditory and visual components
  - identification of words
  - final decision about the meaning of the utterance (Gumul, 2018, p. 18)

- **P – Production:** *all mental representations and planning of the message*
  - initial mental planning and representation of message
  - final message planning and implementation of message delivery

- **M – Memory:** *short-term memory effort*
  - identification of the incoming message
  - *mental reformulation* into TL
  - all language decisions are made or disappears from memory (Gumul, 2018)

- **C – Coordination:** *all of the energy expended on all three efforts above*
  - listening, producing, and memory demands throughout the production of the TL interpretation

Gile then assumes that since the available cognitive processing capacity is limited, the *sum of these efforts must be less than the available processing resources* (which logically means that no one Effort can be greater than the available resources). One task of the interpreter is partly to distribute resources in an efficient way (Pym, 2008, p. 2).

Gile (1995) explains that each interpreter is to manage their resources effectively, because in the event an interpreter fails to utilize their resources appropriately, it will result in an error. In addition, should an interpreter distribute their resources ineffectively across the four Efforts a miscue is likely to result. This might happen, for example, if an interpreter expends too much energy "to produce an elegant reformulation of segment A, and therefore not have enough capacity left to complete a Listening task on an incoming segment B" (Gile cited in Pym, 2008, p. 3).

Pym (2008) explains that the Effort Models are "also able to describe the way in

Chapter 9

NOTES

which simultaneous interpreting differs from consecutive interpreting" (p. 3). Due to the slightly different rendering in simultaneous and consecutive interpreting, one or more Efforts may be used more extensively because of the various constraints that may affect the types of processing capacity available (Pym, 2008).

THE FINER POINTS OF INTERPRETING

ASL/English interpreting is most often done in person, with one or two dDeaf individuals, the interpreter and the non-Deaf individual. The interpreter may already know the dDeaf individual from going to dDeaf community events, or possibly because the interpreter has interpreted for this person previously. Interpreters and dDeaf participants typically meet at the location where the interpretation will take place: at the doctor's office, in the main office at the school, in the lobby at the lawyer's office. Interpreting sometimes takes place remotely via Zoom or another video platform; in addition, many dDeaf people use a video relay service which allows them to dial a specific number connecting them to an interpreter on their videophone. The operator who will answer is an ASL/English or Spanish/ASL/MSL interpreter who will connect the dDeaf caller to the number indicated and interpret the conversation. This service is typically available 7 days a week, 24-hours per day (depending on the particular VRS company).

Another important decision that must be made is whether to use simultaneous or consecutive interpreting. Consecutive interpreting is utilized in numerous settings; this mode of interpretation is *most effective* for one-on-one interactions such as interviews, parent-teacher conferences, doctor appointments, lawyer consultations, essentially between any professional and dDeaf participants. Consecutive mode can also be used during video remote interpreting (VRI), which should not be confused with video relay services (VRS). For this reason, many VRI companies have a dDeaf interpreter on staff to step into a video call when necessary. Consecutive interpreting is also effective when there are negotiations or discussions with small groups or a brief presentation given to a small audience. Consecutive interpreting is encouraged for interactions that are serious or where the outcome of the interaction could have significant consequences to one or more of the participants. In cases where *life* or *liberty* is at risk, you may see a team of interpreters taking abbreviated notes to ensure the inclusion of everything signed or said. Additional examples of situations that are best suited to consecutive work might be a deposition, competency hearing, mental health appointments and ongoing counseling or therapy.

Simultaneous interpreting is the most common form of interpreted communication used by ASL/English interpreters today. It is not uncommon to see sign language interpreters at public and private gatherings interpreting information for medium-to-large audiences. They can be present at any event or location where a dDeaf person would be present, such as staff meetings, town halls, religious gatherings, plays, graduation ceremonies, concerts, tours, conferences, etc. Managing the messages of both parties enables them to communicate effectively. Detailed information, such as numbers, dates, unique or formal names are often difficult to hold in one's short-term working memory; for that reason, the interpreter will often deliver that content quickly to conserve their energy, thus enabling them to process other information. When the interpreter is working with a co-interpreter, they have the added support of their team who can hold onto details from the message and share them as needed.

Interpreting Process Models

NOTES

What are the pro's and con's of simultaneous versus consecutive interpretation? The models of cognitive processing increase an interpreter's understanding of how we, as interpreters, work to produce an accurate interpretation. Furthermore, the various Process Models help us to assess whether a situation requires the use of consecutive or simultaneous interpreting. It is clear that interpreting is not an easy task; this is especially true for interpreters who have acquired American Sign Language as a second language. Even with ASL as a first language, the benefits of working consecutively provides student interpreters with more time to construct something closer to an equivalent message. It is evident that simultaneous interpretations have the potential for a higher number of misinterpretations and omissions of information than consecutive interpretations (Russell, 2005). Considering the cognitive and physical demands of interpreting, providing consecutive instead of simultaneous interpreting, supports appropriate working conditions, giving interpreters a greater opportunity to understand the meaning of the source language and to construct an equivalent message in the target language. There is much to learn about the interpreting processes and your formal learning begins when you embark on your academic journey by enrolling in an interpreter education program.

Research has documented that the closer the interpretation is to the utterance of the source message, reducing processing time, the greater the number of errors and omissions will be present in the interpretation, and the greater likelihood that the grammatical structure of the interpreted message will follow that of the source language, rather than the target language (Cokely, 1992). "Mental fatigue sets in after approximately 30 minutes of sustained simultaneous interpreting, resulting in a significant loss of accuracy" (Segal, & Salazar, 2020, p. 6). Actually, "accuracy may be compromised even before the thirty-minute mark, depending on the complexity of the subject matter, the speaker's speech patterns and speed, and even the time of day" (Segal, & Salazar, 2020,p. 6). This is true for both Deaf and non-deaf interpreters due to the *demand* of simultaneous interpreting on one's brain. It should be known that when working as a coordinated team to ensure the highest quality of service and accuracy each interpreter will interpret for approximately 15-20 minutes, taking turns throughout the event. Even when not actively interpreting, both interpreters are *actually working* throughout the assignment; supporting their colleague by monitoring their interpretation and providing linguistic and cultural help when the speed or density of the presentation warrants it.

> A 1998 study conducted at the École de Traduction et d'Interprétation at the University of Geneva, demonstrated the effects of interpreting over increasing periods of time. The conclusion of the study was that an interpreter's own judgment of output quality becomes unreliable after increased time on task (Gile cited in Erickson, 2007, p. 2).

There are numerous variables that determine how many interpreters are needed at each interpreting assignment and whether there will be a tandem (a dDeaf and hearing interpreting team, for more information see chapter 7). Some of the significant factors that determine number and type of team arrangements are density of content, length of event, type of event (conference with breakout sessions or single topic workshop), age of the participants (young children or adults) and the cognitive functioning of the participants – these are only a few of the variables to be considered.

Chapter 9

NOTES

INTERPRETERS WORKING AS A TEAM

As interpreters, we all "play for the same team," whether we are dDeaf or able to hear, certified or novice, male or female, regardless of the affiliations we hold outside of the profession. We should encourage and support each other. This section of this chapter will discuss the various ways interpreters work together in respectful and supportive ways which leads to successful and effective interpretations that consistently meet the needs of those who use our services. Even when an interpreter is not working as a co-interpreter with someone on a job, interpreters should "have the backs" of their colleagues. Experienced interpreters should encourage and support less experienced interpreters. Novice interpreters should heed the advice and warnings of more experienced interpreters. It should be safe for one interpreter to contact another with questions regarding how to deal with a particular interpreting job, specific settings, ideas for how to prepare for an interpretation, etc.

Each interpreter needs to bring all of their energy and focus to the job when working as co-interpreters. This is done by sharing information with each other if, for example, one interpreter has worked in this setting or with one or more of the participants in the past. It includes: (1) discussing and agreeing on who will take the first turn interpreting and (2) the length of each turn, (3) how each prefers to receive support from the other in the event they miss a bit of information, (4) how they will communicate with each other through the assignment (e.g., by the support interpreter writing notes for the "working" interpreter to read when they change places). Interpreters should have a level of professional trust that will allow honest sharing, support and feedback. This could include, for example, one team member letting their co-interpreter know that they may need support reading signed numbers or fingerspelling; another may suggest 15-minute turns because they have just come from a 3 hour job and are feeling a bit fatigued.

dDeaf/Hearing Teams

Best practices suggest that the Deaf interpreter make introductions to the non-signing participants with the interpreter who can hear providing the interpretation. It is essential, however, that both interpreters arrive between 20-30 minutes in advance of the appointment, particularly if you have never worked as co-interpreters prior to this event. Having not worked together requires both of you to take intentional risks and extend deliberate levels of trust. As much as reasonable, allow some time to get to know each other and exchange a bit of personal history. If either interpreter has worked with any of the participants in this interaction, that information should be shared along with information regarding how those participants manage language. Agreements need to be reached regarding how the dDeaf interpreter prefers to receive the message – ASL, PSE? Communication signals, how does each interpreter prefer to be notified if they need their colleague to pause, repeat or clarify information. Also if the assignment is scheduled to be long, such that it will require breaks, try to identify a location where to wait or transition in order to avoid interaction with any of the participants, this is especially important in certain settings (legal matters, employment hearings, union meetings, etc.). As interpreters we need to avoid any appearance impropriety, lest there be an appearance of favoritism or lack of impartiality. A key element of each assignment, which is often overlooked, is ensuring some time to debrief about the experience of working together, the assignment and how to improve future tandem work. This time can be critical to improving your interpreting work and building alliances for the future.

Interpreting Process Models

NOTES

Hearing Teams

As a courtesy, both interpreters should arrive at the venue a minimum of 15-20 minutes before the event is scheduled to begin. If they know each other or have worked together in the past, part of this time can be used to catch up. But the goal is to share what each knows about the upcoming appointment and if either has cultural or linguistic information about the participants that will help the team be more successful. In addition, negotiate how you want to be supported – a sign, a full sentence, communicate what works best for you? You need to agree on the length of turns, how you will communicate with each other during the interaction, and how each will indicate the need for support from their co-interpreter. Be sure to build in some time to debrief after the appointment.

"Trading Spaces"

When two hearing interpreters work together, they typically change positions from the "working" interpreter to the "support" interpreter several times throughout an assignment. The person in the "support" position should have a clear view of the "on" interpreter in the event there is a need for the support.[5] Of course, any physical movement during the assignment has the potential to become distracting. However, after the first or second "switch" it will cease to be an issue in most situations; it should not become the focus of everyone in the room. If there is an issue with the interpreters' ability to hear or the room is becoming entirely too warm or cold, it is best for the support interpreter to handle all side issues, lighting, room temperature, handouts, and other logistical details. This division of duties allows the working interpreter to continue to interpret without distractions. The same principles apply to all interpreting teams, if you have multiple dDeaf interpreting teams they will also strive to be discreet while trading places.

Wrapping Up

Most of our work is done with little or no supervision, we operate in isolation; this is the nature of our work. Like it or not, you represent every interpreter practicing today, your actions are a reflection on of all of your colleagues, and their actions reflect on you. Recognize that the way you behave and the interactions you have with each participant will shape what people think when they think of the word *interpreter*. How do you want to be remembered when you are finished interpreting in a doctor's office, a WIC appointment, or a town hall meeting? What you do and how you treat your colleagues matters. As a profession, we are not known for being gracious with our colleagues. Let's change that – be as gracious with others as you would like them to be with you. You are the next generation of interpreters – be amazing!

Chapter Review

Each Process Model is important to know for further development as an interpreter. There are many terms that may feel foreign, but they will become familiar the more you work towards your goal. Now that you have gained knowledge of the *process* of *interpreting* the authors want to reinforce the information you have gleaned by providing you with essential information below.

Terms to Know

- **ASL Modality:** As a visual and spatial language, that is time-oriented, based on visual perception and the physical conveyance of ideas, information and *feeling*

---

[5] It is a misnomer to refer to one member of the team as the "on" interpreter and the other as the "off" interpreter. Both interpreters are (or should be) working the entire assignment.

concepts (Humphrey and Acorn, 2007). ASL uses the arms, wrists, hands, face, eyes, head and the torso of the signer to physically produce messages, which are articulated in the space in front of the signer (approximately from shoulder to shoulder width during one-on-one interactions), and is easily perceived visually by the individuals to whom the message is being sent (Klima, & Bellugi, 1979).

- **Bilingualism:** Maftoon, & Shakibafar, (2011) define bilingualism as "the native-like control of two languages" (p. 80). Haugen (1953) goes further and explains that bilingualism is the "ability to produce 'complete meaningful utterances in the other language'" (cited in Mackey, 2000, p. 22).

- **C-language:** This term refers to one who has "picked up" some phrases and simple utterances in a language other than their first or second language.

- **Consecutive Interpretation:** Is defined as "the process of interpreting after the speaker or signer has completed one or more ideas in the source language and pauses while the interpreter transmits that information" into the target language (Russell, 2005, p. 136).

- **Dynamic Equivalence:** "maintaining the speaker's intended impact on the audience; when accomplished in an interpretation, the speaker's goals and level of audience involvement is the same for both the audience who received the message in its original form and the audience who received the message through an interpreter" (Humphrey & Alcorn, 2007).

- **Interpretation:** The result of taking a SL message, identifying the meaning of the affective layer, words or signs used, as well as the signer's/speaker's intent by analyzing the linguistic and paralinguistic elements of the message, then presenting a cultural and linguistic equivalent of the original text produced in the intended TL.

- **Linguistic Fluency:** These terms refer to an individual's strongest language and include: *native language, first language, mother tongue, L1* or *A-language.* This is the language in which one is most fluent.

- **Miscue:** "a lack of equivalence between the source language (SL) message and its interpretation or, more specifically, between the information in an interpretation and the information in the SL message it is supposed to convey" (Cokely, 1992, p 74).

- **Modality:** The physical aspects required to produce each language; often referred to as the method or channel through which a message is expressed, specifically English is auditory/oral while American Sign Language is visual/spatial.

- **Paralinguistics:** The auditory, visual or physical elements associated with signed or spoken messages, which convey additional information above and beyond the words spoken.

- **Prelinguistic Formulation:** When two or more individuals engage in an extemporaneous (non-scripted) spoken or signed interactions, the ideas are

Interpreting Process Models

NOTES

formulated from the initial impressions. The initial impressions of the participants help shape the preliminary ideas of the interpretation.

- **Processing Time:** The time used by an interpreter to complete an analysis of the source language (SL) utterance and to search for cultural and linguistic equivalents before producing an equivalent message in the target language (TL).

- **Prosodic Features:** Prosody is the combination of features in any language that produces the rhythm, accent, and "feel" of the language. In ASL, prosody is a visual spatial image, created by several features. These features include head and body movements, eyebrow movement, mouth movement, speed of signing, sign formation, pacing, and pausing (Winston, 2000, p. 1).

- **Second language, L2 or B-language:** These terms refer to acquisition of a second language, typically acquired by living in another country for several years or by having an immersive experience with a language other than your mother tongue.

- **Sight Translation:** Sight translation usually renders a written document into signed language but at times, an interpreter might be asked to write in English a signed text. Sight translation is typically done "on the spot" with little-to-no advanced notice or preparation.

- **Sign-To-Voice:** Interpreting signed messages from the source language into a spoken target language.

- **Simultaneous Interpretation:** "Is defined as the process of interpreting into the target language at the same time as the source language is being delivered" (Russell, 2005, p. 136).

- **Stakeholders:** include any "individual or group that has an interest in any decision or activity of an organization" (ISO 26000 cited in American Society for Quality, 2020, para 1).

- **Translation:** This is generally done over time and typically with a team directing the development of a translation of a frozen text (written or video) into another language. This is currently an emerging field for dDeaf individuals (e.g. videotaped translations of textbooks, plays and poems) (Forestal & Cole, 2018).

- **Transliteration:** The result of taking a SL message, identifying the meaning, goal and intent of the speaker by analyzing the linguistic and paralinguistic elements of the message, and expressing that message in a different mode of the same language (e.g. PSE or Signed English to spoken English).

- **Voice-To-Sign:** Interpreting from a spoken source language into a signed target language.

Interpreting Models summary of several models by Humphrey and Alcorn (1995):

A. The interpreter takes in the source utterance

157

B. Lexical and semantic units are strung together and held until the interpreter has sufficient units to determine the meaning of what is being said or signed

C. A string of lexical and semantic units (referred to as a chunk) is analyzed to identify the speaker's or signer's intent and communication goal(s), explicit and implicit ideas, and a multitude of sociolinguistic features that impact upon the meaning of the source utterance. This could include gender, power, distance between the speakers, setting, and contextual factors such as the impact or significance of the message on the receiver

D. A search is made for cultural and linguistic equivalents as well as observing cultural norms and the cultural overlays of meaning

E. Then a search is made of the target language to identify the lexical and semantic units and communication behaviors that can be used to produce an utterance in the target language with an equivalent meaning

F. The interpretation is expressed in the target language

G. The interpreter monitors internal and external feedback to check for errors or needed corrections (Russell, 2005, pp. 136-137).

Pochhacker focuses on visualizing how messages are formulated — formal or informal. There are many factors which influence why one chooses to formulate a message, how they will structure that message, the major consideration being the perspective of the person formulating the message and what they believe they know about the person or people with whom they wish to communicate.

Remember, there are many things that influence each interaction you interpret including:

- The people who will be involved
- The relationship they have with one another.
- Consider what a doctor, teacher, or employer might say in the type of interaction you will be interpreting
- What is the purpose or goal of the meeting/appointment
- What does each person hope will result from this encounter

Cokely concluded that interpreters could minimize the occurrence of errors or miscues in their interpretations by identifying the stage where the miscues occurred and determined the cause of those error(s), for the interpreter to stop making those types of errors.

Cokely's research identified the following taxonomy of miscues:

- Omissions
- Additions
- Substitutions
- Intrusions
- Anomalies

Colonomos believes that you cannot master all of the knowledge and skill required to be an interpreter within a 2 year or 4 year academic program. Your academic education is a launching pad to a lifetime journey to build greater bilingual and

Interpreting Process Models

NOTES

bicultural knowledge, as well as interpreting skills, in addition to building on the foundation of your formal education.

Colonomos identifies multiple points at which an interpreter may choose to exit the process in order to return to one of the previous steps in the model:

1. to confirm understanding
2. to elicit additional information needed in order to produce an equivalency
3. once aware of an error, to make a correction.

Gish said it seemed that the "difference between an effective and ineffective interpreting performance often seemed to lie in the use of appropriate pauses, connections and inflections, as well as in the specific grouping of information for presentation" (Gish, 1987, p. 125).

The goal of this approach reflects a foundational truth – interpreters must:

1. *identify* the critical elements of what is being conveyed
2. *extract* the meaning and purpose of the communication
3. *construct* the interpretation into a *meaningful whole*.

Gile work focused on the practice of simultaneous interpreting in monologic conference settings, whereas the models introduced above were applicable to dialogic interpreting.

- **L – Listening and analysis:** *comprehension operations from receipt of SL*
- **P – Production:** *all mental representations and planning of the message*
- **M – Memory:** *short-term memory effort*
- **C – Coordination:** *all of the energy expended on all three efforts above* (Gumul, 2018)

dDeaf and **hearing** team: arrive at any job 20-30 minutes in *advance*.
Hearing team: arrive 15-20 minutes in *advance*.

Competencies identified for interpreters: *https://www.unco.edu/cebs/asl-interpreting/pdf/asl-english-interpretation/entry-to-practice-competencies.pdf*

Remember you represent every interpreter practicing today, your actions reflect on all of your colleagues, and their actions reflect on you.

Consider your strengths and areas of growth as you assess the Processing Models. What areas do you see that could be strengthened by incorporating the knowledge into practice?

159

TERMS TO KNOW:

- dDeaf Plus
- Tadoma
- Intervenors

10 | dDeaf & Differently Abled

An important segment of the dDeaf community is made up of people who are dDeaf with additional challenges, including: intellectual delays or limitations, cerebral palsy, physical challenges, and others on the autism spectrum, to name a few. Approximately 40% of the dDeaf population are disabled (Gallaudet Research Institute, 2005). Often referred to in the literature as **dDeaf plus**, these individuals have norms of communication, attention getting, and connecting with each other that are not always the same as those among the majority dDeaf community. A significant population of individuals who are dDeaf have visual limitations ranging from requiring special lenses in their glasses to being totally blind. As you study to become an interpreter, it is essential that you become familiar with the range of communication requirements when interpreting for those who are dDeaf plus. The goal of this chapter is to introduce you to individuals falling into this category, helping you build a schema for understanding how your interactions with them can be respectful, successful and better informed.

It is vital that the uniqueness of each person be honored and respected. Accommodations are typically focused on providing support for each individual's areas of growth (concern) and assistance for the student or adult as a whole person. If you are interpreting for a child or youth of school age, you will likely be a part of the school's educational team, or as a staff person working with the after-school program or if there are concerns about the student's regression the student could qualify for summer programming. If you are affiliated with a school, there may be additional support available for the student you are working with, in addition access to the child's IEP which will help you understand the spectrum of needs a particular child is dealing with and the agreed upon supports the school will provide. Additionally, you can speak with the special education teacher, regular education teacher, childcare director and other professionals (speech and language, occupational therapy) working with the child/youth to get ideas about how you may need to adapt your approach to interpreting for this specific individual.

On the other hand, you may show up for an interpreting assignment and unexpectedly find the dDeaf participant has additional challenges in addition to being unable to hear. Freelance community interpreting jobs are primarily staffed by a single interpreter, so in the absence of a co-interpreter, it is important for you to get ideas how to approach interpreting for the individual in this situation. Asking other staff who work with the participant and/or their attendant is likely the best

Deaf & Differently Abled

NOTES

source of information. It is absolutely acceptable for you to ask the dDeaf individual:

- What kind of communication do you need?
- Do I need to be closer or further away from you when I sign?
- Shall I sign in a smaller space?
- What kind of lighting is best?

Of course if this is a standing appointment and the physical therapist or dentist will also be able to give you some ideas about what they "normally" do when this individual comes in for an appointment. It is, of course, common for such interactions to take more time to complete the task at hand. Remember, your anxiety can be conveyed to the dDeaf participant and it doesn't create a sense of confidence in you. If you have limited experience working with a person who is dDeaf that may have additional disabilities, remember that you can do anything for an hour (or more). Take a deep breath, and silently say to yourself: "I can do this... what else should I ask to be more prepared? I can do this!"

DEAF AND PHYSICALLY CHALLENGED

Individuals in this group often rely on crutches, a cane, a walker or sometimes a wheelchair to navigate through physical settings. They often move more slowly and require more physical space when entering and exiting a building or office, as well as setting up in the area where communication will be taking place. Everyone involved in the appointment or event with a dDeaf individual who has physical challenges needs to exercise patience in dealing with the challenges of space and movement. As the interpreter, you may be expected to hold the door open while the individual enters or exits the building or to hold the person's crutches once they are seated and settled, placing the crutches in a non-intrusive place. If the dDeaf participant has a full range of upper body movement, it is likely not significant that linguistic modifications will be needed. On the other hand, if this participant displays palsy, paralysis, or other features that limit the physical articulators of ASL, the interpreter can expect some challenges in comprehending what they are signing.

Many dDeaf individuals who have physical challenges live a typical life as children, youth and adults, often participating in Special Olympic events, holding down a job, and being married with children. Others have a combination of physical and medical challenges which sometimes impact their day-to-day life and activities significantly. The best way to approach interpreting with individuals in this category is to be open, explaining that you do or do not have experience working with someone with this particular individual's challenges and asking direct questions for guidance regarding what they need from you in terms of mediating the communication in the setting. If the dDeaf individual is unable to produce signs clearly, making it hard for you to comprehend what is being stated or asked, ask for them to repeat their comment or question. You may need to sign back what you think you are understanding to get confirmation or correction before speaking your interpretation. Be polite, but do not be embarrassed or fail to ask directly for what you need to know. In addition, the staff who may work with the dDeaf person may understand their unique signing style, please do not be afraid to use them as a resource.

You may have some physical limitations yourself, which might inhibit your ability to

161

Chapter 10

NOTES

hold a door open or carry a set of crutches from one side of the car to another. Climbing a flight of stairs may be a challenge and asking whether the building is accessible is essential to know. Be upfront and honest about your personal limitations, particularly before accepting a job where these expectations may be in place.

DEAF AND INTELLECTUALLY DELAYED/CHALLENGED

Intellectual disability (ID) now replaces the term "mental retardation" used in previous editions of the DSM-5. "Intellectual disability involves problems with general mental abilities that affect functioning in two areas:

- intellectual functioning (such as learning, problem solving, judgement)
- adaptive functioning (activities of daily life such as communication and independent living)" (Parekh, 2017, para. 1)

The functioning of each person ranges from mild to severe, with those who have severe intellectual function requiring more support, especially in school settings. Individuals with severe intellectual disabilities often face multiple disabling conditions, each of which can seriously interfere with a person's development, including:

- Cerebral palsy
- Epilepsy
- Vision impairments
- Hearing loss
- Speech and language problems (American Academy of Pediatrics, 2015, para. 15)

"While a...IQ test score is no longer required for diagnosis, standardized testing is used as part of diagnosing the condition. A full scale IQ score of around 70 to 75 indicates a significant limitation in intellectual functioning" (Parekh, 2017, para. 3). Families are typically able to find social service agencies to provide support for their disabled family members, as well as support for the parents dealing with a family member with special needs. Interpreters are often employed to facilitate communication with individuals who are dDeaf with additional challenges. In some cases, those interpreters have received special instruction regarding how to best support the individual's communication and inclusion. Interpreters who are brought into such a setting with no preparation may not know how best to communicate or maintain the focus of the individual who is dDeaf with additional disabilities. In such situations, it is important for interpreters to seek the kind of information and support that will allow them to be successful in the inclusion and participation of the dDeaf individual with special needs. This may come from family members, but is more likely available from the agency staff of the organization offering the services requiring interpretation. The presence of a Deaf interpreter is one of the "best practices" currently encouraged to meet these needs.

Children with intellectual disabilities may take longer to learn to speak, walk, and take care of their personal needs such as dressing or eating. They are likely to have trouble learning in school. They *will* learn, but it will take them longer. There may be some things that cause them to be unable to learn:

- **Genetic conditions.** Sometimes an intellectual disability is caused by

162

abnormal genes inherited from parents, errors when genes combine, or other reasons. Examples of genetic conditions are Down syndrome, fragile X syndrome, and phenylketonuria (PKU).

- **Problems during pregnancy.** An intellectual disability can result when the baby does not develop inside the mother properly. For example, there may be a problem with the way the baby's cells divide as it grows. A woman who drinks alcohol or gets an infection like rubella during pregnancy may also have a baby with an intellectual disability.
- **Problems at birth.** If a baby has problems during labor and birth, such as not getting enough oxygen, he or she may have an intellectual disability.
- **Health problems.** Diseases like whooping cough, the measles, or meningitis can cause intellectual disabilities. They can also be caused by extreme malnutrition (not eating right), not getting enough medical care, or by being exposed to poisons like lead or mercury (Center for Parent Information and Resources, 2017, para. 5).

An intellectual disability is not a disease. You can't catch an intellectual disability from anyone. It's also not a type of mental illness. There is no cure for intellectual disabilities. However, most children with an intellectual disability can learn to do many things. It just takes them more time and effort than other children. Children with severe IDs are more likely to have additional disabilities and/or disorders compared to children with milder IDs.

One's ability to develop *structured communication skills* varies depending on the degree of intellectual challenges each person has. Some are able to communicate fairly well, especially in the area of life needs (expressing hunger and preferences of what to eat, feeling good or ill, and happy or sad). Others are more limited in the levels they are able to engage in conversations or education. Interpreters may work with individuals who have intellectual delays from early childhood through their senior years. The greatest challenge when working with young children is the absence or delayed acquisition of communication skills, which is somewhat similar to working with senior citizens who have this disability because, like many aging adults, they often forget the communication skills they have learned at younger stages in their life.

Settings where an interpreter might encounter dDeaf individuals with delayed intellectual abilities ranges from public and private preschools through highschool, in special day-programs for disabled individuals and sometimes in residential programs where adults live while receiving social, educational, and nutritional support, as well as the opportunity to live in a safe environment. Residential programs often have staff interpreters, ensuring access to the range of programs offered in those settings.

DEAFBLIND

People with extremely limited sight and hearing are considered DeafBlind (DB); the National Association of Regulatory Utility Commissions (NARUC) estimates that 70,000-100,000 people living in the United States are DeafBlind (Committee on Consumer Affairs, 2008). While most DeafBlind people have some useful but not always reliable vision and hearing, some people have little or no usable hearing and vision. One person may be born deaf or hard of hearing and lose their vision later in life; another person may grow up as a blind or visually impaired person and experience a hearing loss later. Some people are born with combined vision and hearing loss, or lose their vision and hearing at an early age.

About 50 percent of individuals in the DB community in the US have Usher Syndrome which is a genetic condition where a person is born deaf or hard of hearing, or sometimes with normal hearing, and loses their vision later on in life from retinitis pigmentosa (RP) (U.S. Department of Health & Human Services, 2017). There are three kinds of Usher Syndrome. If a person has Ushers 1, they are born deaf, and starts to lose their vision usually in the teen years. If a person has Ushers 2, they are born hard of hearing and start to lose their vision by midlife. With Ushers 3, a person is usually born with normal vision and hearing, or with a mild hearing loss, and begins to lose both senses later in life. Other common causes of deaf-blindness include birth trauma, optic nerve atrophy, cataracts, glaucoma, macular degeneration, or diabetic retinopathy. Some people may be born with both hearing and visual impairments through birth trauma or rare causes such as CHARGE Syndrome or cortical visual impairment. Others may become DeafBlind through accidents or illnesses.

Terminology
- **Congenitally DeafBlind** is a term used when people are born DeafBlind or when their combined hearing and vision impairment occurs before spoken, signed or other visual forms of language and communication have developed.
- **Acquired DeafBlindness** People who are born Deaf or hard of hearing and later experience deteriorating sight. People who are born vision impaired or blind and go on to experience hearing loss at a later stage (Senses Australia, 2020, para. 1-4)
- **Dual-Sensory Loss** refers to people who are DeafBind and are categorized as having a "dual sensory loss," but the degree of loss in vision and hearing varies widely, as do the causes of this conduction

Some DB individuals are physically fit and able to move independently; others have additional physical challenges. Depending on the level of auditory/visual loss and other factors, each person's abilities can vary greatly, affecting their ways of communicating, ability to manage independent movement in a familiar setting as well as their ability to manage basic self-care. Throughout history, DB people have maximized their potential for personal development and have inspired those who are able bodied.

You can imagine the level of isolation that results when a person cannot hear or see what is going on around them. However there are a variety of ways for DB individuals to navigate their environment and to communicate. DB people can often travel independently and/or with family, friends or support service providers (SSPs). Many use public transportation like buses or subways, especially if they live in an area where public transportation is available. They can also use paratransit vans or special taxis, especially if they live in rural areas or in an area where public transit is not available. Some may use car or van pools. Others may depend on family and friends for transportation, or travel on foot if they live within walking distance of where they need to go.

TOUCH AND COMMUNICATION

There are varying types of communication needs. Historically, communication with those who are DB has been treated as a special accommodation, rather than a given. But the spirits of DB individuals are indomitable and many live full and rewarding lives.[1]

Each DB person is different and as a result, there are a variety of communication techniques, always depending on what is the best fit for the individual but the types of communication available to individuals who are DB typically include some kind of touch. Touch is highly treasured among members of the DB community and is perhaps the most intimate of the senses. For a DB person, the moment they come in contact with something, they are able to determine the shape, texture, size, and weight of the object they are touching. We now know that the effects of a touch linger in the brain long after the sensory experience ends, and often without our being directly aware of it (Pan, 2019). Surprisingly, large amounts of information are preserved with touch and a single touch has a far greater impact on the mind than one might have ever imagined.

Several forms of communication reflect the creativity and determination of DB individuals to interact with others. For example, **Tadoma** is a method of communicating with the blind and deaf whereby their hands are placed on the lips of the speaker. The person with dual-sensory loss feels the shape of the words as you say them. This is similar to lip reading but done with the fingers, rather than the eyes. Not all people who are DB use Tadoma, and not everyone is comfortable with another person placing a hand on their mouth Other tactile forms of communication include Braille, Tactile symbols and object cues, palm printing, and touch cues.

The Emergence of Tactile ASL

Most recently, a revolutionary form of communication has emerged with the evolution of recently Tactile American Sign Language (TASL). In 2006, the first ever DeafBlind director of the DeafBlind Service Center (DBSC) Seattle, WA, a non-profit organization that provides communication and advocacy services, was employed. She and her staff launched a study to identify the causes encountered by members of the DB community and found it was a single cause: *DeafBlind people do not have enough direct, tactile contact with their environment and the people in their environment.* In an effort to address this problem, DeafBlind participants engaged in a series of workshops in the spring of 2011 focused on tactile communication and all participants were required to communicate tactually. Through this series of workshops, new interactional conventions were established, triggering a grammatical divergence between Tactile American Sign Language and Visual American Sign Language. "The pro-tactile movement has not been driven by metalinguistic reflection or valuation", (Terra Edwards, 2020 interview) instead it has grown from the "need for immediacy and co-presence" (Terra Edwards, 2020 interview). Edwards, goes on to argue that this has resulted in an emerging and distinct language. When people come into our space, they should use PT in the same way that people coming into Deaf spaces should use ASL (Granda, & Nucci, 2018, p. 2).

Members of the Seattle DB community are exuberant in describing the positive changes for them as individuals and as members of the community of people who are DeafBlind. The following comments are taken from the Protactile Vlog (March 2014) in which Jelica Nunncio and AJ Granada, both DB leaders in Seattle, WA, shared their enthusiasm for pro tactile communication.

AJ: *"DeafBlind people are responsible for establishing a positive and solid*

[1]*See DeafBlind Hall of Fame and Frequently Ask Questions in the ToolBox*

relationship with the community. We embrace and value the DeafBlind way and we value ProTactile. We do not want to repeat the struggles the Deaf community endured. We do not want to repeat Deaf history within our DeafBlind community" [*Jelica taps aj's knee in agreement, nods, then turns to face the camera*].

Jelica: We want to ensure that we all work together, as a community. Stand for what we believe in. That's where we are now; we are *advocating for our DeafBlind community to promote a more positive, healthy, and unrestricted future."*

This is being said because visual ASL (VASL) is not accessible to those who cannot see and inspite of years of DB individuals struggling to keep up with conversations, presentations and other presentations in which VASL was used, they were never fully able to comprehend either the content or the affective elements being expressed. The same is true for attempts to use "touch signals," which involve touching aDB person in a particular manner to physically convey information that a glass of water had been placed in a certain place, allowing the DB individual to access whatever the touch signal was set up to convey.

Jelica: *"We need ProTactile (PT) as a part of our empowerment, in order to live our life and make decisions for ourselves. Language is key to our quality of life; In order to achieve autonomy, we need access to language to thrive ... (unlike TouchSignals) PT includes philosophy, attitude, language, and techniques"* [*Jelica gives AJ a high 5*] *These so-called "Touch signals" do not do us justice. They do not benefit us or do us any good.*

AJ: ProTactile philosophy is not just about "accessing" communication. ProTactile affects all areas of life, including DeafBlind culture, politics, empowerment, and language...we want to tell you more about how the ProTactile movement is pushing back against many of the assumptions and practices that oppress members of our DB community.

Jelica compares ProTactile philosophy to a tree: the trunk of a tree is ProTactile ASL and it supports those branches which are (1) *philosophy*, (2) *attitude*, (3) *culture* (4) *language*.

Protactile, like ASL, has evolved over time a − a language that has been developed by the DeafBlind community. Unlike touch signals (TS) and/or haptics, neither of which developed naturally over time. ProTactile *includes back-channeling* (cues for the unspoken/unsigned reactions to the information a dDB individual is receiving tactically). The philosophy behind PT is *innate*, a *natural form of communication that's a part of the DeafBlind culture.*

As Protactile (PT) and Tactile ASL (TASL) are emerging, new research is revealing that touch "generates surprisingly powerful and long-lasting memories (Pan, 2019, para. 2)" Pan (2019) states that "touch is perhaps the most intimate of the senses," noting that "specialized skin cells convey a wealth of information [to the brain], such as shape, texture, size, and weight" (para. 1). It has been thought, however, that tactile information fades fairly quickly, and is therefore only useful "in the moment...especially when compared to the visual system" (Pan, 2019, para. 2). However, some new research has found that "the sense of touch generates memories that are far more complex and long-lasting than previously thought" (Pan, 2019, para. 2). Participants in the study, in which they were blindfolded then asked to pick up and touch a series of kitchen utensils, stationery goods and other items for 10-seconds each, identified the objects they handled with 94% accuracy immediately after the experience. When tested one week later, they had 85% accuracy, proving that tactile memories can endure over the long term.

> It would appear then that the cognitive capacities of touch, which was *among the first of the sensory systems to evolve*, have long been underestimated...touch leaves a memory trace that persists long after the physical sensation is gone. Moreover, information appears to be stored without much conscious awareness. As a result, those memories can manifest in interesting ways (Pan, 2019, para. 7).

It is an exciting time to become acquainted and involved with the DeafBlind community near you. Whereas some choose to ignore the communication used by DB individuals, some even avoid meeting DB people altogether. As a future interpreter, you need to locate DB people near you, develop a level of comfort in interacting with members of this community and take advantage of opportunities to develop skills in the communication techniques used by members of the DB community. Initially, you may feel uncomfortable with the close proximity necessary for communication, but once you acclimate it will be a rich and rewarding experience.

Oppression from Sighted Deaf People – *Distantism*

John Lee Clark (2017), who is DeafBlind has coined some terms that he feels are appropriate to describe the way sighted dDeaf individuals treat DeafBlind folks. Noting that dDeaf individuals have invented words to describe their experience of marginalization, Clark introduces *vidism* and *distantism* marking the ways (1) the sighted community treats blind individuals and (2) the fact that Deaf community members replicate their own oppression in their view of dDB people. Clark identifies the reality that since the evolution and advancements of the Protactile movement in the DeafBlind community which he notes have always been "in the air" but has become more blatant since the evolution of the Protactile movement in 2007. The term *distantism* is used to explain the high value sighted and hearing people place on being able to perceive events and communication that are distant. Clark says, "The English word "distance" comes from 'distantia,' Latin for 'a standing apart. A point could be made that distantism refers to the privileging of distance senses of hearing and vision" (Clark, 2017, para.7). He points out that most cultures around the world have evolved based on the ability to see and hear and as a result have caused world cultures to devalue anyone who could not see or hear, resulting in an attitude of "*distantism*," standing apart, devaluing the sense of touch.

> It is an attitude and a behavior. Many hearing and sighted societies prize it highly, and their members seek to maintain physical distance, however thin those margins may be. Their rulers and heroes stand alone -- the more remote they are, the more highly esteemed they are. Even when the less privileged are squeezed closer together due to poverty, exploitation, or as punishment, distantism manifests itself in the long lines, tight cells or cubicles, and above all, their being removed out of sight and hearing. For all the hype around its ability to connect the world, technology has often served to isolate people in every other way (Clark, 2017, para. 7-8).

Clark declares that people of sight and sound impose their value of *distantism* on

Chapter 10

NOTES

DeafBlind because they are unable to deal with the reality that other human beings so severely disabled due to the lack of sight or hearing could thrive in the world. And as a result, dDB individuals are considered the lowest in society. It is actually the attitude of *distancing* that actually limits the opportunities of dDB people to live a life filled with information and opportunities.

The solution was to provide each dDB person a sighted companion, first in schools and later as assistants to help dDB people around the community. It has been a way to give dDB people "hearing and sight by proxy" (Clark, 2017, para. 14). Initially this was only available in special schools for the dDB, so full access was not accessible but today there are special companions called "Intervenors." Clark notes that while this is a wonderful idea, the real need is to have dDB adults teaching DeafBlind children *DeafBlind ways of being* beginning with young children. Unfortunately as this book goes to press, the field of education of DeafBlind children has never included dDB adults as teachers. For that reason, they are deprived of knowing *dB culture and ways of being.*

Intervenors are trained to work with dDB people, guiding them as they move through the world. They are trained in tactile sign language, tadoma and palm printing in order to meet the communication needs of various dDB individuals. Clark describes intervenors as providing access to sound and things around dDB individuals by proxy (Clark, 2017, para. 14). Determined to live fulfilling lives, with the support of intervenors, dDB people are able to go exploring as intervenors guide, describing things and people they see to the dDB person, letting them know what is happening around them, as well as informing them of other visual information the intervenor believes would be important or of interest. This service is wonderful, but members of the dDB communities long for something better. Intervenors will describe it, let a dDB client touch the object if possible, use the communication system the dDB individual uses...but there is still a sense of isolation experienced by many dDB people.

Clark replies, "There's a whole cultural element involved. There are *distantist* modes of touch and there are *protactile* modes of touch. A *distantist* cannot truly teach or empower DeafBlind children to live and learn as tactile people" (Clark, 2017, para. 17). Yet the field of education of DeafBlind children has never included DeafBlind adults in the early education of dDB children. Not only could dDB children learn about history and mathematics, they would be introduced to DeafBlind culture from members of their own 'people' – guiding the young on the shoulders of those who have experienced the world without sight or sound. This is happening in Deaf schools, public schools and private schools where dDBlind children are helped, kept safe, protected from bad influences and unfortunately exposed daily to see the world from the *distantist ideal* – waiting to be told things rather than finding out things for themselves. "If it was its goal to succeed completely in educating us, it would embrace our *tactilehood* and value [dDB individuals] as teachers and leaders. Instead, *distantism* is the first condition, and for that to make sense, the field needs its work to be difficult and expensive, not easy and effective" (Clark, 2017, para. 21).

One dDB man friend shared an experience he had with a yoga activity at a popular "DeafBlind" retreat. The yoga instructor wanted the group to do it in Protactile style so there was a happy clustering, and people helped each other and passed on information. But one of the SSPs standing back intervened by going to her "client" to correct his position. As soon the other SSPs slipped into the group there was a nice straight row, everyone paired off and standing apart.

Orientation and Mobility specialists reinforce the importance of "independence," "freedom," and "safety." Unfortunately, in ASL all three are said the same way – a challenge for interpreters or intervenors to convey to dDB clients. "The bubbles they put us in are sometimes so thick they are more like tanks. I cannot count the times I would approach a DeafBlind friend and get the feeling I'd just interrupted their process " (Clark, 2017, para. 31) of moving through the world. Clark goes on to say, "That's why I have worked on making my bubble as thin as possible, ready to pop the instant there's an opportunity for connection. For me, this has meant finding the right cane: a slender beauty made of fiberglass. It's so light that I can hold it like a pencil if I wanted to, with just two fingers" (Clark, 2017, para. 31).

Needless to say, intervenors working with dDB clients need to be students, asking how the dDB child or adult prefers to be led, what information they want, as well as how and when they want those cues and information, rather than telling them how you are going to provide the support services they require.

Chapter Review

The career of an interpreter can span more than simply mediating language between one culture to another. There are many distinct avenues to work with people who are dDeaf. Now that you have gained a deeper understanding of an interpreter and a slightly different track of interpreting, hopefully it has broadened your understanding. Below are terms that you should become familiar with and opportunities to always consider.

Terms to Know

- **dDeaf Plus:** Individuals who are dDeaf and have other disabilities or another disability.

- **Intervenors:** Are trained to work with dDB people, guiding them as they move around indoors or out. They are trained in tactile sign language, tadoma and palm printing in order to meet the communication needs of various dDB individuals.

- **Tadoma:** Is a method of communicating with the blind and deaf whereby their hands are placed on the lips of the speaker.

When working with a dDeaf child, teen or adult, remember to ask for their preferences in how you are to work with them. It is acceptable for you to ask:

- What kind of communication do you need?
- Do I need to be closer or further away from you when I sign?
- Shall I sign in a smaller space?
- What kind of lighting is best?

Accommodations are typically focused on providing support for each individual's areas of growth (concern).

Intervenors working with dDB clients need to become the students, asking how the

Chapter 10

NOTES

dDB child or adult prefers to be led, what information they want, as well as how and when they want those cues and information, rather than telling them how you are going to provide the support services they require.

Check all that apply:

Children with intellectual disabilities may take longer to….

___ Swim
___ Walk
___ Knowing their address
___ Counting money
___ Be able to dress themself independently
___ Climb a ladder
___ Run
___ Speak or sign

What qualities are necessary for an interpreter to work well with children who are dDeaf and have additional disabilities?

Qualities you possess

How do you reconcile the two

Qualities that are necessary

11 | Where the Jobs Are

When do you become a professional interpreter? Cody Simonsen, the owner of an interpreting agency in Utah was asked this question and he said "Anytime an athlete is paid, we call them a professional. This also applies to interpreting, anytime we pay someone for their services, we are calling them professional" (C. Simonsen, personal communication, July 15, 2019). The minute you are paid, you are considered a professional, and you should be ready for the professional world.

As you graduate and start looking for a job as an interpreter, there are three settings that new interpreters entering the field can be found, depending on their mastery of American Sign Language and English. These are education, freelance or contract with interpreting agency, and working in the VRS/VRI industry. This chapter will expound on these three settings, what you will likely encounter and the requirements of each. We will also discuss considerations you need to have in mind, as well as some tips that will prepare you as you start working professionally.

Rural, Suburban or Metropolitan
One's pay is dependent primarily on: a) your readiness, b) the setting where you are working c) your location, d) experience and e) certification. If you will be working in a metropolitan setting, you can generally expect greater competition for the available assignments and an increase in demand for interpreting services. Of course, the cost of living will be higher in a large city than in rural areas. In addition, there is less demand for interpreters in rural settings and as a result, job availability and demand for interpreters is less and the pay scale may be lower. At the same time, the cost of living is typically lower in rural areas compared to the large city. Living in metropolitan Los Angeles, CA compared to living in Raleigh, NC is significantly different, simply because the cost of living in California is significantly higher. Of course, as a result, pay rates will be higher in California compared to those in North Carolina because of the difference in the cost of living. The same is true if you choose to work in Toronto versus working in Winnipeg.

It is a good idea to start thinking about that now. When you are placed in practicum or field work, you might request a certain location so you can get a feel of the area where you might want to live upon graduation.

Full Time versus Part Time
The challenge of finding full-time work depends on a number of factors, one of which is the population of dDeaf people in the area where you will be working. dDeaf individuals often

choose to live in the city where they attended a Provincial or State school for the dDeaf following high school or after completing college. The same is true in areas near well known post secondary programs geared for dDeaf adults. As a result, these cities are usually flush with interpreting jobs.

Employee versus Freelance Work

Large urban areas are attractive for dDeaf adults because of the range of job opportunities in diverse fields of work, which often make it possible for individuals in relationships to find work. In today's economy, a majority of large cities also have multiple interpreting agencies filling requests for interpreting services. However, finding full-time work can be difficult immediately after graduation. If you need the stability of full-time work (typically 30 hours/week), there are typically interpreting jobs in the educational sector in both rural and metropolitan areas. Remember, schools are off for the summer so you will need to decide how to pay your bills during that break. Depending on the school district you work for you may be able to have your 10 month salary divided into 12 months, it will lower your monthly income, but provided financial stability for the entire year. Unfortunately, this is not available for every school district in the US.

School districts, as well as colleges and universities, often have full-time staff work for interpreters, as do certain industries which employ dDeaf workers. This will vary by the number of dDeaf employees and types of business/industries. The benefit of being an employee is that you have guaranteed hours, which may be less than 40 hours per week but they are guaranteed. In addition, employees normally have paid holidays, sick leave and medical insurance. If there is frequent driving expected in your job, the company may reimburse you based on mileage. Employees typically have state/provincial taxes deducted from their checks so they don't have to pay their taxes quarterly.

Being self employed is your other option. If this is your choice, remember that you need to collect evidence of all business expenses for tax purposes: mileage, meals, parking, tolls, etc. If 40% of the miles put on your car for interpreting you can claim 40% of your car payment, auto insurance, etc. for business deductions. For this make sure you have a tax person who is knowledgeable about self employment taxes.

VRI/VRS companies: may have work available for you, depending on the strength of your skills upon graduation. This work most likely will start with only a few supervised hours each week, but could have the potential of expanding into full or regular part-time employment. VRS/VRI companies often have mentors on-site to work with recent graduates; most of these companies also provide professional development opportunities "in house" for their employees. If you think you might be interested in this type of work, you should make some contacts while you are still a student. Ask for a tour or if possible, meet with management personnel, even before graduation, and show an interest in the services they offer. In a few cases, students can often observe interpreting work in VRS/VRI settings during their internship/practicum. You never know what might open up.

Interpreting Agencies: It is rare for a recent graduate from interpreter education programs to be offered interpreting jobs with an agency, because of the type of jobs agencies typically fill. Unless the agency has a "ready to work program," which will hire recent graduates (most often with exceptional skills) to mentor as they prepare for certification. Agencies typically call on interpreters who have some

Where the Jobs Are

NOTES

"miles under their belts." Agencies often send job opportunities to freelance interpreters who depend on part or full time employment as an interpreter. However, there are other jobs in agencies, including taking interpreting requests and calling/paging interpreters to assign those jobs, as well as secretary or bookkeeper positions. Working in these support roles may allow you to earn a living wage while getting a different take on the job market, and developing your interpreting skills.

Self employed interpreters: do not have the benefits of paid vacation or sick leave. However they are able to deduct most of their business expenses from their total income, often significantly reducing the amount of state/provincial or federal taxes paid. As a freelance interpreter, it is possible to deduct a percentage of miles you put on your car for business, reducing the total income on which taxes are based. The same is true of meals, parking, tolls paid – even a percentage of your car payment and auto insurance. Some states will allow a percentage of rent and utilities paid for your home office, so long as you use that area specifically for your interpreting business. If you pay for someone to do your taxes, the portion involving your business expenses can be deducted. Of course, you have to be sure to hang on to receipts and to keep good records in the event of an audit, but there are many advantages to being self employed.

Downfalls for the freelance interpreter include the fact that work is more scarce in the summer because school and college interpreters are off and they are competing for freelance work. In addition, you most likely will need to purchase individual medical insurance to cover doctor visits and the cost of prescriptions. Your taxes must be paid quarterly.

New Graduate versus Experienced Interpreter
There is no guaranteed way around this challenge. As a recent graduate from an interpreting program, you may need to take a reliable, part-time job outside of interpreting in order to cover your essential bills as you build your experience and credibility in the interpreting field. It is possible that you could qualify to interpret in a K-12 classroom setting, or at least have your name put on the substitute list.

If you are considering having your home base in a rural area, you need to consider the added challenge of being able to attend training and workshops opportunities which are essential for you as a new interpreter; those educational opportunities typically take place in larger cities, although more and more are offered online. Just keep this need in mind as you make these decisions.

Ongoing Education and Professional Growth Opportunities
You want to seek out interpreting colleagues as quickly as possible in the area where you expect to be living while still a student, as well as after graduation. ASL interpreters tend to be very supportive of new interpreters, willing to show you the ropes, give you tips about where you might find work, etc. The most important connection to make is finding and joining the local, regional and state/provincial interpreting organization. You should consider doing volunteer work to support the organization as another way of connecting with colleagues. This is key to getting additional training, workshops, and meeting your colleagues in the field. Continuing your professional growth in a supportive interpreting community as a recent graduate is one of the most important post-graduate goals you should have.

If you work for a school system or a VRI/VRS company, you will probably find that

Chapter 11

NOTES

they often have funds to support the fees required by outside learning opportunities. In addition, they sometimes sponsor continuing education for their employees. For that reason, you may want to consider employment with a school district, agency or VRI/VRS company. Just remember your moral obligations: if you choose to work in a school setting, you are usually the only ASL model that child will get. Are you qualified and ready for that?

INTERPRETING IN EDUCATIONAL SETTINGS

Educational interpreting includes elementary, secondary, and post-secondary environments. Post-secondary settings can be further divided into adult education or upgrading courses, vocational training, and academic settings from college through university graduate-level courses. Elementary schools serve children from preschool to 5th or 6th grade (typically ranging from ages 2 to 12); secondary schools include middle school and high school (typically from ages 12 to 18) and post-secondary serves anyone from ages 17 and up.

The probability of full time employment is greater in educational settings (full time is often defined as 30-hours per week, but it often includes sick pay, as well as pay on days the school is closed for holidays. In this setting, you are likely to find a job that offers stability, with a regular schedule, benefits such as medical and dental insurance and flexible pay with time off on holidays and summer vacation. The average pay for educational interpreters typically ranges from $15k to $45k, depending on the location, your experience and certification may also influence where you fall on the pay scale; many educational settings are willing to employ interpreters who are not yet certified.

If you choose to work in K-12 educational settings, it is important to know that the goals of integrated education is for dDeaf students includes: a) maintaining grade-appropriate academic progress, b) becoming independent, empowered, and integrated with dDeaf and hearing peers while c) developing a healthy sense of themselves as dDeaf individuals. Ideally, this includes exposure to and an understanding of dDeaf history and heritage, the culture of dDeaf people, and exposure to the rich linguistic tradition of American Sign Language. Unfortunately, a majority of mainstream educational settings fail to meet or address all of these goals. This is due, in part, to the lack of qualified instructional and support personnel, including interpreters, teaching assistants and note takers.

It is the practice in many school districts to hire a teacher's aide when a dDeaf or hard of hearing student is added to a regular education classroom. Unfortunately, in many cases, these individual aides are assigned to multiple responsibilities, including but not limited to:

- Assisting the teacher in the classroom with all of the students
- Tutoring the dDeaf student
- Interpreting for the dDeaf student
- Teaching ASL

Elementary Schools

If you accept work in an elementary school, it is important to remember that students will see you as an adult – as a teacher. Given their age, these children aren't able to discriminate between a teacher, a classroom assistant or an interpreter. They will ask you for help for simple things such as tying their shoes or

174

Where the Jobs Are

NOTES

lifting them to reach the water fountain just because you are an adult. It's okay to tie their shoes and do other simple tasks that they are not yet able to do due to their age. In addition, while working in elementary schools, you will find a huge variety of language and family backgrounds among the children. You will encounter children from multicultural and multilingual backgrounds, including some who have little to no formal English at all. You will find that some children who are trying to learn a spoken language (LSL) are transferred into an ASL program, for a range of reasons.

If you are applying to work as an interpreter in elementary settings, be sure to *read the job description carefully*. If the description includes "other duties as assigned," in addition to interpreting, be prepared to do a range of tasks that have nothing to do with being an interpreter. Because it is in your job description ("other duties as assigned"), you must comply regardless even if the request is outside the scope of a sign language interpreter. You may see yourself as an interpreter, but the school simply sees you as an employee. Other duties as assigned can be recess and lunch duty, tutoring and working with other students that can hear.

This practice is laden with problems. Because teacher's aides are considered unskilled labor, the pay rate is usually minimal, as well as the required education training and experience to qualify for employment. Further, an "educational assistant" is *not* educated as an interpreter, so full inclusion of the dDHH student is often limited, at best. The presence of a dDeaf child should justify the hiring of a qualified interpreter, not an educational aid. Unlike some students with disabilities, dDeaf children can open doors, handle books, and go to the bathroom independently. Hiring an aide often fosters the perception that deafness is a defect. It also lets the school district maintain the *appearance* of optimal support services for mainstreamed students while using unqualified, low paid personnel.

When you start working as an educational interpreter, you have to recognize that as a new, inexperienced interpreter, you are most likely putting the child you work with at a linguistic disadvantage; this is particularly true if you only started learning ASL in college and/or high school. You may think that the consequences of your late language acquisition are not significant because those you work with are still young, but the truth is that you will become the primary language model for the child you work with. You are providing access to education, as well as their access to social skills and development. You must set a primary goal of doing everything in your power to constantly be improving and expanding your ASL knowledge and skills, as well as ASL concepts related to the topics you are interpreting.

dDeaf and hard of hearing students require the services of an interpreter to maximize access, integration, equality, and empowerment for everyone in this setting. However, the actual role of an interpreter will vary dramatically depending on whether they are working with elementary, secondary or post secondary students.

Secondary Schools

Like elementary settings, secondary schools will have a range of dDeaf and hearing students, some from non-English speaking homes, some recent immigrants with minimal fluency in written or spoken English, and with both dDeaf and hearing students who need a range of academic supports throughout each day in school.

However, as you work with youth in middle and high schools, your role will typically

175

be different than that found in elementary schools, giving you more opportunities to be in an interpreter role. Should you become a staff interpreter, assigned to work with a specific dDeaf student for all their classes, consider:

- While transitioning from class to class, will you walk with the student or meet them in the next class? What kind of boundaries do you think would be appropriate between you and the student that you see everyday?

- What interpreting concerns might you have if the student's class is going on an all day field trip which includes a 3-hour tour of the local museum?

- If the school where you work is not air conditioned and the temperature for the next week is going to be over 95 degrees F., how would you modify your work clothes to accommodate that heat?

It is important to think about these kinds of situations because you will not only be the student's primary language model, you will be modeling appropriate boundaries between dDeaf individuals and interpreters as they move into adulthood.

Post-secondary Education

Post secondary education is considered public education if it is required by law. The experience of working in a post-secondary educational setting is very diverse. If you work for a college or university, you will most likely have the same classes throughout the year such as English 101, History 200 and the basic core requirements to get a degree. However, once students declare their majors, you may be working at internship sites, vocational settings, technical skills classes and other areas of trade. Regardless of which courses the student is taking, as the interpreter you need a copy of the syllabus for each class, in addition to copies of all textbooks for each class you will be interpreting so you can properly prepare for each class. You need to insist that these books be provided by the college and be on loan to you through the end of each quarter/semester, not something you have to share or are only able to access when you are on site.

Post-secondary education has a range of required interpreting skills. Most colleges and universities require a certification of some sort before hiring an interpreter, but this often varies. It is important to realize that having a certification does not mean you are qualified for the job. For example, medical school is a form of higher education that requires significant knowledge of medical terminology, surgical procedures, and human anatomy, however, you also have to be able to tolerate the sight of blood, having to wear a surgical mask for 6 hours per day, potentially being exposed to diseases, among many other challenges. Other classes might require that you interpret for a student in a welding class, which requires you to use safety equipment, in addition to having some knowledge of welding tools and materials. Copies of textbooks, as well as safety equipment should be paid for by the college.

The pay range is often a little higher in postsecondary settings compared to elementary and secondary schools, even within the same geographical area, however the chances of getting a full time job as a staff interpreter is less likely compared to elementary and secondary educational settings.

A word of caution: It is important to note that oftentimes, when an interpreter stays within the same field and same job over a period of time, their skills often plateau or deteriorate, preventing an overall improvement in their interpreting skills. School districts often do not systematically encourage professional development for sign language interpreters, classroom assistants and other support personnel. As a result, those individuals lack any encouragement to improve over time. There is often a general lack of any urgency to improve the support staff of dDeaf students; unfortunately less skilled and/or unqualified employees stay in these positions because the job is stable, and they are usually not in danger of losing the position once hired. The authors encourage you to set goals for yourself upon graduation from your interpreting program, including to consistently seek to improve your skills, expand your knowledge and to network with other interpreters in order to maximize your interpreting skills.

VRS/VRI INTERPRETING

A video relay service (VRS), also sometimes known as a video interpreting service, is a video telecommunication service that allows dDeaf, hard-of-hearing, and speech-impaired individuals to communicate over video telephones and similar technologies with hearing people in real-time, via a sign language interpreter. Video Remote Interpreting, in contrast to educational or community interpreting, requires that individuals you are interpreting for *not* be in the same room. By law, VRS is allowed to interpret calls between a Deaf person and a hearing person *only if they are in different locations*. The Federal Communications Commissions (FCC) funds the VRS companies, reimbursing them for the total minutes the VRS company provides interpreting services.

By contrast, Video Remote Interpreting facilitates communication between dDeaf and hearing people who are in the same location. VRI companies are paid by the hiring company or agency setting up video interpreting service.

Before VRS/VRI emerged as a profession, interpreters rarely got to see, much less interpret for intimate conversations. Families never had a convenient way to talk to their dDeaf family members, except in person or through print-based relays (TTY). Professional interpreters often only saw the professional or business side of the dDeaf community, but once the VRS/VRI became available, it allowed interpreters to gain the experience and the honor of interpreting for the heart of the language of the dDeaf community between dDeaf individuals and their families and friends.

Working for VRS and VRI companies present some unique challenges, including:
- Interpreters get no advanced information about what is to be interpreted before the interpreting begins, thus no opportunity to prepare
- The hours are long and require interpreters to stay in their stations, with headphones on, ready to take the next call that pops up on their computer, except for taking one 10 minute break per hour.
- This setting requires that interpreters work with callers in a flat, 2D world, rather than a 3D setting
- You never know where the next call will from or what type of setting you will find yourself in and the variety can be quite significant
- Your work is only as good as the internet connectivity
- Interpreters are challenged to interpret personal conversations, including sign names, explicit language, references to locally known businesses
- You will also interpret intimate conversations, including name signs, locations, and other things that are very familiar to the people talking to each other but not the interpreter

Chapter 11

NOTES

The exciting thing about VRS interpreting is that you will be able to experience a wide range of jobs every day and exposure to a variety of different clients and numerous spoken/signed dialects.

VRS/VRI companies often provide professional development opportunities for their interpreters but they also typically require certification before allowing you to apply, and most companies have a screening process that you will be required to go through. There have been instances where an educational interpreter who has worked in schools for many years applies and fails to get a job in the VRS/VRI industry. This happens because those interpreters lack the range of skills required to manage spontaneous conversations, and often they have not continued their growth in interpreting or expanding the cultural knowledge required to support their developing skills. Unfortunately, these interpreters end up plateauing.

Video Remote Interpreting (VRI) is a controversial topic as this book goes to press. Many companies, hospitals and professionals are starting to provide VRI services because it is more cost effective and less of a scheduling headache. However, there are situations where VRI is not ideal, such as the birth of a baby, a dissertation defense and legal proceedings which require having an interpreter present in the room. If you work for a VRI agency, be aware of these situations and make a judgement call as to whether a situation should have an onsite or VRI interpreter. However, VRI makes sense in rural areas where getting an interpreter is almost impossible and expensive.

The pay for the VRS interpreting is dependent on your certifications, experience, and geographical location. VRS pays on average from $25 an hour to $45 an hour. VRI interpreters may earn approximately the same but the range is usually wider because it is more similar to freelance work. VRI interpreter pay will range from $18 an hour to $65 an hour.

In the VRS setting, you will be interpreting calls that range from ordering pizza to work calls and from parole calls to calling the social security office. There will be days where you will be doing non-stop interpreting and other days where you will be put on hold for most of the day. You will be interpreting arguments and intense conversations which will require that you to match the tone and emotion of the callers. You will have times where you will call 911 for the caller and must make sure you understand everything, which is difficult when the caller is in distress. You will handle job interviews over the phone and have to sound professional and competent, "knowing your stuff" because the caller "knows their stuff."

FREELANCE INTERPRETING

Unless you grew up with ASL as one of your childhood languages and have an exceptional mastery of spoken English, you will not be qualified to work as a freelance interpreter for several years after graduating from an interpreter education program. Many sign language interpreters prefer to work with an interpreting agency, either on a contract basis or as a staff interpreter, rather than being a self-employed practitioner. Freelance interpreters are guaranteed opportunities to work in a variety of settings; they rarely work for the same client two days in a row, they are constantly going into new environments with different dDeaf and hearing people. In addition, they have full control over their own schedules and can decide whether they work 40-hours a week or 15-hours a week. They just have to make enough money to support themselves.

178

Where the Jobs Are

NOTES

Pay rates for freelance practitioners are as varied as the number of interpreter jobs on any given day. The pay tends to reflect the geographical area of employment. Further, there are several ways in which interpreters can assess fees for service. Some interpreters charge by the hour, some by the job, or others by the full or half-day. If you are living in an area where the cost of living is high and you are being paid by the hour, the rate of pay might range from $30.00 - $75.00 per hour. If you are living in a rural, low cost of living area, you may be paid $12.00 to $30.00 per hour.

When working freelance jobs, interpreters typically charge a minimum of two-hours which covers the cost for travel, parking, preparation time and administrative work. If the job is longer than an hour, you will need to request a team (depending on the complexity or density of the content), as well as a fixed hourly rate. Further, if you are working one job for more than three hours, you may want to negotiate half-day and all day-rates. Some settings will offer a flat rate for working all day. Examples of this type of work include working for a multi-day conference, in a court hearing, or for new employee orientations.

Determining Your Rates

There are many variables in determining your rate of pay. As stated above, the cost of living in a geographic area is one factor. Other critical factors include the level of education attained by the interpreter, the years of interpreting experience, as well as the type of certifications you have obtained. Interpreters working as staff or contract interpreters should take the cost of doing business into consideration when setting rates wi th the agency. Consider the following expenses wh en you calculate your rates:

- Auto registration and insurance, depreciation of your car, gas, oil, toll fees, and parking or expenses related to public transit
- Office expenses, including stationary, envelopes, postage, business cards, telephone, fax, cell phone, email, computer hardware and software, office rent, office supplies
- Taxes, retirement fund, disability insurance these are all required for the private practice interpreter
- Billing/booking time: time to make calls to confirm jobs, complete and mail invoices, etc. because when you are in the office doing these tasks, you are not working (i.e. earning money) so the cost of this time needs to be figured into the cost of doing business
- Business clothing, any shoes, safety gear or clothing used exclusively when working in the role of an interpreter
- Insurance personal health, business and liability
- Press releases, website and advertising for business

If your agency is not covering these expenses, you need to work out something with them.

In addition, contract or self-employed interpreters must plan for those weeks (months) when business is light, because their income will be reduced as a result. For example, it is sometimes challenging to get freelance jobs in the summer because all the educational interpreters are vying for jobs

Other business skills are important in order to establish, grow and expand your business opportunities. This will include:

Chapter 11

NOTES

1. Development of resumes
2. Skills in writing business letters
3. Basic bookkeeping, techniques for developing invoices and collecting money owed to you
4. Schedule maintenance, booking appointments at appropriate intervals, confirming jobs
5. Development of business policies

Before you accept assignments from an agency, be sure to confirm what the job pertains to and consider whether you are ready for that kind of assignment. For example, if someone asks you to do a legal assignment that requires you to interpret for a court hearing, you should refer them to an appropriate interpreter who is legally certified and legally approved to work in courts. Do not accept something like this without proper experience, certification and special training. A side note related to resumes, most agencies are primarily interested in evidence of your certification, if you are not certified as of yet make sure you have a resume ready to go.

OTHER THOUGHTS

There are a few things that could cause you to leave the field of interpreting prematurely. It is imperative that you are aware of these factors as you enter the field and plan for your ongoing well being.

Repetitive Strain Injury (RSI)

There has been a frightening surge in the rate of repetitive strain injury or repetitive motion injuries (also known as overuse syndrome) among sign language interpreters as work opportunities have increased over the years. RSI tends to result in carpal tunnel syndrome, tendonitis, tennis elbow and/or brachial neuralgia, all of which can lead to total disability. Be sure to see the stretching exercises in the Toolbox. The best prevention for RSI includes:

- Proper warm up before working: warming up the hands and arms prior to work and during any extended breaks in a job; special care must be taken by interpreters working in cold climates or in air conditioned buildings.
- Regular exercise and good nutrition: interpreting is a physical activity involving the muscles and tendons of the arms, face, neck, shoulders and upper body. Further, interpreters sometimes stand for long periods of time requiring back and lower body stamina. Maintaining overall physical conditioning and nutrition will increase your longevity as an interpreter.
- Check your signing habits: some interpreters develop particular signing and fingerspelling habits which stress the muscles and tendons in the wrists and arms. Be aware of your ergonomic or lack of ergonomic behavior. Some individuals actually try to change hand dominance. Ask a teacher or colleague to look at you while signing to see if there are any signing features you should modify to prevent damage to your body. Often, new signers try to develop their own "signing style" as they are developing their new identity as an interpreter which frequently puts a strain on your hands and arms. This must be avoided.
- Insist on appropriate working conditions: Interpreter should take a 10-minute break for every 50 minutes worked. Further, if a job is longer than two hours in length, two interpreters should work the job as a team. You must advocate actively to obtain working conditions in accordance with these restrictions, because the alternative could be an end to your career as an interpreter.

Emotional Burnout

Working with people day in and day out is stressful. Interpreting requires working with people, many of whom do not understand your work or the languages or cultures involved. In addition, interpreting often takes us into situations which involve emotional extremes, going from the exhilaration of the birth of a baby, to a diagnosis with a fatal disease, or the agony of interpreting as someone is being fired from a job. We go into settings that are stressful in themselves: prisons, lock-up psychiatric wards and intensive care units, among others.

Consider all of these factors as you work toward becoming an interpreter, it is essential that you have well developed stress management regimen and support systems in place. The failure to do so may result in emotional burnout and an early departure from the field.

Chapter Review

Three work settings have been discussed in this chapter. Describe the pro's and con's of each of those settings below, which one appeals to you and why?

- Educational

- VRS/VRI

- Staff Interpreter/Freelance

Public education has three levels. Summarize the differences in these settings and factors interpreters should consider before taking work there.

- Preschool

- Elementary

- Secondary to Post-secondary

Explain the similarities and differences between work in VRS/VRI settings. Explain why you are/or are not ready to do this type of work.

What settings do freelance interpreters often work in find? List 5-6 settings. Explain why you are/or are not ready to do this type of work.

TERMS TO KNOW:

- Role Space
- Ethics
- Morality
- Teleological
- Deontological

12 | Principles of Practice

This chapter addresses the ethical and professional behavior expected of all sign language practitioners, how they should interact with dDeaf and hearing participants, as well as their interpreter colleagues. However, before we get into the details of ethical decision making and behavior. We will offer you some very *practical* advice that should make your journey as an interpreter a little bit easier. First, the years you spend in school, whether two or four years, will be over in a blink of an eye – exhaust yourself acquiring new skills. Do not pass up any opportunities. Here are some things you can do to grow your skills, your reputation and your opportunities:

- **Attend:** Go to as many workshops, trainings, and learning opportunities as you can afford, may your face be recognized by every presenter and professional (this leads to the second point)
- **Network:** Don't simply attend, mingle, chat, introduce yourself, it is best not to hang in a comfortable cluster with your classmates – get known
- **Join:** Become a member – join your local and national interpreting organization, if your state does not have a local affiliate, join the dDeaf organizations. It is what we do
- **Mentor:** Find a mentor for your language or your interpreting or both. Offer to buy them lunch, you are a student after all. Finding a mentor while you are a student is courageous and shows your commitment

Oh yes, one more thing, if you make a mistake own it, apologize and try to make it right. Everyone makes mistakes, but not everyone takes responsibility for them. Be different, be better.

The information in this chapter is critical to know and apply in all of your professional interactions. Candidly, you will not likely *master* the norms and expectations outlined here for some time; this content provides an introduction to the norms and expectations required of all interpreters. It will take years of practice. You will make mistakes, but learn from them – grow into the expectations outlined here. After graduating from your interpreter education program, you will need to keep learning, growing and doing. As a new interpreter, engage in educational opportunities and attend professional development training – it is expected and will be a healthy habit for the life of your career.

Principles of Practice

NOTES

A knowledgeable interpreter will be more apt to think through the challenges of ethical dilemmas. Your reputation is closely tied to your competence and ethical decision making. It is essential to develop the ability to *think critically,* to apply meta-ethical principles and apply RID's Code of Professional Conduct or CASLI's Code of Ethics and Guidelines for Professional Conduct to your daily work and decision making process. The authors of this text have a total of more than 200 years of experience as interpreters and we are still on a learning curve. We invite you to join us in this ever challenging application of principles of professional practice.

As you grow in your professional practice, you will realize there are no easy or simplistic answers to the important issues and decisions that you will encounter. With time, and experience, your sense of options and appropriate responses will grow and support your ability to make appropriate decisions in the moment. It is rare if you are given time to think through an ethical dilemma. It is important to recognize the value of working with more experienced interpreters as colleagues and mentors. It is essential to regularly engage in ongoing dialogue with your colleagues as you encounter more complex and multi-layered interpreting situations that are loaded with ethical challenges. This is one path, among many, that will lead to developing a firm foundation as a professional interpreter. Consider workshops, mentoring, classes and self study, all of which help prepare you to face real ethical situations.

WHAT DISTINGUISHES PROFESSIONALS?

Before embarking on an in-depth discussion on ethics and decision making, it is essential to understand what it means to be a *professional* and its relevance to sign language interpreting. To illustrate this further, think of other "professions" that are looked at with a degree of skepticism. For example, when a used car salesman tells you, "That car is perfect for you!" or the sales clerk in the store says, "That dress is stunning on you!" – you are fully aware that their flattery or persuasion is solely because they want your money (they too, must make a living). On the other hand, when a doctor tells you, "You really need this surgery" or the interpreter coordinator says, "This job requires six interpreters," you assume their recommendation stems from their professional judgment based on what is best or necessary. "Professionals, by the very definition, are individuals in a position of trust, who are called...to judiciously and ethically use the power inherent in their positions" (Humphrey, 1999, p. i). Professionals, like doctors, social workers, and mental health counselors work in the human service profession to strengthen, support and empower individuals by keeping their interests paramount. Sign language interpreting professionals are committed to promoting the well being of the dDeaf community by ensuring that people who are dDeaf have communication access and, in doing so, are empowered to live a rich and meaningful life.

Humphrey (1999) explains that being a *professional* means we are in the position of holding a sacred trust and with that trust comes a measure of power. The combination of trust, power and expertise generate specific standards which the general public comes to expect. "Those we refer to as 'professionals' generally possess knowledge and/or skills that their clients, patients, or students do not have. Further, they are in a position to profit from that disparity of knowledge and/or skills" (p.5).

That is that very reason that we find ethical violations from those we hold in such regard are heinous. Sadly, we are reminded almost daily that this is not always the

Chapter 12

NOTES

case. Just watch the media and you will find the clamor of allegations and denials regarding tax evasion, corruption, fraud, influence peddling, sexual impropriety, insider trading, and drug abuse that raises disturbing questions about clergy, teachers, government leaders and others in professional roles. As a result, the subject of ethics has emerged as one of the most fundamental issues confronting our society today.

Furthermore, it is the *intention* of the professional to offer quality services, yet to practice without the necessary competence or evidence of competence is to take advantage of those being served as there is a level of trust inherent in the position of interpreter. Adherence to professional standards of credentialing is evidence of competence and capacity to practice. There are numerous credentialing systems, yet "it is estimated that approximately 55% of the identifiable workforce remains uncertified" (Witter-Merithew, & Johnson, 2004, p. 12). If employment, as an interpreter, does not require a practitioner to obtain state or national certification what evidence can be offered for their competence? To practice without informing those you serve that you do not possess credentials is an abuse of trust.

> Levy (1993) points out that if the person receiving professional services is weaker, more vulnerable, less intelligent, more dependent, less capable of exercising good judgement, or disadvantaged, and the professional's position or role makes it possible to exploit such deficits, the degree of ethical responsibility on the professional escalates proportionality (Cited in Humphrey, 1999, p. 7).

It is our interactions with dDeaf people that make what we do as interpreters potentially harmful or helpful to that community. For this reason, the public holds practitioners to a standard of professionalism and ethical practice. Practitioners distinguished themselves by certain essential characteristics:

1. Professional practitioners have specialized skills and knowledge that is unique and as such, they are in the position to provide a particular service which requires credentialing (licensure, certification or both)
2. Professional practitioners are expected to have studied a specialized body of knowledge, and are authorized to operate within a defined scope of practice
3. Professional practitioners are required to adhere to a clearly articulated set of values or a code of ethical conduct (Humphrey, 1999)

Furthermore, because of their status as a professional, it is assumed that they know how to perform their duties, that they will come to the task prepared, and they are worthy of the trust placed in them by their clients, patients, parishioners or students. Professionals are expected to deal with sensitive information in a discrete manner and they are expected to avoid emotional entanglements that would likely be detrimental to their clientele. In addition, most professionals work in the privacy of an office or in settings where no one will question their decisions. It is critical, then, that a professional has a well developed sense of ethical conduct.

For the sake of time and space we will not unpack all of the theoretical elements of character, values and beliefs. However, those ideals will likely be addressed as they arise during our analysis of some of the related concepts such as morality and integrity. Additionally, as a sign language practitioner, you will find there are no easy or simplistic answers and your sense of appropriate decisions and responses will grow and change with experience.

Principles of Practice

NOTES

At this juncture the authors would like to offer a bit of clarification. In this chapter the word *professional* will be used often in relation to interpreters and their behavior. Our emphasis to make it evident that our behaviors should be different from untrained persons and that we are held to a higher standard. We do not recommend when you introduce yourself as an interpreter that you say that you are a "professional sign language interpreter," rather than engender trust it may have the opposite effect. Consider how you would feel if your doctor introduced themselves as a "professional doctor."

ROLE SPACE

What are the accepted behaviors of interpreters when they are working? What distinguishes them from any of the other participants attending who knows how to sign? For the first 35-plus years of practice the answer to this question has been fairly rigid; ASL/English interpreters presented themselves as though they were *invisible* in the very event where they were facilitating communication between individuals who used different languages. The unwritten rules of conduct are *rooted* in the history of the profession, limiting the behaviors of professional interpreters by deeming certain actions acceptable while others were considered unacceptable. To further remove us from the interpreted event we contrived philosophical names (models) to describe our behavior; conduit, machine, facilitator, telephone, ghost (Martinez-Gomez, 2015). However, it was not always this way (for additional information on the history of interpreting see chapter 2).

> Historically, interpreters were anything but invisible – allies in explorations and conquests, partners in diplomacy and trade, helpers in private affairs. However, with the advent of training and the development of interpreting as a profession, role models such as the ones described through these metaphors took hold (Martinez-Gomez, 2015, p. 175).

Essentially, the many facets of the interpreter were reduced into a rigid and prescriptive role (Lee, & Llewellyn-Jones, 2011). This restrictive construct is visible by our continued *over emphasis* on the behavior of the interpreter. As interpreters, we are expected to either ask permission or inform participants that we need to "step out of role" to obtain or share information critical to the work we are performing. Also disconcerting is that as a whole, interpreters, speak of their role separate from their responsibilities. Simply put, one cannot have a role without the accompanying responsibilities. The construct of the interpreter role and responsibilities must be reinvented and redesigned to demonstrate that our behavior as an interpreter is not fixed or static, but fluid and continually adapting to meet the needs of the interpreting environment (Llewellyn-Jones & Lee, 2011)

> There cannot be one right approach to all interactions. To talk of "stepping out of role" is to miss the point. Interpreters are human beings with specialist communication skills and one can't step out of being a human being. Is it possible that the notion of "role" is simply a construct that interpreters have hidden behind to avoid their individual responsibility for professional decision-making? (Llewellyn-Jones & Lee, 2009, p. 6).

It is evident that the notion of the invisible and disempowered interpreter as "an uncontested principle, has recently started to be deconstructed in favour of the image of the interpreter as an active third party in the interaction" (Martinez-Gomez, 2015, p. 175). To illustrate the idea that the interpreter's role is an

Chapter 12

NOTES

unrealistic and untenable construct – consider visiting your doctor for an appointment, would your physician *ever* say, "I'm going to step out of my role to share some advice with you." No, that idea is ridiculous – instead he would likely say, "In my professional opinion I recommend..."

Fortunately, several researchers started exploring and suggesting changes concerning these archaic and unrealistic restrictions and expectations (Wadensjo, 1998; Metzger, 1999; Roy, 2000). Llewellyn-Jones & Lee (2011) addressed principles concerning role space in ways that provide a practical guide to interpreter practices. These ideals, long overdue, will impact our current and future behavior. Rather than outlining a litany of "appropriate and inappropriate behaviors" for interpreters to follow unquestioningly, this approach calls on interpreters to act with *integrity*. Furthermore, by accepting the role and responsibilities, interpreters become an active, dynamic participant acting on behalf of those whom they serve by "managing the myriad of factors that foster successful interactions" (Llewellyn-Jones, & Lee, 2011, p. 1).

It is obvious that interpreters are required to make linguistic, interpersonal, cognitive and cultural decisions, however, to date, there has been no overt recognition that interpreters are, in fact, interactants in the events they interpret, along with other participants (Cokely, 1992; Dean, & Pollard, 2001). Llewellyn-Jones and Lee (2011) proposed that the integral role of interpreters necessitates they make active and ongoing decisions while working, which reflects on the multi-dimensional nature of an interpreter's role, stating that interpreters are "acting with integrity and making informed decisions appropriate for the domain goals and characteristics of the interlocutors" (p.3), which is required for interpreted interactions to be successful. They referred to this model as **Role Space.** A closer look reveals that the very roles taken on by an interpreter, when successfully mediating cross lingual and cross cultural interactions, involve three elements: (1) presentation of self, (2) interaction management, and (3) participant alignment. Let's take a closer look at three dimensions of interpreter behavior.

Presentation of Self

This phrase is used to identify those linguistic and non-linguistic behaviors in which the interpreter speaks for and acts on their own behalf; for example, an interpreter introducing themself or answers questions directed at them, even when not related to the interpretation per se. Another way of stating this is that they behave like everyone else in the room and by doing so do not call undue attention to themselves. Typical interactions interpreter's encounter while at an interpreting assignment could include being invited to get coffee or snacks when not interpreting. Responding directly to a question asked of them or making a comment regarding the temperature of the room (Llewellyn-Jones, & Lee, 2011).

Interaction Management

Interpreters are often put in a position of managing or encouraging the progress of an interpreted interaction, such as asking an attendee to repeat something they said because the interpreter was unable to hear the statement or perhaps the interpreter is uncertain if they understood the comment made or question posed. Such a request would be made because failing to do so might change the outcome of the interaction, if omitted or not accurately interpreted. It is important to note that another participant present could make the same type of requests (repetition or clarification), but for *different reasons*. "The crucial difference is the reason why the interpreter makes such requests; specifically that they are requesting to change.

something in the interaction that is impeding effective interpretation" (Llewellyn-Jones, & Lee, 2011, p. 5).

Participant Alignment

If an interpreter behaves in a stoic or disconnected manner while interpreting human interactions, there is a possibility that the participant(s) who can hear will feel uncomfortable due to an atypical reaction. For example, directly looking at the person who is speaking or reacting to something that an interlocutor may have said by smiling when something humorous is conveyed or showing a sad emotional reaction to something tragic that is communicated. This element refers to *how much* the interpreter is directing their communication to a participant or a group of participants (Llewellyn-Jones, & Lee, 2011).

The term "role space," refers to the increased awareness of the various dimensions occupied by an interpreter at any point during an interpreted interaction and recognizes the work and presence of an interpreter in any setting always has some level of impact on that interaction. That impact is less in certain settings where interpreters are limited to a very restricted role space such as in court. In other settings, however, such as a family reunion, interpreting in elementary school or interpreting the gathering of family and friends following a funeral, the interpreter is present in all three of dimensions, dealing with the presentation of self, using interaction management as needed and supporting participant alignment. Though interpreters are attendees in meetings for other reasons, such as communication access, it is important that interpreters behaviors "are consistent with, rather than counter to, the expectations of the participants. By normalizing their own communicative behaviors, and by acting in ways that are similar to the other participants, interpreters can be more effective in facilitating successful interactions" (Llewllyn-Jones, & Lee, 2013, p. 59).

> The evolution of the interpreting profession *requires* that interpreters acknowledge their presence and potential impact on interpreted interactions. Further, the choices and behaviors of "interpreters should be guided by the size and shape of the 'role space' they take up in each interaction to determine the most appropriate and effective behavior" (Lee, & Llewellyn-Jones, 2011, p. 6).

WHAT ARE ETHICS?

We will provide a simple, yet foundational definition of **ethics** in order to build a greater understanding of the term. Ethics are, "the basic concepts and fundamental principles of *decent human conduct* [emphasis added]" (WebFinance Inc., 2020, para. 1). Ethical behavior encompasses the way we treat one another, how we behave (publicly and privately), and what we do with what we know. Ethics also give consideration to the higher principles, behaviors and ideals that guide the thinking and actions of all individuals. "It includes...the essential equality of all men and women, human or natural rights, obedience to the law of land, concern for health and safety and, increasingly, also for the natural environment" (WebFinance Inc., 2020, para. 1).

Ethical guidelines are shaped by the principles of right and wrong which influence the practice and behavior of professionals. The principles, guidelines and standards of *decent human conduct* are then codified in the broadest sense so that the application of the tenets are not prescriptive. Rather than adhering to tenets in a literal, inflexible and unyielding manner, we espouse that interpreters have the autonomy to apply the ethical tenets and guidelines in such a manner that they result in the best outcome for each participant. Attorneys, doctors, counselors, teachers and sign language interpreters, (among other professionals), are all expected to abide by a set of standards that guide their decisions and behavior in each field of professional practice.

Ethics are not related to one's feelings, religious beliefs or the law. It is important to clarify that ethics are not synonymous with **morality**. Morality can be expressed as the principles of right and wrong as defined by culture or society; when codified, they are most often called laws or ordinances. Moreover, behaving ethically is not the same as following what society accepts as right or wrong. Rather, ethics refer to well-founded standards of appropriate and inappropriate behaviors that dictate how individuals should act and react in their professional interactions with clients. Ethics are guidelines for behavior, principles of conduct, and state of goodness guided by moral principles (Seymour, 1990).

It should be apparent that the abstract nature of *ethics*, much like culture, has numerous definitions, perspectives and interpretations. However, in this text, we will contain our definition of **ethics** to a *set of principles that characterizes the appropriate and decent conduct guiding one's professional obligations and behavior toward others.* As an interpreter, it is not enough for you to memorize the RID or CASLI Guidelines for Professional Conduct. Rather, it is necessary for you to internalize the tenets and guidelines to create a solid understanding of your moral and ethical beliefs, which translates into principled professional conduct. It is the obligation of interpreting practitioners to integrate these ideals into their daily decisions, actions, and interactions.

For these reasons, CASLI and RID have developed guidelines for professional behavior, articulating the standards that define what is judged as appropriate conduct in the field of sign language interpretation. Professionals function in the real world, where we must exercise our judgment concerning issues that often have no easy answers (Stromberg, 1990). Our codes of professional conduct provide guidelines to assist us as we make, review and evaluate our professional decisions. It is hoped that the adherence to a code of conduct would foster a sense of trust from those who utilize interpreting services. However, understanding the intricacies of the codes of conduct make it difficult for community members to interpret and apply the tenets in meaningful and effective ways. Lou Fant, renowned interpreter and pioneer in the field of sign language interpreting, noted that standards of conduct elicit trust from consumers toward interpreters because they know that "we will always act morally in our dealings with them." During the early days of our profession that may have been the case, unfortunately, the history of the interpreting profession has shown otherwise. Wayne Betts, Jr., Co-Founder and Chief Strategic Officer for *Convo,* shared some of his experiences at *StreetLeverage,* 2016:

> The Deaf community shares information. The community knows and shares the interpreters to avoid, those who should never be permitted to interpret. This information sharing goes on all the time...As we watch the interpreter in these situations, the resentment stirs and builds with each request for clearer communication while we try to make do (Betts, 2016, para. 4).

Some interpreters may not have acted morally in the past, but today is a new day, let us strive to never, ever be one of "those" interpreters.

Principles of Practice

NOTES

Both the RID and CASLI codes identify competent, ethical and professional behaviors. These codes expect that interpreting practitioners will apply critical thinking skills and decision making skills in order to come to well reasoned decisions. Those skills must be honed and well rehearsed enabling interpreters to make good decisions even when working under difficult or stressful conditions.

NAD-RID CODE OF PROFESSIONAL CONDUCT

The authors encourage you to learn the meta-ethical principle for each tenet (listed in bold capital letters) in the NAD-RID Code of Professional Conduct (CPC) which will enable you to recall the guiding force behind each tenet and illustrative behavior. Embodied in the code is the driving principle that every interpreter will *do no harm*. dDeaf and hearing people have a right to *expect* the following from every interpreter hired to provide interpreting services.

1. **PRIVACY:** Interpreters adhere to standards of confidential communication.
2. **COMPETENCE:** Interpreters possess the professional skills and knowledge required for the specific interpreting situation.
3. **BOUNDARIES:** Interpreters conduct themselves in a manner appropriate to the specific interpreting situation.
4. **RESPECT:** Interpreters demonstrate respect for consumers.
5. **TEAMWORK:** Interpreters demonstrate respect for colleagues, interns and students of the profession.
6. **PROFESSIONALISM:** Interpreters maintain ethical business practices.
7. **SELF-EVOLUTION:** Interpreters engage in professional development (Adopted 2005).[1]

The tenets of the RID Code of Professional Conduct are to be viewed holistically and as guiding principles for professional behavior. Because of the breadth of these tenets there is no need for a separate code for each area of interpreting. In their ongoing effort to practice professionalism, it is the responsibility of every interpreter to exercise judgment and critical thought when applying lessons learned in practical experience to future actions. Further application of these principles to their conduct, should be governed by a *reasonable interpreter* standard. "This standard represents the hypothetical interpreter who is appropriately educated, informed, capable, aware of professional standards, and fair-minded" (Registry of Interpreters for the Deaf, 2005).

CANADIAN ASSOCIATION OF SIGN LANGUAGE INTERPRETERS (CASLI)

CASLI's current Code of Ethics and Guidelines for Professional Conduct was developed by the Association of Visual Language Interpreters of Canada (AVLIC). Practitioners began by *first* identifying the values upon which each standard of conduct was based, then elaborated on the expectations of professional practitioners more fully. They also overtly state the purpose of the Code of Ethics in the preamble and values below.

CASLI CODE OF ETHICS

Preamble
The purpose of the Code of Ethics is to provide guidance for interpreters, and in so

---

[1]*For more information on the RID Code of Professional Conduct see: https://rid.org/ethics/code-of-professional-conduct/*

Chapter 12

NOTES

doing, ensure quality of service for all persons involved. Adherence to the following tenets is essential for maintaining national standards; professional discretion must be exercised at all times.

The Canadian Association of Visual Language Interpreters expects its members to maintain high standards of professional conduct in their capacity and identity as an interpreter. Members are required to abide by the Code of Ethics and to follow the Guidelines for Professional Conduct as a condition of membership in the organization. The document articulates ethical principles, values, and tenets of conduct to guide all members of CASLI in their pursuit of professional practice. It is intended to provide direction to interpreters for ethical and professional decision making in their day-to-day work. The Code of Ethics and Guidelines for Professional Conduct is the mechanism by which the public is protected in the delivery of service.

VALUES OF THE CASLI CODE OF ETHICS & GUIDELINES FOR PROFESSIONAL CONDUCT

1. **Professional accountability:** Accepting responsibility for professional decisions and actions.
2. **Professional competence:** Committing to provide quality professional service throughout one's practice.
3. **Non-discrimination:** Approaching professional service with respect and cultural sensitivity.
4. **Integrity in professional relationships:** Dealing honestly and fairly with consumers and colleagues.
5. **Integrity in business practices:** Dealing honestly and ethically in all business practices.[2]

Members are to understand that each of these core values and accompanying sections are to be considered when making professional and ethical decisions in their capacity and identity as an interpreter. These values are of equal weight and importance. The complete ethical guidelines for the RID and CASLI codes can be found on their websites.

KNOWING YOURSELF: THE FOUNDATION OF ETHICS

Ethical behavior grows out of a strong moral sense, the ability to think critically and the courage to do the right thing. Everyone has misbeliefs about themselves, the world around them and their place in it. Addressing your misbeliefs aids in your overall moral development and your ability to consciously make good decisions – the cornerstone of becoming an ethical person. Many of our decisions and behaviors, in fact, are motivated by subconscious factors stemming from a lifetime of experiences, both good and bad. A personality formed in a negative environment of excessive control may not be prepared to adapt to an adult way of life. Wounded individuals are often left with basic problems of trust, autonomy, and initiative (Herman Lewis, 1997). As interpreters, it is wise to deal with the experiences we have gone through on our way to adulthood, many such experiences shape our self concept (Minirth, Meier, Hemfelt, Sneed, & Hawkins, 1990). Many of us come to adulthood with characteristics such as:

- Poor self esteem, struggling with feeling of shame

---

[2]*For more information on the CASLI Code of Ethics see: https://www.avlic.ca/ethics-and-guidlines/english#overlay-context=user/285*

Principles of Practice

NOTES

- Covering or compensating for a poor self concept through actions of perfectionism, caretaking, controlling, judgmental attitudes toward others or hyper responsibility/hyper irresponsibility
- People pleasing
- Changing what you believe based on your peer group
- Struggling to be assertive (Bradshaw, 1990)

It should be self evident why these internal struggles could negatively impact your ability to be an effective sign language interpreter. It is essential you deal honestly with who you are today and how you got to be that person. The failure to deal with these issues may result in applying the Code of Professional Conduct in the most simplistic, dogmatic, rule oriented approach. Furthermore, the reasons for becoming an interpreter may be rooted in your need to care for others by getting overly involved in their lives. Both of these responses are detrimental to you as an interpreter, the dDeaf community, and the profession as a whole.

LEARNING TO MAKE ETHICAL DECISIONS

As an interpreter, you will find yourself in situations that require you to make difficult decisions regarding behavioral, linguistic, cultural or professional conflicts (to name a few). It should be evident at this point *every decision* made while interpreting is loaded with ethical implications that can impact members of the dDeaf community. These conflicts require ethical decision making skills based on your ability to think quickly and critically. This section of the chapter provides you with an introduction to help you develop those skills. A word of encouragement, these skills should be applied often throughout your education and professional practice.

As you become an interpreter, please do not settle, instead become an introspective, reflective and an analytical thinker – learn to question your solutions, both positive and negative. This ongoing retrospective thinking fosters opportunities to discover better options and outcomes. However, if you find that you repeatedly are unable to make appropriate, ethical choices, the problem may be due to:

- Lack of clarity regarding expectations of professional interpreters across multiple facets
- Uncertainty or personal conflict regarding how to deal with client demands, employer expectations, the expectations identified in the Code of Professional Conduct, as well as your personal values, moral and principles
- Ignorance or naivete resulting from lack of experience
- Lack of awareness regarding both short and long term consequences of decisions made

It is imperative that you can live with each and every decision you make, you must look at yourself in the mirror every morning and every evening and you need to be okay with you. In addition, irrespective of the decisions you make, you must be able to live the consequences of that decision. For these reasons, frequent practice is a must throughout your education and beyond. Consistent practice will only improve your ability in identifying ethical and professional challenges. As an interpreter, you will encounter complex, delicate and potentially frustrating situations in which you must make decisions. A renowned ethicist cautions us that:

191

we may be tempted to do wrong – but only because the wrong appears, if only in some small way and perhaps momentarily, to be right. For most people, some sober reflection is all that's required to recognize a wolflike moral temptation masquerading in the lamb's clothing of a seemingly ethical dilemma (Kidder, 1992, p. 75).

Some situations will proffer fairly obvious right versus wrong choices; some actions (or lack of action) are widely understood to be wrong. However, you will also encounter situations which present you with right versus right choices; these are some of the toughest choices you will encounter in both your personal or professional life. "They are genuine dilemmas precisely because each side is firmly rooted in one of our...core values" (Kidder, 1992, p. 75). We will state some facts related to the conflicts that we, as interpreters, face on a regular basis.

- FACT: Interpreters deal with multiple demands, some of which are intricate, occasionally contradictory, and most are difficult to deal with
- FACT: There is rarely one single right answer or correct response. For that reason, it is important to develop the ability to identify and weight your options
- FACT: Interpreters don't always have time to research the *correct, appropriate,* or *ethically responsible* decision in real time

For that reason, you must (1) learn to distinguish between a right versus right dilemma and right versus wrong issues; (2) listen to interpreters who have been in the field for some time regarding some of the challenges they have faced, what decisions they made and how they reached those decisions; (3) engage in frequent practice with classmates and if your solutions are significantly different, use "energetic self-reflection" (Kidder, 1992, p. 71) to determine why.

It is important that you *deliberately* work with those who do not think like you do; choose different critical thinking partners. Work through scenarios, do not give up if it becomes challenging, work until each of you comes to a satisfactory conclusion. Understand that a *satisfactory conclusion* does not mean you will be happy or content with the outcome. As you begin to address each scenario take the time to identify the type of dilemma – whether it is a right versus right or right versus wrong issue. If there is disagreement among your classmates, spend the time to come to a resolution. As you are working with your colleagues/classmates reflect on your process, review your responses, as well as your patterns of thinking. Try to come up with a variety of responses and the ability to defend those choices; identifying where your process broke down (if it did). In addition, adhere to best practices while answering questions during role plays so you will be ready to face demanded made of you.

FACT: You are human so you will make some mistakes and some poor choices. As a professional, you must take responsibility when that happens. It is essential that you begin applying deliberate "energetic self reflection" to these experiences. Practice how you can (1) deal with an event after making an error or poor choice (2) review how to avoid repeating that mistake.

Mistakes are part of life; the goal is to learn from them and make NEW mistakes, rather than repeating them the same mistakes.

FACT: It takes time to develop professional discretion and judgment. Be patient with yourself and with your fellow students. Remember to extend the grace you want to receive.

Principles of Practice

NOTES

What's the Issue?

Kidder (1992) explains that we all face tough choices, and we are inclined to avoid difficult situations, it is atypical to move toward difficult choices but avoiding conflict is also a decision.

> Sometimes we simply brood endlessly over possible outcomes or agonize about paths to pursue. And even if we do try to resolve them, we don't always do so by energetic self reflection. Sometimes we simply bull our way through to a conclusion by sheer impatience and assertive self-will as though getting it *resolved* were more important than getting it *right* (Kidder, 1992, p. 71).

Right versus Wrong

For most of us, when faced with the issue of comparing a blatant moral "wrong" against a moral "right," there is little doubt of which side to take. When people in positions of trust violate that trust – the right and wrong in those matters are often without debate. Teachers are entrusted with the educational well being of our children and when a teacher uses their position of authority and takes advantage of a child or teen it is recognized as an atrocious ethical violation. In recent years this type of violation has become almost commonplace. Inappropriate teacher-student relationships have dramatically increased according to the data released by the Texas Education Agency (TEA). "In 2016-2017, the agency opened 302 investigations into improper relationships. During the 2018 to 2019 fiscal year, TEA tracked 442 inappropriate relationships" (Iracheta, 2019, para. 2). It is obvious that such actions are not only illegal, but they are morally wrong and likely will have lasting implications for the students who have been wronged. In situations that are so obviously *inappropriate* we do not wrestle with the moral or ethical implications – it is wrong, plain and simple. However, when a situation is about a right versus right dilemma that is when we are torn and our ethical prowess is truly tested.

Right vs Right

Because most of us are inclined to believe that most people are good, holding core values of honesty, integrity and fairness, we are predisposed to believe that they will choose the right course of action. What happens when there are two rights, which one is *more right*? These issues arise in all areas of life, whether corporate, professional, personal, civil, educational, or religious. Review the situations on this and the previous page. Both of the situations above remain unresolved. Please understand that all right versus right dilemmas fall into one of four categories, which we will get to in a moment. Kidder (1992) advises that a right versus right choice is one in which either option is "right" or "good," in light of your personal core beliefs of morality and ethical behavior. Therefore, either choice would be

Hannah has just bought a new dress, it has a deep plunge on the back of the dress, nearly to her waist. It also has a rather low cut in the front. She loves the dress, the color, the cut, how it hugs her shape. However her best friend, Cassandra thinks the dress is anything but flattering. They are going out on a double date this weekend and Cassandra does not want Hannah to wear the dress.	
RIGHT: It is right to be honest and truthful and tell your friend if what they are wearing does not make them look as good as they think it does.	**RIGHT:** It is also right to protect their feelings, and if you speak up it could hurt her and maybe your friendship. Maybe the "ugly dress" is only ugly in your head.
Both are right – which one is more right?	

193

Chapter 12

NOTES

> Thomas and Becky live in subsidized housing, yet the rent is still quite high. Thomas has a fairly good job as a package delivery driver for a large company, he is also in recovery. Becky is receiving a monthly disability check because she injured her back; her disability check will expire 60-days after the birth of her child, this is a high risk pregnancy and her injury is related to the pregnancy. They use the disability check to pay their rent. Thomas relapsed and stole Becky's check and now they do not have enough money to pay the rent. Furthermore, since it is government housing they have a strict no tolerance policy.
>
> | **RIGHT:** It is right to extend equal social services to everyone equally, especially to those who have been historically marginalized due to race or ethnic origin. | **RIGHT:** It is also right to expect that people who are receiving social services and governmental assistance will not use those benefits to purchase illegal drugs. |
> | --- | --- |
>
> *Both are right – which one is more right?*

right, but which of the two choices is *more right?* Only you can decide – your colleagues may feel the exact opposite way.

Use situations such as these to sharpen your decision making skills, you are not permitted to abstain from making a decision. You must choose and thus you are faced with a genuine dilemma. In this case, Kidder explains that right versus right situations can be one of four *dilemmas paradigms*. Consider the above scenarios in light on the following dilemma paradigms:

1. **Truth versus Loyalty:** Kelly and Sondra are coworkers and both work for the same company. Sondra is the administrative assistant for the vice-president. Kelly has worked on the assembly floor but has recently applied for clerical receptionist position in operations. Sondra's boss tells her who has been selected for the position, and it is not Kelly, but he has sworn her to secrecy. At lunch that day Kelly asks Sondra if she has heard about the clerical receptionist position. Sondra is now in a *truth versus loyalty bind*. This bind occurs when you are bound to keep information confidential but due to a strong sense of loyalty, but you feel conflicted because to maintain your loyalty you will have to sacrifice the truth. Or you could tell the truth and violate your sense of loyalty.

2. **Individual versus Community:** Eric grew up in foster care, and he struggled with school attendance. But he finally finished school to become an interpreter. He was pretty rough and wild in his teen years having several brushes with the law, but he genuinely has changed his life. He earned his interpreter certification one week before his twenty-first birthday. He and a group of his friends went out to celebrate his birthday and his certification. They were drinking and Eric was driving when they inadvertently hit and killed an elderly man who was considered a pillar of the community. Eric received a felony charge for vehicular manslaughter, he served 1 year, but was put on probation. Recently, it has been proposed (and likely will pass) that felons no longer be permitted to hold certification. You feel very conflicted because you know Eric, but for the interpreting profession to move to the next level the question about whether felons should be allowed practice must be answered. This is an *individual versus community bind* – it is right to protect the community from felons, but what about protecting each individual?

3. **Short Term versus Long Term:** Andrew graduated with a four-year degree in

194

Principles of Practice

NOTES

interpreting, he was the top of class, not just academically, but his interpreting skills were stellar. Shortly after graduation he obtained his NIC. When Andrew graduated from school his 3 boys were ages 5, 7 and 8 years old and he has been interpreting for approximately for 7 years. For the last year he has been doing legal interpreting and he has recently obtained his SC:L. He has also applied for and has been *tentatively* accepted for a faculty position at the college he graduated from because of his skill, knowledge and overall personable nature. There is one stipulation – he must return to school to obtain his Master of Arts degree. The school will cover his financial costs for college; the only cost will be his *time.* His concern is that he is *very close* to his boys and they are now in their teen years – a time they regularly look to him for guidance. This is the *short-term versus long-term bind* since being a full-time teacher and carrying a three-quarter load at a Masters level would consume all of his free time, but he will finish school in a little more than three years. Long term benefits for his family are significant: free college tuition for his boys and significant increase in salary, however, the boys need him *now.*

4. **Justice versus Mercy:** You are an educational interpreter for a small town school with a thriving dDeaf education partner program. Unlike many public schools, your school has a wonderful partnership with the residential school for the Deaf. Many of the advanced placement students take their classes in the mainstream setting. It just so happens a brilliant dDeaf student, Jessica, has moved into town. She quickly rose in popularity and she takes advanced placement (AP) classes – she is one of the top students in both schools. She is quite overwhelmed with the attention and the increased expectation from her parents. She is close friends with Tiffany, another girl in the AP program. Jessica is so nervous about her grades, her performance and popularity that she has become a little anxious. One day in class she is panicked because she cannot find her homework. Tiffany slides her paper to Jessica to copy. It is at this point you walk in the room and see Jessica copying Tiffany's paper. You confront her and she starts to tear up and is visibly shaken. You know this so unusual for her – she begs you to "let it go." You are in a *justice versus mercy bind.* You know she is under a great deal of pressure and she is afraid what will happen to her if she is caught cheating. It is right to show mercy and let it go, but it is also right to exact justice for cheating. Yet, all of us desire mercy, not solely the firm hand of justice.

Please return to the initial dilemmas concerning Thomas and Becky and Hannah and Cassandra. It is your job to "finish the stories" by deciding what you think should happen. Often what you think you *would* do and what you *should* do are not the same – why do you think that is true? Even more importantly, thoroughly explore the right versus right dilemma paradigms and decide which paradigm their stories fit into the best. Sometimes, it will seem as though the situation can fit into more than one paradigm (and it may). However, it will usually fit into one paradigm the most clearly. Working with your classmates, discuss whether there are additional considerations that should be given attention. It is *imperative* that you make a decision based on the facts you have – do not presuppose additional "story elements" to make the event more palatable. As an interpreter, when you are faced with a right versus right dilemma you will have to make a decision based on the knowledge you possess in that moment. Please understand it is normal, even good, that you feel conflicted concerning the (simple) scenarios above. Though the above situations are unrelated to interpreting, there will be many times when events like this happen *while* you are interpreting and you will feel the conflict. Interpreters are

Chapter 12

NOTES

not to discuss the details of any assignment, including who the dDeaf and hearing participants are or the contents of an assignment, it is wise to find healthy ways to deal with the inner conflict created at an interpreting assignment.

As we wrap up the discussion on right versus right dilemma paradigms, we will share two more very brief scenarios to help illustrate the differences between right versus right and right versus wrong. Imagine you are interpreting for an employee owned company that holds the contract for the "school photo days" for five school districts. You donate your services as an interpreter for a small share of the company stock; this is an in-kind form of payment you have agreed to because they have a good number of dDeaf employees. You are called to interpret on Monday and while there you happen to learn, while interpreting, they are planning to divide the stock on Friday and the prices will fall moderately on your shares. As you leave the assignment, you are very tempted to sell your shares before Friday at the higher price. This inner conflict is NOT caused by a right versus right dilemma, rather it is caused by a *moral temptation* to do wrong instead of right. *What would you do?*

One final illustration: Pam, a Pennsylvanian college student, works as a receptionist in an apartment building for elderly persons. Last winter, many of the building's tenants, who had become Pam's friends, complained to her that their apartments were cold. When she relayed these comments to her boss, Pam was told to tell the seniors that the furnace was under performing, but was scheduled to be repaired. However, Pam knew that her boss had simply turned down the central thermostat to save money on heating bills. Pam hates lying to the tenants, but is certain she will lose her much needed job if she refuses to keep up the ruse.

Please consider the elements of this story and consider if it fits the principles of a right versus right dilemma paradigm and if it does, decide which paradigm Pam's story fits into the best. For the answer to this dilemma see the last page in this chapter.

Practicing our Principles

The exercises in this section are intended to help you develop the ability to identify whether the events described are, in fact, right or wrong, good or bad, but more importantly how will you align what you know you *should* do and what you really think you *would* do. Your *ideal self* would like to be bold, brave and call out wrong doing, whereas your *real self* may not have the same intestinal fortitude to do that very thing. There is an old saying, "There is never a wrong time to do the right thing" (Anonymous, 2008).

Teleological versus Deontological Thinking

As you develop your ability to make decisions as an interpreter, we encourage you to develop a **teleological** approach. Teleological thinking is an approach to ethical reasoning that "is focused on the outcomes or consequences of one's decisions" (Cokely cited in Dean, & Pollard, 2011, p. 157). Compare this with **deontological** thinking, which "is concerned with adherence to pre-ordained rules" (p. 157). You must use your developing critical thinking skills to evaluate the possible *outcomes* of each situation or dilemma you encounter while interpreting. It is essential that as interpreting students and colleagues, you consider the multiple options, consequences or outcome of each course of action, to the best of your ability. It is essential to note that teleological thinking is significantly more adaptable, as is necessary, within complex interpreting situations where, "the individual is continually evaluating potential and actual decisions with respect to the outcomes these decisions may, or are, causing" (Dean, & Pollard, 2011, p. 157).

Principles of Practice

NOTES

One way to identify your thinking process is to analyze your approach to complicated situations. Do you ask yourself, "What would happen if I did this..." or do you think, "Every time this happens, I have to do this..." Utilizing absolute language (terms like always, never, every) is a strong indicator that the thinker does *not* employ critical thinking, rather they are deontological in their thinking. One way of explaining deontological thinking is, "the rule is always right." For example, is it *always* wrong to kill? No, we understand that in general it is clearly wrong to take someone's life, but in situations of self defense – kill or be killed, or during times of war the rules are interpreted differently because of the context or circumstances. Deontological thinkers apply the RID Code of Professional Conduct or the CASLI Code of Ethics and Guidelines for Professional Conduct as though they were fixed, black and white immutable rules. Whereas teleological thinkers recognize that the codes of conduct influence our thinking, compelling us to consider the potential *outcomes* in light of the context and circumstances. Unfortunately, even the language of the codes of conduct are infused with deontological (absolute) language.

Defending Your Decision

Using the principles of *deontology* (rule oriented) and *teleology* (outcome oriented) apply your critical thinking skills to the situations below. If there are clear ethical violations, please think about how you *should* handle the situations, and discuss how you think you *would* really handle the situations (would and should are the keywords). If there is a difference, what can you do to reconcile the two responses? Below are some suggestions to help you resolve your potential conflicting feelings.

- Unless urgent action is required, take the time to gather the facts, review and confirm what you know about the situation.
- Consider what you believe is the best course of action; contemplate the potential outcomes based on your decision.
- Would your actions be in line with or consistent with the code of ethics and standards of practice? You need to take the time to predict the possible consequences for each of the individuals involved in the interpreting event.

Seek input from trusted colleagues, not only your peer group, but those with more experience than you. Know that you need to keep your circle of confidants small, but it is important to have the perspectives of others to prevent you from overlooking details. A word of advice: as you anticipate the decisions that must be made, it is wise to rehearse those situations in advance so you have several alternative responses readily available to you. It is also critical that you realize that with a few exceptions, there is rarely *one* correct response.

In the situations you will encounter, there may be several options available to you, depending on the setting, the clients, and numerous other contextual factors. Once again consider ALL the possible options, start from the untenable moving all the way to the most probable and likely decision. After making your final decision, reflect on and evaluate the appropriateness of your action(s) before you go forward. Is your final decision *defensible,* do you have a tenet to support your decision and is the decision logical and focused on the outcome, rather than the rule?

Activity for Situations 1 & 2: There are several steps to the following activity. It is best if you can practice the following situations with a partner. Begin by reading one of the scenarios, then each of you should respond to that scenario, then more to the next.

1. Write down two or three possible ways for you to handle the situation. One of

Chapter 12

NOTES

your goals is to make decisions as *quickly* as possible, using the information you have.

2. Now *take the time* to look over the Code of Professional Conduct and cite the potential violations (if any) for each decision. Be attentive to the illustrative behaviors.

3. Once you have determined *if* your decision is genuinely supported by the code then *determine* whether it is more in line with teleological or deontological thinking, this is another one of your goals.

4. Prioritize your decisions, place them in order, first, second and so on, take turns sharing your outcomes with your partner.

Please allow time for energetic discussion and self reflection. Your colleague may not agree with you, but practice allowing for the freedom to share one another's thoughts with respect. You may need to drop back to one of your other options; you may need to rethink and come up with other options and consequences as the events unfold.

As you conclude this activity, understand that numerous organizations have codes of conduct to safeguard the community from unethical and potentially harmful practitioners. Below are some of the most salient principles that have clearly stated purposes:

1. Deter inappropriate or immoral conduct by professionals.
2. Establish a standard professional expectation in order to discipline offenders.
3. Provide information to the public outlining acceptable and unacceptable practice.
4. Protect the public from unethical practitioners.

PRECEPTS OF THE CODES

As we conclude this chapter there are several precepts that embody the RID and CASLI codes which we have addressed below with some explanation regarding the interpretation and application of the specific principles. The code of conduct

---

SITUATION ONE: You are a relatively new interpreter with only five years of interpreting experience. You would like to get into theatrical interpreting. A seasoned interpreter, with an amazing reputation contacts you and asks you to team with them for an upcoming play, explaining that it will be a volunteer opportunity since the small community theatre has no funds to pay for interpreters. You consider this an opportunity to grow, you ask some clarifying questions about when you will get a script, if the interpreters will be able to practice during the planned dress rehearsals, etc. and based on the answers you receive, you accept! You practice and meet with your co-interpreter on several occasions to agree on how to divide the interpreting.

On the evening of the interpreted performance, things go very well; the 27 dDeaf individuals who attended enjoyed themselves. The following week, you receive a phone call from the theatre manager, asking for your social security number. When you ask why she needs that information, she replies she has to file documents to report the $500 fee the theatre paid to you and your co-interpreter. Confused, because it was your understanding that you were donating your services, you ask for clarification. The stage manager says, "We gave your colleague two envelopes containing $250 cash in each envelope prior to the interpreted performance." *What do you do?*

Principles of Practice

NOTES

> **SITUATION TWO:** You live in a rural community and have been interpreting for nearly 10 years. For the past year and a half you have been doing some medical and mental health interpreting, and you find it very rewarding. Lately, you have been interpreting for a 9 year old dDeaf girl named Nina; she is wrapping up her therapeutic regime. At the one of final appointments the therapist explains that they are going to play a game. She explains that they will sit on the floor and roll the ball back and forth and each time they roll the ball they will say one thing that they learned in therapy. Nina excitedly signs, "I want the interpreter on my team – I will roll the ball to her!" *What do you do?*

identifies competent, appropriate behavior that delineates what the field of interpretation has defined as professional, ethical and moral. They also assume that practitioners are able to apply critical thinking and good decision making skills as they come to a reasoned decision regarding their professional conduct, even when working through challenging conditions.

Confidentiality/Privacy

People *expect* that interpreters will keep the information they learn while interpreting private. Participants enter into a trust relationship with interpreters who provide services. It is akin to the reasons we are willing to disrobe in front of our physician, we bare our souls to our psychiatrist, confess to our priest, essentially making ourselves vulnerable. We do that knowing our physical, emotional, or spiritual problems will not be the topic of someone's dinner conversation. Further, we know that if we encounter our physician, psychiatrist, priest, or interpreter at a social function, there ought not be a facial expression that will "give us away" to others in the room. If that understanding is violated, the ethical standards we expected are also breached. As professionals, we realize that the failure to guard all interpreting and quasi-interpreting information closely, will rob our clients of the power to control personal and professional information.

As sign language interpreters, we are even more sensitive to the need for confidentiality due to the close-knit nature of the dDeaf community in which it only takes a minimum of information to identify the parties involved in an interpreted situation. Please understand, there are specific situations in which it is necessary and appropriate for us to discuss the specifics of an assignment with another colleague. When this is the case, we must behave in an ethically responsible manner, using *great discretion* in sharing only information that is critical to the effective functioning of the professional team in order to provide the highest quality of service to the clients involved. Remember, when we share information with others, we are talking about the people to whom that information belongs.

Purchase of Services

As professionals, it is our obligation to respect the right of the participant to have interpreter preferences. Every dDeaf person has their favorite interpreters, if you are not that person – deal with it. There are some occasions when it is appropriate for professionals to donate or volunteer their services. Therefore, interpreters need to be judicious when determining if it is appropriate to offer their services pro bono.

Professional Distance

It is important to maintain a healthy, professional distance from those individuals we provide interpreting services for, however, we know that the dDeaf world is quite small and interpreting for those you may know will likely happen on occasion.

199

It is unwise and inappropriate for the interpreter to become emotionally close to the participants in an interpreting assignment. It is best practice if we refrain from interpreting in settings where family members, good friends or close professional associates are involved.

Professional Competence

Know your limits – physically, emotionally, experientially, linguistically, culturally, and in other areas of your personal and professional life. If you are interpreting for a dDeaf person who has a mobility disorder that impairs their sign production and as they sign you do not understand them, do not *speculate* what you *think* they are saying. Explain what is happening and ask to reschedule the appointment. If the complexities of an interaction require the knowledge and skills of a highly experienced individual, and you are asked to interpret (with less than five years experience), you likely do not possess the competency. As professionals, we must demonstrate that the interest or well being of the participants is paramount. One of the most honorable and professional actions one can take is to know your limitations and to decline an assignment you are not capable of doing well.

Competence is defined by the CASLI Code of Ethics means the following:

- Linguistically capable to determine the intent and spirit of a speaker or signer and able to express that intent and spirit in an equivalent manner and in the target language and culture.

- Flexible enough to adjust communication methods so that services can be provided in a manner the participants prefer.

- Committed to continuing one's professional development, in order to expand interpreting competence and to be better able to serve dDeaf and hearing clientele.

BEYOND GRADUATION

Competence also means working as a certified practitioner. Certification provides evidence of your competence and commitment to professionalism. As a graduate of an interpreter education program, you have the required foundation or knowledge, some field experience in the Deaf community and you should have completed an internship. This experience should provide you with limited opportunities for paid work in your community. You are just embarking on an exciting future career, and this text, along with your classes, will have laid a foundation for entry into the field of interpreting. There will be expectations of you, going forward – from the Deaf community, from your interpreting colleagues, and from the settings where you may work.

Promote the Profession

Become an active member of the interpreting community. Attend dDeaf events and build a rapport with dDeaf community members. Do not stop learning, attend professional development opportunities and talk to your colleagues about changes and trends impacting the profession. Do not wait for someone to offer to mentor you – ask people if they are willing to pour into you. As a recent graduate and new interpreter, you need to become an active member in your professional associations. Many local CASLI/RID chapters allow students to serve on the board and some chapters have a position on their board for student interpreters. Consider serving on your local board in spite of your "beginner" status. In addition to organizational meetings, your professional association will offer workshops and other professional development opportunities to support your continuing education. Attendance at various trainings, workshops and conferences will improve your skills and will help you identify potential mentors.

Give Back

A mentor is typically a Godsend for recent graduates. Select a mentor who possess some years of experience, and together you will determine your goals and the kind of support you desire. You will learn ways of working together, your mentor will outline appropriate times and ways to contact him/her and the anticipated length of the mentorship. Obviously, these initial agreements are typically open for discussion and possible revision as you both navigate the waters of mentoring. The great thing about working with a mentor is the ability to speak confidentially about situations, sharing more details about location, clients, types of information being interpreted, etc. The support and encouragement from a mentor is priceless.

As you enter the field of sign language interpreting, it is important that you get the kind of guidance and support needed to be *out in the real world.* This includes asking a mentor "Do you think I am ready for that assignment?", as well as talking through your ethical dilemmas and decisions. You will encounter many situations armed with limited experience and will need support applying discretion, judgment and professionalism. Consider asking the more seasoned interpreters in your life questions that allow them to share their experience and wisdom with you. Such as, "If you could give me *any* advice what would you tell me?", or "If you could do anything differently what would it be?" Learning from others is important, but it is just as important to learn *about* yourself. On this path of self development, take the time to be kind to yourself. In the days to come you will have good and bad days and it will take a lot out of you, extend yourself a little grace on your journey to excellence. Though it may not seem like it right now, the time will come for you to help the "newbie", look back and remember your some of the most meaningful tidbits of wisdom and pass them along.

NOTE: The answer concerning Pam's situation, her dilemma is not a dilemma, it is a moral temptation there is nothing right about her behavior.

It is essential to consider ethical dilemmas because those decisions will weigh heavily on you. Make sure is it a decision you can live with even if the consequences are great and always focus on "doing no harm". This chapter discusses crucial information you will need as an interpreter and below are some tools to take with you as you continue to learn and grow.

Terms to Know

- **Deontological:** "is concerned with adherence to pre-ordained rules" (p. 157).

- **Ethics:** "the basic concepts and fundamental principles of *decent human conduct* [emphasis added]" (WebFinance Inc., 2020, para. 1). Ethical behavior encompasses the way we treat one another, how we behave (publicly and privately), and what we do with what we know.

Chapter 12

NOTES

- **Morality:** as the principles of right and wrong as defined by culture or society; when codified, they are most often called laws or ordinances.

- **Role-Space:** Llewellyn-Jones and Lee (2011) proposed that the integral role of interpreters necessitates they make active and ongoing decisions while working. This reflects on the multi-dimensional nature of an interpreter's role, stating that interpreters are "acting with integrity and making informed decisions appropriate for the domain goals and characteristics of the interlocutors" (p.3).

- **Teleological:** Is an approach to ethical reasoning that "is focused on the outcomes or consequences of one's decisions" (Cokely cited in Dean, & Pollard, 2011, p. 157).

Interpreters *must*:

- **Attend:** Go to as many workshops, trainings, and learning opportunities as you can afford
- **Network:** Mingle, chat, introduce yourself, *don't* cluster with your classmates – get known
- **Join:** Join your local and national interpreting organization, if your state does not have a local affiliate, join the dDeaf organizations.
- **Mentor:** Find a mentor for your language or your interpreting or both. Offer to buy them lunch, you are a student after all.
- **Own it:** Accept responsibility for your mistakes and try to right your wrong.

Practitioners *distinguish* themselves by:

1. Have specialized skills and knowledge that is unique – they are in the position to provide a particular service which requires credentialing (licensure, certification or both)
2. Are expected to have studied a specialized body of knowledge, and are authorized to operate within a defined scope of practice
3. Are required to adhere to a clearly articulated set of values or a code of ethical conduct (Humphrey, 1999)

According to Role Space, successfully mediating cross lingual and cross cultural interactions involve:

1. Presentation of self
2. Interaction management
3. Participant alignment

Presentation of Self is used to identify those linguistic and non-linguistic behaviors in which the interpreter speaks for and acts on their own behalf, such as an interpreter introducing themself or answers questions directed at them, even when not directly related to the interpretation.

Interaction Management: Interpreters are often put in a position of managing or encouraging the progress of an interpreted interaction, such as asking an attendee to repeat something they said because the interpreter was unable to hear, etc. Failing to do so might change the outcome of the interaction, if omitted or not accurately interpreted.

Principles of Practice

NOTES

Participant Alignment: This element refers to *how much* the interpreter is directing their communication to a participant or a group of participants (Llewellyn-Jones, & Lee, 2011).
Interpreters:

- Deal with multiple demands, some of which are intricate, occasionally contradictory, and most are difficult to deal with
- There is rarely one single right answer or correct response. For that reason, it is important to develop the ability to identify and weight your options
- Don't always have time to research the *correct, appropriate,* or *ethically responsible* decision in real time

To balance the demands above, interpreters must:

1. *Learn* to distinguish between right versus right dilemma and right versus wrong issues
2. *Listen* to interpreters who been in the field for some time regarding some of the challenges they have faced, what decisions they made and how they reached those decision
3. *Engage* in frequent practice with classmates

Kidder (1992) discusses "right" dilemmas:

1. Right versus Loyalty
2. Individual versus community
3. Short term versus long term
4. Justice versus Mercy

To gain a better understanding of the ethical dilemma's above, read *How Good People Make Tough Choices* by Rushworth Kidder.

Ways to resolve potential conflicting feelings:

- Unless urgent action is required, *take the time* to gather the facts, review and confirm what you know about the situation.
- *Consider* what you believe is the best course of action; contemplate the potential outcomes based on your decision.

What are the benefits to networking as a sign language interpreter? Can you name 10 people who have an excellent reputation that you have connected with?

_____

_____

_____

_____

_____

_____

_____

_____

_____

_____

_____

_____

13 | International Perspectives

If you are reading this textbook, you are most likely studying in the US or Canada, and your goal is probably to work as an interpreter in North America. However, we close this text with a look at the education and the practice of interpreting across the globe. In this chapter, we will introduce information regarding Deaf communities and interpreters who, like members of those groups you have read about in earlier chapters, are seeking recognition and inclusion in their own countries.

As interpreters in a North American context, you are likely more familiar with organizations at state, regional, or national levels. The Oregon Registry of Interpreters for the Deaf (ORID) or the Texas Society of Interpreters for the Deaf (TSID), for example, are state organizations, whereas the Canadian Association of Sign Language Interpreters (CASLI) and the Registry of Interpreters for the Deaf (RID) are examples of national interpreting bodies. When we think of "international" interpreting, we know there is a fairly long experience of sign language interpreters from the US and Canada crossing borders and coming together, attending meetings of CASLI (formerly known as AVLIC) or having Canadian signed language interpreters attending state, regional and national RID events in the US.

It is easy to focus on the local and national issues arising in our own country, such as: interpreter education, opportunities and challenges for collaboration among professional practitioners, standing up for the inclusion and respect for members of diverse Deaf communities, and the inclusion and support for expanding the work of Deaf interpreters. But have you contemplated how sign language interpreters across Europe have interfaced with European and international interpreting organizations, some for many more years that of US and Canadian interpreters? It is important to look, then, at the profession and work of sign language interpreting outside of your national bubble.

This is a cursory look at international Deaf communities and interpreters working globally. In this chapter, we introduce the current status of interpreting, interpreter education and the recognition of Deaf communities on the international stage, and in selected countries. We will share information regarding the structure and activities of international interpreting organizations, in addition to looking at interpreters from a transnational perspective. This is where you find multiple organizations working across multiple countries, often on the same continent. The African Forum of Sign Language Interpreters (AFSLI), or the European forum of sign language interpreters (efsli) are such organizations.

We will also look at the pathways to interpreter education found in different parts of the globe. Here our purpose is to draw your attention to the different interpreter education models that have emerged across the global South versus those of the global North. *Income poor* countries around the world are often *knowledge rich*, and even though they have benefited from some of the early advances in North America and Western Europe, they are often able to teach us new, creative, and enhanced educational approaches. For this reason, we will draw upon some diverse and elegant examples of interpreter education around the world which are embedded in the empowerment of Deaf communities and other stakeholders.

Our attention will then move to exploring some of the differences in interpreting practices found outside of the North American context. We will contrast the practices in North America where there is often a focus on interpreters within cities or states, with those at the international level where interpreting services are provided.

We will conclude with a discussion of some things to consider when interpreting overseas. These thoughts stem from our own experiences of travelling the globe and working within teams of multinational interpreters, reflecting diverse cultures and language communities. Our insights and advice regarding this topic is not exhaustive and serves only to present some of the joys and jolts of working abroad.

INTERNATIONAL INTERPRETING ORGANISATIONS

Sign language interpreters are found in virtually every country in the world, working with *"people of the eye"* in the same kinds of activities as those found in North America, including education, health care, cultural events, and accessing information critical for survival during times of war and civil upheaval. Interpreters from around the globe have been involved with international interpreting organizations for almost as long as these organizations have been in existence. However, our globe continues to "shrink" as a result of greater access to international travel (Covid-19 withstanding), the expansion of the internet, and increased calls for global organizations committed to world peace to include Deaf voices. Members of Deaf communities are involved in many international gatherings and a number of interpreter related organizations have come into being over the years. In this section, you will get a sense of the various organizations through which interpreters are able to conduct their business, as well as a range of both signed and spoken language interpreting organizations, their organizational goals and structure, as well as a summary of their evolution.

The United Nations was founded in 1945, at the end of World War II, as an international organization promoting world-wide peace and global cooperation. The UN are best known for intervening in the breakout of wars and attempting to ensure the health and safety of individuals across the globe. The United Nations *Convention on the Rights of Persons with Disabilities* (CRPD) is one such action, addressing the rights of Deaf people to participate in all aspects of civil society, including education, justice, government, and culture. This is the first UN convention to explicitly mention the recognition of sign languages and the need for *professional* interpreters for deaf people (Stone, 2013). Countries that have signed and ratified the UN CRPD are held to account for the ways in which the rights of their deaf citizens are supported through professional interpreting services and can access society. This requires countries to implement sign language research and provide opportunities for interpreter education. As a result, the World Federation of the Deaf (WFD) and the World Association of Sign Language Interpreters (WASLI) have had opportunities to influence the education and training of signed language interpreters internationally, in turn making it possible for countries to comply with this crucial expectation and be in compliance with the UN CRPD.

World Federation of the Deaf (WFD) is the oldest international non-governmental organization (INGO) of persons with disabilities in the world. The WFD has worked closely with the United Nations since its' founding in 1951, promoting the human rights of Deaf people worldwide. A nonprofit organization with a focus on Deaf people who use sign language and their family and friends . Since 1951, WFD has held a World Congress in venues around the world which is attended by thousands of Deaf people, most recently by participants from 133 countries, as well as a large contingency of signed language interpreters. At the Congress, the *General Assembly* is convened; there is also a large cultural component including performances and exhibitions.

The International Federation of Translators (FIT) | **The Federation Internationale des Traducteurs** (FIT), founded in 1953 with support of the United Nations Educational, Scientific and Cultural Organisation (UNESCO), is a federation of national associations of spoken language interpreters, translators, and terminologists. FIT joined WASLI in signing a *Memorandum of Understanding* (MOU) in 2015, agreeing to collaborate on various initiatives, such as lobbying for: the safety of signed and spoken language interpreters working in conflict zones (via the RedT coalition), and for economic measures to support interpreters during the COVID pandemic.

The International Association of Conference Interpreters (AIIC) *L'Association Internationale des Interpreters de Conference* is a professional association of (historically spoken) language conference interpreters, established in 1953, and functions today as both a professional association and as a trade union, with committees that focus on research, staff interpreters, interpreters in conflict zones, distance interpreting, and more recently a Sign Language Interpreting Network. Originally funded at the request of interpreters working in INGOs the purpose of AIIC is to represent conference interpreters in negotiations regarding working conditions. This includes negotiated working conditions for interpreters working in the UN and its' related organizations, the European Union (EU) and EU bodies, as well as global union federations and world customs organisations (Thiery, 2009). The work of AIICC has been similar to that of WASLI, although WASLI wasn't formed until 2005. The AIIC ethos has always been competition on quality not price and is one that has stood the test of time.

Association of Visual Language Interpreters of Canada (AVLIC), established in 1979, is a non-profit professional association for interpreters whose working languages include a sign language. AVLIC has eight affiliate chapters across Canada. In 2019, AVLIC changed its name to the **Canadian Association of Sign Language Interpreters** (CASLI). An active association of sign language interpreters in Canada , they have developed several position papers and offer a range of educational opportunities across Canada. Their website offers links to their provincial chapters and information about upcoming workshops and other events. The authors

International Perspectives

NOTES

encourage US-based students to consider applying for a student membership in CASLI, as well as attending some of their conferences and events.

European Forum of Sign Language Interpreters (efsli) was established through efforts of the former WFD Regional Secretariat (now the European Union of the Deaf – EUD) to bring interpreters together across European countries. efsli has held annual conferences for interpreters since 1994 at various locations in Europe which are open to interpreters from across the globe. Their first conference received support from (a) the EUD, (b) the Commission of the European Communities – Integration of Disabled People and (c) a community action programme for Disabled Europeans Citizens who are living independently in an open society

World Association of Sign Language Interpreters (WASLI) WASLI, was established in 2005 as the culmination of international gatherings at WFD Congresses and Conferences. WASLI represents the interests of signed language interpreters globally and since its establishment there have been increased educational opportunities for signed language interpreters world-wide.

WASLI's organizational structure includes (1) the membership of national interpreter associations (voting members) and (2) the selection of regional representatives at a continental level, who work at the multi-country level to support the development of interpreter associations and the education of interpreters in each country or region. In 2015, eight regions were added (mirroring the regions set up by WFD), including Africa, the Asia Pacific, the Balkans, North America, Latin America & the Caribbean, Europe, Transcaucasia, and Oceania. In 2019, another region was added which included the 22 Arab speaking nations.

In 2011, WASLI released a philosophy statement on the education of signed language interpreters and they have created a framework on how to best meet educational needs of interpreters. This has been useful for several countries, particularly those that have ratified the United Nations' Convention on the Rights of Persons with Disabilities (the CRPD).

WASLI signed a Memorandum of Understanding (MOU) with WFD (2007, updated 2017) spelling out clear mandates for both organizations declaring: (1) sign language instruction and related activities rightly belongs to Deaf people under the purview of Deaf organizations; (2) issues related to interpreter education falls under the purview of WASLI. This document serves as a model for national Deaf and interpreter organizations seeking to adopt similar frameworks, solidifying their relationships, and ensuring that collaboration is at the heart of the work.

Working closely with the WFD, a number of initiatives have been set in place and opportunities for education and training which support Deaf communities and sign languages globally, including:

- Developing standard practices documents such as:
    - guidelines for hiring interpreters for international conferences
    - best practices for dealing with media and communication access during times of national emergencies
- Developed an International Sign interpreters accreditation system

Critical Link International (CLI) was founded in Canada in 1992 by both signed

207

language and spoken language interpreters and interpreter educators after identifying their common goal of enhancing the training opportunities and working conditions of community interpreters internationally. They were instrumental in the development of an international standard (ISO) for community interpreting (ISO 13611:2014). CLI hosts international conferences every three years for community interpreters and other stakeholders in the delivery of community/public service interpreting. It also showcases practical training and community-based research from both spoken and signed language interpreters and educators. Since its founding, it has morphed into an international network of researchers, practitioners and educators.

INTERPRETER EDUCATION AROUND THE GLOBE

The United States has a long history of having state associations and a national interpreter association which has long offered testing and accreditation processes to sign language interpreters. It is fair to say that other places also have long histories, such as the UK (from the 1920s - Simpson, 1990) and Russia (former USSR). Similarly, many countries have followed this path for interpreter education.

While countries such as the United States and Brazil (amongst others) have programs based at universities offering Bachelor's and Master's degrees from programs in sign language interpreting and interpreting studies, Napier (2004) identifies that educational opportunities for signed language interpreters globally range from countries having:

- no training available
- short-term workshops and courses that last a few weeks
- college-level 2- and 3-year programs

Within this context of dramatically different opportunities for learning to become a signed language interpreter, there are also generally no standard requirements for becoming certified and working as an interpreter. In some countries there are no qualifying systems and no professional bodies that represent interpreters (Bontempo, 2015).

While most Western Europe countries require interpreters to obtain a Bachelor's degree in interpreting to be able to work, in many countries this degree provides entry onto the national list/register which is required for an interpreter to be paid with government funds. In the Nordic countries, and much of Northern Europe, the government pays for all interpreting services and the list/register regulates the education and market of interpreters quite effectively. In Southern Europe interpreter education is often run by Deaf Associations who are tasked with holding the list/register. Testing may also be available via a professional interpreter association as opposed to a University, an independent registration body, or a Deaf Association.

In Canada, interpreter education is delivered at six post-secondary institutions. There is one BA level interpreting program and another that offers a BA degree in linguistics with a minor in interpretation. The other programs are three-year programs that have a strong requirement of sign language proficiency prior to entering the program. In 2019, the University of Quebec at Montreal began delivering a more robust French-LSQ interpreting program in order to prepare interpreters to serve the Francophone Deaf community in Quebec and New Brunswick.

International Perspectives

NOTES

Global Development in Interpreter Education

Let's look at two examples to highlight some current global developments, considering first interpreter education in Kosovo and secondly in Brazil.

Kosovo

In Kosovo, we have seen the development of an interpreter education program from scratch. It is an excellent example of how interpreter education/training can be relevant and meaningful for a country while remaining firmly embedded in the Deaf community. The first step in setting up this program was when the country secured support from the Finnish Association of the Deaf (FAD), who assisted Kosovo in documenting their signed language in linguistically sound ways. Deaf linguists worked with local Deaf leaders to video the language in natural contexts, identifying the structure, lexicon, and variations within the linguistic data.

After this crucial first phase, the development of an interpreter education program began. A local multilingual sign language interpreter, Selman Hoti, who was raised by and well-respected in the Deaf community, became the first interpreter educator. The FAD supported Selman and an international advisor, Susan Emerson, was recruited to provide additional expert advice. By strategically pairing these two people, the country was able to prepare their first cohort of eight interpreters, all of whom were already fluent in Kosovo Sign Language and ready to begin providing community-based interpreting. This was something that had been not been possible during the civil war in former Yugoslavia during the 1990s.

Since this work started, the community has expanded its program to offer a longer format which is still delivered by the Deaf association and local interpreter educators (both Deaf and hearing). This has continued to embed interpreting education and interpreting practice firmly within the Deaf community. This model also included the creation of an Interpreter Working Group who have designed a professional code of conduct and documents that described suitable working conditions for interpreters, along with best practices for educating the wider community on how to work with an interpreter. This group produced valuable documents that were suitable for the context in which the interpreters found themselves working.

Although this model may be viewed as non-traditional by countries with long-established educational opportunities at the college and university level, it is a model that works well in start-up locations and can be easily replicated internationally where no interpreter education programs exist. Furthermore, this model is in keeping with WASLI's Philosophy for Interpreter Educators, which stresses that if international educators are needed they should work together with local interpreters and Deaf community members to ensure the designing of effective education practices relevant to the communities they are designed to serve.

Brazil

By contrast, Brazil has approached the education of interpreters from a strategic top down approach. This was led in large part by Dr. Ronice Müller de Quadros who, after completing her PhD in linguistics, returned to her home country. Using her native signed language, Libras, and her relationship with the Deaf community, plans were made for massive educational reforms. Working collaboratively with Deaf communities and organizations of the Deaf, a plan was launched to change the laws and policies of Brazil leading to the official recognition of Libras as an official

209

language and for it to be a requirement for all university students to take at least two classes in that language.

This legal recognition and educational requirement opened the door for many Deaf people to teach at University, and for Deaf people to earn BAs, MAs and PhDs. Simultaneously, they engaged in researching many of the aspects of Libras that had never before been examined. This created networks of Deaf academics studying and contributing to Libras scholarship. Their research centered on linguistics, education, social reform, translation, and interpreting.

The next strategic aspect was to implement interpreter education at the university level. Given the vastness of the country, Brazil quickly adopted video conferencing technology for the delivery of interpreter education courses. This allowed universities to deliver blended courses with face-to-face training at universities in major cities, delivered from Dr Quadros' university UFSC. Twenty years of planned research and education has resulted in thousands of interpreters being able to earn their BA, MA and PhD degrees, all of whom have strong relationships with Deaf communities. The main sign language translation and interpreting conference in Brazil (TILS) is a Libras-medium conference rather than using spoken Portugese with interpreters for deaf access. These professionals and scholars are currently contributing to the advancement of the profession, not only in Brazil but throughout the world.

THE REALITY OF INTERPRETING OUTSIDE OF NORTH AMERICA

You might wonder what significant differences exist between interpreting in large US and Canadian cities compared with interpreting in other areas of the world? Let's take a look.

Historic Control by Deaf Community Centers
For all countries around the globe, interpreting services have historically been delivered by the national, state, or regional associations of the Deaf with interpreters employed through those venues to provide interpreting services to the broader Deaf community. Examples include North America, Latin America, Asia, most European and Scandinavian countries, as well as many former Soviet countries. In all of these regions, Deaf organizations and associations had a long history of Deaf people managing community interpreting services and this approach has served them well.

Movement Away from Deaf Centered Service Centers
With the passage and ratification of the United Nations *Convention on the Rights of Persons with Disabilities* (CRPD) and the increasing number of countries who have ratified this convention, there has been a move away from Deaf associations holding governments accountable for interpreting services. As a result, the management of funds and interpreter contracts by Deaf associations have been relocated, having the government or other non-deaf agencies take over that role instead. Unfortunately, this has resulted in the loss of historic Deaf-centered oversight which vetted interpreters based on appropriate language and culture requirements. In many respects, interpreting services have been socialised much like healthcare in Canada or the UK.

Further, in many of these income-poor/knowledge-rich regions that have traditionally had limited opportunities for formal education for interpreters, a push

International Perspectives

NOTES

for increased access to training and increased educational opportunities has resulted in interpreters in those countries demanding higher salaries and wages. In addition, after increased contact among interpreters across borders and regions, more and more interpreters in these countries are shifting their sights to working as freelance practitioners or setting up their own interpreter businesses, rather than working as an interpreter under the auspices of a Deaf agency. Unfortunately, these changes have resulted in increased movement of the oversight of interpreting quality away from the Deaf community – a loss of essential quality control and gatekeeping.

Lithuania

An example of this shifting landscape can be seen in Lithuania. Historically, government funding for interpreting services went directly to an organization with strong ties to the national association of the Deaf, in which all of the interpreters worked full time for an interpreter service agency in each region of the country, with interpreters receiving informal vetting from members of the local Deaf community. Instead, two interpreters have attempted to disrupt the traditional delivery of interpreting services by setting up freelance contracts which has caused tension among stakeholders.

Columbia

Provides another example highlighting how these competing approaches can create challenges that do not benefit the Deaf community. The Colombian Association of the Deaf has historically held the mandate for providing interpreting services across the country, including face-to-face community appointments, as well as the delivery of video relay services. In recent years, however, the interpreter association has competed to administer the provision of interpreting services, resulting in tension between the two associations.

In both of these examples the disruption has not benefited the local Deaf communities or the interpreting professional as a whole.

The African Continent

Some of the countries that comprise the African continent are often considered income poor, although we would note that they are *knowledge rich*. These countries face continued struggles to establish and support the ongoing operation of medical, educational, political, and other infrastructures; other African countries such as Uganda which was the first country to constitutionally recognize its sign language, or South Africa have university-based interpreter education programs. The education of sign language interpreters, still in its infancy in many countries, generally starts by teaching sign language, then moving on to teach interpreting itself.

It is no surprise, then, to find in some contexts there are still struggles with making the curriculum accessible to deaf students, or that indigenous signed languages/or rural signed languages are generally undocumented (much like the scant documentation of Indian Plain Sign Language). There are organizations of (1) Deaf individuals, established due primarily to the capacity building of the World Federation of the Deaf and (2) sign language interpreters, due primarily because of the support of WASLI and the WFD.

211

Chapter 13

NOTES

INTERNATIONAL TRENDS THROUGH A PERSONAL LENS

Personal Reflections Both Debra Russell and Christopher Stone, the authors of this chapter, have a great deal of experience at the international level serving in leadership roles with the World Association of Sign Language Interpreters (WASLI). Within that context, they state they have traveled to six continents and to over 80 countries. Here are some common trends observed across these counties, including:

- Increasing pressure on governments to recognise the human rights of Deaf citizens
- Following the requirements for qualified *professional* interpreters to be used when providing interpreting services
- These demands have gathered steam due to the increased visibility of sign language interpreters on televised proceedings, such as presidential addresses, parliamentary debates, daily briefings, and during times of natural disasters such as earthquakes or the 2020 fires in Australia, or most recently during the Covid pandemic

Within a ***rights-based frame of reference***, Deaf communities are increasingly using their political knowledge and the power of social media to engage decision-makers and political figures in public debate to effect change. There are multiple examples of Deaf community organizations using social media to engage politicians as well. This includes the Twitter campaigns and circulating hashtags that promote the official recognition of signed language, as seen in the Philippines (https://www.facebook.com/philadeaf/). Or, to open letters critiquing policies, such as the campaign to create an Accessibility Act in Canada (http://cad.ca/media-centre/).

The Use of Deaf Interpreters
There is also an increase of Deaf interpreters in many countries. Discussions abound regarding the role of Deaf interpreters and moving from a traditional conceptualization to that of becoming the (political) face of signed language access. Whereas non-deaf interpreters have historically been the visible face of signed languages internationally, this is changing rapidly and is, quite honestly, an area that is controversial among some interpreters who can hear. We can see that the British Broadcast Corporation (BBC) has a team of both Deaf interpreters (working with an autocue/teleprompter rather than a with hearing co-interpreters) and hearing interpreters providing 5% of their programming within interpretation.

In the Fijian government's decided to employ Deaf interpreters for daily government broadcasts while working closely with a team of interpreters who can hear. Formal training for any sign language interpreters has been severely restricted in the Oceania region, an area where the concept of working with Deaf interpreters is an exceptional model, as it is in other countries.

In China, for example, hearing interpreters have been on television "providing access" to the daily news, but research has shown that a majority of Deaf people report very little if any comprehension of those interpretations (Xiao et al 2015). While this research is based in China, there is good reason to suggest that these findings might well apply equally to other countries as well.

International Perspectives

NOTES

Growing Demand for Interpreter Education & Advanced Interpreting Abilities

The demand for quality interpreter training is a common theme across every country we have visited, and the rise of Deaf professionals across a range of professions goes hand-in-hand with the need for interpreters to have solid academic backgrounds and sophisticated interpreting abilities. Across Europe, the demand for interpreters to work in high-level meetings (HLM) is on the rise. Such meetings are typically found in political contexts such as the European Union which regularly works with signed language interpreters when interacting with Deaf politicians. The United Nations in Geneva alone provides over 100 days of International Sign interpreting each year.

Connections with the Deaf Community

Another disturbing trend noted in our travels is that as interpreters acquire professional status, their relationships with the Deaf community often weaken. Individuals are typically urged to become interpreters based on their relationship with their local Deaf communities precisely because those early experiences lay the foundation, in large part, for ongoing involvement in local, national and international Deaf communities. When interpreters cut or significantly reduce those ties and commitments, they can expect that interpreting skills, as well as continued understanding of the norms and expectations of Deaf individuals, will suffer stagnation. Unfortunately, there is a trend of interpreter education programs having minimal connections to the Deaf community, with few or no Deaf faculty members and programs that do not require students to be active members of the local Deaf community. These same programs are guilty of fostering a model of interpreting solely as a business transaction which gives reason to be seriously concerned about the future of interpreting.

If we lose our connection to the Deaf community or fail to develop and nurture that connection through education that is embedded in the Deaf community via internships and in-service training, how will interpreters be able to provide interpretation that is rooted in cross-cultural knowledge and experience? How likely is it that Deaf interpreters will feel welcomed and supported to work in the field?

A Word for Interpreters Wishing to Work Outside of Their Home Country

As active members of the international community of sign language interpreters, one of the most frequently asked questions we receive is *"How do I become an international sign (IS) interpreter?"* We point to the section on IS interpreting on the WASLI website for a fuller discussion of this question (www.wasli.org). WASLI's response to international sign interpreting is deeply rooted in the WASLI philosophy that interpreters can only excel as interpreters if they are active in their local Deaf community, specifically their mastery of their local/regional/national signed language(s). These solid, life-long experiences provide opportunities to establish the critical foundations which support one's ability to understand high level meetings and academic conferences, which are largely the two domains where we see IS interpreters working.

WASLI also requires IS interpreters to have more than two spoken languages and/or two signed languages. Having multiple languages allows interpreters to have a greater range of options in understanding participants and constructing interpreted target texts that provide the maximum opportunity for effective interaction.

Chapter 13

NOTES

Use of International Signs

WASLI recognizes that in some contexts IS is not a viable practice and it should not be assumed or provided to all *international* events. For that reason, *WASLI and the WFD continue to challenge the default use of IS interpreters for international events*. Truthfully, IS interpretation does not provide complete access to information for many Deaf attendees at international conferences or Deaf events; the use of the national signed languages of the attendees provides greater inclusion and access for Deaf participants at international events. National signed languages must be valued, supported, and used *as the first option* wherever possible and practicable. In contexts where this is not possible, such as deaf-led events like the WFD congresses or the Deaflypmics, then IS serves a purpose.

Teaching or Researching in International Settings

While the opportunity to travel and share one's knowledge is exciting, it can have negative effects. Our North American/Minority World lens can sometimes prevent us from recognizing how much we can learn from knowledge rich countries of the Majority World. If an opportunity arises to do some work in another country, you should only accept that opportunity if you can work with local Deaf community members in addition to local interpreters. It is critical that we not impose American Sign Language or other 'killer languages' (see Skutnabb-Kangas 2003) on countries where national signed languages are in use. And it is important to avoid delivering a one-off workshop with little capacity for the community to develop its own educators on the topic.

Unfortunately, too often we see interpreters stepping up to help countries "research sign language" without the following consideration:

> Interpreter educators working in countries where they do not know the local sign language are advised to work with local Deaf associations and Deaf people who are the "experts" in their language. To assume that a country does not have a sign language is to risk language colonization as clearly described in Philemon Akach's (2005) paper in the Proceedings of the Inaugural Conference of WASLI. Spoken language interpreters and linguists can play an important role in helping to document the sign language used by local communities. Finally it is important to also document and respect the language variation that may exist in a country or region, thus supporting all of the diverse ways that language exists in the country.

When you travel, be cautious, and politically astute. Think deeply about the damage caused when one brings a "colonizer" mindset when visiting other countries and cultures.

Concluding Thoughts

As you begin your journey to becoming an interpreter, we wish you every success — it's a rewarding and worthwhile journey. Remember, there is a great amount to learn when considering interpreting work in international settings, and it is best learned in collaboration with local Deaf and interpreter communities all working towards common goals. Our hope is that as you transition into your interpreter career, you will be more aware of interpreting and interpreting organizations that operate at an international level. We hope that you might some day join us at a WASLI conference.

- **Income Poor are often Knowledge Rich:** Though individuals have benefited from some of the early advances in North America and western Europe, they are often able to show us the way to enhanced educational approaches.

- **Video Relay Services (VRS):** Phone interpreter

Organizations:

- **The World Association of Sign Language Interpreters (WASLI)** is an international organization that represents signed language interpreters.

- **The World Federation of Deaf (WFD)** has been instrumental in bringing interpreters together and holds conferences every four years.

- **European Forum of Sign Language Interpreters (efsli)** holds yearly conferences throughout Europe and these are attended not only by those members living in Europe but by interpreters from other countries as well.

- **Memo of Understanding (MOU):** WASLI and WFD signed a Memo of Understanding in 2007, and this cooperation agreement was then updated in 2017. Those agreements spell out the clear mandates for both organizations.

- **United Nations Convention on the Rights of Persons with Disabilities (UNCRPD)** addresses Deaf people's rights to participate in all aspects of society, including education, justice, government, and culture; sign language is addressed in several of the articles.

- **International Federation of Translators (FIT)** is a federation of national associations of spoken language interpreters, translators, and terminologists, rather than individual members

- **The International Association of Conference Interpreters (AIIC)** is a professional association of conference interpreters and functions as a professional association and as a trade union.

- **Critical Link** organization hosts international conferences for community interpreters and other stakeholders in the delivery of community/public service interpreting.

- **Red T** protects the lives and interests of linguists, interpreters, translators and journalists that work in conflict zones.

- **International Sign (IS):** WASLI requires interpreters to have more than two spoken languages and/or two signed languages.

WASLI and WFD has mandates and an example is:

- Sign language instruction rightly belongs to Deaf people and associated activities fall under Deaf organizations purview, whereas interpreter education

Chapter 13

NOTES

issues are a WASLI matter

Napier (2004) identifies that educational opportunities for signed language interpreters range from countries having:

- no training available,

- short-term workshops and courses that last a few weeks,

- college-level 2- and 3-year programs.

In some countries there is no *qualifying system and no professional bodies that represent interpreters (Bontempo, 2015)*.

Video Relay Service (VRS) – a few companies are Sorenson Communication and Convo.

- A dDeaf person makes a phone call through their video phone and sees an interpreter who connects the line to a non-deaf person who, often, does not sign. The dDeaf person signs to the interpreter and the interpreter speaks to the non-deaf person. After the dDeaf person's message has been interpreted, the non-deaf person will speak, and the interpreter will sign what the non-deaf person said.

Country Requirements:

- The United States and Brazil have programs based at universities offering bachelor's, master's, and programs in sign language interpreting/interpreting studies.

- Some countries have no qualifying system and no professional bodies that represent interpreters (Bontempo, 2015).

Questions for Further Reflection:

1. In what ways can you foster a greater connection to your local dDeaf community?
2. What might it mean to be an effective sojourner when travelling and meeting dDeaf people and interpreters from other countries?
3. What are the major international organisations supporting the development of the interpreting profession?
4. Why is it so important that WASLI and WFD work closely together?
5. What are your two "take away" messages from reading this chapter?

TOOLBOX

Tool A: Historical Philosophies — 218

Tool B: Claggett Statement — 222

Tool C: Interpreter Certifications — 225

    CASLI — 225

    RID — 227

    BEI — 230

    NAD — 234

Tool D: DeafBlind Hall of Fame — 235

Tool E: Interpreter Stretches — 239

Tool F: Language Continuum — 240

Tool G: Colonomos — 241

    CRP — 241

    Integrated Model of Interpreting (IMI) — 242

    IMI Supplementary Notes — 243

    Constructing Meaning — 246

HISTORICAL PHILOSOPHIES OF INTERPRETING

The Registry of Interpreters for the Deaf (RID) was established in 1964 as the first professional association of sign language interpreters in the world. Prior to its establishment and in the early days of RID's existence, the common approach to delivery of service for interpreters was the philosophical frame. Deaf people were generally viewed as handicapped, limited, and unable to fully manage their personal and business affairs. Thus, it fell to the interpreter to be a caretaker to some extent.

The philosophical frames include (chronologically listed):
- Helper
- Conduit (or machine)
- Facilitator
- Bilingual-bicultural
- Ally, Deaf-centered
- Accomplice

Helper Philosophy
The benefactor often takes on a proprietary and caretaker attitude toward members of the oppressed group (Freire, 1973, 1970 and Freire & Vasconcillos, 1989). There is an intense need on the part of the power group for everything to work out well, yet there is a corresponding lack of trust in the abilities of the minority group to do well on their own. It becomes necessary, then, for the family member who can hear or for the professional who is not Deaf to take charge and to be in control – making decisions for the Deaf person, assuming he or she is unable to do or to learn certain things.

Parents or childcare counselors may assume that Deaf children and youth are unable to develop an internal locus of control. Therefore, they do everything for them: wake them up every morning, set their schedules for them, dole out their money, permit or forbid one student to interact socially with other specific students, and so on, as they deem appropriate. All of these behaviors foster unhealthy dependence in the child and damage his or her self esteem.

The Helper Philosophy in Action
A prime example of this model can be told through the eyes of two fictional people whose experience resonates with the truth of the model. George is a Deaf man who has a doctor's appointment. His friend's daughter, Sarah, is his interpreter and his ride to the doctors. When the two arrive at the doctors Sarah asks him what's been going on. Slightly embarrassed, George says he's been having a lot of pain with his bowel movements and he's concerned the blood in his stools could be cancer.

When the nurse calls him in, the doctor asks him how he is. As George begins to sign, Sarah steps in and takes over, answering the question for him and continuing to explain George's problem. George watches as the two converse, unsure about what is being shared. When the doctor asks questions that Sarah does not have answers to, she summarizes her discussion with the doctor to George then asks him the question before continuing her discussion with the doctor.

While George is changing into an examining gown, the doctor turns to Sarah and asks how she knows sign language. The two continue to chat while the doctor examines George. The doctor asks George the name of any medication he is taking and Sarah interrupts before informing the doctor that George's medications are in his briefcase in the waiting room. She pats George's hand and tells him she will get the briefcase for him.

After the appointment ends and the two are heading home, Sarah mentions how her parents' friend had the same issue that George is experiencing. She asks George if his wife knows about the pain and mentions that if it is cancer there are things he needs to figure out. George doesn't quite understand what she means, but Sarah continues speaking. Sarah says he should check his life insurance benefits and adds she will call and make those appointments for him. She also points out that if he dies in an accident his insurance will pay twice as much than death by cancer. She adds that there is a new stomach cancer drug that can be purchased on the black market and if he's interested, she can hook him up with a guy who brings it from Mexico.

The illustration above shows an interpreter following the helper philosophy, which is overly involved in the personal lives of Deaf people and patriarchal. The interpreter may move out of their role of interpreting to advise, direct, teach, or cajole Deaf and hearing clients. The idea behind the interpreter's actions are founded in the belief that Deaf people are incapable of understanding or participating in the world around them, due to their limited experiential base or intolerance of most people. Thus, this influences the transition for the interpreter to become an interloper. This model represents the early days of interpreting when interpreters were volunteers with no formal training and whose primary roles were parent, child, teacher, VR counselor, or clergy.

The RID Code of Ethics was developed partially in response to the presence of helper model interpreters in the field. The RID founders felt the behaviors described above resulted in inappropriate boundaries that imbalanced the power between Deaf and hearing people (which gave people who can hear power). Deaf professionals would no longer tolerate the paternalistic care-taking attitudes exhibited by the interpreters they encountered. Through this, eight principles emerged known as the Code of Ethics, which were intended to guide the decisions made by interpreters in the field.

Conduit (Machine) Philosophy

The beginning model (helper) began with extreme over involvement and was viewed as inappropriate and oppressive. To combat this over involved model, the machine model was introduced. The dynamics between machine and helper were on opposite ends of the spectrum. The machine (conduit) philosophy became accepted as the most appropriate model for interpreters. This machine mindset interpreted the Code of Ethics as a rigid set of rules. The philosophical frame inverters followed the rules; denying that their presence had an influence on the dynamics and often unaware of the inequality resulting from the history of oppression experienced by Deaf people.

When looking at the work of an interpreter functioning from this philosophical frame, you would see a verbatim transmission of words/signs. Interpreters focused on volume, being sure to sign every word spoken and to speak every sign produced. Unfortunately, consumers often saw a torrent of signs or heard a great number of words – from which it was often difficult to derive meaning. Interpreters took on an almost robot-like role in the communication process, assuming no responsibility for the interaction or communication dynamics taking place between clients.

It was also during this time that interpreters began to describe themselves as equivalent to a telephone wire – simply relaying information from one receiver to another. The following scenario captures an interpreter working from a *machine philosophical frame*.

The Conduit (Machine) Philosophy in Action

George, a Deaf man, has a doctor's appointment. He arranged an interpreter through a referral agency. When he arrives at the hospital, the interpreter is waiting for him. George identifies himself as the Deaf client and asks for the interpreter's name. The two sit to chat while waiting for George to be called back.

George asks the interpreter, Steve, how he got involved with interpreting before asking if he has Deaf parents. Steve looks up from his magazine and shakes his head, trying to avoid any unnecessary personal interaction with his client before reading again. George is confused about Steve's actions and considers the possibility that Steve is shy. However, George knows how important it is that the two can properly understand one another and a nervous interpreter may not understand him. George decides to inform Steve about what's been going on and tells him he's been having pain with his bowel movements and has had blood in his stools. He tells Steve he's afraid he might have colon cancer, like his friend.

Steve puts his magazine down and tells him that they cannot discuss George's medical condition in the waiting room and that Steve is not a retainer of information. Steve adds that George should think of him as a telephone wire that passes information without emotions, feelings, or personal involvement. After he finishes, Steve picks his magazine up.

George feels unsettled by Steve's words and is worried whether or not he can understand Steve or trust him to accurately convey the message. Other concerns prompt George to question if Steve understands the Deaf community, and if he understands George as a Deaf man.

Soon after, the nurse calls George into the doctor's office. Steve conveys everything that is said into sign language and everything that is signed into spoken English. After the initial questions are over, the doctor moves George into an examining room. While George is changing, the doctor turns to Steve and asks him how he learned sign language. Steve responds by saying he isn't allowed to engage in personal dialogue while working. In turn, the doctor feels embarrassed by Steve's response.

When George returns, the examination begins. At one point, the doctor mumbles something to the nurse and Steve asks the doctor to repeat what was said. The doctor mentions it wasn't important, just a comment to the nurse. Steve vocalizes his disagreement by demanding to know what was said because he must convey everything to George.

Later in the examination, the doctor asks Steve to hand him a bottle of medication that George has in his pants pocket. Steve refuses and tells the doctor it isn't his role.

The two models are a on the opposite ends of a pendulum swing. The "inappropriate" behavior was modified, and many interpreters became insensitive to the human dynamics within the interpreting setting. They became rigid and inflexible. They also began to refer to themselves as "professionals" and perhaps they thought this because they displayed "involved but separate" attitudes which were demonstrated by some hearing professionals. However, in many ways, interpreters became clock-punching, insensitive appendages within Deaf and hearing interactions. In a human service profession, people must recognize their presence impacts situations.

Facilitator Philosophy

In the early to mid-1970s, interpreters became aware of the field of communications and another shift was made in the philosophical frame, which migrated away from the machine philosophy and toward the communication facilitation philosophy. Within this philosophy, the base of ethical decision making was not significantly impacted. However, interpreters became more aware of the need for appropriate placement, lighting, background, etc. They began to indicate who was speaking since the realization had now dawned that this was an important component in the communication dynamics.

Interpreters became more aware of the need for proper physical placement within proximity of the speaker so Deaf clients could see both the speaker and the interpreter in one visual intake. It was during this period that interpreters adopted solid colored smocks to contrast with the tone of their skin as "uniforms". Finally, the interpreter's personal appearance was analyzed in light of the characteristics that would undergird professional status of the practitioner. They began to exclude those features that could hamper communication. It was expected that interpreters would not have beards, mustaches, fingernail polish, patterned clothing, and most jewelry.

For example, utilizing the doctor scenario above, the interpreter would likely put on a smock before entering the doctor's office and would remove the smock before doing any non-interpreting activities, like using the restroom. The interpreter would place himself or herself behind the doctor's desk alongside the doctor to facilitate eye contact between the doctor and her patient, whether or not this was an uncomfortable invasion of the doctor's personal and professional space. While in the examination room, the interpreter might go to great efforts to be sure he or she was "appropriately" placed and to direct an adequate amount of lighting on the area where interpreted communication was taking place.

It is the opinions of the authors that when observing the work of an interpreter functioning from a communication facilitator philosophical frame, the output looked much like that of a machine model interpretation – rigid. The focus continued to be on volume (quantity) of signs and words. While interpreters were sensitive to communication dynamics in a physical sense, they were still making ethical and communication decisions that resulted in a lack of equality in terms of access and participation for Deaf consumers.

Bilingual Bicultural

In recent times, interpreters work primarily from a *bilingual bicultural* philosophical frame when approaching their jobs. This is a direct result of the recognition of American Sign Language (ASL) as a language and the accompanying research validation of Deaf culture.

The bilingual bicultural philosophy of interpreting has emerged in an effort to achieve a midpoint between the two extremes of interpreter behavior: overinvolved (helper) and invisible (machine). In the bilingual bicultural philosophy, the interpreters are sensitive to physical communication dynamics, indicate who is speaking, place themselves appropriately, etc. They are also keenly aware of the inherent differences in the language, cultures, norms for social interaction and schema of the parties using interpreting services.

Interpreters utilizing this philosophy are often more mindful of people involved in interpreting situations. This method is aware of goals outside the interpreters themselves. For example, interpreters practicing the bilingual bicultural philosophy is aware that a speaker has individual goals and uses words to accomplish his or her goals. However, interpreters know that these goals are accomplished differently in each language and culture and he or she identifies this goal to help analyze the text and select appropriate target language elements.

Bilingual bicultural philosophy is vastly different from the prior philosophies introduced during the earlier years. This philosophy is far more aware of the needs of participants (Deaf and hearing alike). The bilingual bicultural philosophy has learned from previous models and explored new ideas of supporting without over imposing. The emphasis on culture and linguistic mediation has aided this approach to gain an understanding of both cultures to equivalently convey accurate messages across the different cultures and languages.

Ally Philosophy

The Ally philosophy is the current philosophy utilized by the majority of sign language interpreters. It grows out of the bilingual bicultural philosophy. An Ally can be defined as "one who supports the goals of the community and accepts leadership...from the oppressed group" (Baker-Shenk, p. 9). Interpreters practicing this philosophy recognize that Deaf people retain experiential knowledge beyond their scope and that Deaf people are capable of making their own decisions (Baker-Shenk). This philosophy balances the power dynamics between hearing and Deaf and across the interpreting philosophies.

This philosophy encompasses more than "facilitating communication". The role does not encroach on "helper" by being overinvested in lives nor does it cater to machine, pretending one is invisible. Instead, this model follows a healthy line between the two which allows the interpreter to be a human that impacts a setting. For example, an interpreter named Carol is working at an elementary school where she interprets for a Deaf girl. One of the Deaf girl's friends runs up to Carol and presents her untied shoe. The girl asks Carol to tie it because she hasn't learned how. If Carol were to follow the machine philosophy, she would ignore the girl or tell her to find a teacher. However, Carol is an ally and participates in the world of both Deaf and hearing, thus she ties the girl's shoe.

Accomplice Philosophy

The Accomplice philosophy encourages interpreters to not simply "support" the Deaf community, but to stand with them and fight for them; when injustice happens, the expectation is that the interpreters will stand with the Deaf community and support, whether by interpreting or by utilizing their platform to invoke justice (Webb, 2017). It is imperative that people who can hear use their "hearing" privilege to create an equal space for the Deaf to voice their concerns (Webb, 2017). People in the social justice sphere have begun to adopt this philosophy by working with the Deaf community in an attempt toward equity (Webb, 2017). Jonathan Webb, the founder of this philosophy, is reframing the word "accomplice" to become a positive support system between people who can hear and people who are Deaf as they march toward equity for all (Webb, 2017).

THE CLAGGET STATEMENT

*The following document was developed by a group of Deaf and hearing
individuals in 1984 to openly recognize the historic oppressed experience
of dDeaf individuals in relation to churches throughout North America.*

WE BELIEVE:

God created the world and saw that it was good. God created women and men to live with dignity and self-respect as children of God. God wants people to live together with justice, equality, freedom and mutual love.

Instead of trusting God's plan, people made themselves into false gods, oppressing each other and creating injustice, wars, suffering and death. But God did not give up on them (us). God sent Jesus as a visible sign of God's liberating love.

Jesus grew up poor. He loved and intimately associated with poor and oppressed people. He knew their suffering and their needs. In relation with these poor and oppressed ones, Jesus showed us God's compassionate love and God's desire for us all to live with justice and freedom.

Instead of accepting Jesus' way, people rejected the Truth. And Jesus suffered the depths of human pain, degradation, and death. But praise be to God who enabled Jesus to break through the shackles of deceit and death, and raised Jesus to new life. The Holy Spirit too can break through the shackles of arrogance and oppression.

WE RECOGNIZE:

A variety of experiences of hearing loss. Some people are deafened as adults; some as children; and some are deaf from birth. All have suffered.

Many deaf people share a common culture, a common language (American Sign Language or "ASL" in the United State and many parts of Canada) and a common heritage of oppression. These deaf people, collectively, are often called the Deaf community.

Deaf people have long been shackled, often by the "good" intentions of hearing people who haven't understood them. Deaf people lack meaningful representation and leadership in the major educational, professional, and political institutions that affect their lives. This lack grows out of both the intentions and ignorance of the hearing people in power and the "successfully oppressed" condition of deaf people who experience themselves as powerless and incompetent.

Beginning at a young age and continuing into adulthood, deaf people characteristically view themselves as intellectually, emotionally and spiritually inferior to hearing people. This low sense of self-worth is widely known in the psychological studies in deafness.

The majority of deaf children have hearing parents who did not want to have a deaf child and who grieve over their child's deafness. Large numbers of these parents do not accept their child's deafness for a long time. Some never accept it. Many, perhaps most, of the medical, social service and educational institutions which "serve" deaf children and adults encourage the parents to resist acceptance of the child 's deafness. They are encouraged to try in every new way possible to make the child look and act like a hearing person.

This regularly takes one of two general forms: The first is the extreme oralist position of the Alexander Graham Bell Society, which insists deaf children can and should learn to hear and speak. The second is the so-called "total communication" position of the majority of educators in the United States and Canada. This second approach tolerates the use of signs because they are considered necessary for the acquisition of language. Language, in this context, always means English. The type of signing usually prescribed in this context is some form of signed English.

Deaf children attend school in a variety of educational settings. In residential schools for the deaf, the teachers typically are hearing persons who do not understand the children's peer language, do not know American Sign Language, and believe the children to be intellectually and psychologically inferior to hearing children. The primary focus of their educational program is the acquisition of spoken, written and/or signed English. Often, the children do not understand the teachers. Most communication is one way, teacher to student.

Most deaf children mainstreamed into public schools are partially or completely isolated from groups of other deaf children like them. Thus, they do not experience the comforting reassurance of sameness and peer group identity. Most schools do not provide interpreters for these children and they miss much or most of what is being taught and said in their classes. Many try to catch up by frantic reading outside the classroom.

Some deaf children do have access to interpreters. However, most interpreters are not even minimally conversant in American Sign Language. The majority simply try to code the spoken English into a signed form of English (which many argue does not make meaningful sense). Most deaf children have very limited skills in English, and have a hard time understanding a (presumably) signed form of English. However, even those who have good reading and writing skills often say they have a hard time with English-based forms of signing.

Most deaf adults do not understand most interpreters. But deaf people have become accustomed to not understanding. They tolerate it, usually because they blame themselves – blame their own presumed ignorance. With so few interpreters fluent in ASL, the majority of deaf people have never seen spoken English properly interpreted into a form of communication they readily understand. Also, because most interpreters are unable to accurately convey the meaning of an ASL message into spoken English, most deaf people have never had the opportunity to express themselves as freely in a hearing context, and often have been misinterpreted in important settings. These instances of misinterpretation have furthered the myths that deaf people are inferior, inarticulate, immature, etc.

Most (signing) deaf people marry people who are also deaf, and socialize primarily with other deaf people. The language they use for such social interaction is usually American Sign Language. However, most of them do not believe that their indigenous language is really a language but rather that it is an inferior, make-do form of communication. This is what they have been taught by their hearing teachers, counselors, speech therapists, audiologists, and other professionals. ASL is rarely, if ever, taught to any deaf children in school. Instead, they learn it from deaf children of deaf parents, older students, and deaf adults. Generally, deaf people do not realize that their community has a culture and a language which is central to that culture.

MANY DEAF PEOPLE:

Reject the Church because its representatives have been as oppressive as their teachers and therapists. Religion has become one more place where deaf people feel they are told to stop being "deaf" and try to be "hearing". They must try to fit into hearing forms of worship with its heavy emphasis on music, its wordy English liturgies and its love for ancient phrases – all through an interpreter they frequently can't understand.

Unfortunately, even the separate deaf churches and/or programs, there has been little development of indigenous worship forms that reflect the experience of deaf people. All of this has led to alienation and/or superficial involvement in the Church. Clearly, the situation has not encouraged any real understanding of God and the message of Jesus. Exceptions exist, of course, but unfortunately the exceptions are all-too-few.

The Church generally has not looked upon deaf people as a potential gift or resource to the broader Christian community. The Church has considered deaf people to be "handicapped" and, relatedly, has thought deaf people to be intellectually and morally inferior, unable to learn properly and/or spiritually inhibited by a lack of adequate language. Burdened with such stereotypes, deaf people have not been accepted as equal members of the Body of Christ. The Church has not recognized deaf people as persons equipped with theological and cultural gifts with which to enrich the life of the whole Church.

WE BELIEVE:

That the message of Jesus is a message of liberation – not liberation from deafness, per se, but liberation from all forms of oppression, which include the denial of basic human needs for things like unencumbered communication, healthy human interaction, self-esteem, positive recognition of one's culture and language, and meaningful education.

We do not view deafness as a sickness or handicap. We view it as a gift from God, which has led to the creation of a unique language and culture, worthy of respect and affirmation.

We believe that it is necessary to stop trying to communicate the Gospel through hearing people's eyes, through their interpretation and understanding of the Bible, and through their methods. Deaf people have a right to know the Gospel in their own language and relevant to their own context.

We believe that American Sign Language is indeed a language – and a worthy and powerful vehicle for expressing the Gospel.

We believe the Holy Spirit is leading all of us to work for a new day of justice for all deaf people. We believe the Holy Spirit is leading deaf people to develop indigenous forms of worship that can adequately convey the praise and prayers of the deaf Christian community.

We stand in solidarity with the oppressed people of the world. We believe that God empowers the oppressed to become free. By the act of attaining their own freedom, the oppressed can also help liberate those who have oppressed them.

We believe that God is calling the Church to a new vision of liberation of both deaf and hearing people. This vision is deeply rooted in the Gospel of Jesus Christ, and in an understanding of the spiritual, socio-economic, political, and educational struggles of the deaf community.

We believe God has given deaf people a unique perspective and unique gifts. The Body of Christ remains broken and fragmented while deaf people are separate and their gifts unknown and strange to most Christians. We believe God is calling us to wholeness.

We commit ourselves to this vision, and trust God's Spirit to lead, to strengthen, and to empower us in this task. And we call upon deaf and hearing Christians alike to join together in this struggle toward freedom.

Participants/Co-authors:

Dr. Charlotte Baker-Shenk, ASL Linguist, Teacher, Author
Dr. Jan (Kanda) Humphrey, Interpreter, Teacher, Author
Dr. Mary Weir, Theologian, Teacher
Ella Mae Lentz, ASL Teacher, Translator, Poet
Patrick Graybill, Teacher, Actor, ASL Translator, Deacon in Roman Catholic Church
Bill Millar, Pastor
Mary Anne Royster, Interpreter, Teacher
Pam Dintaman, Christian Ministries
Shelia Stopher Yoder, Social Worker in Christian Ministry
Susan R. Masters, Interpreter, Social Worker

INTERPRETING CERTIFICATIONS

CANADIAN ASSOCIATION OF SIGN LANGUAGE INTERPRETERS (CASLI)

For updated information see: https://www.avlic.ca/ces

Becoming Certified in Canada

The national certification process is referred to as the Canadian Evaluation System (CES) and is only available to CASLI members (see Membership Information page for details on becoming a member). CASLI members who have successfully completed the CES process are awarded the Certificate of Interpretation (COI). In Canada, it is not required to have this certification to work as an interpreter (however some employers do require you to have certain phases in order to work), but it is recommended that all CASLI members work towards this certification. Members agree to abide by the Code of Ethics and Guidelines for Professional Conduct when they become a member and one of the tenets reads as follows:

Members will incorporate current theoretical and applied knowledge, enhance that knowledge through continuing education throughout their professional careers and will strive for CASLI (AVLIC) certification.

The CES is a four-phase system offered to Active, ASL-English CASLI members. CASLI members can find more details about the CES by signing into their member sign in/members only accounts and then clicking on the following link: www.avlic.ca/members/ces. Interpreters move through the four phases in the following sequence:

Phase One: Written Test of Knowledge (WTK)
- 73 question multiple choice test which ensures the candidate has the appropriate background knowledge in the field ASL-English interpretation
- Offered on the third Saturday of May, August and November.
- Student members of CASLI can apply if in their final semester of their program

Written Test of Knowledge Reading List (https://www.avlic.ca/sites/default/files/docs/2015-12_WTK_Reading_List.pdf)
Written Test of Knowledge Study Tips (https://www.avlic.ca/sites/default/files/images/2014-02%20WTK%20Study%20Tips.pdf)

Please note: Certification is granted upon successful completion of Phases One through Three to ASL-English interpreters who have had continuous Active CASLI membership. Passing the Written Test of Knowledge in no way constitutes any form of certification and may not be considered as partially certified.

Phase Two: Preparation
- Development Resource Online Clearinghouse – Coming Soon!

Phase Three: Test of Interpretation (TOI)
April 29, 2019: In keeping with the recommendations provided in the CES Phase Three: Rating Review Report, the TOI will not be offered until the test can be delivered in a way that is consistent with effective testing principles AND is, at minimum, cost-recoverable for CASLI.

- Candidates are evaluated on their ability to provide message-equivalent interpretations between American Sign Language and English
- Focuses on interpretation samples from ASL to English, English to ASL and two interactive interpretations
- Under the guidance of a facilitator, samples are rated by three deaf raters then three certified interpreters
- Successful completion of this phase awards the Certificate of Interpretation (COI)

Phase Four: Certification Maintenance
- Currently under development
- Individuals must maintain membership in order to keep their CES status valid (see Motion WP14G-06 for more details). A list of current members can be viewed here: (https://www.avlic.ca/index.php)

To learn more about becoming a member of CASLI please click here. (https://www.avlic.ca/index.php)

REGISTRY OF INTERPRETERS FOR THE DEAF (RID)

Current Certifications

NIC Certification (National Interpreting Certification)
This certification is currently recognized and offered by RID. In order to receive this certification, one must demonstrate:
1. professional knowledge of the field of interpreting
2. ability to make ethical decisions
3. ability to meet or exceed the minimum professional standards necessary to perform in a broad range of interpretation and transliteration assignments.

This credential has been available since 2005.

NIC Certification Process
While RID is responsible for setting eligibility requirements and issues interpreting credentials, the actual administration and grading of exams is done by the **Center for the Assessment of Sign Language Interpretation, LLC** (CASLI). CASLI has been responsible for the ongoing development and maintenance of RID's interpreting exam since 2016. Candidates will need to contact both RID and CASLI at different points in the certification process.

Detailed information is available on: the CASLI FAQ page *(https://www.casli.org/2016/07/01/casli-faqs/)*

In order to obtain NIC Certification, you must:
1. Review all pertinent NIC web pages on the CASLI website: https://www.casli.org/
2. Apply for the NIC Knowledge Exam
3. Pass the NIC Knowledge Exam
4. Provide RID with evidence of meeting the educational requirement
5. Apply for the NIC Interview and Performance Exam
6. Take and pass the NIC Interview and Performance Exam

STEP ONE: Take and pass a multiple-choice NIC Knowledge Exam which can be taken before the candidate is ready to take the skills portion of the exam. To take the Knowledge Exam, candidates must be at least 18 years old.

STEP TWO: Take the NIC Performance Exam
In order to take this exam, candidates must:
1. Provide evidence that you hold a Bachelor's degree (with any major) or submit an approved Alternative Pathway to Eligibility application (updated July 2012); these submissions must be recorded in your RID/CASLI record prior to taking any RID performance-based exam, whether this is your first RID Performance Exam or if you already hold other RID certifications.
2. Take and pass the written exam within 5 years of taking the NIC Performance Exam.

What does the NIC Performance Exam look like: This is a vignette-based assessment using videos to deliver and record the assessment.

There are two portions of the NIC Performance Exam:
1. an interview regarding professional ethical standards and
2. an interpreting test in which you will demonstrate your interpreting skills.

Previously Offered RID Certifications

These RID Certifications are fully recognized; however, the exams are no longer available.

NIC Advanced

Individuals who achieved the NIC Advanced level certificate have passed the NIC Knowledge Exam, scored within the standard range of a professional interpreter on the interview portion of the NIC Interview and Performance Exam and scored within the high range on the performance portion of the NIC Interview and Performance Exam.

NIC Master

Individuals who achieved the NIC Master level have passed the NIC Knowledge Exam and scored within the high range on both portions of the NIC Interview and Performance Exam. The NIC with level credential was offered from 2005 to November 30, 2011.

Certificate of Interpretation (CI)

Holders of this certification are recognized as fully certified in interpretation and have demonstrated the ability to interpret between American Sign Language (ASL) and spoken English for both sign-to-voice and voice-to-sign tasks. The interpreter's ability to transliterate is not considered in this certification. Holders of the CI are recommended for a broad range of interpretation assignments. This credential was offered from 1988 to 2008.

Certificate of Transliteration (CT)

Holders of this certification are recognized as fully certified in transliteration and have demonstrated the ability to transliterate between English-based sign language and spoken English for both sign-to-voice and voice-to-sign tasks. The transliterator's ability to interpret is not considered in this certification. Holders of the CT are recommended for a broad range of transliteration assignments. This credential was offered from 1988 to 2008.

Comprehensive Skills Certificate (CSC)

Holders of this certification have demonstrated the ability to interpret between American Sign Language (ASL) and spoken English and to transliterate between spoken English and an English-based sign language. Holders of this certification are recommended for a broad range of interpreting and transliterating assignments. This credential was offered from 1972 to 1988.

Master Comprehensive Skills Certificate (MCSC)

The MCSC examination was designed with the intent of testing for a higher standard of performance than the CSC. Holders of this certification were required to hold the CSC prior to taking this exam. Holders of this certification are recommended for a broad range of interpreting and transliterating assignments. This credential was offered until 1988.

Reverse Skills Certificate (RSC)

Holders of this certification have demonstrated the ability to interpret between American Sign Language (ASL) and English-based sign language or transliterate between spoken English and a signed code for English. Holders of this certification are deaf or hard-of-hearing and interpretation/transliteration is rendered in ASL, spoken English and a signed code for English or written English. Holders of the RSC are recommended for a broad range of interpreting assignments where the use of an interpreter who is deaf or hard-of-hearing would be beneficial. This credential was offered from 1972 to 1988.

Interpretation Certificate (IC)

Holders of this certification have demonstrated the ability to interpret between American Sign Language (ASL) and spoken English. Holders received scores on the CSC exam which prevented the awarding of CSC certification or IC/TC certification. The interpreter's ability to transliterate is not considered in this certification. Holders of the IC are recommended for a broad range of interpretation assignments. The IC was formerly known as the Expressive Interpreting Certificate (EIC). This credential was offered from 1972 to 1988.

Transliteration Certificate (TC)

Holders of this certification have demonstrated the ability to transliterate between spoken English and a signed code for English. Holders received scores on the CSC exam which prevented the awarding of CSC certification or IC/TC certification. The transliterator's ability to interpret is not considered in this certification. Holders of the TC are recommended for a broad range of transliterating assignments. The TC was formerly known as the Expressive Transliterating Certificate (ETC). This credential was offered from 1972 to 1988.

Specialist Certificate: Performing Arts (SC:PA)
Holders of this certification were required to hold the CSC prior to sitting for this examination and have demonstrated specialized knowledge in performing arts interpretation. Holders of this certification are recommended for a broad range of assignments in the performing arts setting. This credential was offered from 1971 to 1988.

Oral Interpreting Certificate: Comprehensive (OIC:C)
Holders of this certification demonstrated both, the ability to transliterate a spoken message from a person who hears to a person who is deaf or hard-of-hearing and the ability to understand and repeat the message and intent of the speech and mouth movements of the person who is deaf or hard-of-hearing. This credential was offered from 1979 to 1985.

Oral Interpreting Certificate: Spoken to Visible (OIC:S/V)
Holders of this certification demonstrated the ability to transliterate a spoken message from a person who hears to a person who is deaf or hard-of-hearing. This individual received scores on the OIC:C exam which prevented the awarding of full OIC:C certification. This credential was offered from 1979 to 1985.

Oral Interpreting Certificate: Visible to Spoken (OIC:V/S)
Holders of this certification demonstrated the ability to understand the speech and silent movements of a person who is deaf or hard-of-hearing and to repeat the message for a hearing person. This individual received scores on the OIC:C exam which prevented the awarding of full OIC:C certification. This credential was offered from 1979 to 1985.

Certified Deaf Interpreter-Provisional (CDI-P), retired 1999
Holders of this provisional certification are interpreters who are dDeaf or hard-of-hearing and who demonstrated a minimum of one year of experience working as an interpreter. They have shown evidence of at least eight hours of training on the NAD-RID Code of Professional Conduct. They have completed eight hours of training in general interpretation, as it relates to functioning as a dDeaf or hard-of-hearing interpreter. Holders of this certificate were recommended to interpret in a broad range of assignments where an interpreter who is dDeaf or hard-of-hearing would be beneficial.

Conditional Legal Interpreting Permit (CLIP), retired 1999
Holders of this conditional permit completed an RID recognized training program designed for interpreters and transliterators who worked in legal settings. To qualify for this certificate the interpreter had to hold a valid CI and CT or CSC certification prior to enrolling in the training program. Holders of this conditional permit were recommended for a broad range of assignments in the legal setting during the development of the SC:L certification.

Provisional Specialist Certificate: Legal (Prov. SC:L), retired 1998
Holders of this provisional certification hold CI and CT or CSC and have completed RID approved legal training. Holders of this certificate were recommended for assignments in the legal setting.

As of April 2020, the above content was current and accurate, for more information see the following websites:

https://rid.org/rid-certification-overview/certification-archives/previously-offered-rid-certifications/
https://rid.org/rid-certification-overview/certification-archives/nad-certifications/
https://rid.org/rid-certification-overview/certification-archives/rid-retired-certifications/
https://rid.org/rid-certification-overview/available-certification/nic-certification/
https://rid.org/rid-certification-overview/available-certification/cdi-certification/
https://rid.org/rid-certification-overview/certifications-under-moratorium/

BOARD OF EVALUATION OF INTERPRETERS (BEI)
Texas Health and Human Services
Certification Program

A BEI certified interpreter is a person who provides sign language interpreter services. To work as a BEI certified interpreter, a person must have the skills, experience, education, and other job related requirements of the position. The person must also be able to perform the essential job functions. BEI certification testing costs and an annual renewal payment is required to maintain your certification

The Office of Deaf and Hard of Hearing Services (DHHS) Board for Evaluation of Interpreters (BEI) certification program is responsible for testing and certifying the skill level of individuals seeking to become certified interpreters in Texas. The primary goal of the BEI certification program is to ensure that prospective interpreters are proficient in their ability to meaningfully and accurately comprehend, produce, and transform ASL to and from English.
Additional functions of the BEI program are to:
- Improve the quality of interpreter services for Texans who are deaf, hard of hearing or who are hearing by administering testing materials that are valid, reliable and legally defensible.
- Protect the interests of consumers who use interpreter services by regulating the conduct of interpreters certified by the program.
- See the Complaint Process at BEI Manual, Chapter 2
- (https://hhs.texas.gov/laws-regulations/handbooks/bei/chapter-2-complaints-against-a-bei-certificate-holder)

How to Apply for Testing
Applicants may submit a completed application form for the desired test and include:
(https://hhs.texas.gov/doing-business-hhs/provider-portals/assistive-services-providers/board-evaluation-interpreters-certification-program/bei-forms)
- An applicable testing fee in the form of a check or money order.
- A copy of driver's license.
- A copy of valid certificate card, if applicable
- An official college transcript.

Applicants may request a test online using the BEI Registry.
(https://hhs.texas.gov/doing-business-hhs/provider-portals/assistive-services-providers/board-evaluation-interpreters-certification-program/bei-registry-interpreters)

Please contact the BEI office for further assistance at dhhs.bei@hhsc.state.tx.us.

Section A: To apply for or to take any examination for a BEI Certificate, an applicant must
- be at least 18 years old;
- have earned a high school diploma or its equivalent; and
- not have a criminal conviction that could qualify as grounds for denial, probation, suspension, or revocation of a BEI certificate, or other disciplinary action against any holder of a BEI certificate.

Section B: To take the written Test of English Proficiency, an applicant must have
- met all the criteria above; and
- earned at least 30 credit hours from an accredited college or university, with a cumulative GPA of 2.0 or higher.

Section C: To take a BEI performance test, an applicant must have
- met all the criteria in subsection A of this section;
- earned a passing score on the Test of English Proficiency, unless the applicant is applying for a specialty certificate; and
- earned an associate degree and/or a minimum of 60 credit hours from an accredited college or

university, with a cumulative GPA of 2.0 or higher, unless the applicant is applying for a specialty certificate or except as provided in subsections E and F of this section.

Section D: To apply for and to be issued a BEI certificate, an applicant must have

- met all criteria in subsection (a) of this section; and
- earned an associate degree and/or a minimum of 60 credit hours from an accredited college or university, with a cumulative GPA of 2.0 or higher, except as provided in subsections E and F of this section; and
- earned a passing score on the requisite examination for the certificate level sought.

Section E: A BEI certificate holder who holds an active and valid BEI certificate awarded as a result of proceedings initiated before January 1, 2012, is exempt from the educational or degree requirements in subsections B, C, and D of this section, as long as the BEI certificate remains active and valid.

Section F: A BEI certificate holder who holds an active and valid BEI certificate awarded as a result of proceedings initiated before January 1, 2012, and who applies for an additional BEI certificate level after January 1, 2012, may be exempt from the educational or degree requirements of subsections B, C, and D of this section, if, at the time the certificate holder applies for, takes, and passes any BEI examination for the additional certificate, the BEI certificate holder

- has an active and valid BEI certificate that is fully compliant with BEI's annual certificate renewal and five-year recertification rules and requirements;
- is not under any type of active or pending disciplinary action from BEI or DHHS; and
- satisfies all other rules and requirements applicable to the additional BEI certificate level sought.

Section G: A certified interpreter wanting to take a higher level BEI performance test must have the following prerequisite certificate for the corresponding BEI performance test:

Prerequisite Certificate	
BEI—Level I, Basic, Level II, Level III, Level IV, Level V RID—Comprehensive Skills Certificate (CSC), Certificate of Interpreting (CI), Certificate of Transliteration (CT), National Interpreter Certification (NIC), NIC Advanced, NIC Master	Advanced
BEI—Level III, Level IV, Level V, OC:C, or Advanced RID—CSC, CI/CT, NIC Advanced or NIC Master	Master
Level III Intermediary	Level IV Intermediary
Level I Oral or OC:B	Oral Certificate: Comprehensive (OC:C)

Holders of RID, NIC, or certification from another state must submit a copy of their certification for verification purposes if applying for the Advanced or Master Performance test.

There is an initial testing fee.

Once certified, interpreters must satisfy annual continuing education credits and pay an annual fee to maintain the certification

What the BEI is measuring

A BEI-certified non-Deaf interpreter must have the following physical, cognitive, cultural, linguistic, and professional abilities and attributes.

Essential Physical Abilities

- **Hearing**: able to hear, identify, and understand the speech of another person without relying on visual assistance
- **Speech:** able to speak clearly so that the speech is understandable to a listener
- **Vision:** able to see details of another person's hand shapes, hand movements, and facial expressions from a distance of three to six feet
- **Facial expression:** able to control the muscles of the face in order to manipulate the eyebrows, cheeks, mouth, and nose
- **Manual dexterity:** able to quickly make coordinated movements of one hand, a hand together with its arm, two hands, or two hands together with arms
- **Finger dexterity:** able to make precisely coordinated movements of the fingers of one or both hands
- **Wrist-finger speed:** able to make fast, simple, repeated movements of the fingers, **hands, and wrists**
- **Limb movement:** able to move the arms to place the hands slightly above the head, and to extend the arms away from the front of the body and to the sides of the body
- **Limb movement speed:** able to quickly move the arms
- **Dual-limb coordination:** able to coordinate movements of both arms while sitting or standing
- **Head:** able to control the head in order to nod and to turn it from side to side
- **Physical stamina:** able to endure moderate physical exertion without getting winded or out-of-breath for at least 30 minutes

Essential Cognitive Abilities of a nondeaf interpreter

- **Critical thinking**: able to use logic and analysis to assess communication in order to make adjustments in approaches to interpretation
- **Self-monitoring:** able to monitor and assess the interpretation during and after a task
- **Selective attention:** able to concentrate and be undistracted while performing a task, and to sustain that attention over a period of time
- **Auditory attention:** able to focus on a single source of auditory information in the presence of other distracting sounds
- **Visual attention:** able to focus on a single source of visual information in the presence of other distracting movements in the surrounding area
- **Mental Attention:** able to sustain a significant amount of mental processing without fatigue or breakdown for at least 30 minutes
- **Working Memory:** able to remember information such as concepts, words, and numbers for a brief time while interpreting
- **Information management:** able to track and arrange information in a certain order
- **Pattern inference:** able to the ability to quickly make sense of information even when parts of that information may appear to be missing
- **Time management:** able to efficiently shift between two or more activities or tasks, and between two or more sources of information
- **Problem sensitivity:** able to recognize when something is wrong or is likely to go wrong

English language

- knowledge of the structure and content of the English language including the meaning and spelling of words, rules of composition, and grammar
- able to listen to and understand information and ideas presented through spoken words
- able to communicate information and ideas by speaking so that others will understand

Written English

- able to read and understand information and ideas presented in writing
- Able to communicate information and ideas in writing so that others will understand

American Sign Language

- knowledge of the structure and content of American Sign Language including the meaning of

lexical and phrasal items, rules of grammar, and articulation
- the ability to watch and understand information and ideas presented through signs, gestures, classifiers, and finger spelling
- the ability to communicate information and ideas through signs, gestures, classifiers, and finger spelling so that others will understand

Essential Cultural Knowledge and Linguistic Abilities
of a nondeaf interpreter are described below:

Fluency of ideas: able to generate a number of ideas about a given topic (this concerns the number of ideas produced and not the quality, correctness, or creativity of the ideas)

Breadth of knowledge: an acquaintance or understanding, at the introductory level or higher, of a broad variety of topics and fields of interest

Culture: a BEI-certified interpreter must have an in-depth understanding of the cultural norms and mores of the American English-speaking and the American deaf communities.

Essential Professional Attributes of a nondeaf interpreter are described below:
- **Social perceptiveness:** aware of and sensitive to others' reactions, and the ability to understand why others react as they do
- **Independence:** able to develop independent approaches to doing things and to work with little or no supervision
- **Interpersonal relationships:** able to develop constructive and cooperative working relationships with others, and to maintain them over time
- **Adaptability and flexibility:** able to adapt to considerable variety in the workplace and be flexible and accepting of positive and negative change
- **Emotional well-being**: able to exercise emotional control and stability in order to fully use intellectual abilities and good judgment
- **Self-control:** able to maintain composure, keep emotions in check, control anger, and avoid aggressive behavior, even in difficult situations
- **Professional decorum:** able to show respect and act in a professional manner during all interactions
- **Problem solving:** able to make complex decisions, including the ability to identify problems, collect information, establish facts, and draw valid conclusions
- **Organizing, planning, and prioritizing work:** able to develop specific goals and plans, and to prioritize, organize, and accomplish goals
- **Conflict resolution:** able to identify and resolve conflicts related to the meanings of words, concepts, practices, or behaviors
- **Time management:** able to manage time well and to respect the time of others

Ethical standards: able to follow the Code of Professional Conduct as set forth by the Registry of Interpreters for the Deaf. The tenets of the code are as follows:

1. Interpreters adhere to standards of confidential communication.
2. Interpreters possess the professional skills and knowledge required for the specific interpreting situation.
3. Interpreters conduct themselves in a manner appropriate to the specific interpreting situation.
4. Interpreters demonstrate respect for consumers.
5. Interpreters demonstrate respect for colleagues, interns, and students of the profession.
6. Interpreters maintain ethical business practices.

NATIONAL ASSOCIATION OF THE DEAF (NAD) CERTIFICATIONS

In 2003, RID began to recognize interpreters who hold NAD III, NAD IV and NAD V certifications as certification for interpreters. These credentials were offered by the National Association of the Deaf (NAD) between the early 1990s and late 2002. In order to continue to maintain their certification, NAD credentialed interpreters must have had an active certification and registered with RID prior to June 30, 2005. These interpreters are required to comply with all aspects of RID's Certification Maintenance Program, including the ongoing professional development to maintain certification status.

NAD III (Generalist) – Average Performance

Holders of this certification possess above average voice-to-sign skills and good sign-to-voice skills. They have demonstrated the minimum competence needed to meet the generally accepted interpreter standard. Occasional words or phrases may be deleted but the expressed concepts in their interpretations are accurate. An individual with this certification displays good grammatical control of their second language and is generally accurate and consistent but is not qualified for all situations.

NAD IV (Advanced) – Above Average Performance

Holders of this certification possess excellent voice-to-sign skills and above average sign-to-voice skills. These individuals have demonstrated above average skill in any given area. Their interpreting performance is consistently accurate and expressed fluency in the target language with few deletions. Deaf individuals have no doubt of the candidate's competency. Holders of this certification should be able to interpret in most situations.

NAD V (Master) – Superior Performance

Holders of this certification possess superior voice-to-sign skills and excellent sign-to-voice skills. Those with this certification have demonstrated excellent to outstanding ability in any given area of interpreting. Individuals holding this certification demonstrate a minimal number of flaws in their performance and demonstrated evidence of interpreting skills necessary in almost all situations.
https://rid.org/rid-certification-overview/certification-archives/nad-certifications/

DEAFBLIND HALL OF FAME

"Approximately 15 percent of adults in the United States over the age of 18 have some difficulty hearing. Around 8.5 percent of adults between the ages of 55 and 64 have disabling hearing loss. For people between the ages of 65 and 74, the rate jumps to 25 percent, and for those older than 75, disabling hearing loss affects 50 percent."

Before Helen Keller, there [were]…deafblind children – who had also managed to accomplish quite a bit at a time when the odds were seemingly against them.

Sanzan Tani (1802-1867)
Sanzan Tani became deaf as a child while growing up in Japan and devoted most of his time to reading the great books. The more he learned, the more curious he became about the world. As an adult, Tani was known for his excellent knowledge and was awarded a prestigious teaching position by the government of Japan. He began to lose his eyesight and became deafblind. Tani continued to teach about the great books and communicated with his students through touch.

Laura Bridgman (1829-1889)
Bridgman is known as the first deafblind person to be successfully educated, an accomplishment that lead to the education of Helen Keller. Her education became an experiment that her teacher, Samuel Howe, hoped would support his own controversial ideas about the body, mind, and soul. The life of Laura Bridgman has been the inspiration of several books.
- *Child of the Silent Night* (Houghton Mifflin Company; ISBN: 0395068355)
- *The Education of Laura Bridgman: First Deaf and Blind Person to Learn Language* (Harvard University Press; ISBN: 0674005899)
- *The Imprisoned Guest: Samuel Howe and Laura Bridgman, the Original Deaf-Blind Girl* (Picador USA; ISBN: 0312420293)

Julia Brace
The name of Laura Bridgman is remembered today as Dr. Howe's greatest teaching success, as well as for the indirect role her accomplishments played in opening the doors of education for the twentieth-century deaf-blind humanitarian, Helen Keller. That of Julia Brace is all but forgotten. Yet it was because of a visit to the Hartford Asylum for the Deaf and Dumb (now the American School for the Deaf), where Dr. Howe met Julia Brace, that he conceived a plan for the education of the deaf-blind and undertook the training of Laura Bridgman, Oliver Caswell, and eventually Julia Brace herself.

Helen Keller (1880-1968)
In her will, Helen Keller bequeathed her papers and memorabilia to the American Foundation for the Blind (AFB).
- Braille Bug Helen Keller Biography (http://www.afb.org/braillebug/helen_keller_bio.asp)
- Helen Keller Archival Collection (http://www.afb.org/helenkeller.asp)
  The Helen Keller Archival Collection contains The Helen Keller Papers, The Helen Keller Artifacts and Memorabilia Collection, The Helen Keller Photograph Collection, and Books from Helen Keller's Library. All except the books are available online at no charge.
- Biography.com profile on Helen Keller (http://search.biography.com/print_record.pl?id=16451)
- The Truth About Helen Keller (http://www.rethinkingschools.org/archive/17_01/Kell171.shtml)
- The Socialist Legacy of Helen Keller (http://www.marxists.org/reference/archive/keller-helen/intro.htm)

Robert (1925-) and Michelle (1947-) Smithdas
Robert Smithdas was born on June 7th in 1925. He became the first deaf-blind person in America to receive a master's degree, fifty years after another renowned deaf-blind advocate, Helen Keller, became the first deaf-blind person to receive a bachelor's degree. Smithdas ran Services for the Deaf-Blind at the Industrial Home for the Blind in New York as a director. He also published two works: Life at My Fingertips, an autobiography and City of the Heart, a collection of poetry. Smithdas went

on to earn three honorary degrees, one from Gallaudet College, one from Western Michigan University and one from John Hopkins University in 1980. (Gannon, Jack R. (1981). Deaf Heritage: A Narrative History of Deaf America. Maryland: National Association of the Deaf)

- 20/20 Interview of Bob and Michelle Smithdas – Barbara Walters' most memorable interview was "a man I interviewed more than 25 years ago. He was a teacher and a poet, and the most inspirational person I have ever met. His name is Robert Smithdas.' Now, more than 30 years later, Walters revisits Smithdas, who is now married to a woman who, like him, is deaf and blind. She reports how they manage to live independently; cooking by touch, using teletype-style phones and computers, wearing pagers that vibrate to signal the ringing of the telephone or the doorbell."
- Bob and Michelle Smithdas, Both Blind and Deaf, Lead Lives Full of Love, Work, Hobbies and Humor (http://www.redwhiteandblue.org/news/bins/SMITHDAS.HTM)

Georgia Griffith (1931-)

Born during the Great Depression, Georgia Griffith was at first blind, then later became deaf. After some time at the Ohio School for the Blind, she graduated cum laude in 1954 from Capital University in Columbus, Ohio with a degree in music education. Griffith was the first blind student at that university, her graduation with Phi Beta Kappa honors.

After graduation, Georgia returned home to Lancaster, teaching blind students in public school and teaching private music lessons. By the 1960's her hearing had deteriorated enough to cause Griffith to consider a second career. So in 1970, she began proofreading Braille music for the Library of Congress, earning the top certification. In her spare time during that period, she also proofread all nine Beethoven symphonies, because, according to an account, she felt blind people needed to have the experience of playing Beethoven.

While working for the Library of Congress, Griffith taught herself ten different languages (German, French, Russian, Italian, Spanish, Portuguese, Swedish, Danish, Slovak, and Greek) as she corresponded with people from different countries. This feat bloomed out of a small venture helping one of her friends write a Braille music dictionary. Funding for her proofreading job was cut in 1981, bringing her to the Internet.

A year earlier, Georgia Griffith had discovered the VersaBraille machine, which is no longer manufactured. Friends in the music world raised money to help cover the $5,000 cost of the text-to-Braille machine, and an eager Griffith soon appeared in cyberspace.

In 1982, CompuServe, then one of the largest internet service providers, hired Griffith as a systems operator/independent contractor to moderate several forums, providing information to users. The forums include: Issues, IBM Special Needs, Political Debate, and White House, in addition to three religion forums: Religion, Religious Issues, and Christian Fellowship. CompuServe's decision to hire her as a Wizard came after executives realized how often they and subscribers asked Griffith to help. The forums had over 200,000 users, and internet chats sponsored by her forums would appear with the byline, "A Georgia Griffith Presentation."

Griffith worked out a small office in her home. In 2000 her setup involved two desks and a variety of equipment furnishing the room. Main features included two PCs, one laptop, and a Blazie Engineering Versapoint embosser. Telesensory's ScreenPower for Windows 95, the only Windows product developed for braille first, speech second, was her first choice for accessing a Windows environment at that time. Griffith's main screen reader then was Henter-Joyce's JAWS for Windows, the backup Syntha-Voice's Window Bridge.

The home where Georgia Griffith lives was built on land that her parents owned when she was born. The house itself came up after her father's death. The walls are decorated with awards, letters from notables such as Presidents Reagan and Clinton, and photographs of Georgia with people like Colin Powell, a former governor of Ohio, and Senator Mike DeWine. She lived with her mother for many years until her mother's death. Currently her sister, neighbors, and friends lend their services, enabling her to live independently.

Her interpersonal communication methods include having speakers write the alphabet in her hands, speaking for herself, and using a Versa-Braille printer nicknamed the "Versy." She does not read American Sign Language tactually. Interviews with the media usually come through e-mail. Griffith has been described as a quick wit and as having a plain-spoken manner.

She has been given several notable recognitions. In 1991 she received the Fred L. Sinclair award from the California Transcribers and Educators of the Visually Handicapped. The Ohio Women's Hall of Fame inducted her in 1994 under the achievement category of Arts, Music, and Journalism. Colin Powell gave the keynote address at a 1996 luncheon where Griffith received the Great Communicators award from the Columbus Speech and Hearing Center.

Griffith has also served on the Board of Directors for the National Braille Association. A display on her life and achievements now resides in the Smithsonian Museum of American History among others who have contributed to the advancement of information technology in the Permanent Research Collection on Information Technology. In addition to the display, the Smithsonian Innovation Network honored Georgia Griffith with a medal in 1997.

Griffith has self-published a book about her life through Xulon Press, titled *Running Around in Family Circles With Friends in Pursuit*. She runs her own business: GG Technical Services is found online at http://www.ggtechservices.com.

Her VersaBraille now retired in favor of a Telesensory Power Braille 40, Georgia Griffith, the New York Times' "Net Queen," continues to roam the internet world.

John J. Boyer (1936-)
History of John J. Boyer and his company, Computers to Help People (CHPI) (http://www.chpi.org/history.htm)
The founder and Executive Director of Computers to Help People (CHP), John J. Boyer, is himself both deaf and blind. He started the company in 1981 after earning a master's degree in Computer Science from the University of Wisconsin at Madison. His main duties are writing special software for people with disabilities, especially for the Technical Braille Center, business development and fundraising.

John J. Boyer is not only a computer programmer and business owner, but also a lay minister. This page describes his life, religion, and avocation.
- Godtouches Internet Ministry (http://www.godtouches.org/history.htm)

Danny Delcambre (1959-)
The deaf-blind community in Seattle is extraordinarily vibrant, with a strong sense of pride and independence. That is why Danny Delcambre moved there. Deaf from birth and steadily losing his sight, Danny suffers from Usher syndrome. The region in Louisiana he left behind has the highest concentration of Usher syndrome in the world. This program takes a sensitive look at this degenerative condition, as neurologist/author Oliver Sacks and Danny explore the nature of deaf culture and the marvelous richness of American Sign Language, which includes a sophisticated touch-based variation called tactile signing. ("The Ragin' Cajun: Usher Syndrome" Video, available from Films for the Humanities and Sciences)
- DELCAMBRE'S Ragin Cajun Restaurant – official web site (http://www.theragincajun.com/) of Delcambre's restaurant, which is now closed, provides a full description of the restaurant and its DeafBlind founder and owner.
- Danny Delcambre – If I Can, You Can (http://www.washington.edu/doit/Newsletters/Dec97/06.html)
  An article from DO-IT (Disabilities, Opportunities, Internetworking & Technology) at the University of Washington. Danny Delcambre, the first Deaf-Blind founder and operator of a Seattle restaurant, gave an inspirational speech on his accomplishments...All of Danny's stories made for a very entertaining hour and a half...Danny made his fantastic speech in American Sign Language where most of the people in the room could only understand him through a voice interpreter.

Khaled Alvi (1963-)
(http://www.khaled-alvi.co.uk)
Born in Lucknow, India, in 1963. Alvi moved to London, England in 1965 with his parents. During their stay in London, Alvi's hearing loss and tunnel vision was diagnosed, so his family remained in England instead of returning to India. His life was changed by a visiting teacher from Arizona. He was learning to draw and paint in his senior year at school when the teacher saw his talent and encouraged him to become a painter. Alvi's subsequent education included a stint at City Lit College at Holborn learning art history, print making and landscape painting. His favorite mediums include oil, acrylic, watercolors, pencil, black chalk, pastel, and felt-tip markers. His work ranges across modern life, landscapes, wildlife, cubism, and still life, with Alvi's favorite artists being Leonardo Da Vinci, Picasso, Monet, and Van Gogh.

His first oil painting entitled "Fruit and Glass Tumbler," created in 1992, sold to Sheridan Russell gallery in 1998. His first solo exhibition of eighty drawings and paintings was in Kanpur, India 1995.

Thomas Lafferty
http://www.rnib.org.uk/xpedio/groups/public/documents/publicwebsite/
public_frcasestudy_thomas.hcsp
Thomas Lafferty builds models from visual and tactile memory. Each model he builds has a story behind it, such as his 'Bygone Days' double-decker bus sculpture. Lafferty says it represents the number 17 bus he used to ride to work on before going blind.

Lafferty did not pursue model-making until after retirement. His first model was a ship, made from the memory of when he was 18 years old and saw a big ship. Another fairly recent model is 'Country Cottage,' a combination of his grandmother's home and the current home he lives in.

Born deaf, Lafferty lost his sight by age 32. His current communication mode involves using the deafblind manual alphabet or having block letters traced on the palm. He has had his work displayed in local libraries and at the BALTIC Centre for Contemporary Art. The British Empire Medal was given to him in 1983, recognizing Thomas Lafferty's achievements.

INTERPRETER STRETCHES

Improve Your Range of Motion

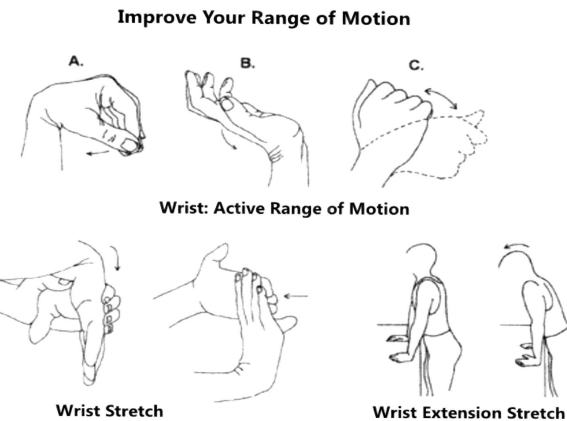

Wrist: Active Range of Motion

Wrist Stretch

Wrist Extension Stretch

Wrist Flexion Stretch

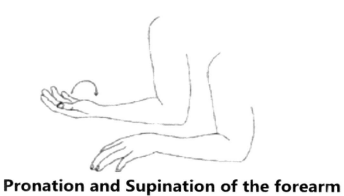

Pronation and Supination of the forearm

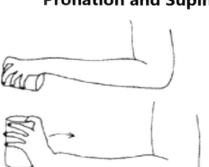

Wrist Flexion Stretch

Wrist Extension Stretch

Grip Strengthening

Copyright © 1997, 2001 McKesson Health Solutions, LLC. All rights reserved.

STRINGHAM: LANGUAGE CONTINUUM (2019)

240

COLONOMOS: INTERPRETING MODEL

Comprehending, Representing, Preparing/Planning (CRP)

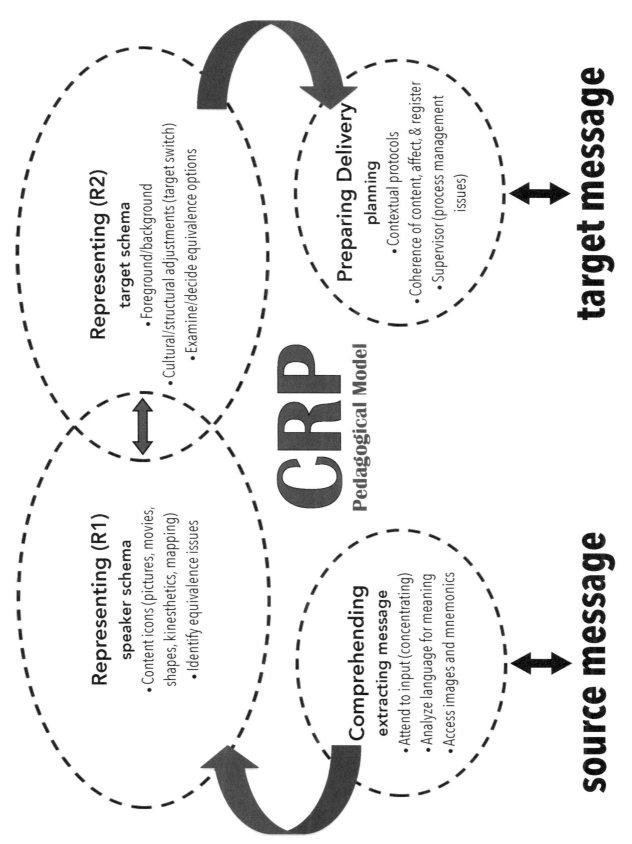

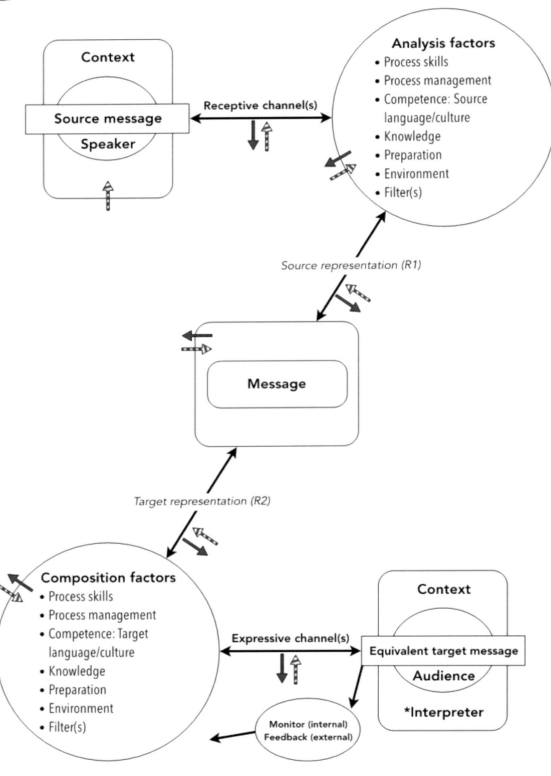

Copyright © 1989, 2016 by Betty M. Colonomos, Bilingual Mediation Center, Inc.

IMI Supplementary Notes

Supplementary notes on the IMI

A. Source/Target Message

Boxes include the components of message meaning in the handout *How do we construct meaning (the message)?* Refer to it for more information.

B. Receptive/Expressive Channels

These areas refer to the channel(s) of transmission from the speaker (receptive) or expression from the interpreter (expressive). For example, the speaker may be speaking English (auditory channel to the interpreter), but may also be pointing/gesturing/ posturing (which conveys meaning) through the visual channel. For these reasons it is important to hear and see the speaker whenever possible. Practicing interpreting from audiotape limits the interpreter's ability to discern meaning.

C. Analysis and Composition Factors

The following items (1-7) are an expansion of the items, which are listed under **Analysis Factors** and **Composition Factors** in the process model, to assist the reader in understanding the scope of each factor. These factors significantly affect (perhaps determine) the degree to which successful interpretation can be accomplished.

1. Process Skills

Analysis Factors refers to the interpreter's ability to quickly and accurately derive meaning from the source message; it includes attending (blocking distraction), analysis and synthesis, ability to access short-term memory, ability to access long-term memory for knowledge (see below), and retaining form when appropriate (e.g. proper names).

Composition Factors refers to the interpreter's ability to quickly and accurately construct language forms from the Message; it includes retrieval of linguistic and cultural knowledge, ability to access short-term memory, ability to access long-term memory for knowledge (see below), as well as planning the production of the target message.

2. Process Management

This element of the process is responsible for "supervisory" functions and overseeing numerous sub-tasks, such as:

- allotting and modifying process (lag) time to allow for analysis/composition
- chunking message units into manageable sections
- monitoring the sequence of operations
- making decisions about obtaining clarification/restatement from the speaker (in **Analysis** stage)
- making decisions about repairing a portion of the target message (in **Composition** stage)
- making decisions about reliance on an external monitor (team member)

243

3. Competence in Source/Target Language and Culture

Language refers to both knowledge about grammatical rules, vocabulary repertoire, discourse styles, and phonological constraints as well as the ability to perform functions in these languages appropriate to context.

Culture refers to both knowledge about norms, values, rules, traditions, and beliefs held by members of the culture as well as the ability to behave in culturally appropriate ways in various contexts.

In addition to the individual languages/cultures, it is necessary for the interpreter to have an understanding of the ways in which the languages and cultures are similar and are different (cross linguistic/cultural competence). This knowledge assists the interpreter in "flagging" particular linguistic or cultural elements which may need to be acted upon (e.g. recognizing that an item is uninterpretable) by the supervisor (see **Process Management**).

4. Knowledge

This term refers to the stored (long-term memory) experiences and learning that the interpreter has accumulated in all sensory and intellectual contexts. Knowledge may be stored non-linguistically, some in only one language/culture, and sometimes knowledge is stored cross-linguistically/culturally. For any given assignment, this refers specifically to knowledge relevant to the message being interpreted.

5. Preparation

This item refers to any means the interpreter has used to prepare for the task at hand, either prior to the assignment or during it. It includes:

- physical dimensions (e.g. sleep, exercise, nourishment)
- emotional/psychological dimensions (e.g. confidence, stress management)
- content-related dimensions (e.g. meeting with speaker, researching topic)
- contextual dimensions (e.g. finding out about the participants, environment)
- task-related dimensions (e.g. meeting with team members, coordinator)

6. Environment

This refers to any and all conditions that exist at the time of the interpretation. External environmental factors include:

- physical factors (e.g. lighting, temperature, time of day, proximity to speaker/ audience/team member, noise)
- psychological factors (e.g. stress, emotional displays)
- cultural factors (e.g. conflicting behaviors and/or expectations)

Internal environmental factors include:

- physical (e.g. fatigue, illness)
- psychological (e.g. perceived evaluation, bonding with speaker)
- emotional (e.g. reaction to speaker/topic, audience) state(s) of the interpreter

7. Filter(s)

This item refers to the interpreter's own "baggage" which may filter in, filter out, or distort any aspect of the message as well as process factors listed above. Despite claims to the contrary, interpreters (as human beings) have their own biases, beliefs, personalities, and habits that do affect how they perceive people, situations, and meaning. The ability to recognize when filters may be hindering one's own performance and accessing the resources necessary to intervene (or make some other decision), may be crucial to the outcome.

D. Message

Message refers to the meaning of the speaker's message, represented through non-linguistic (ideally) means, which has been extracted by the interpreter during the analysis phase of the process. The absence of linguistic symbols frees the interpreter from the constraints of language meanings so that they may optimally recreate the message using target language forms that most appropriately convey message equivalence. Certain language forms, however, cannot be separated from their meanings (such as proper names).

Source Representation (R1) refers to the non-linguistic representation from the source message perspective. Keeping the message in the speaker's frame of reference prevents the interpreter from prematurely representing the message from the target audience's point of view, which may result in a loss of meaning. It also helps the interpreter more readily identify which aspects of the speaker's meaning may need modification or adjustment.

Target Representation (R2) refers to the non-linguistic representation from the perspective of the target audience. Shifting the message to the audience's frame of reference facilitates the interpreter in composing an equivalent message into the target language. This switch in representation may also help to identify aspects of the speaker's message that need expansion or clarification. For example, if the English speaker is describing an accident they may be using prepositions such as "near" or "across from" without providing enough spatial information to allow an accurate rendition into ASL. This stage of the process allows the interpreter to recognize the need for more information and obtain it from the speaker.

E. Monitor/Feedback

After the segment of text is interpreted, there are both internal and external forces that may prompt the interpreter to act on their just-completed production. The internal one is called the **Monitor** (which operates throughout the process as well), and it may signal the interpreter that repair is needed. For example, if the interpreter realizes that her/his English interpretation was not a complete thought, the Monitor may revert to the composition stage and complete the sentence. Another way this may be accomplished is through external feedback. This feedback may come from the interpreter's team member or the audience. For example, the interpreter fingerspells a name and a Deaf

person in the audience corrects it for the interpreter. The interpreter may repair the spelling, if the internal monitor decides that is appropriate or possible to do (e.g. if the interpreter is falling too far behind or is preoccupied with a processing a difficult segment of the text, they may decide not to repair.)

F. Arrows

The two-sided arrows (⟷) between phases of the process show that these stages are not separate and strictly sequential. In other words, there may be interaction between the analysis and representation (message) stages before the interpreter moves on to composition.

At any stage in the process the interpreter may access an earlier stage. The solid gray arrows (⟶) indicate that the interpreter has chosen to exit the process at that point and access an earlier stage. The striped arrows (⇢) indicate access to a particular part of the process. For example, if the interpreter knows they did not see/hear something the speaker signed/said, they would exit at receptive channel (gray arrow) and access the speaker (striped arrow) or their team member (not shown) for the information that was missed.

Copyright © 1992, 2016 by Betty M. Colonomos, Bilingual Mediation Center, Inc.

Constructing meaning (message)

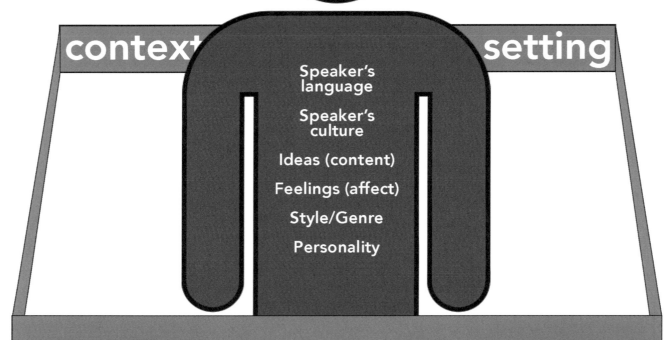

Speaker's language Community language plus individual's form of language, which is affected by age, gender, ethnic background, social class, geographic area, education, occupation, race, and other factors.

Speaker's language Primary affiliation and individual's identification with other groups (e.g. ethnic or racial, lgbt, religious, vocational, recreational, and others) that may modify behaviors, norms, and values.

Setting Type: *school, office, conference.* Location: *rural, urban.* Milieu: *stressful, relaxed.*

Languages Similarities and/or differences between speaker and audience.

Cultures Match to speaker's culture(s): *norms, behaviors, expectations.*

Participants Relationship to the speaker: *familiar, peer, power differentials.*

Copyright © 1998, 2016 by Betty M. Colonomos, Bilingual Mediation Center, Inc. • Do not reproduce or distribute without permission. (16b01)

References

Ackerman, C. S. (2020, April 15). *87 Self-Reflection Questions for Introspection*. Retrieved July 11, 220, from Positive Psychology: https://positivepsychology.com/introspection-self-reflection/

Adam, R., Carty, B., & Stone, C. (2011). Ghostwriting: Deaf translators within the Deaf community. *Babel, 57*(4), 375-393. doi:https://doi.org/10.1075/babel.57.4.01ada

Adler, R., & Towne, N. (1998). *Looking out/looking in: Interpersonal communication (2nd Edition).* New York: Holt, Rinehart, and Winston.

Akamatsu, T. C. (1993). Teaching Deaf Asian and Pacific Island American Children. In K. M. Christensen, & G. L. Delgado (Eds.), *A Multicultural Approach to Education of Children Who Are Deaf.* White Plains: Longman.

Akkus, B., Postmes, T., & Stroebe, K. (2017, September 28). Community Collectivism: A social dynamic approach to conceptualizing culture. *PLoS ONE*, 1-29. doi:https://doi.org/10.1371/journal.pone.0185725

Alakhunova, N., Diallo, O., Martin del Campo, I., & Tallarico, W. (2015). Defining Marginalization: An Assessment Tool. *Elliott School of International Affairs & the World Fair Trade Organization-Asia*, 1-20. Retrieved April 7, 2020, from https://elliott.gwu.edu/sites/g/files/zaxdzs2141/f/World%20Fair%20Trade%20Organization.pdf

Alcorn, B. (1986). *Interviews "Off the Record".* (unpublished).

Alcorn, R. (1996). *Dominion.* New York: Waterbrook Multnomah.

Allen, R. L. (2001). Consequences of the Black sense of self. *Journal of Black Psychology, 27*, 3-28.

Allerton, C. (2016, August 25). *Occupational Health & Wellbeing*. Retrieved June 24, 2020, from Personnel Today: https://www.personneltoday.com/hr/deaf-workers-one-four-quit-job-discrimination/

Alley, E. (2014). A Follow-Up Survey to Determine Competencies and Skills Needed for Effective Trilingual Interpreting. In P. G. Annarino, M. Aponte-Samalot, & D. Quinto-Pozo (Eds.), *Toward Effective Practice: Interpreting in Spanish-influenced Settings* (pp. 127-134). National Consortium of Interpreter Education Centers.

American Academy of Pediatrics. (2015, December 18). *Children with Intellectual Disabilities*. Retrieved from Healthy Children: https://www.healthychildren.org/English/health-issues/conditions/developmental-disabilities/Pages/Intellectual-Disability.aspx

American Deaf Culture. (2015). Retrieved July 24, 2020, from from Laurent Clerc National Deaf Education Center: https://www3.gallaudet.edu/clerc-center/info-to-go/deaf-culture/american-deaf-culture.html

American Psychological Association, Task Force on Resilience and Strength in Black Children and Adolescents. (2008). *Resilience in African American children and adolescents: A vision for optimal development.* Washington, DC. Retrieved June 14, 2020, from ttp://www.apa.org/pi/cyf/resilience.html

American Society for Quality. (2020). *What are Stakeholders?* Retrieved July 28, 2020, from What Do You Want to Do?: https://asq.org/quality-resources/stakeholders

American Sociological Association. (2020). *Race and Ethnicity*. Retrieved May 30, 2020, from American Sociological Association: https://www.asanet.org/topics/race-and-ethnicity

Annarino, P. G., Aponte-Samalot, M., & Quinto-Pozos, D. (Eds.). (2014). *Toward Effective Practice: Interpreting in Spanish-Influenced Settings.* The National Consortium of Interpreter Education Centers. Retrieved May 29, 2020, from http://www.interpretereducation.org/wp-content/uploads/2014/04/Toward-Effective-Practice-Interpreting-in-Spanish-Influenced-Settings.pdf

Annarino, P., Casanova de Canales, K., & Trevino, R. (2014). Defining Trilingual Interpreting and Its Practitioners. In P. G. Annarino, M. Aponte-Samalot, & D. Quinto-Pozos (Eds.), *Toward Effective Practice: Interpreting in Spanish-Influenced Settings.* (pp. 1-8). The National Consortium of Interpreter Education Centers. Retrieved June 16, 2020, from http://www.interpretereducation.org/wp-content/uploads/2014/04/Toward-Effective-Practice-Interpreting-in-Spanish-Influenced-Settings.pdf

Antonini, R. (2015). Unseen forms of interpreting: Child language brokering in Italy. (D. Katan, & C. Spinzi, Eds.) *Cultus: the Intercultural Journal of Mediation and Communication, 8*, 96-112. Retrieved May 27, 2020, from https://www.researchgate.net/publication/303701781_Unseen_forms_of_interpreting_Child_language_brokering_in_Italy

Anynonmous. (2008, April 6). *Some great quotes*. Retrieved from Fire Engineering: https://community.fireengineering.com/group/quotes/forum

Assael, M. Y., Shillingford, B., Whiteson, S., & de Freitas, N. (2016, December 16). LipNet: End-to-end sentence-level lipreading. *Google Deepmind & CIFAR CANADA*, 1-13. Retrieved May 16, 2020, from https://arxiv.org/pdf/1611.01599.pdf

Association of Visual Language Interpreters of Canada. (2011). *AVLIC Policy & Procedure Manual.* Policy & Procedure Manual. Retrieved April 27, 2020, from https://www.avlic.ca/sites/default/files/docs/2011-12%20P&P%20Manual%20Section%201%20-%20History.pdf

Association of Visual Language Interpreters of Canada. (2014). Benefits Afforded to Active and Student Membership Types and to the Subscription Service. Retrieved March 23, 2020, from https://www.avlic.ca/sites/default/files/docs/2014-11Summary_of_Benefits.pdf

Association of Visual Language Interpreters of Canada. (2016, April 24). In-Lieu-of-Affiliate Chapter Membership. *IN-LIEU-OF-AFFILIATE CHAPTER MEMBERSHIP*, 1-2. AVLIC. Retrieved June 28, 2020, from https://www.avlic.ca/sites/default/files/images/II%20-%209.0%20In-Lieu-of-Affiliate%20Chapter%20Membership%20-%20POLICY%20-%2024%20April%202016.pdf

Association of Visual Language Interpreters of Canada. (2018). *2018 Annual Report.* Toronto: www.avlic.ca. Retrieved April 27, 2020, from https://www.avlic.ca/sites/default/files/images/2018-06-21%20Annual%20Report.pdf

Association of Visual Language Interpreters of Canada. (2018, August). *Board of Directors (Members).* Retrieved from Association of Visual Language Interpreters of Canada: https://www.avlic.ca/members/directors

Association of VIsual Language Interpreters of Canada. (2018, July 14). *Vision, Mission, Core Values and Bylaws*. Retrieved from Association of VIsual Language Interpreters of Canada: https://www.avlic.ca/about/vision_mission_bylaws#Core%20Value

Baker-Shenk, C. (1985). Characteristics of oppressed and oppressor peoples: Their effect on the interpreting context. In M. McIntire (Ed.), *Interpreting: The art of cross cultural mediation* (pp. 45-53). RID Publications. Retrieved May 23, 2020, from http://www.interpretereducation.org/wp-content/uploads/2016/01/Baker-Shenk-Opression-Article.pdf

Baker-Shenk, C. (1992). The Interpreter: Machine, Advocate, or Ally? *National Consortium of Interpreter Education Centers*, 1-18. Retrieved July 2020, from http://www.interpretereducation.org/wp-content/uploads/2014/04/The-Interpreter-Machine.pdf

Bauman, H.-D. L., Nelson, J. L., & Rose, H. M. (Eds.). (2006). *Signing the Body Poetic: Essays on American Sign Language Literature.* Los Angeles, California: University of California Press. Retrieved July 17, 2020, from https://content.ucpress.edu/pages/9424/9424.ch01.pdf

Beckerman, J. (2018, June 1). *Recognizing Caregiver Burnout*. Retrieved April 12, 2020, from WebMD: https://www.webmd.com/healthy-aging/caregiver-recognizing-burnout#1

Bell, N. D. (2007, January). How native and non-native English speakers adapt to humor in intercultural interaction. *Humor, 20*(1), 27-48. doi:10.1515/HUMOR.2007.002

Bentley-Sassman, J., & Dawson, C. (2012). Deaf-Hearing Interpreter Teams: A Teamwork Approach. *Journal of Interpretation, 22*(1).

Bernstein , L. E., Demorest, M. E., & Tucker, P. E. (2000). Speech perception without hearing. *Perception & Psychophysics, 62*(2), 233-252. Retrieved May 16, 2020, from https://link.springer.com/content/pdf/10.3758/BF03205546.pdf

Betts, J. W. (2016, April 15-17). *The Speed of Change: Is Sign Language Interpreting Keeping Pace?* Retrieved August 4, 2020, from StreetLeverage: https://streetleverage.com/live_presentations/speed-change-sign-language-interpreting-keeping-pace/

Bienvenu, M. (1987, APril 6). The Third Culture: Working Together. Hyattsville, Maryland: RID Publications. Retrieved June 20, 2020, from http://intrpr.info/3330/3330_bienvenu_thirdculture.pdf

Bienvenu, M. (1992). *personal communications*.

Biography.com, E. (Updated 2020, January 13). *W.E.B. Du Bois Biography*. (A&E Television Networks) Retrieved April 10, 2020, from The Biography.com website: https://www.biography.com/activist/web-du-bois

Birner, B. (n.d.). *Is English Changing?* Retrieved March 28, 2020, from Linguistic Society of America: https://www.linguisticsociety.org/content/english-changing

Bishop, A. (1994). *Becoming an Ally: Breaking the Cycle of Oppression.* Halifax: Fernwood Publishing.

Black, L. L., & Stone, D. (2005). Expanding the Definition of Privilege: The Concept of Social Privilege. *Journal of Multicultural Counseling and Development, 33*(4), 243-255.

Boam , D. H. (2019, Winter). It Should Have Always Bothered Me. (J. Wardle, Ed.) *VIEWS, 36*(1), 2-52. Retrieved April 10, 2020, from https://issuu.com/ridviews/docs/february19_views

Boaz, D. (2015). *The Libertarian Mind: A Manifesto for Freedom.* New York: Simon & Schuster.

Bontempo, K. (2015). SIgned language interpreting. In H. Mikkelson, & R. Jourdenais (Eds.), *The Routledge handbook of interpreting* (pp. 112-128). London, UK, Routledge.

Boudreault. (2005). *Topics in Sign Language Interpreting: Theory and Practice.* J. Benjamins Publishing Company.

Bowleg, L. (2012, July). The Problem With the Phrase Women and Minorities: Intersectionality - an Important Theoretical Framework for Public Health. *American Journal of Public Health, 102*(7), 1267-1273. doi:10.2105/AJPH.2012.300750

Bradshaw, J. (1990). *Homecoming: Reclaiming and championing your inner child.* New York: Bantam Books.

Brown, S. (n.d.). *Deaf Interpreter Rupert Dubler On His Role During The Coronavirus Crisis.* WBUR News. Retrieved from https://www.wbur.org/news/2020/04/17/rupert-dubler-asl-interpreter-baker

Burdick, E., & Lederer, W. J. (1958). *The Ugly American.* New York. Retrieved June 27, 2020

Burke, D. (2019). Deaf education: The past, present, and future. *Senior Honors Projects, 2010-current*, 655. Retrieved July 5, 2020, from https://commons.lib.jmu.edu/honors201019/655

Cagle, K. (2020, July 3). Faculty. (W. F. Ross III, Interviewer)

Canada. (2011). Retrieved from Infoplease: https://www.infoplease.com/world/countries/canada

Carbin, C. F., & Smith, D. L. (1996). *Deaf Heritage in Canada: A Distinctive, Diverse, and Enduring Culture.* New York: McGraw-Hill Ryerson. Retrieved from ttps://glottolog.org/resource/languoid/id/mari1381

Casanova de Canalas, K., & Trevino, R. (2014). Trilingual Interpreting Domains and Competency Statements. In M. A.-S.-P. Annarino (Ed.), *Toward Effective Practice: Interpreting in Spanish-Influenced Settings.*

(pp. 107-125). The National Consortium of Interpreter Education Centers. Retrieved June 19, 2020, from http://www.interpretereducation.org/wp-content/uploads/2014/04/Toward-Effective-Practice-Interpreting-in-Spanish-Influenced-Settings.pdf

Casanova de Canales, K., & Trevino, R. (2014). Identifying the Skills and Competencies of Trilingual Interpreters Through the Use of Focus Groups. In P. G. Annarino, M. Aponte-Samalot, & D. Quinto-Pozos (Eds.), *Toward Effective Practice: Interpreting in Spanish-Influenced Settings* (pp. 57-106). The National Consortium of Interpreter Education Centers. Retrieved June 19, 2020, from http://www.interpretereducation.org/wp-content/uploads/2014/04/Toward-Effective-Practice-Interpreting-in-Spanish-Influenced-Settings.pdf

Census in Brief. (2016). *Linguistic diversity and multilingualism in Canadian homes.* Statistics Canada. Retrieved July 7, 2020, from https://www12.statcan.gc.ca/census-recensement/2016/as-sa/98-200-x/2016010/98-200-x2016010-eng.pdf

Center for Parent Information and Resources. (2017, 16 2017). *Intellectual Disability.* Retrieved August 6, 2020, from Supporting the Parent Centers Who Serve Families of Children with Disabilities: https://www.parentcenterhub.org/intellectual/#def

Cherry, K. (2019, September 23). *The Role of a Schema in Psychology.* (S. Gans, MD, Editor) Retrieved May 1, 2020, from Verywell mind: https://www.verywellmind.com/what-is-a-schema-2795873

Cherry, K. (2020, March 24). *Individualistic Cultures and Behavior.* Retrieved June 16, 2020, from Very Well Mind: https://www.verywellmind.com/what-are-individualistic-cultures-2795273

Christensen, K. M. (1993). A Multicultural Approach to Education of Children Who Are Deaf. In K. M. Christensen, & G. L. Delgado (Eds.), *Multicultural Issues in Deafness.* White Plains.

Christenson, D. (2020, March). In a Glass Box: Clarke School for the Deaf Alumni Detail Decades of Abuse. *Daily Hampshire Gazette.*

Clark, J. L. (2017, August). *Notes from a DeafBlind Writer.* Retrieved August 7, 2020, from Distantism: https://johnleeclark.tumblr.com/post/163762970913/distantism

Cokely, D. (1986). The Effects of Lag Time on Interpreter Errors. *Sign Language Studies*, 341-375. doi:10.1353/sls.1986.0025

Cokely, D. (1992). *Interpretation: Towards A Sociolinguistic Model.* Burtonsville: Linstok Press.

Cokely, D. (2001). Interpreting Culturally Rich Realities: Research Implications for Cuccessful Interpretations. (D. Watson, Ed.) *Journal of Interpreting*, 1-45. Retrieved March 18, 2020, from https://sites.google.com/site/ridpublicationsproject/home/journal-of-interpretation/joi-2001

Cokely, D. (2008, December). Shifting Positionality: A Critical Examination of the Turning Point in the Relationship of Interpreters and the Deaf Community. 1-36. doi:10.1093/acprof/9780195176940.003.0001

Colonomos, B. (1989; 2002). *About IMI.* Retrieved August 1, 2020, from Bilingual Mediation Center: https://www.visitbmc.com/index.php/from-bmc/integrated-model-of-interpreting-imi

Coltrane, B. (2012). *What is Audism?* Retrieved April 6, 2020, from deafchoice.com: http://deafchoice.com/faq/what-is-an-audist/

Committee on Consumer Affairs. (2008, February 20). *Resolution to Support Equal Access to Communication Technologies by People with Disabilities in the 21st Century.* Retrieved August 6, 2020, from NARUC: National Association of Regulatory Utility Commissioners: https://pubs.naruc.org/pub.cfm?id=53A057F7-2354-D714-5154-282DC15A9914

Commonground. (n.d.). *Aboriginal, Indigenous or First Nations?* Retrieved June 4, 2020, from Common Ground: https://www.commonground.org.au/learn/aboriginal-or-indigenous

Conceptually Accurate Signed English (CASE). (2019, Reviewed, March 21). Retrieved May 4, 2020, from Hearing Loss in Children: https://www.cdc.gov/ncbddd/hearingloss/parentsguide/building/case.html

Crossman, A. (2020, February 11). *Ethnicity Definition in Sociology.* Retrieved May 29, 2020, from ThoughtCo.: https://www.thoughtco.com/ethnicity-definition-3026311

Crossman, A. (2020, February 11). *The Sociology of Race and Ethnicity.* Retrieved May 31, 2020, from ThoughtCo.: thoughtco.com/sociology-of-race-and-ethnicity-3026285

Daniels, R. (2020, March 24). personal communications. (J. Featherstone, Interviewer)

Darwish, A.-F. E., & Huber, G. L. (2003). Individualism vs Collectivism in Different Cultures: a cross-cultural study. *Intercultural Education*, 47-55. doi:10.1080/1467598032000044647

de Bruin, E., & Brugmans, P. (2006). The Psychotherapist and the Sign Language Interpreter. *Journal of Deaf Studies and Deaf Education, 11*(3), 360-368. Retrieved July 5, 2020, from https://academic.oup.com/jdsde/article/11/3/360/2530033

Dean, R. K., & Pollard, Jr, R. Q. (2001, January). Application of Demand-Control Theory to Sign Language Interpreting: Implications for Stress and Interpreter Training. *Journal of Deaf Studies and Deaf Education, 6*(1), 1-14. doi:doi.org/10.1093/deafed/6.1.1

Dean, R. K., & Pollard, R. Q. (2011). Context-based Ethical Reasoning in Interpreting: A Demand Control Schema Perspective. *The Interpreter and Translator Trainer, 5*(1), 155-182. Retrieved August 5, 2020, from http://intrpr.info/library/dean-pollard-context-based-ethical-reasoning-in-interpreting.pdf

Department of Economic and Social Affairs. (2009). Culture. In N. Kipuri, *State of the World's Indigenous Peoples* (pp. 12-250). New York: United Nations. Retrieved May 28, 2020, from https://www.un.org/esa/socdev/unpfii/documents/SOWIP/en/SOWIP_web.pdf

DesGeorges, J. (2016, April). *Avoiding Assumptions: Communication Decisions Made by Hearing Parents of Deaf Children.* Retrieved March 21, 2020, from AMA Journal of Ethics: https://journalofethics.ama-assn.org/article/avoiding-assumptions-communication-decisions-made-hearing-parents-deaf-children/2016-04

Dictionary.com. (2020, July). *context.* Retrieved from Dictionary.com: https://www.dictionary.com/browse/context

Dymoke, S., & Harrison, J. (Eds.). (2008). *Reflective Teaching and Learning: A Guide to Professional Issues for Beginning Secondary Teachers.* Thousand Oaks: SAGE Publications. Retrieved July 11, 2020, from https://www.bookdepository.com/Reflective-Teaching-Learning-Sue-Dymoke/9781412946476

Ellis, N. (2020, February 25). *Descendants.* Retrieved June 13, 2020, from The Washington Post: https://www.washingtonpost.com/nation/2020/02/25/lost-lineage-quest-identify-black-americans-roots/?arc404=true

Emory University. (2009). *African Origins.* Retrieved June 13, 2020, from African Origins: Portal to Africans Liberated from Transatlantic Slave Vessels: https://legacy.african-origins.org/

Erickson, A. (2007, March 1). NAJIT Position Paper: Team Interpreting in the Courtroom. Seattle, Washington: National Association of Judiciary Interpreters & Translators.

Ericsson, K. A. (2006). The Influence of Experience and Deliberate Practice on the Development of Superior Expert Performance. In N. C. K. A. Ericsson (Ed.), *The Cambridge handbook of expertise and expert performance* (pp. 683-703). Cambridge University Press. doi:https://doi.org/10.1017/CBO9780511816796.038

Fant, L. (1990). *Silver Threads.* Silver Springs: RID Publications.

Federal Interagency Forum on Child and Family Statistics. (2019). *America's Children: Key National Indicators of Well-Being.* Washington, DC: U.S. Government Printing Office. Retrieved May 28, 2020, from https://www.childstats.gov/pdf/ac2019/ac_19.pdf

Ferguson, S. (2014, September 29). *Privilege 101: A Quick and Dirty Guide.* Retrieved April 10, 2020, from Everyday Feminism: https://everydayfeminism.com/2014/09/what-is-privilege/

Forestal, E., & Cole, J. (2018). Deaf Translation: Socio-Cultural Perspective. *2018 Biennial Conference – Reaching New Heights in Interpreter Education: Mentoring, Teaching, and Leadership* (pp. 188-199). Conference of Interpreter Trainers. Retrieved July 30, 2020, from http://www.cit-asl.org/new/wp-content/uploads/2018/10/14-Forestal-Cole-2018.pdf

Freire, P., & Ramos, M. B. (1970). *Pedagogy of the oppressed.* New York: Continuum.

Funk, K. (2001, March 21). *What is a Worldview?* Retrieved July 25, 2020, from Oregon State University: College of Engineering: http://web.engr.oregonstate.edu/~funkk/Personal/worldview.html

Gannon, J. (2012). *Deaf Heritage: A Narrative History of Deaf America* (Vol. 7). Washington, District of Columbia: Gallaudet University Press.

Gelman, S. A., & Roberts, S. O. (2017). How language shapes the cultural inheritance of categories. In A. Whiten (Ed.), *Proceeds of the National Academy of Science of the United States of America. 114: 30*, pp. 7900-7907. Irvine: PNAS. doi:10.1073/pnas.1621073114

Gish, S. (1987). I understood all the words, but I missed the point: A goal-to-detail, detail-to-goal strategy for text analysis. *RID Publication*, 125-137.

González Ávila, T. (2020, March 27). personal communication. (J. Featherstone, Interviewer)

Gooda, M. (2011, September 11). *Social Justice Report 2011.* Australian Human Right Commission. Retrieved July 5, 2020, from Australian Human Right Commission: https://humanrights.gov.au/sites/default/files/content/social_justice/sj_report/sjreport11/pdf/sjr2011.pdf

Granda, A., & Nuccio, J. (2018). *Protactile Principles.* Seattle: Tactile Communications.

Gravetter, F. J., & Forzano, L.-A. B. (2019). *Research Methods for the Behavioral Sciences* (6th Edition ed.). Cengage Learning. Retrieved from https://www.cengage.com/c/research-methods-for-the-behavioral-sciences-6e-gravetter/9781337613316/?filterBy=Higher-Education#compare-buying-options

Griffiths, H., & Keirns, N. (2015). *Introduction to Sociology 2e.* Houston, Texas: OpenStax. Retrieved March 20, 2020, from Racial, Ethnic, and Minority Groups: https://courses.lumenlearning.com/sociology/chapter/racial-ethnic-and-minority-groups/

Guardino, C. A. (2008, Spring). Identification and Placement for Deaf Students With Multiple Disabilities: Choosing the Path Less Followed. *American Annals of the Deaf, 153*(1), 55-64. Retrieved from https://www.jstor.org/stable/26234488

Guerrero, L. K., & Floyd, K. (2006). *Nonverbal Communication in Close Relationships.* (S. Duck, Ed.) London: Lawrence Erlbaum Assocaites Publishers. Retrieved July 7, 2020, from https://www.academia.edu/36261723/Laura_K.Guerrero_Kory_Floyd_-_Nonverbal_Communication_in_Close_Relationships.pdf

Gumul, E. (2018). Searching for Evidence of Gile's Effort Models in Retrospective Protocols of Trainee Simultaneous Interpreters. *Między Oryginałem a Przekładem, 24*(42), 17-39. doi:doi.org/10.12797/MOaP.24.2018.42.02

Hall, B. J. (2017). Cultural Communication Norms. In Y. Kim (Ed.), *The International Encyclopedia of Intercultural Communication.* doi:doi.org/10.1002/9781118783665.ieicc0116

Hall, E. T. (1976). *Beyond Culture.* New York: Bantam Doubleday Dell Publishing.

Hall, E. T. (1989). Deaf Culture, Tacit Culture and Ethnic Relations. *Sign Language Studies, 65*, 291-304. Retrieved June 27, 2020, from www.jstor.org/stable/26204018

Happynook, T. M. (2000). Cultural Biodiversity: Indigenous Relationships within Their Environment. *International Institute of Fisheries Economics and Trade (IIFET)*, (pp. 1-3). Corvalis.

Happynook, T. M. (2000, April, May, June). Indigenous Whalers and Traditional Resource Management Knowledge. *Indigenous Affairs(2)*, 1-88. International Work Group for Indigenous Affairs. Retrieved June 10, 2020, from https://www.iwgia.org/images/publications/IA_2-00.pdf

Harvey, M. (2015). Reaping the Benefits of Vicarious Trauma. *International Journal of Interpreter Education, 7*(2), 5-20. Retrieved April 12, 2020, from http://www.cit-asl.org/new/wp-content/uploads/2015/11/c-Reaping-VT-benefits-Harvey.pdf

Harvey, M. A. (1984, June). Family Therapy with Deaf Persons: The Systemic Utilization of an Interpreter. *Family Process, 23*(2), 205-221. doi:10.1111/j.1545-5300.1984.00205.x

Haugen, E. (1953). *The Norwegian Language in America.* Philadelphia, Pennsylvania: Pennsylvania University Press.

Higgins, M., & Lieberman, A. M. (2016). Deaf Students as a Linguistic and Cultural Minority: Shifting Perspectives and Implications for Teaching and Learning. *Journal of Education, 196*(1), 9-18. doi:https://doi.org/10.1177/002205741619600103

Hill, R. (1999). *The Strengths of African American Families: Twenty-five Years Later.* Maryland: University Press of America, Inc.

History.com Editors. (2018, November 16). *History.* Retrieved June 13, 2020, from Black History Milestones: Timeline: https://www.history.com/topics/black-history/black-history-milestones

Hofstede, G., & Bond, M. H. (1984, December 1). Hofstede's Culture Dimensions: An Independent Validation Using Rokeach's Value Survey. *Journal of Cross-Cultural Psychology, 15*(4), 417–433. doi:https://doi.org/10.1177/0022002184015004003

Holcomb, T. (2013). *Introduction to American deaf culture.* New York: Oxford University Press.

Horvath, R. J. (1972, February). A Definition of Colonialism. *Current Anthropology, 13*(1), 45-57. Retrieved May 31, 2020, from https://www.jstor.org/stable/2741072

Humphrey, J. H. (1997). Chopping down and Reconstructing a Tree. *Meta: Translators' Journal,, 42*(3), 515-520. Retrieved June 19, 2020, from https://www.academia.edu/4386771/Chopping_Down_the_Tree_Humphrey

Humphrey, J. H. (1999). *Decisions? Decisions! A Practice Guide for Sign Language Professionals.* Amarillo: H & H Publishers.

Humphrey, J., & Alcorn, B. (2007). *So You Want to be An Interpreter? An introduction to Sign Language Interpreting.* (4th Edition ed.). Seattle: H & H Publishing.

Humphries, T. (1075). *The Making of a Word: Audism.*

Intercultural Communication: High- and Low-Context Cultures. (2020). Retrieved July 10, 2020, from Southeastern University: https://online.seu.edu/articles/high-and-low-context-cultures/

Introduction to Language. (n.d.). Retrieved March 28, 2020, from Luman - Boundless Psychology: https://courses.lumenlearning.com/boundless-psychology/chapter/introduction-to-language/

Iracheta, M. (2019, November 27). Texas educators accused of inappropriate relationships with minors. *Houston Chronicle.* Retrieved August 5, 2020, from https://www.chron.com/news/houston-texas/houston/article/Bad-Teacher-Texas-school-officials-who-ve-been-14867357.php

Isenhath, J. O. (1990). *The Linguistics of American Sign Language.* Jefferson: Mcfarland & Co Inc Pub.

Isham, W. P. (1985). The Role of Message Analysis in Interpretation. *Interpreting: The Art of Cross Cultural Mediation* (pp. 111-122). RID Publications.

Johnson, L., Witter-Merithew, A., & Taylor, M. (2004). A National Perspective on Entry-to-Practice Competencies for ASL-English Interpreters. In E. M. Maroney (Ed.), *Proceedings of the 15th National Interpreter Trainers Convention* (pp. 30-42). Washington: Conference of Interpreter Trainers. Retrieved July 28, 2020, from https://www.cit-asl.org/new/wp-content/uploads/2014/07/CIT-2004.pdf

Johnson, L., Witter-Merithew, A., & Taylor, M. (2004). *Entry–to–Practice Competencies for ASL/English Interpreters.* University of Northern Colorado, at Lowry Campus , National Distance Learning Center for Interpreter Education. Denver: Distance Opportunities for Interpreter Training Center. Retrieved

July 28, 2020, from https://www.unco.edu/cebs/asl-interpreting/pdf/asl-english-interpretation/entry-to-practice-competencies.pdf

Joos, M. (1967). *The Five Clocks: A linguistic excursion into the five styles of English usage.* New York: Harcourt, Brace & World.

Kelly, C. D., & Varghese, R. (2018, June 25). Four contexts of institutional oppression: Examining the experiences of Blacks in education, criminal justice and child welfare. *Journal of Human Behavior in the Social Environment, 28*(7), 874-888. doi:https://doi.org/10.1080/10911359.2018.1466751

Kelly, L. (1979). *The true interpreter: A history of translation theory and practice in the west.* New York: St. Martin's Press.

Kidder, R. M. (1992). Institute for Global Ethics. In R. M. Kidder, *How Good People Make Tough Choices* (pp. 71-90).

King, Jr, M. (1963, April 16). *"Letter from a Birmingham Jail [King, Jr.]".* (A. B. Ali-Dinar, Editor) Retrieved July 5, 2020, from African Studies Center - University of Pennsylvania: https://www.africa.upenn.edu/Articles_Gen/Letter_Birmingham.html

Klima, E., & Bellugi, U. (1979). *The Signs of Language.* Cambridge: Harvard University Press.

Kurz, K. B. (2018). Deaf Eyes on Interpreting. In T. K. Holcomb, & D. H. Smith (Eds.), *The Heart of Interpreting from Deaf Perspectives.* GU Press. Retrieved March 7, 2020

Ladd, P. (2005, October 1). Deafhood: A concept stressing possibilities, not deficits. *Scandinavian Journal of Public Health, 33*(Suppl 66), 12-17. doi:10.1080/14034950510033318

Lane, H. (2005, Summer). Ethnicity, Ethics, and the Deaf-World. *Journal of Deaf Studies and Deaf Education, 10*(3), 291-310. doi:10.1093/deafed/eni030

Lane, H. L., & Hoffmeister, R. B. (1996). *A journey into the deaf-world.* San Diego: Dawn Sign Press.

Lawrence, S. (2003). Interpreter Discourse: English to ASL Expansion. 1-15.

Leal, M., Martinez, C., Stockton, P., & Bose, N. (n.d.). Transcription: What is reflective practice? *Cambridge Professional Development.* Cambridge. Retrieved June 20, 2020, from https://cambridge-community.org.uk/professional-development/gswrp/ReflectivePractice_transcript1.pdf

Lee, J. (1995). *Marginality: The Key to Multicultural Theology.* Minneapolis: Fortress Press.

Letourneau, R. (2009). Reflections: AVLIC 2008 – Connecting Minds and Communities. *AVLIC News, 24(Fall/Winter),* 2. Retrieved April 27, 2020, from https://www.avlic.ca/sites/default/files/docs/2009-11%20AVLIC%20News%20Fall-Winter%202009.pdf

Levinson, S. C., & Torreira, F. (2015, June 12). Timing in turn-taking and its implications for processing models of language. *Frontiers in Psychology, 6*(731). doi:10.3389/fpsyg.2015.00731

Lewis Herman, J. (1997). *Trauma and Recovery: The Aftermath of Violence - From Domestic Abuse to Political Terror.* New York: Basic Books.

Little, B. (2017, August 16). *How Boarding Schools Tried to Kill the Indian' Through Assimilation.* Retrieved June 6, 2020, from HIstory: https://www.history.com/news/how-boarding-schools-tried-to-kill-the-indian-through-assimilation

Little, W. (2016). *Introduction to Sociology - 2nd Canadian Edition.* Retrieved from https://opentextbc.ca/introductiontosociology2ndedition/

Livingston, S., Singer, B., & Abramson, T. (1994, Spring). Effectiveness Compared: ASL Interpretation vs. Transliteration. *Sign Language Studies, 82*, 1-54. doi:10.1353/sls.1994.0008

Llewellyn-Jones, P., & Lee, R. G. (2009). The 'Role' of the Community/Public Service Interpreter. *Supporting Deaf People Online Conference*, (pp. 1-7). 2009.

Llewellyn-Jones, P., & Lee, R. G. (2011). Re-visiting Role: Arguing for a multi-dimensional analysis of interpreter behaviour. *Supporting Deaf People Conference*, (pp. 1-7).

Llewllyn-Jones, P., & Lee, R. G. (2013). Getting to the Core of Role: Defining Interpreters' Role-Space. *International Journal of Interpreter Education, 5*(2), 54-72.

Locker, R. (1990). Lexical Equivalence in Transliterating for Deaf Students in the University Classroom: Two Perspectives. *Issues in Applied Linguistics, 1*(2), 167-195. Retrieved April 17, 2020, from http://intrpr.info/library/locker-lexical-equivalence-deaf-students-transliteration.pdf

Loeffler, S. C. (2016, Spring). *Unit 4: Deafhood, Linguistics, and Colonialism*. Retrieved May 31, 2020, from Deaf Culture: http://deafstudiesonline.weebly.com/4-deafhood--colonialism.html

Lopez, G., Ruiz, N. G., & Patten, E. (2017, November 8). *Key facts about Asian Americans, a diverse and growing population*. Retrieved June 19, 2020, from Pew Research Center: https://www.pewresearch.org/fact-tank/2017/09/08/key-facts-about-asian-americans/

LTI, Language Testing International. (2020). *Heritage Speakers Frequently Asked Questions*. Retrieved June 18, 2020, from LTI, Language Testing International: https://www.languagetesting.com/heritage-speakers-frequently-asked-questions

Lumen - Introduction to Sociology. (n.d.). Retrieved March 20, 2020, from Minority Groups: https://courses.lumenlearning.com/cochise-sociology-os/chapter/minority-groups/

Lynch, H. (2020, February 26). African Americans. *Encyclopædia Britannica*. Encyclopedia Britannica, Inc. Retrieved June 13, 2020, from https://www.britannica.com/topic/African-American

Mackey, W. (2000). The description of bilingualism. In L. Wei (Ed.), *The Bilingualism Reader* (pp. 22-50). New York: Routledge. Retrieved from https://vulms.vu.edu.pk/Courses/ENG512/Downloads/[Li_Wei]_The_Bilingualism_Reader(BookFi).pdf

Maftoon, P., & Shakibafar, M. (2011). Who Is a Bilingual? *Journal of English Studies, 1*(2), 79-85. Retrieved July 29, 2020, from https://www.researchgate.net/publication/296695511_Who_Is_a_Bilingual

Mahadi, T. S., & Jafari, S. M. (2012, September). Language and Culture. *International Journal of Humanities and Social Science, 2*(17), 230-235. Retrieved July 24, 2020, from https://pdfs.semanticscholar.org/15f9/293128638a978f6c589643cbc92ab288958a.pdf

Martinez-Gomez, A. (2015). Invisible, visible or everywhere in between? Perceptions and actual behaviours of non-professional interpreters and interpreting users. 175-194. Retrieved August 2020, from https://pdfs.semanticscholar.org/060c/78725333a633e9ba726335fef22fe27c9dc0.pdf

Mathers, M. C., & Witter-Merithew, A. (2014). The contribution of Deaf interpreters to GATEKEEPING within the interpreting profession: Reconnecting with our roots. *Conference of Interpreter Trainers* (pp. 158-253). University of Northern Colorado, Mid-America Regional Interpreter Education Center. Retrieved May 2, 2020, from http://www.cit-asl.org/new/wp-content/uploads/2014/10/2014-23-Mathers-Witter-Merithew.pdf

Mathews, E. S. (2015). Towards an Independent Future: Life Skills Training and Towards an Independent Future: Life Skills Training and. *Irish Journal of Applied Social Studies, 15*(1), 1-14. doi:10.21427/D7442K

Mathis, S. (2020, March 21). personal communications. (J. Featherstone, Interviewer)

McCombs School of Business; The University of Texas at Austin. (2020). *Moral Relativism*. Retrieved August 4, 2020, from Ethics Unwrapped: https://ethicsunwrapped.utexas.edu/glossary/moral-relativism

McCoy, R. (2011, Fall). Ritual in Later Life: Its Role, Significance, and Power. *Generations: Journal of the American Society on Aging, 35*(3), 16-21. Retrieved June 16, 2020, from https://www.jstor.org/stable/pdf/26555789.pdf?refreqid=excelsior%3A2165df0f94599754b505882c1367ca17

McDermid, C. (2008). *Brief History of Canadian ASL_English Interpreting*. York University. Retrieved April 27, 2020, from https://eric.ed.gov/?id=ED502281

McDermid, C. (2014). Evidence of a "Hearing" Dialect of ASL while Interpreting. *Journal of Interpretation, 23*(1), 1-25. Retrieved July 28, 2020, from http://digitalcommons.unf.edu/joi/vol23/iss1/2

McKay-Cody, M. (2020). Protocol for Sign Language Interpreters Working in North American Indigenous Settings. (J. Wardle, Ed.) *VIEWS, 1*(37). Retrieved May 20, 2020, from https://issuu.com/ridviews/docs/february20_views

McLeod, S. (2018). *Jean Piaget's Theory and Stages of Cognitive Development.* Retrieved February 25, 2013, from Simply Psychology: https://www.simplypsychology.org/piaget.html

McLeod, S. (2018). *Lev Vygotsky's Sociocultural Theory.* Retrieved from SImple Psychology: https://www.simplypsychology.org/simplypsychology.org-vygotsky.pdf

Merriam-Webster. (2020). *Microaggression.* Retrieved April 4, 2020, from Merriam-Webster.com Dictionary: https://www.merriam-webster.com/dictionary/microaggression

Merriam-Webster. (2020). *Oppression.* Retrieved April 9, 2020, from Merriam-Webster.com dictionary: https://www.merriam-webster.com/dictionary/oppression

Metzger, M. (1999). *Sign language interpreting: deconstructing the myth of neutrality.* Washington: Gallaudet University Press.

Meusburger, P., Freytag, T., & Suarsana, L. (2016). Ethnic and Cultural Dimensions of Knowledge: An Introduction. In P. Meusburger , T. Freytag, & L. Suarsana (Eds.), *Ethnic and Cultural Dimensions of Knowledge* (1st ed., pp. 1-486). Springer. Retrieved March 28, 2020

Miles, J. F. (2019, January 06). *Oral tradition.* (Encyclopædia Britannica, inc.) Retrieved March 03, 2020, from Encyclopædia Britannica: https://www.britannica.com/topic/oral-tradition

Mindess, A. (2006). *Reading Between the Signs: Intercultural Communication for Sign Language Interpreters.* Boston: Intercultural Press.

Minirth, F. M. (1990). *Love Hunger.* nASHVILLE: Thomas Nelson Publishers.

Minister of Industry. (2017). *Ethnic and cultural origins of Canadians: Portrait of a rich heritage.* Statistics Canada. 2017. Retrieved May 30, 2020, from https://www12.statcan.gc.ca/census-recensement/2016/as-sa/98-200-x/2016016/98-200-x2016016-eng.pdf

Models of deafness. (2015, December 6). Retrieved April 11, 2020, from Canadian Hearing Services: https://www.chs.ca/models-deafness

Moore, M. S. (1993). *For Hearing People Only: Answers to Some of the Most Commonly Asked Questions about the Deaf Community, Its Culture, and the "Deaf Reality".* Rochester: Deaf Life Press.

Mousley, V. L., & Chaudoir, S. R. (2018). Deaf Stigma: Links between stigma and well-being among deaf emerging adults. *Journal of Deaf Studies and Deaf Education, 23*(4), 341-350. doi:10.1093/deafed/eny018

Myers, D. (2013, Spring-Summer). Looking Back to Ball State: Birthplace of RID. *VIEWS.*

Napier, J. (2004). Sign language interpreter training, testing and accreditation: An international comparison. *American Annals of the Deaf, 149*(4), 350-359.

Napier, J. (2012). *Sign language brokering: A survey of hearing and deaf Codas.* Macquarie University. Macquarie University. Retrieved May 5, 2020, from http://www.codaukireland.co.uk/uploads/1/3/0/0/13000270/languagebrokeringsurveysummaryoffindings.pdf

Napoli, D. J., Mellon, N. K., Niparko, J. K., Rathamann, C., Mathur, G., Handley, T., . . . Lantos, J. D. (2015, June). Should All Deaf Children Learn Sign Language. *Pediatrics, 136*(170), 170-176. doi:10.1542/peds.2014-1632

National Association of the Deaf and Registry of Interpreters for the Deaf, Inc. (2005). *Code of Professional Conduct.* Retrieved from https://rid.org/: https://drive.google.com/file/d/0B-_HBAap35D1R1MwYk9hTUpuc3M/view

National Consortium of Interpreter Education Centers. (2016). *What is a Deaf Interpreter?* Retrieved July 17, 2020, from Deaf Interpreter Institute: http://www.diinstitute.org/what-is-the-deaf-interpreter/

NCCJ - National Conference for Community and Justice. (2020, July 4). *Social Justice Definitions*. Retrieved from NCCJ: https://www.nccj.org/resources/social-justice-definitions

NCIEC. (2016). *Deaf Interpreter Curriculum*. Retrieved from National Consortium of Interpreter Education Centers: http://www.interpretereducation.org/specialization/deaf-interpreter/

Newell, W., & Caccamise, F. (2006, June). Sign Language Proficiency Interview (SLPI) Rating Scale. 1-2. Rochester, New York: Rochester Institute of Technology. Retrieved January 2020, from https://www.rit.edu/ntid/slpi/sites/rit.edu.ntid.slpi/files/page_file_attachments/RatingScale%20and%20Analyzing%20Function%202020a.pdf

Nguyen, A. T., & Pendleton, M. (2020, 23March 23). *Recognizing Race in Language: Why We Capitalize "Black" and "White"*. Retrieved June 24, 2020, from Center for the Study of Social Policy: https://cssp.org/2020/03/recognizing-race-in-language-why-we-capitalize-black-and-white/

Nkomo, T. S. (2017, August 4). The Influence of Socio-Cultural Beliefs in Chris Hani Baragwanath Academic Hospital (Chbah): A Social Work Perspective. *Open Journal of Social Sciences, 5*, 46-59. doi:10.4236/jss.2017.58004

Noble, L. L. (1961). Can St. Paul's Methods be Ours? *Practical Anthropolgy*, 180-185.

Noe-Bustamante, L., & Flores, A. (2019, September 16). *Facts on Latinos in the U.S.* Retrieved June 17, 2020, from Pew Research Center Hispanic Trends: https://www.pewresearch.org/hispanic/fact-sheet/latinos-in-the-u-s-fact-sheet/#top-three-states-by-share-of-u-s-hispanic-population-2017

Nordquist, R. (2018, December 4). *Professional Communication Definition and Issues*. Retrieved July 29, 2020, from ThoughtCo.: https://www.thoughtco.com/professional-communication-1691542

Nordquist, R. (2019, November 4). *Definition and Examples of Native Languages: Glossary of Grammatical and Rhetorical Terms*. Retrieved April 19, 2020, from Thought Co.: https://www.thoughtco.com/native-language-l1-term-1691336

Nordquist, R. (2019, July 25). *ThoughtCo.* Retrieved July 1, 2020, from What Is Register in Linguistics?: https://www.thoughtco.com/register-language-style-1692038

Omidvar, I. (2001). Oppression, emotions, and the institutional definition of critical thinking. *Retrospective Theses and Dissertations*, 1-187. Retrieved from https://lib.dr.iastate.edu/cgi/viewcontent.cgi?article=17153&context=rtd

Online Etymology Dictionary: aborigine (n.). (2001-2020). Retrieved June 4, 2020, from Online Etymology Dictionary: https://www.etymonline.com/word/aborigine

Pan, S. C. (2019, January 8). *A Touch to Remember*. Retrieved July 19, 2020, from Scientific American: https://www.scientificamerican.com/article/a-touch-to-remember/

Paneth, E. (1957, April). An Investigation into Conference Interpreting. *Translators' Journal, 3*(1), 35–38. Retrieved July 31, 2020, from https://www.erudit.org/fr/revues/jtraducteurs/1958-v3-n1-jtraducteurs04707/1061456ar.pdf

Parekh, R. (2017, July). *What is Intellectual Disability?* Retrieved August 6, 2020, from American Psychiatric Association: https://www.psychiatry.org/patients-families/intellectual-disability/what-is-intellectual-disability

Patrie, C. J. (2000). *The Effective Interpreting Series: Cognitive Processing Skills in English.* San Diego: Dawn Sign Press.

Payne, R. K. (1995). *A Framework for Understanding and Working with Students and Adults from Poverty.* RFT Publishing. Retrieved July 1, 2020

Pew Research Center. (2007, April 25). *Changing Faiths: Latinos and the Transformation of American Religion.* Retrieved June 18, 2020, from Pew Research Center: Latino Trends:

https://www.pewresearch.org/hispanic/2007/04/25/changing-faiths-latinos-and-the-transformation-of-american-religion/

Pew Research Center. (2013). *The Rise of Asian Americans.* 4: April. Retrieved June 19, 2020, from https://www.pewsocialtrends.org/wp-content/uploads/sites/3/2013/04/Asian-Americans-new-full-report-04-2013.pdf

Pew Research Center. (2017, September 8). *Indians in the U.S. Fact Sheet.* Retrieved June 19, 2020, from Pew Research Center: Socail & Demographic Trends: https://www.pewsocialtrends.org/fact-sheet/asian-americans-indians-in-the-u-s/

Philip, M. (1993). Cross-Cultural Comparisons: American Deaf Culture and American Majority Culture. Colorado: Front Range Community College. Retrieved March 2020

Pochhacker, F. (2004). *Introducing Interpreting.* London: Routledge.

Pollard, K. M., & O'Hare, W. P. (1999, September). America's Racial and Ethnic Minorities. *Population Bulletin, 54*(3), 52. Retrieved March 14, 2020

Polstra, T. (2020, April 17). Executive Director of Silent Blessings. (W. F. Ross III, Interviewer)

Population Reference Bureau; citing U.S. Census Bureau, Population Estimates Program (accessed June 2019). (2020). *United States Indicators.* Retrieved May 29, 2020, from PRB: https://www.prb.org/usdata/indicator/race-ethnicity/snapshot

Porter, R. (2020, March 11). *The Psychology Behind Sense of Entitlement.* Retrieved April 10, 2020, from Better Help: https://www.betterhelp.com/advice/personality-disorders/the-psychology-behind-sense-of-entitlement/

Pronovost, M., & Harrison-Boisvert, C. (2015). *Cultural mediation.* (L. Picard, Ed.) Retrieved July 25, 2020, from Culture pour tous!: https://www.culturepourtous.ca/en/cultural-professionals/cultural-mediation/wp-content/uploads/sites/18/2015/09/Toolkit_Evaluation_projects_CPT_mai2015.pdf

Pym, A. (2008). On omission in simultaneous interpreting. Risk analysis of a hidden effort. In H. Gyde, A. Chesterman, & H. Gerzymisch-Arbogast (Eds.), *Efforts and Models in Interpreting and Translation Research* (pp. 83-105). Amsterdam/Philadelphia. Retrieved August 1, 2020, from https://usuaris.tinet.cat/apym/on-line/translation/2008_omission.pdf#:~:text=Gile%E2%80%99s%20Effort%20Models%20portray%20the%20key%20ways%20in,what%20must%20be%20happening%20in%20the%20interpreter%E2%80%99s%20brain.

Quinto-Pozos, D., Martinez, M., Suarez, A., & Zech, R. (2018). Beyond Bilingual Programming: Interpreter Education in the U.S. Amidst Increasing Linguistic Diversity. *International Journal of Interpreter Education, 10*(1), 46-59. Retrieved May 28, 2020, from https://www.cit-asl.org/new/wp-content/uploads/2018/07/f-IJIE-10-1-quinto-pozos.pdf

Race and Ethnicity. (2020). Retrieved May 30, 2020, from American Sociological Association: https://www.asanet.org/topics/race-and-ethnicity

Redfield R, Linton R, & M., H. (1936). Memorandum on the study of acculturation. *American Anthropology, 38*, 149–152.

Registry of Interpreters for the Deaf. (2005). *NAD-RID Code of Professional Conduct.* Alexandria: RID Publications.

Registry of Interpreters for the Deaf, Inc. (n.d.). *Join or Renew Membership.* Retrieved March 20, 2020, from Registry of Interpreters for the Deaf: https://rid.org/membership/join/#certifiedmember

Registry of Interpreters for the Deaf, Inc. (n.d.). *Member Benefits.* Retrieved March 22, 2020 , from Registry of Interpreters for the Deaf: https://rid.org/membership/benefits/

Registry of Interpreters for the Deaf, Inc. (n.d.). *RID Board of Directors.* Retrieved March 19, 2020, from Registry of Interpreters for the Deaf: https://rid.org/about-rid/mission-vision-statements/board-of-directors/

Rendel, K., Bargones, J., Blake, B., Luetke, B., & Stryker, D. S. (2018). Signing Exact English: A Simultaneously Spoken and Signed Communication Option in Deaf Education. *The Journal of Early Hearing and Detection and Intervention, 3*(2), 18-29. Retrieved May 4, 2020, from https://digitalcommons.usu.edu/cgi/viewcontent.cgi?article=1080&context=jehdi

Riabinin, A. (2020, March 21). personal communication. (J. Featherstone, Interviewer)

Ricks, J. (1976). *MIss Lillian*. Amarillo: Published Janice Ricks.

Rockymore, M. (2006). *A Practical Guide for Working with African American Families in the Child Welfare System*. Minneapolis: Minnesota Department of Human Services. Retrieved June 14, 2020, from http://centerforchildwelfare.fmhi.usf.edu/kb/cultcomp/Practice%20Guide%20for%20African%20American%20families.pdf

Rodriguez, M. P. (n.d.). Cultural Influences on Interpersonal Relationships. In J. D. Wright (Ed.), *International Encyclopedia of the Social & Behavioral Sciences* (Vol. 5, pp. 426-432). Oxford: Elsevier.

Ross III, W. (1992, Summer). *personal communication.*

Ross, M. E., & Karchmer, M. A. (2004). Chasing the Mythical Ten Percent: Parental Hearing Status of Deaf and Hard of Hearing Students in the United States. *Sign Language Studies*, 138-163. doi:10.1353/sls.2004.0005

Rothe, E. M., Tzuang, D., & Pumariega, A. J. (2010). Acculturation, Development, and Adaptation. *Child and Adolescent Psychiatric Clinics of North America, 19*, 681-696. doi:10.1016/j.chc.2010.07.002

Roy, C. (2000). *Interpreting as a discourse process*. Oxford: Oxford University Press.

Russel, D. (2018). International Perspectives on Interpreting: Isn't everything just like at home? In L. Roberson, & S. Shaw (Eds.), *Signed Language Interpreting in the 21st Centre* (pp. 173-198). Washington DC: University Press.

Russell, D. (2005). Consecutive and simultaneous interpreting. In T. Janzen (Ed.), *Topics in Signed Language Interpreting* (pp. 135-163). Philadelphia: John Benjamins North America. Retrieved July 2016, from https://www.academia.edu/4666592/Consecutive_and_simultaneous_interpreting

Sadanand, S. (2017). *Block - 3 Basic Issues in Development - II*. Retrieved April 7, 2020, from eGyanKosh: http://egyankosh.ac.in//handle/123456789/39252

Sapir, E. (1956). *Selected Writings in Language, Culture and Personality*. Berkeley: University of California Press.

Sarigül, E. (2000). Why Don't We Teach Different Registers In The Foreign Language Classroom? *Selçuk University Journal Of Social Sciences Institute, 6*, 413-421.

Schawbel, D. (2016, April 26). *Patrick Lencioni: 3 Indispensable Virtues That Make Teams Successful*. Retrieved July 22, 2020, from Forbes: https://www.forbes.com/sites/danschawbel/2016/04/26/patrick-lencioni-3-indispensable-virtues-that-make-teams-successful/#1ae2c0717fdc

Schemas in Psychology: Definition, Types & Examples. (2015, May 13). Retrieved July 3, 2020, from Study.com: https://study.com/academy/lesson/schemas-in-psychology-definition-types-examples.html

Schoeneman, T. (1997). Individualism Versus Collectivism: A Comparison of Kenyan and American Self-Concepts. *Basic Applied Social Psychology, 19*(2), 261-273. doi:10.1207/s15324834basp1902_7

Schwartz, S. (2007). *Deaf Life*. Retrieved July 7, 2020, from Through Deaf Eyes: https://www.pbs.org/weta/throughdeafeyes/deaflife/index.html

Segal, G., & Salazar, T. (2020, May). Position Paper: Team Interpreting in Court-Related Proceedings. Atlanta, Georgia: National Association of Judiciary Interpreters and Translators. Retrieved August 3, 2020, from https://najit.org/wp-content/uploads/2016/09/Team-Interpreting-5.2020.pdf

Seleskovitch, D. (1978). *Interpreting for International Conferences: Problems of Language and Communication*. Washington, DC: Penn and Booth.

Senses Australia. (2020). *About Deafblindness*. Retrieved August 6, 2020, from Welcome to the Deafblind Information Hub: https://www.deafblindinformation.org.au/about-deafblindness/

Seymour, C. (1990, May). The hunt for absolute goodness. *In Reflections on ethics: A compilation of articles inspired by the ASHA ethics colloquium.*

Simonsen, C. (2019, Summer). personal communication. (J. Featherstone, Interviewer)

Simpson, T. (n.d.). A stimulus to learning; A measure of ability. In 1990, S. Gregory, & G. Hartley (Eds.), *Constructing Deafness* (pp. 217-225). London: Conyinuum.

Siple, L. A. (1997, July 1). Historical Development of the Definition of Transliteration. (M. L. McIntire, & S. Wilcox, Eds.) *Journal of Interpretation*, 77-100. Retrieved April 17, 2020, from https://sites.google.com/site/ridpublicationsproject/home/journal-of-interpretation/joi-1997

Skutnabb-Kangas, T. (2003). *Linguistic diversity and biodiversity: The threat from killer languages. The Politics of English as a World Language.*

Smith, E. (1946). *Knowing the African.* London: Lutterworth Press.

Smith, J. W. (2014, January). Emoting Emotions. 1-48. Minneapolis, Minnesota.

Statistics Canada. (2019). *Canada's Population Estimates.* Retrieved July 7, 2020, from https://www150.statcan.gc.ca/n1/daily-quotidien/190930/dq190930a-eng.htm

Stavenhagen, R. (2004). *Report of the Special Rapporteur on the situation of human rights and fundamental freedoms of indigenous people.* United Nations, Economic and Social Council. Commission of Human Rights. Retrieved June 8, 2020, from https://digitallibrary.un.org/record/539597?ln=en

Stokoe, W. C. (1960). ign Language Structure: An Outline of the Visual Communication Systems of the American Deaf. *Studies in linguistics: Occasional Papers, 8.*

Stone, C. (2009). *Toward a Deaf Translation Norm.* Gallaudet University Press.

Stone, C. (2013). The UNCRPD and 'professional' sign language interpreter provision. In C. Schäffner, & K. Kredens (Eds.), *Interpreting in a Changing Landscape.* Amsterdam: John Benjamins.

Stringham, D. (2019, September). Comparative American Sign Language/English Continuum. Retrieved May 4, 2020, from https://www.researchgate.net/publication/335636080_Comparative_American_Sign_LanguageEnglish_Continuum_2019

Stromberg, D. (1990, May). Key Legal Issues in Professional Ethics. In Reflections on ethics. *ASHA Ethics Colloquium.*

Swenson, K. (2017, August 9). 'Long time coming': Army returns remains of Arapaho children who died at assimilation school. *The Washington Post.* Retrieved June 6, 2020, from https://www.washingtonpost.com/news/morning-mix/wp/2017/08/09/a-long-time-coming-army-returns-remains-of-arapaho-children-who-died-at-assimilation-school-in-1800s/

Szarkowski, A., & Brice, P. (2018). Positive Psychology in Research with the Deaf Community: An Idea Whose Time Has Come. *Journal of Deaf Studies and Deaf Education, 23*(2), 111-117. doi:doi:10.1093/deafed/enx058

Tannen, D. (1986). *That's Not What I Meant.* New York: Harper Collins.

Tannen, D. (1995). The Power of Talk: Who Gets Heard and Why. *Harvard Business Review, 5*, p. 5.

Tannen, Deborah. (2013). Language and Culture. In R. Fasold, & J. Connor-Linton (Eds.), *An Introduction to Language and Linguistics* (pp. 343-372). New York: Cambridge University Press. Retrieved July 2, 2020, from https://repository.stkipgetsempena.ac.id/bitstream/531/1/An_Introduction_to_Language_and_Linguistics.pdf

The Canadian Cultural Society of the Deaf, the Canadian Association of The Deaf, and Canadian Association of Sign Language Interpreters. (2010). *Joint Communication Team.* Retrieved May 7, 2020, from

Association of Visual Language Interpreters of Canada: https://www.avlic.ca/sites/default/files/docs/2010-07_JCT_Joint_Statement-eng.pdf

Thiery, C. (2009, March 10). *How it all started: thoughts for the opening of the AIIC Assembly in Nice.* Retrieved November 20, 2019, from aiic.net: http://aiic.net/p/3202

Tse, L. (1996, Summer/Fall). Language brokering in linguistic minority communities: the case of Chinese- and Vietnamese-American students. *The Biblingual Reseach Journal, 20*(3 & 4), 485-498. Retrieved April 18, 2020, from https://www.sandberglaw.com/wp-content/uploads/sites/49/2016/05/McQuillan-Tse-Child-Language-Brokering-in-Linguistic-Minority-Communities-Effects-on-Cultural-Interaction-Cognition-and-Literacy-Language-and-Education-93-at-195-215-1995.pdf

U.S. Department of Health & Human Services. (2017, March 16). *Ushers Syndrome.* Retrieved August 6, 2020, from National Institute on Deafness and Other Communication Disorders: https://www.nidcd.nih.gov/health/usher-syndrome

United Nations Educational, Scientific and Cultural Organization. (2013). *Intercultural Competences Conceptual and Operational Framework.* (W. Hurwitz-Leeds, & K. Stenou, Eds.) Pris, France: UNESCO.

University of Minnesota. (2016). *Communication in the Real World: An Introduction to Communication Studies.* Minneapolis, Minnesota: M Libraries. Retrieved July 1, 2020, from Communication in the Real World: file:///C:/Users/wmfro/AppData/Local/Temp/Communication-in-the-Real-World-An-Introduction-to-Communication-Studies-1538667550.pdf

Useem, J., Donoghue, J. D., & Useem, R. H. (1963, Fall). Men in the Middle of the Third Culture: The Role of American and Non-Western People in Cross-Cultural Administration. *Human Organization, 22*(13), 169. Retrieved June 20, 2020, from https://search.proquest.com/openview/a749eeabd6f606c5d29b99410abbc666/1?pq-origsite=gscholar&cbl=1821032

Veditz, G. W. (Director). (1913). *Preservation of the Sign Language* [Motion Picture]. National Association of the Deaf. Retrieved July 3, 2020, from https://www.loc.gov/item/mbrs01815816/

Vidor, N. (2020, February 24). School for the Deaf Reports Dozens of Decades Old Sexual Abuse Cases. *New York Times.*

Wadensjö, C. (1998). *Interpreting as Interaction.* New York: Longman Press.

Wagner, C. (2020). *President Report About NAD-RID Transcript.* Retrieved from National Association of the Deaf : https://www.nad.org/about-us/board/president-report-about-nad-rid-transcript/

Wallis, D., Musselman, C., & MacKay, S. (2004). Hearing Mothers and Their Deaf Children: The Relationship between Early, Ongoing Mode Match and Subsequent Mental Health Functioning in Adolescence. *Journal of Deaf Studies and Deaf Education, 9*(1). doi:10.1093/deafed/enh014

Wang, J. (2008). A Cross-cultural Study of Daily COmmunication between Chinese and American - from the Perspective of High Contexr and Low COntext. *Asian Social Science, 4*(10), 151-154. Retrieved March 21, 2020

WASLI. (n.d.). *WASLI Training Guidelines.* Retrieved from http://wasli.org/wp-content/uploads/2018/03/WASLI-Training-Guidelines-Aug-2017-1.pdf

Webb, J. (2017, October 18). The Field of Sign Language Interpreting Needs an Accomplice Not an Ally. (B. Arthur, Interviewer) Retrieved June 2020, from https://streetleverage.com/podcasts/the-field-of-sign-language-interpreting-needs-an-accomplice/

Webb, J. (2020, February). President's Report. (J. Wardle, Ed.) *VIEWS, 1*(37). Retrieved June 20, 2020, from https://issuu.com/ridviews/docs/february20_views

WebFinance Inc. (2020). *BD Dictionary-Eethics.* Retrieved from http://www.businessdictionary.com/: http://www.businessdictionary.com/definition/ethics.html

Western Intepreting Network. (2020). *Definitions & Explanations*. Retrieved July 19, 2020, from Western Interpreting Network: https://www.westerninterpreting.net/win_defs.cfm

What is Culture? (2019, April 9). Retrieved March 18, 2020, from Center for Advanced Research on Language Acquisition (CARLA): https://carla.umn.edu/culture/definitions.html

Wilber, R. B. (2009). Effects of Varying Rate of Signing on ASL Manual Signs and Nonmanual Markers. *Language and SPeech, 52*(Pt. 2-3), 245-285. doi:doi.org/10.1177/0023830909103174

Wilcox, S., & Wilcox, P. (1985). Schema theory and language interpretation: a study of sign language interpreters. *Journal of Interpretation*, 84-93. Retrieved from https://drive.google.com/drive/folders/0B3DKvZMflFLdcEtUM1BNb2Z5WFE

Winston, B. (2000). It just doesn't Look Like ASL! Defining, Recognizing and Teaching Prosody in ASL. *CIT at 21: Celebrating Excellence, Celebrating Partnership* (pp. 1-20). Portland: RID Publications. Retrieved July 30, 2020, from https://tiemcenter.org/wp-content/uploads/2012/06/Doesnt-Look-Like-ASL-Prosody-2000.pdf

Wirth, L. (1945). The Problem of Minority Groups. In R. Linton (Ed.), *The Science of Man in the World Crisis*. New York: Columbia University Press. Retrieved July 13, 2020, from http://fadak.ir/?1000318

Witchel, A. (1994, October 27). GOING HOME WITH: Heather Whitestone; Placing the Person Ahead of the Crown. *The New York Times*. New York, new York, United States. Retrieved May 10, 2020, from https://www.nytimes.com/1994/10/27/garden/going-home-with-heather-whitestone-placing-the-person-ahead-of-the-crown.html

Witter-Merithew, A. (2002). Understanding the Meaning of Texts and Reinforcing Foundation Skills Through Discourse Analysis. *Distance Opportunities for Interpreter Training (DO IT) Center* , 1-15.

Witter-Merithew, A., & Johnson, L. (2004). Market Disorder Within the Field of Sign Language Interpreting: Professionalization Implications. *Journal of Interpretation*, 1-35.

Wixstrom, C. (1988). Two Views of Deafness. (J. M. Smith, Ed.) *The Deaf American, 38*(1), pp. 1-28. Retrieved July 6, 2020

Xiao, X. (2013). Sign language interpreting on Chinese TV: A survey on user perspectives. *Perspectives: Studies in Translatology, 21*(1). Retrieved from (In English. with F. Li)

Xiao, X. (2015). Chinese Deaf viewers' comprehension of signed language interpreting on television: An experimental study. *Interpreting: International Journal of Research and Practice in Interpreting, 17*(1). Retrieved from (In English. with X. Chen & J. Palmer)

Yamada, A.-M., Marsella, A. J., & Yamada, S. Y. (1998). The Development of the Ethnocultural Identity Behavioral Index: Psychometric properties and validation with Asian Americans and Pacific Islanders. *Asian American and Pacific Islander Journal of Health, 6*(1), 35-45. Retrieved May 24, 2020, from https://www.researchgate.net/publication/11781515_The_Development_of_the_Ethnocultural_Identity_Behavioral_Index_Psychometric_Properties_and_Validation_with_Asian_Americans_and_Pacific_Islanders

Yellow Bird, M. (1999). What We Want to Be Called: Indigenous Peoples' Perspectives on Racial and Ethnic Identity Labels. *American Indian Quarterly, 23*(2), -21. doi:10.2307/1185964

Yngve, V. (1970). On Getting a Word in Edgewise. *Papers from the Sixth Regional Meeting of the Chicago Linguistic Society*, (pp. 567-577).

Yoel, J. (2009). *Canada's Maritime Sign Language*. University of Manitoba.

INDEX

A

ableism 63
Aboriginal 75, 81, 84, 86, 101
Acculturation 81, 85, 101, 102
African Forum of Sign Language Interpreters (AFSLI) 205
AFSLI (see African Forum of Sign Language Interpreters)
AIIC (see International Association of Conference Interpreters)
allies 65, 69, 185
ally 59, 65, 68, 69, 74, 77, 79, 114
American Sign Language (ASL) 5, 11, 19, 21, 23, 24, 26, 31, 43, 44, 49, 51, 52, 53, 57, 60, 67, 78, 81, 82, 95, 97, 100, 106, 112, 118, 119, 133, 134, 135, 136, 138, 139, 143, 148, 153, 156, 165, 171, 174, 214
apartheid 31
Asian-American 71, 83, 84, 99, 100, 102
ASL (see American Sign Language)
ASL modality 132, 138, 155
assessment 7, 9, 19, 21, 27, 46, 58, 107
assimilation 85–87
assumptions 41, 60, 68, 79, 126, 166
attention-getting 52
atypical 36, 37, 187, 193
audism 59–61, 63, 72, 78
audist 59, 60, 62, 72, 73, 77, 78
autonomy 61, 166, 188, 190
Association of Visual Language Interpreters of Canada (AVLIC)16, 21–23, 189, 190, 204, 206
AVLIC (see Association of Visual Language Interpreters of Canada)

B

B-language (also see second language) 132, 134, 157
backchanneling 28, 36, 57, 124, 166
balance 10, 11, 13, 63, 88, 107, 116, 203
barriers 18, 45, 74, 107, 109, 118, 130
beliefs 2, 7, 10, 12, 21, 22, 29, 31, 34, 37, 41–43, 45–47, 50, 51, 53–55, 59–64, 67, 68, 71, 72, 75, 78–80, 82–85, 88, 93, 94, 97, 100, 101, 107, 119, 120, 133, 147, 184, 188, 194
benefactors 59, 64, 72–74, 77, 79, 80
benefits 20, 23, 62, 63, 78, 88, 153, 173, 174, 194, 195, 203
bias 54, 91, 100, 107, 114, 116
Bible 14, 135
bicultural 30, 146, 159
bilingual 23, 47, 52, 121, 134, 135, 146, 147, 158
bilingualism 48, 132, 135, 156
black 31, 47, 71, 83, 84, 90, 91, 93, 94, 99, 100, 102, 110, 111, 197
blind 1, 7, 12, 80, 160, 163–65, 167, 169
boundaries 7, 11, 84, 90, 108, 118, 176, 189
brokers 14, 15, 26, 81, 82
burnout 10, 66, 181

business 5, 19, 22, 34, 72, 109, 125, 126, 129, 172, 173, 177, 179, 180, 189, 190, 205, 213
bylaws 5, 17, 21

C

Canada 3, 5, 16–18, 21–24, 27, 39, 43–45, 62, 64, 72, 81, 82, 84, 87, 88, 95, 100, 119–21, 126, 189, 204, 206–8, 210, 212
Canadian 5, 15, 16, 18, 21–24, 27, 47, 48, 51, 55, 65, 81, 82, 84, 189, 190, 204, 206, 210
Canadian Association of Sign Language Interpreters (CASLI) 5, 15, 16, 21–24, 27, 188–90, 197, 199–201, 204, 206, 207
caregivers 48, 66, 74, 92
CASE (see Conceptually Accurate Signed English)
CASLI (see Canadian Association of Sign Language Interpreters)
CASLI (see Center for Assessment of Sign Language Interpreters)
CDI 108, 113–16
Center for Assessment of Sign Language Interpreters (CASLI) 19, 21, 27
certification 5, 16, 18–21, 23–26, 98, 99, 106, 116, 171, 172, 174, 176, 178–80, 184, 194, 200, 202
certified 19, 20, 25, 105–7, 154, 174, 180, 200, 208
characteristics 3, 11, 31, 32, 37, 46, 47, 51, 56, 58, 63, 70, 72, 73, 78, 80, 83, 86, 99, 101, 102, 124, 184, 186, 191, 202
citizen 9, 16, 43, 46, 118, 119, 130, 163, 205, 207, 212
civil 17, 62, 71, 93, 120, 121, 194, 205, 209
civil rights 17, 62, 71, 93, 120, 121
C-language 132, 135, 156
client 4, 33, 64, 107, 108, 110, 112–15, 123, 137, 149, 168, 169, 178, 183, 184, 188, 191, 197, 199, 201
close-vision 111–13
CODA 82, 97, 98, 114
code 17, 18, 20, 21, 109, 183, 184, 188–91, 197–200, 202, 203, 209
code of conduct 188, 199, 209
code of ethics 17, 21, 183, 189, 190, 197, 200, 203
code of professional conduct (CPC) 18, 183, 189, 191, 197, 198
cognitive 44, 55, 64, 106, 123, 143, 145, 151, 153, 167, 186
co-interpreter 3, 94, 111, 138, 152, 154, 155, 160, 198
collaboration 21, 22, 106, 116, 133, 204, 206, 207, 214
colleagues 2–4, 6, 7, 25, 32, 54, 61, 64, 67, 68, 79, 80, 82, 90, 91, 94, 110, 113, 116, 133, 148, 153–55, 159, 173, 180, 182, 183, 189, 190, 192, 194, 197–200
collectivist 39, 50–52, 56, 81, 92, 94, 101
collectivist culture 50, 56
collectivistic 41, 49–51, 54, 56, 95
collectivist norm 81, 92, 101
colonialism 75, 81, 85, 86, 101
communication 1–3, 5–9, 11, 12, 14–19, 22, 25, 26, 28,

263

29, 31–37, 39, 43, 45, 48–51, 53, 56, 62, 65, 66, 70, 73, 74, 76, 77, 79, 85, 89, 93, 96, 97, 100, 102, 106, 108–10, 114, 116, 118, 121–26, 130–33, 136–39, 141–44, 148–50, 152, 154, 158–69, 171, 177, 183, 185, 187–89, 200, 203, 207, 216

communication norms 1, 6–8, 11, 35, 53, 65, 121

competence 3, 5–8, 21, 25, 29, 52, 54, 98, 132, 133, 135, 139, 159, 183, 184, 189, 190, 200

complementary schismogenesis 28, 35, 36, 39

concepts 28, 31, 41, 45, 61, 76, 84, 93, 100, 118, 134, 138, 140, 150, 156, 175, 184, 187, 191, 201, 212

Conceptually Accurate Signed English (CASE) 19, 26

condition 42, 54, 55, 59, 65, 71, 73, 119, 153, 162–64, 168, 180, 189, 190, 199, 206, 208, 209

conference 5, 16, 20, 21, 23, 107, 111, 115, 116, 125, 137, 140, 145, 149, 151, 152, 153, 159, 179, 201, 206, 207, 208, 210, 213-215

confidentiality 66, 67, 80, 115, 189, 194, 199

consecutive 111–13, 132, 136, 144, 152, 153, 156

consequences 29, 63, 152, 175, 191, 196–98, 201–3

construct 34, 126, 133, 141, 148, 153, 159, 185, 186

consultative 33, 39, 137

consumer 38, 64, 109, 110, 133, 149, 163, 188–90

contact 7, 8, 19, 24, 26, 30, 32, 35, 53, 68, 70, 85, 89, 91, 101, 103, 112, 113, 120, 123, 127–29, 138, 154, 165, 201, 211

contact varieties 19

content 28, 33, 35, 54, 97, 113, 139, 141, 148–50, 152, 153, 166, 179, 182, 192

context 7, 8, 12, 32, 33, 37, 43, 44, 47, 50, 52, 61, 82, 85, 96, 118, 119, 123, 126, 130, 141, 150, 190, 197, 204, 205, 208, 209, 211–14

contextual factors 141, 144, 158, 197

contextualized 118, 119, 121, 130

contextual settings 44

control 7, 9, 11, 32, 60–62, 85, 135, 156, 178, 190, 199, 210, 211

conversation 8, 28, 29, 32–34, 36, 37, 45, 48, 53, 57, 64, 70, 109, 111, 114, 115, 121, 122, 127, 129, 134, 141, 149, 152, 163, 166, 177, 178, 199

core 5, 22, 29, 40, 42, 47, 176, 190, 192–94

CPC (see Code of Professional Conduct)

credentials 20, 116, 184

critical 3–7, 9, 17, 31, 32, 35, 42, 52, 60, 67, 69, 78, 84, 92, 96, 97, 100, 118, 129, 137, 146, 148, 151, 154, 159, 179, 182, 184, 185, 189, 192, 196, 197, 199, 205, 207, 213–15

Critical Link 207, 215

cross 6, 12, 126, 130, 186, 202

cross-cultural 7, 54, 85, 89, 102, 213

cultural 1, 3, 4, 6–9, 11, 12, 22, 24, 29–32, 35–47, 49–57, 62, 64, 67, 69, 70, 73, 75–78, 81–97, 101–3, 106, 115, 118, 120–26, 128, 130–32, 135–37, 141, 144, 145, 153, 155–58, 168, 178, 186, 190, 191, 202, 205, 206

cultural differences 50, 56, 101, 125, 130, 131

cultural diversity 76, 81, 88, 120

cultural duality 41, 46

cultural frames 41, 43-46, 50, 54, 67, 141

cultural group 6, 7, 11, 29, 41, 43, 47, 52, 55, 73, 83, 123

cultural identities 29

cultural identity 47, 76

cultural norms 6, 8, 24, 29, 35, 36, 40, 43, 47, 49, 53, 69, 77, 83, 88, 89, 94, 95, 103, 121, 130, 144, 145, 158

culture 1, 2, 4–8, 12, 14, 15, 24, 25, 28–32, 34–57, 59, 60, 62, 64, 65, 67, 69–76, 78, 79, 81–102, 104, 106, 110, 118–22, 124, 126–28, 130, 131, 133, 136, 138, 139, 141, 143, 144, 147, 150, 151, 166–69, 174, 181, 188, 200, 202, 205, 210, 214, 215

culture (way of being) 14

customs 8, 29, 30, 37, 45, 50, 56, 67, 72, 89, 120, 206

D

DBSC (see DeafBlind Service Center)

dDB 166–70

dDBlind 168

dDDb 2, 43, 132, 143, 147

dDeaf 1–5, 7–9, 12, 14–18, 20, 21, 23–26, 29–32, 34–36, 39, 40, 42, 43, 45, 47–62, 64–80, 82–86, 88–95, 97, 100, 102–9, 111–30, 132, 134–36, 138, 139, 141–43, 147–49, 152–55, 157, 159–63, 167, 169–72, 174–78, 182–84, 189, 191, 195, 196, 198–200, 202, 216

dDeaf community 3–5, 7, 9, 14, 15, 18, 21, 24–26, 29–31, 35, 36, 39, 42, 43, 47–53, 55, 56, 59, 60, 64–69, 71–78, 84, 85, 104, 105, 107, 115, 116, 118, 120, 123, 124, 136, 152, 160, 177, 183, 191, 199, 200, 216

dDeaf culture 7, 14, 15, 25, 35, 39, 40, 47, 50, 52, 54, 56, 65, 67, 69, 79, 85, 118–20, 124, 127

dDeafDB 82

dDeaf-dDDb 43

dDeaf-hearing 60, 113

dDeaf interpreter 24, 15, 64, 104–7, 108, 111–17, 138, 152, 154

dDeaf plus 160, 169

dDeaf-World 118

dDHH 175

deaf 1, 5, 12, 14–18, 20–24, 26, 34, 37–40, 42, 44, 47, 48, 50, 51, 54–57, 65, 67–70, 73–78, 82, 85, 94, 96–99, 101, 104–11, 113, 115–17, 119–21, 126, 134–37, 148, 153, 154, 161–69, 177, 188, 189, 195, 200, 204–15

deafblind 1, 2, 18, 42, 43, 47, 97, 112, 143, 163–69

DeafBlind Service Center (DBSC) 165

Deafcentric 35, 37, 39, 40, 49

deafhood 73, 81, 85, 101

Deaf-World 42, 52, 119

deontological 182, 196-198, 201

dialects 83, 94, 98, 178

dialogue 28, 33, 36, 37, 39, 124, 125, 136, 149, 150, 183

disabilities 47, 57, 121, 161–63, 169, 170, 175, 205–7, 210, 215

disability 18, 20, 31, 47, 48, 62, 64, 70, 76, 121, 162, 163, 169, 179, 180, 194 disabled 60, 65, 69, 71, 74, 78, 160, 162, 163, 168, 207

discrimination 31, 59, 69, 71, 72, 74, 80, 87, 88, 91, 99, 103

disenfranchisement 59, 77, 79, 91

distantism 167, 168

duality 41, 46

dual-sensory 164, 165

dynamic equivalence 132, 133, 143, 156

dynamics 42, 49, 54, 96, 100, 106, 111, 121

E

education 3–5, 8, 12, 15, 18, 20–25, 29, 35, 38, 47, 59, 62–64, 67, 68, 70–75, 77, 79, 82, 93, 105–7, 116, 118, 120, 132, 133, 141, 145, 146, 153, 158–60, 163, 168, 171–76, 178, 179, 181, 182, 191, 193, 195, 200, 201, 204–11, 213, 215

effective 6, 8, 9, 32, 52, 53, 97, 98, 101, 106, 110, 122, 133, 137, 148, 152, 154, 159, 168, 178, 187, 188, 191, 199, 209, 213, 216

effective communication 9, 32, 53, 106, 133

emotional dependence 50, 79

emotional development 92

emotional health 6, 66

emotive value 118, 122, 130, 131

English 1, 4, 5, 12, 15, 18, 19, 21, 23, 24, 26, 38, 42, 43, 52, 60, 61, 63, 71, 73, 81, 82, 84, 95–97, 99, 100, 107, 113, 129, 133–36, 138, 139, 143, 145, 146, 148, 152, 156, 157, 167, 171, 175, 176, 178, 185, 190

entry-to-practice-competencies 159

environment 8, 42, 44, 45, 49, 67, 74, 75, 77, 88, 111, 123, 125, 144, 145, 163–65, 185, 187, 190

equal 68, 71, 76, 93, 97, 103, 108, 110, 114, 115, 190, 194

equality 17, 18, 68, 74, 77, 79, 103, 175, 187

equivalence 132, 133, 143, 146, 156

equivalent 9, 60, 61, 133, 135, 137, 143–45, 147, 150, 151, 153, 156–58, 200

error 6, 9, 14, 21, 67, 144–47, 151, 153, 158, 159, 163, 192

esfli (see european forum of sign language interpreters)

ethical 5, 18, 19, 21, 22, 25, 26, 98, 107, 182–84, 187–94, 196, 197, 199, 201–3

ethics 17, 21, 64, 182–84, 187–90, 197, 200, 201, 203

ethnic 46–48, 50, 56, 62, 63, 70–72, 75, 79, 81, 83, 84, 87, 95, 99, 100, 108, 110, 194

ethnicity 10, 32, 37, 47, 49, 57, 62, 81, 83, 84, 101, 110, 141

ethnocentrism 1, 6, 7, 12

ethnocultural identity 59, 70, 77, 78, 84

european forum of sign language interpreters (esfli) 207, 215

evaluation 18, 23, 24, 26, 98, 99, 107

expectations 3, 6–9, 13, 24, 25, 29, 44, 46, 49, 54, 58, 64, 72–74, 88, 94, 126, 162, 182, 186, 187, 189, 191, 200, 213

experience 1–4, 9, 10, 13, 17, 30–35, 37–39, 41, 42, 44, 45, 47–49, 51, 55, 59, 62, 64–67, 69–73, 76, 78, 79, 85, 87, 88, 91, 94, 96, 99, 101, 102, 104, 106–8, 114, 116, 118, 120, 128, 130, 132, 134, 137, 139, 141, 142, 144, 149, 150, 154, 157, 161, 164, 165, 167, 168, 171, 173–80, 183, 184, 188–92, 197, 198, 200, 201, 204, 205, 212, 213

explicit 7, 12, 47, 60, 66, 123, 138, 144, 158, 177

expressions 3, 7, 8, 30, 34, 38, 39, 51, 60, 78, 92, 94, 96, 112, 117, 119, 122, 123, 128, 130–32, 135, 139, 199

extralinguistic 139

eye 7, 8, 14, 15, 28, 34, 53, 57, 81, 83, 89, 91, 112, 113, 120, 123, 124, 127–29, 138, 139, 156, 165, 182, 205

eye contact 7, 8, 53, 89, 112, 113, 123, 127–29, 138

F

face 25, 74, 75, 86, 95, 107, 122, 129, 138, 143, 148, 156, 162, 166, 180, 182, 183, 192, 193, 211, 212

facial 3, 8, 34, 35, 39, 60, 78, 109, 112, 119, 122, 128, 130, 131, 135, 138, 139, 199

facial affect 35, 135

facial expression 3, 8, 34, 39, 60, 78, 112, 119, 122, 128, 130, 131, 135, 139, 199

facilitate 1, 14, 26, 89, 114, 126, 162

facilitating 106, 109, 114, 185, 187

features 8, 19, 28, 29, 34, 37, 46, 51, 58, 83, 124, 132, 138, 139, 144, 157, 158, 161, 180

federation 206, 211, 215

feedback 6, 32, 36, 51, 96, 144, 154, 158

field 2–5, 11, 17, 19, 24, 25, 54, 62, 66, 81, 105, 109, 111, 115, 133, 135, 144, 145, 157, 168, 171, 173, 176, 180, 181, 188, 192, 199–201, 203, 213

field of interpreting 3, 5, 17, 19, 66, 111, 133, 180, 200

field of sign language interpreting 17, 81, 188, 201

fingerspelling 12, 33, 34, 48, 49, 122, 154, 180

FIT (see Federation of Translators)

flexibility 2, 3, 12, 106, 144

fluency 2, 12, 24, 29, 95, 101, 107, 121, 134, 135, 138, 148, 156, 175

foundation 8, 29, 119, 132, 133, 145, 146, 159, 183, 190, 200, 213

frame 41, 43–46, 50, 54, 67, 141, 145, 212

frame of reference 44, 45, 67, 212

framework 41, 44, 45, 47, 55, 148–50, 207

freelance 160, 171–73, 178, 179, 181, 211

frequently 15, 33, 42, 61, 62, 64, 72, 83, 92, 95, 134, 146, 165, 180, 213

friend 8, 11, 34, 39, 45, 66, 96, 115, 148, 168, 169, 193

friendships 14, 25, 69, 80, 120, 124, 193

function 2, 14, 15, 26, 59, 61, 100, 126, 151, 162, 138, 199

fundamental 87, 88, 98, 184, 187, 201

265

G

gatekeeping 14, 15, 26, 211
gender 5, 32, 34, 37, 41, 46, 47, 55, 57–59, 62, 63, 72, 79, 141, 144, 158
generation 3, 24, 29, 43, 48, 49, 51, 52, 55, 73, 86, 88, 90, 92–94, 105, 120, 155
gestures 8, 21, 33, 34, 38, 48, 49, 60, 65, 119, 125, 127, 128, 139, 143
ghostwriter 14, 15, 26
goal 5, 9, 11, 18, 24, 26, 28, 30, 62, 83, 98, 109, 110, 113, 123, 124, 126, 134–38, 140–44, 148–50, 155–60, 168, 173–75, 177, 186, 192, 198, 201, 202, 204, 205, 208, 214
greetings 89, 102
guidelines 5, 89, 183, 187–90, 197, 207

H

hand 6, 46, 52, 101, 111, 125–27, 134, 137–39, 143, 160, 161, 165, 180, 183, 195
hands 1, 41, 53, 90, 113, 119, 127, 128, 138, 156, 165, 169, 180
hard-of-hearing 42, 106, 177
hardship 62, 76
harm 91, 109, 189, 201
harmful 66, 184, 198
health 6, 9, 17, 24, 32, 46, 64, 66, 67, 77, 93, 97, 106, 152, 163, 164, 179, 183, 187, 199, 205
healthy 9–12, 66, 71, 107, 166, 174, 182, 196, 200
hearing 1, 4, 14, 15, 18, 21, 24, 25, 30, 31, 35, 38–40, 42, 47–49, 53–55, 57, 59–61, 64, 65, 68–70, 72, 75–79, 89, 91–93, 95, 97, 98, 103, 105, 106, 108, 112–16, 119–21, 124–26, 128, 129, 137, 138, 141, 147, 148, 152–55, 159, 162–64, 167, 168, 174, 175, 177–80, 182, 189, 196, 200, 209, 212
hearing impaired 1, 48, 65
hearing interpreter 106, 105, 108, 113-115, 116, 138, 155, 212
hearing loss 1, 31, 42, 48, 54, 55, 61, 162, 164
Hearing Loss Association of America (HLAA) 48
hearing majority 60
hearing parents 48, 77, 92
hearing privilege 64, 72
hearing teams 106, 108, 114, 154, 155, 159
helpless 74
helplessness 59, 74, 77
heritage 47, 48, 55, 81, 82, 84, 88, 90, 91, 94, 97, 101, 174
heritage speakers 81, 97, 101
high 7, 10, 12, 35, 39, 50, 63, 93, 106, 126, 137, 166, 167, 172, 174, 175, 179, 190, 194, 213
high-context 1, 6, 7, 12, 50, 56, 126
high school 35, 63, 172, 174, 175
Hispanic 47, 83-85, 94–97, 99, 102, 110
HLAA (see Hearing Loss Association of America)
home 30, 37, 42, 43, 46, 48, 49, 51, 63, 67, 74, 81, 82, 87, 95, 97, 103, 122, 125, 134, 173, 209, 213
home culture 30, 37, 46

home language 87, 134
home signs 48, 49
horizontal violence 79

I

identity 10, 29, 30, 39, 41–47, 49–51, 53–55, 57, 59, 63, 70, 74–79, 84, 86, 90, 92, 93, 104, 119, 120, 180, 190
immigrant 82, 84, 99, 175
indigenous 15, 71, 75, 81, 83, 86–90, 101–3, 211
indigenous cultures 89, 102
indigenous ddeaf peoples 86, 89, 102
indigenous peoples 71, 75, 81, 86–90, 101, 102
individualism 49, 50, 81, 93, 101
individualistic 41, 49–51, 55, 56, 92
individualistic culture 41, 49, 50, 56
inequality 59, 62, 63, 78, 79, 84, 88
in-groups 49, 50
ingroup speak 28, 35, 37, 38
injustice 68, 71, 77, 100
institutionalized 41, 45,55,71, 72, 78
institutionalized oppression 41, 45, 55, 71, 72, 78
integrity 6, 23, 144, 184, 186, 190, 193, 202
intellectual 64, 123, 130, 160, 162, 163, 170
interact 1, 4, 7, 11, 12, 29, 32, 36, 42, 43, 46, 53, 58, 85, 105, 107, 121, 128, 130, 165, 182
interaction 2–4, 6, 8, 9, 12, 14, 15, 29, 32, 34, 35, 37, 39, 42, 43, 46, 51, 52, 54, 55, 58, 67, 85, 89, 97, 100, 103, 106, 109, 115, 116, 118, 120, 121, 125–28, 130, 134, 136-138, 140–43, 148–50, 152, 154, 155, 156, 158, 160, 161, 182, 184–88, 200, 202, 203, 213
interlocutors 28, 37, 186, 187, 202
international 5, 9, 18, 47, 82, 97, 204–9, 211–16
International Association of Conference Interpreters (AIIIC) 206, 215
International Federation of Translators (FIT) 206, 215
International Sign (IS) 207, 213-215
Interpretation 4, 5, 9, 10, 14, 16, 20, 21, 24, 27, 33, 35, 36, 38, 67, 82, 89, 102, 103, 114, 122, 124, 129, 132, 133, 134, 135, 136, 137, 139, 140, 142, 143, 144, 145, 146, 148, 150, 151, 152, 153, 154, 156, 157, 158, 159, 161, 162, 186, 187, 188, 199, 202, 208, 212, 213, 214
interpreter 1–12, 14–17, 19, 21–26, 28–30, 32–36, 38, 42, 46, 47, 49, 51, 54, 59–61, 64–67, 69, 72, 76, 80, 82, 85, 89–91, 95, 97–119, 121–26, 128–63, 167, 169–92, 194–96, 198–211, 213–16
interpreter certification 25, 98, 99, 194
interpreter education 8, 15, 21–25, 47, 82, 98, 106, 118, 132, 145, 153, 172, 178, 182, 200, 204–11, 213, 215
interpreter institute 104, 106
interpreter organizations 23, 207, 215
interpreter preparation 17
interpreter team 3, 113, 116
intersectionality 5, 41, 47, 55, 57
intervenors 160, 168, 169
IS (see International Sign)

J

jargon 28, 35–38
job 2-4, 16, 23, 61, 63, 64, 72, 73, 100, 107–12, 114-116, 125, 138, 141, 149, 154, 159, 160-162, 171–81, 183, 194–96
journal 11, 20, 47, 130, 141
justice 5, 68, 74, 75, 77, 91, 166, 195, 203, 205, 215

K

knowledge 4, 5, 9, 11, 12, 19, 22, 25, 32–34, 39, 44, 47, 50, 51, 55, 56, 65, 77–79, 85, 88, 89, 95, 97, 101, 102, 107, 108, 116, 122, 124, 130, 132, 133, 137, 146, 148–50, 155, 158, 159, 175–78, 183, 184, 189, 195, 196, 200, 202, 205, 211–15

L

L2 (see second language or B-language)
La Language de Signes Quebecoise 21, 24, 43, 134
language 1–12, 14–19, 21–34, 36–39, 41–44, 46–57, 59, 60, 62, 64–78, 81–87, 89, 90, 94–98, 100–102, 105–7, 110, 112–14, 116, 118–24, 128–39, 141, 143–48, 150–58, 160, 162, 164–66, 168, 169, 171, 174–78, 180, 182–85, 188–91, 197, 199–216
language broker 14, 15, 26, 81, 82
Latino 47, 94, 95, 98
Latinx 47, 71, 83–85, 94–97, 99, 102, 110
learned 11, 24, 29, 32, 41, 59, 64, 74, 77, 97, 119, 163, 189, 199, 214
learned helplessness 59, 74, 77
linguistic choices 34, 37, 150
linguistic equivalents 135, 144, 157, 158
linguistic features 19, 139
linguistic fluence 132
linguistic register 12, 28, 33, 95, 149
lipread 48, 61, 70, 77–79
lived 31, 35, 62, 64, 76, 85, 91, 95, 97, 104, 125
lived experience 31, 35, 85, 104
low 7, 12, 13, 34, 50, 126, 175, 179, 193
low-context 1, 6, 7, 12, 50, 126
loyalty 34, 49, 50, 194, 203
LSM (see Mexican Sign Language)
LSQ (see la Langue de Signes Quebecoise)

M

mainstream 30, 38, 46, 50, 51, 60, 70, 78, 126, 174, 195
mainstreamed 35, 65, 175
mainstreaming 48
marginalization 59, 67, 77, 78, 80, 85–88, 167
marginalized 54, 55, 59, 61, 62, 71, 72, 74, 86, 194
meaning 22, 28, 29, 34–41, 43, 44, 46, 51, 54, 55, 58, 74, 89, 100, 102, 106, 114, 119, 121–24, 126, 128–30, 133–

139, 143, 144, 146, 148–51, 153, 156–59
...anings 28, 29, 38, 41, 46, 144
mediate/mediation 14, 26, 28, 82, 96, 118, 119, 121, 122, 124-126, 128, 130, 131, 142
medical model 59, 65, 77, 79, 85
membership 18–20, 22, 23, 45–47, 49, 54, 55, 57, 58, 62, 84, 94, 107, 190, 207
mental health 17, 24, 64, 67, 106, 152, 183, 199
mentor 12, 104, 172, 182, 200–202
message 9, 19, 26, 28, 29, 32, 34–36, 38, 44, 53, 60, 71, 100, 113, 114, 119, 121, 122, 123, 127–29, 132–36, 138–41, 143–48, 150–54, 156–59, 216
metalinguistic 165
metamessages 28, 29, 34, 37, 38, 39, 60
method 19, 26, 57, 66, 85, 107, 136, 156, 165, 169
Mexican 1, 24, 95, 110
Mexican Sign Language 110
microaggressions 41, 54, 55, 57, 58
minorities 71, 73, 87, 99
minority 17, 28, 31, 37, 46, 52, 59, 61, 69–73, 75, 77, 78, 80–84, 91, 100–102, 119, 120, 214
minority culture 31, 72, 102, 119
minority group 17, 28, 31, 37, 46, 59, 71, 72, 73, 77, 78, 80, 83, 84, 91, 120
miscue 132, 145, 146, 151, 156, 158
modality 19, 132, 136, 138, 139, 155, 156
mode 31, 56, 77, 96, 135, 152, 157
model 21, 48, 59, 65, 70, 76, 77, 79, 85, 87, 101, 111, 132, 135, 137, 139, 140, 141, 143–49, 151, 153, 155, 157, 159, 174–76, 185, 186, 205, 207, 209, 212, 213
moral 2, 133, 174, 188, 190–93, 196, 199, 201
morality 182, 184, 188, 194, 202
movement 51, 60, 61, 71, 85, 93, 96, 119–21, 129, 138, 139, 155, 157, 161, 164–67, 210, 211
multicultural 3, 6, 43, 81, 82, 105, 107, 110, 121, 175
Multiculturalism 81
multilingual 6, 81, 82, 95, 105, 107, 110, 135, 175, 209

N

NAD (see National Association of the Deaf)
NAD-RID 18, 189
narrative 51, 52, 55, 75, 76, 94, 104
National Association of the Deaf (NAD) 17, 28, 99
native 1, 8, 24, 29, 30, 47, 67, 72, 84, 86–88, 97, 98, 101, 102, 107, 110, 115, 125, 134, 135, 156, 209
native language 8, 72, 107, 134, 156
native-like 122, 135, 156
network 46, 75, 113, 116, 177, 182, 202, 206, 208
networking 5, 6, 16, 22, 115, 203
networks 210
non-deaf 15, 16, 23–25, 73, 121, 124, 126, 128, 152, 153, 210, 212, 216
norms 1, 3, 6–8, 11, 24, 25, 29, 30, 35–37, 40, 42, 43, 46, 47, 49, 50, 52–56, 60, 64, 65, 67, 69, 72, 73, 77, 78, 82–84, 88, 89, 92, 94, 95, 101–3, 121, 123–26, 130, 138,

267

141, 144, 145, 149, 158, 160, 182, 213
normalize 59, 70, 77, 78, 187
nuances 44, 53, 98, 112, 115, 122, 134, 144
number 18, 24, 29, 31, 35, 59, 65, 74, 99, 105, 109, 112, 120, 122–24, 127, 129, 136, 140, 143, 146, 152, 153, 171, 172, 179, 196, 198, 205, 207, 210

O

observe 30, 37, 67, 69, 71, 72, 89, 92–94, 102, 103, 172, 212
obstacles 6, 12, 93, 113
omissions 9, 146, 153, 158
open-minded 12
opportunities 4–6, 16, 20, 23, 31, 32, 59, 62, 63, 70–74, 77, 78, 93, 100, 101, 115, 124, 167–69, 172–74, 176, 178–80, 182, 191, 200–202, 204, 206–9, 211, 213, 216
oppressed 31, 61, 65, 67–69, 71, 72, 74, 75, 79, 80, 85, 87, 91, 100
oppression 31, 41, 45, 47, 55, 59, 61–80, 85, 91, 92, 101, 108, 167
oppressive 46, 59, 62, 67, 68, 71, 72, 77–80
oppressors 67, 68, 73, 79, 80
oral 21, 31, 41, 51, 55, 59, 70, 73, 74, 78, 94, 120, 136, 156
oral education 70, 73, 74
oralism 70, 72, 73
oral lore 51, 55
orally 51, 55
oral program 70, 78
oral traditions 41, 51, 55
organization 5, 15–24, 27, 35, 37, 38, 41, 45, 47–50, 59, 73, 77, 120, 132, 141, 148, 149, 157, 162, 165, 173, 182, 190, 198, 202, 204-207, 210-212, 215
outcomes 85, 106, 109, 121, 152, 186, 188, 191-193, 196–98, 202, 203
outsiders 7, 12, 15, 35–37, 89, 118

P

pandemic 206, 212
paradigm 5, 194-196, 196
paralinguistics 132, 135, 139, 144, 156, 157
participant 3, 9, 17, 32–34, 37–39, 46, 64, 85, 94, 97, 100, 108, 109-113, 115, 116, 121, 122, 126–29, 131, 133, 137, 140, 141, 143, 148–50, 152–55, 157, 160, 161, 165, 167, 182, 185–88, 196, 199, 200, 203, 206, 213, 214
pathological 65, 69, 70, 72, 77, 78
pathology 76
patterns 3, 29, 35, 36, 63, 85, 93, 120, 134, 153, 192
performance 4, 5, 9, 19, 88, 99, 107, 148, 149, 159, 195, 198, 206
personality 2–4, 11, 41, 55, 63, 111, 141, 190
personally 66, 67, 91, 107
perspective 2, 10, 29, 36, 46, 49, 64, 69, 71, 76, 85, 93, 101, 104, 123, 127, 128, 130, 132, 140, 141, 158, 188,

197, 204, 205, 207, 209, 211, 213, 215
philosophy 73, 89, 118, 131, 166, 207, 209, 213
phonemes 43
Pidgin 19, 26
platform 33, 111, 112, 127, 128, 137, 152
policy 21, 70, 71, 86, 98, 132, 180, 194, 210, 212
polite 64, 126, 131, 161
politeness 7, 8, 12, 28, 49
political 5, 33, 37, 41, 59, 62, 72, 87, 90, 211–13
population 4, 60-62, 70, 72, 73, 75, 81–84, 87, 91, 94, 95, 98-100, 119, 120, 160, 171
position 20, 23, 29, 31, 46, 58, 63, 65, 67, 68, 75, 78, 80, 85, 91, 96, 100, 118, 119, 128, 141, 150, 155, 168, 173, 177, 183, 184, 186, 193–95, 201, 202, 206
positionality 118
positive 22, 42, 54, 66, 67, 71, 76, 79, 85, 89, 91–93, 101, 103, 106, 125, 141, 165, 166, 191
post-secondary 63, 174, 176, 181, 208
poverty 86, 88, 93, 167
power 7, 10, 11, 31, 59, 61–63, 65–69, 71–73, 75–77, 79, 80, 84, 85, 93, 100, 101, 106, 114, 121, 135, 144, 158, 175, 183, 199, 212
powerful 33, 53, 67, 73, 76, 92, 93, 96, 100, 119, 123, 166
powerless 71, 79
powerlessness 66, 75
practicum 171, 172
practitioners 9, 18, 21, 24, 65, 97, 132, 133, 145, 179, 182, 184, 188, 189, 198, 199, 202, 204, 208, 211
preference 5, 33, 93, 101, 107, 113-115, 134, 143, 163, 169, 199
prejudice 54, 55, 57, 59, 71, 78
preparation 3, 17, 25, 94, 136–38, 157, 162, 179
prepare 3, 13, 16, 35, 44, 53, 69, 88, 94, 109, 111, 116, 119, 122, 142, 143, 154, 161, 171, 172, 175, 176, 177, 183, 184, 190, 208, 209
prerequisite 23, 118, 123, 147, 151
presumption 14, 61
privacy 50, 184, 189, 199
privilege 20, 31, 47, 59, 61–65, 67, 69, 71–79, 85, 89, 91, 100, 101, 109, 115, 116
privileged 62–64, 100, 167
processing time 132, 135, 146, 153, 157
profession 1, 5, 11, 15, 16, 18–20, 22, 24, 36–38, 54, 72, 77, 105, 110, 132, 154, 155, 177, 183, 185, 187–89, 191, 195, 200, 204, 210, 216
professional 3–6, 9, 15–18, 21–25, 36, 37, 61, 66, 68–70, 72, 73, 79, 80, 82, 85, 95, 97, 100, 104–6, 109, 110, 115, 116, 129, 132, 133, 142, 152, 154, 171–73, 177, 178, 182–86, 188–94, 197–201, 204–6, 208, 209, 211–13, 215, 216
propositions 150
prosodic features 132, 138, 139, 157
prosody 138, 139, 157
ProTactile 165–68
protocol 89, 90, 102

Q

quality 18, 21, 30, 46, 62, 65, 71–73, 77, 92, 105, 124, 132, 133, 135, 153, 157, 166, 184, 190, 199, 206, 211, 213
quasi-interpreting 199
question 2, 4, 33, 34, 39, 55, 64, 76, 112, 115, 121, 124, 125, 127-129, 133, 137, 140, 142, 144, 154, 161, 165, 171, 184-186, 191, 192, 195, 198, 201, 202, 213, 216

R

race 10, 47, 57, 71, 72, 81, 83, 84, 87, 91, 100-102, 194
reaction 3, 85, 54, 64, 66, 129, 130, 143, 149, 166, 187
reality 6, 31, 43, 45, 49, 60, 63, 66–68, 82, 83, 86, 108, 121, 147, 167, 168, 210
recipient 28
reciprocating 25
reciprocity 15
Red T 215
refer 7-9, 18, 26, 27, 33, 35-39, 42, 48, 50, 54, 55, 65, 66, 69, 71, 73, 75, 77, 78, 81, 83-86, 94, 97, 101, 106–8, 110, 113, 115, 122-124, 130, 133-136, 155–57, 164, 167, 180, 183, 187, 188, 203
reference 44, 45, 49, 67, 83, 84, 91, 141, 212
referred 3, 7, 14, 44, 58, 59, 70, 97, 129, 131, 135, 136, 140, 144, 156, 158, 160, 186
reflect 2, 3, 9, 11, 24, 43, 45, 47, 64, 103, 114, 120, 132, 155, 159, 165, 179, 192, 197
reflection 10, 25, 26, 40, 67, 114, 155, 165, 192, 193, 198, 216
reframe 76, 85
refugee 46, 58
region 8, 15, 24, 83, 86, 87, 106, 134, 207, 210, 211, 212, 214
regional 5, 16, 18, 20, 22, 24, 134, 173, 204, 207, 210, 213
register 12, 28, 33, 34, 37, 39, 71, 95, 149, 208
registry 5, 15–18, 20, 21, 23, 26, 99, 189, 204
Registry of Interpreters for the Deaf (RID) 5, 15–21, 23, 26, 98–100, 115, 116, 188–90, 197, 199, 201, 204
rehabilitation 18, 65
relationship 2, 8, 12, 15, 17, 18, 24, 25, 29, 32, 34, 37, 38, 44, 45, 48, 49, 51, 54, 60, 67, 85, 92, 101, 110, 114, 116, 118, 123, 124, 130, 141, 142, 146, 148, 149, 150, 158, 166, 172, 190, 193, 199, 207, 209, 210, 213
religion 10, 45, 64, 79, 84, 93, 96, 102, 131
religious 24, 29, 35, 45, 87, 92–94, 96, 97, 109, 120, 152, 188, 194
rendered 17, 22, 33, 35, 39
rendering 19, 26, 38, 144, 152
repeat 129, 134, 154, 161, 166, 186, 203
reputation 53, 94, 182, 183, 198, 203
requirement 3–5, 19, 25, 99, 106, 109, 124, 132, 160, 171, 176, 208, 210, 212, 216

research 14, 29, 44, 61, 73, 95, 96, 99, 100, 104, 105, 139, 144–46, 153, 158, 160, 166, 192, 203, 206, 208, 210, 212, 214
residential 35, 40, 45, 48, 70, 74, 120, 163, 195
resilience 92, 93
resistance 100
resolution 23, 192
resources 4, 62, 63, 72, 78, 92, 97, 151, 163
respect 4, 11, 42, 49, 53, 66, 69, 76, 83, 85, 89, 91, 92, 96, 102, 103, 116, 133, 189, 190, 197–99, 204, 214
response 6, 15, 26, 28, 36, 39, 81, 110, 123-125, 128, 129, 140, 141, 183, 184, 191, 192, 197, 203, 213
responsibility 4, 6, 9, 10, 43, 60, 63, 64, 74, 85, 89, 93, 95, 125, 126, 143, 174, 182, 184-186, 189–92, 202
result 1, 9, 10, 12, 15, 28, 29, 31, 35, 44, 45, 54, 60, 62, 63, 66, 68, 71, 72, 77, 79, 85, 87, 93, 96, 98, 109, 119-21, 127, 128, 129, 130, 135, 142, 151, 153, 156–58, 163-165, 167, 168, 171, 172, 177, 179–81, 184, 188, 191, 205, 206, 210, 211
review 4, 54, 77, 130, 132, 188, 192, 194, 197, 203
revolutionary 17, 121, 165
RID (see Registry of Interpreters for the Deaf)
rights 17, 18, 62, 71, 86, 87, 90, 93, 111, 120, 121, 187, 193, 205–7, 210, 212, 215
risk 11, 106, 108, 152, 194, 214
rituals 88, 93, 120
role 3-5, 15, 20, 46, 49, 58, 67–69, 74, 76, 80, 85, 92, 93, 111, 112, 115, 116, 118, 120, 126, 129, 137, 141, 173, 175, 176, 179, 182, 184–87, 192, 202, 210, 212, 214
role space 5, 182, 185–87, 202
rules 7, 8, 11, 12, 30, 33, 34, 41, 43, 52, 118–21, 126, 134, 137, 138, 185, 196, 197, 201

S

sacrifice 61, 113, 194
safeguard 9, 198
scenario 7, 98, 125, 126, 129–31, 141, 192, 194, 196, 198
schema 44–46, 55, 58, 96, 97, 144, 160
schismogenesis 28, 35, 36, 39
second language 8, 24, 25, 29, 132, 134, 135, 153, 156, 157
segregation 31, 91, 92
self 9, 32, 49, 81, 85, 92, 93, 117, 172, 173, 183, 186, 187, 190–93, 196–98, 201, 202
self-assessment 9
self-care 9, 10, 12, 13, 80, 108, 164
self-expression 109
self-identify 1, 81, 84
self-reflection 3, 67, 68, 80, 192
semantic 35, 37, 39, 144, 158
sense of entitlement 59, 63, 78, 79
sensitive 8, 28, 29, 43, 46, 49, 53, 91, 112, 122, 144, 149, 184, 199
sensitivity 5, 6, 28, 52, 53, 69, 89, 97, 102, 190
sensory 52, 64, 164, 165, 167

269

sermon 94, 120, 137, 141

service 3, 4, 9, 22, 23, 68, 110, 116, 125, 132, 152, 153, 162, 164, 165, 168, 177, 179, 183, 184, 190, 199, 202, 208, 210, 211, 215, 216

services 15–18, 21–24, 26, 32, 49, 63, 65, 71, 72, 74, 77, 93, 94, 98, 105, 106, 108, 121, 126, 136, 152, 154, 162, 164, 165, 169–72, 175, 177, 178, 184, 188, 189, 194, 196, 198–200, 205, 206, 208, 210–12, 215

setting 2-5, 8, 17, 24, 32, 33, 34, 37–39, 44, 45, 47, 51, 55, 57, 58, 72, 82, 89, 90, 92, 94, 96, 97, 100, 102, 103, 107, 110-112, 121, 125, 128, 133, 134, 137, 138, 141, 142, 144, 145, 150-152, 154, 158, 159, 161-163, 164, 171–79, 181, 184, 187, 195, 197, 200, 209, 211, 214

sexism 47, 60, 63

shared 7, 8, 14, 29, 32, 33, 35, 39–41, 44, 49, 56, 70, 77, 78, 82–84, 95, 114, 143, 149, 150, 154, 165, 168, 188

shifting 31, 84, 129, 211

short-term 151, 152, 159, 195, 208, 216

sight 2, 53, 111, 132, 136, 157, 163, 164, 167, 168, 176

sight translation 132, 146, 157

sign 1–3, 5–8, 11, 14–19, 21–34, 36, 38, 42–44, 48, 49, 51–57, 60, 62, 64–68, 70–74, 76–78, 81–83, 85, 89, 90, 95–98, 100, 102, 106, 107, 110, 112, 113, 118, 119, 121–23, 128, 131–36, 138–40, 143, 148, 149, 152, 153, 155–57, 161, 165, 168–71, 174, 175, 177, 178, 180, 182–85, 188, 189, 191, 199–201, 203–16

signals 35, 44, 52, 123, 127, 128, 138, 146, 154, 166

signed 1–5, 15, 18, 19, 21, 25, 26, 28, 30, 33–36, 39, 40, 43, 44, 48, 51, 52, 82, 96, 107, 118–20, 122, 123, 127, 129, 130, 134–36, 138–40, 143–45, 148–50, 152, 154, 156–58, 164, 178, 204–9, 211–16

signed communication 15, 19, 43, 139

Signed English 19, 26, 135, 157

signed language 1, 48, 118, 134–36, 157, 204, 206–9, 212, 213, 215, 216

signer 26, 35, 51, 96, 112, 136, 138, 139, 145, 156, 200

signing 1, 19, 26, 28, 33, 43, 49, 73, 89, 103, 113, 115, 127–29, 132, 134, 135, 138, 157, 161, 180, 206

sign language 1, 2, 5–8, 11, 14–19, 21–33, 36, 38, 42–44, 48, 49, 51–57, 60, 62, 64–68, 71–74, 76–78, 81–83, 85, 89, 90, 95–98, 100, 102, 106, 107, 110, 112, 113, 118, 119, 121–23, 128, 131–36, 138, 139, 143, 148, 152, 153, 156, 165, 168, 169, 171, 174, 175, 177, 178, 180, 182–85, 188, 189, 191, 199, 201, 203–16

Sign Language-Spanish 97

signs 4, 19, 26, 28, 33, 34, 39, 42, 44, 48, 49, 60, 78, 89, 103, 113, 119, 122, 125, 129, 130, 133–35, 138, 139, 148, 150, 156, 161, 177, 199, 214, 216

sign-to-voice 132, 136, 137, 148, 157

SignWriting 51

simultaneous 111, 112, 132, 136, 142, 144, 145, 151–53, 157, 159

simultaneous interpretation 136, 151, 157

simultaneous interpreting 112, 151–53, 159

situations 4, 8, 32, 33, 34, 37, 44, 46, 49, 50, 53, 58, 61, 64, 65, 67, 71, 75, 88, 91, 96, 103, 106-8, 113-116, 119,

121, 129, 130, 131, 136, 140, 152, 153, 155, 160, 162, 176, 178, 181, 183, 188, 189, 191–99, 201, 203

skills 1, 2, 5, 7–12, 14, 15, 21–23, 25, 26, 30, 32, 34, 52, 74, 79, 82, 92, 95, 97, 98, 100, 101, 104–7, 109, 110, 113–16, 119, 122, 124, 132–34, 146, 158, 159, 163, 167, 172, 173, 175–80, 182–85, 189, 191, 194–97, 199–202, 213

social 3, 5–9, 11, 12, 17, 24, 29, 32–37, 41–43, 45–47, 50, 52, 55, 56, 58, 59, 62, 63, 68, 71, 75–79, 82–84, 86–88, 90–94, 96, 101, 102, 118, 120, 123, 130, 134, 141, 162, 163, 175, 178, 183, 194, 198, 199, 210, 212

social inequality 59, 62, 63, 78, 79

society 1, 13, 22, 31, 32, 35, 37, 38, 43, 45, 46, 52, 55, 59, 61–63, 68, 69, 71, 75, 77–79, 81, 82, 84, 100, 101, 132, 157, 168, 184, 188, 202, 204–7, 215

sociolinguistics 28, 32, 33, 37, 38

solution 66, 97, 111, 126, 168, 191, 192

sound 14, 15, 30, 31, 45, 53, 64, 69, 70, 77, 123, 124, 126, 127, 167, 168, 178, 209

source 9, 41, 84, 93, 100, 114, 135, 136, 143–46, 153, 156–58, 161

space 5, 18, 33, 35, 49, 72, 76, 100, 101, 122, 129, 131, 132, 138, 156, 161, 165, 169, 182, 184–87, 202

Spanish 1, 18, 24, 38, 43, 82, 83, 94–98, 134, 136, 152

Spanish-English 98

Spanish-English-American 97

Spanish-English-ASL 82

Spanish-speaking 43, 96, 97

speech-impaired 177

speechreading 21, 61, 77

spiritual 5, 41, 55, 71, 90, 93, 96, 103, 131, 199

spoken 1–5, 7, 8, 14–16, 18, 19, 21, 25, 26, 28–31, 33, 38, 44, 48, 61, 76, 82, 95–97, 101, 118, 119, 122, 123, 130, 133–36, 139, 140, 143, 145, 148–50, 156, 157, 164, 175, 178, 205, 206, 208, 210, 213–15

stability 41, 63, 118, 172, 174

stakeholders 132, 157, 205, 208, 211, 215

standardize 19, 71, 162

standards 21, 24, 73, 132, 133, 183, 184, 187–90, 197, 199, 203

statement 22, 34, 66, 119, 128, 149, 186, 207

status 7, 41, 47, 52, 55, 63, 64, 72, 78, 79, 86, 94, 100, 125–27, 133, 135, 184, 201, 204, 213

stereotype 42, 57

stereotyping 41, 45, 55, 69, 72

stigmatized 73, 75

stigmatizes 75

stigmatizing 48

stimuli 45, 52, 123

stimulus 105

storytellers 104

storytelling 51, 120

strategies 66–68, 80, 92, 113

struggle 44, 65, 69, 71, 73, 75, 97, 101, 148

study 3, 5, 11, 35, 71, 98, 104, 118, 139, 146, 147, 153, 160, 165, 167, 183

styles 3, 5, 29, 33, 35, 94, 96, 102, 132
subculture 41, 43-45
superior 2, 7, 9, 24, 29, 50, 60, 62, 78, 119, 122, 134
support 5, 18, 20, 25, 26, 38, 61, 66, 67, 69, 70, 74, 76, 80, 87, 89, 91, 93, 103, 108, 109, 111, 115, 130, 136, 147, 152, 154, 155, 160, 162–64, 168–70, 173–75, 177, 178, 181, 183, 197, 201, 204, 206, 207, 209, 211, 213
symbols 29, 165
syndrome 70, 163, 164, 180
synonymous 133, 188
systems 16, 18, 19, 21, 26, 47, 51, 59, 67, 71, 85, 88, 101, 122, 167, 181, 184, 208

T

tacit culture 1, 7, 12
tactile 104, 111–13, 165–69
Tactile American Sign Language 165
tactile communication 165
tactile interpreting 104, 113
tactile symbols 165
tadoma 160, 165, 168, 169
talk 4, 32, 44, 45, 53, 61, 66, 76, 96, 97, 110, 115, 129, 149, 177, 185, 200
talking 10, 14, 35, 36, 53, 64, 69, 101, 108, 109, 111, 125, 127, 129, 177, 199, 201
tandem 108, 153, 154
tandem of interpreters 104
target 9, 19, 59, 65, 114, 135–37, 143–45, 147, 150, 153, 156–58, 200, 213
task 2, 20, 23, 61, 69, 75, 93, 100, 151, 153, 161, 184
TASL (see Tactile American Sign Language)
taxes 172, 173, 179
team 3, 22, 36, 38, 105, 106, 108–16, 136, 137, 138, 152–55, 157, 159, 160, 179, 180, 198, 199, 205, 212
team interpreting 114
teammates 105, 106
teamwork 116, 189
techniques 49, 54, 56, 57, 82, 165–67, 180
technology 5, 51, 70, 77, 96, 99, 167, 210
teleological 182, 196–98, 202
term 1, 4, 8, 9, 11, 14, 19, 20, 25, 26, 28, 29, 33, 35-42, 47, 48, 54, 55, 57, 59, 60, 62, 64, 65, 70, 77, 81, 84-86, 94, 101, 104, 108, 110, 118, 130, 132, 134, 135, 137, 141, 146, 150, 155-157, 160-162, 164, 167, 182, 187, 191, 1997, 195, 201, 203
terminology 4, 5, 33, 36, 37, 40, 94, 134, 137, 164, 176
test 5, 16, 19, 24, 98, 99, 106, 107, 129, 162, 206
testing 5, 20, 24, 66, 97, 162, 208
theatre 110, 198
theological 94
theoretical 47, 93, 184
theory 75, 91, 133, 146
thoughtless 9
thought 7, 10–12, 32, 34, 51, 53, 59, 63, 64, 66, 67, 69, 80, 100, 101, 104, 111, 115-117, 119, 122, 130, 139, 140,

141, 144, 150, 166, 180, 189, 198, 205, 214
tokenism 111
tolerance 127, 194
tolerate 176
tolerated 3
tongue 82, 97, 101, 134, 156, 157
toolbox 10, 13, 19, 43, 106, 146, 147, 165, 180
topic 2, 5, 8, 18, 19, 34, 37, 38, 43, 67, 72, 107, 122, 127, 129, 132, 134, 137, 140–42, 153, 175, 178, 199, 205, 214
traditional 73, 87, 88, 90, 96, 149, 211, 212
traditions 1, 41, 43, 44, 48, 51, 52, 55, 67, 70, 78, 87, 93, 96, 102, 104, 119, 120, 174
training 5, 19, 21, 22, 89, 93, 104, 106, 115, 116, 126, 137, 173–75, 180, 182, 185, 201, 202, 206–13, 216
transformation 66
transformative 68
transgendered 47
translation 14, 26, 19, 82, 106, 132, 135, 136, 157, 210
transliterating 14, 18–20, 26
transliteration 19, 21, 106, 132, 135, 136, 157
trauma 66, 100, 108, 164
treatment 31, 59, 61, 62, 91, 100, 103
trends 19, 200, 212
trilingual 81, 82, 95, 97–99, 101, 102
trilingual interpreters 81, 95, 97, 102
trust 4, 15, 25, 26, 112, 115, 133, 140, 154, 183–85, 188, 190, 193, 199
trusted 14, 15, 197
Trustees 120, 121
truth 45, 67, 87, 90, 140, 148, 159, 175, 194
turn 7, 10, 50, 52, 62, 65, 74, 91, 108, 120, 122, 126–28, 149, 154, 206
turn taking 3, 7, 120, 126–28, 137

U

unethical 198
UNCRPD (see United Nations Convention of the Rights of Persons with Disabilities)
uninitiated 40, 57, 59, 65, 69, 78, 79, 128
United Nations Convention on the Rights of Persons with Disabilities (UNCRPD) 205, 207, 210, 215
United Nations Educational, Scientific and Cultural Organization (UNESCO) 41, 49, 206
UNESCO (see United Nations Educational, Scientific and Cultural Organization) unqualified 24, 175, 177
users 9, 31, 33, 34, 43, 74, 118, 134, 138, 139
utterance 36, 44, 123, 128-130, 135-139, 143-145, 150, 151, 153, 156-158

V

value 6, 13, 22, 32, 41, 50, 51, 53, 55, 60, 68, 71, 76, 85, 101, 109, 114, 118, 122, 130, 131, 166–68, 183
values 1, 2, 5, 7, 29, 30, 32, 41–43, 46, 47, 49–51, 53, 54, 56, 67, 70, 71, 75, 82, 83, 85, 89, 92–94, 96, 97, 102,

271

119, 120, 133, 141, 184, 189–93, 202
variations 32, 33, 37, 38, 49, 83, 124, 134, 209
varieties 19, 95
variety 12, 21, 32, 33, 43, 46, 49, 98, 120, 122, 133, 134,
164, 165, 175, 177, 178, 192
verbal 7, 33, 36, 94, 126–28, 138, 140
verbatim 19, 26, 33, 35, 39
vicarious trauma 66, 100, 108
video 51, 105, 125, 135, 137, 141, 152, 157, 177, 178,
209–11, 215, 216
violence 75, 79, 108
visible 7, 8, 12, 49, 60, 74, 97, 109, 122, 130, 131, 143,
185, 212
visibly 2, 195
vision 1, 5, 20, 30, 52, 63, 69, 113, 132, 162–64, 167
visual 16, 21, 25, 28, 31, 45, 51–53, 60, 76, 78, 96, 106,
113, 120, 127, 128, 134–36, 138, 139, 143, 151, 155–57,
160, 164–66, 168, 189, 190, 206
vocabulary 3, 12, 40, 44, 55, 83, 100, 134, 137, 149
vocalization 60, 78
voice 28, 34–36, 38, 39, 45, 77, 122, 129, 130, 135
voice-to-sign 132, 136, 137, 148, 157
vote 18–20, 22, 23, 71, 91
VRI 152, 171–74, 177, 178, 181
VRS 125, 126, 152, 171–74, 177, 178, 181, 215, 216

W

war 16, 17, 91, 197, 205, 209
WASLI (see World Association of Sign Language
Interpreters)
WebFinance 187, 202
website 22, 72, 98, 104, 106, 179, 206, 213
welfare 51, 92, 93, 101
wellbeing 11, 50
well-being 18, 36, 72, 87
WFD (see World Federation of the Deaf)
World Association of Sign Language Interpreters (WASLI)
206, 207, 211–16
World Federation of the Deaf (WFD) 206, 207, 211, 214–
16
workshops 5, 115, 165, 173, 182, 183, 201, 202, 206,
208, 216
worldview 69, 73, 88, 118, 123, 130, 131

Z

Zoom 152